the unpublished
lectures of
William Morris

the unpublished lectures of

Williyam Morris

edited and compiled by
EUGENE D. LEMIRE
UNIVERSITY OF WINDSOR

WAYNE STATE UNIVERSITY PRESS
DETROIT / 1969

Published simultaneously in Canada
by The Copp Clark Publishing Company
517 Wellington Street, West
Toronto 2B, Canada.

Library of Congress Catalog Card Number: 69–19307
Standard Book Number: 8143–1394–9

CONTENTS

179861

ACKNOWLEDGMENTS

This work has been published with the help of a grant from the Humanities Research Council of Canada, using funds provided by the Canada Council. In an earlier version it was submitted as a thesis at Wayne State University. I am indebted to the University, to the Society of Antiquaries (holders of the Morris copyright), and to the British Museum (owner of the manuscripts) for permission to publish portions of that thesis and the manuscript lectures.

Other organizations and a host of individuals generously assisted my effort to compile a calendar and bibliography of Morris's lecturing career. Among the organizations, help came from the British Museum's Newspaper Library at Collindale, the Bodleian Library, the Morris Museum at Walthamstow, the Fales and Tamiment Libraries of New York University, the Pierpont Morgan Library, the Huntington Library, the Miriam Lutcher Stark Library at the University of Texas, the Berg Collection at the New York Public Library, the Victoria and Albert Museum, the National Library of Iceland, the International Institute of Social History (Amsterdam), the Beinecke Rare Book and Manuscript Library at Yale University, the Society for the Protection of Ancient Buildings, the Art Worker's Guild, and the William Morris Society.

From the many individuals who loaned materials or gave freely of their advice and support, some public thanks must be given: to Professor William E. Fredeman of the University of British Columbia; the late Sir Sydney Cockerell; Mr. R. C. H. Briggs, Secretary of the William Morris Society; the late Mr. Freeman Bass; Mr. Graeme Shankland; Mr. Philip Henderson; Mr. Vincent Brome; Professor Edward P. Thompson of the University of Warwick; Professor David Hettich of the University of Nevada; Professor Charles Holt of the State University of New York, Long Island; Professor Helmut Gerber of Northern Illinois University; and Professor and Mrs. Norman Kelvin, City University of New York.

I am especially grateful to Mr. Wilfred Blunt for permission to quote from S. C. Cockerell, and to Sir Basil Blackwell for permission to use passages from *William Morris: Artist, Writer, Socialist* by May Morris.

The unpublished lectures printed here are the copyright of the Society of Antiquaries of London and cannot be reproduced again without the written consent of the Society.

E. D. LeM

LIST OF ABBREVIATIONS

Organizations

ACES   Arts and Crafts Exhibition Society
DF   Democratic Federation (became the Social Democratic
        Federation at the annual conference of August, 1884)
EQA   Eastern Question Association
FS   Fabian Society
HSS   Hammersmith Socialist Society
LEL   Labour Emancipation League
LLL   Law and Liberty League
LRL   Land Restoration League
NAAA   National Association for the Advancement of Art and Its
        Application to Industry
NSS   National Secular Society
SDF   Social Democratic Federation
SL   Socialist League
SLLL   Scottish Land and Labour League
SPAB   Society for the Protection of Ancient Buildings

Sources

(Abbreviations used in this volume are to the left of the dash; full citations are to the right.)
Architecture, Industry and Wealth—Architecture, Industry and Wealth: Collected Papers by William Morris, ed. Sydney C.

Cockerell and Robert G. C. Proctor and printed at the Chiswick Press in Morris's Golden Type (London, 1902; popular edition published in the same year). Italian translation, Bari, 1963.

Artist, Writer, Socialist—May Morris, *William Morris: Artist, Writer, Socialist,* 2 vols. (Oxford, 1936). Reprinted, New York, 1966.

Cockerell Papers—*The Diaries and Correspondence of Sydney Carlyle Cockerell,* 151 vols. B.M. Add. Mss. 52623–52773.

Collected Works—*The Collected Works of William Morris,* ed. May Morris, 24 vols. (London, 1910–1915). Reprinted, New York, 1966.

Dual Golden Type Edition—8-volume, large quarto edition of Morris books not printed at the Kelmscott Press. Edited by Sydney C. Cockerell and Robert G. C. Proctor and printed at the Chiswick Press (London, 1901–1902). Vol. VII combines *Hopes and Fears for Art* and *Signs of Change;* Vol. VIII introduced a new collection, *Architecture, Industry and Wealth* (see above).

Glasier—J. Bruce Glasier, *William Morris and the Early Days of the Socialist Movement* (London, 1921).

Ham. Min. Book—*The Hammersmith Minute Books,* SL and HSS, B.M. Add. Mss. 45891–45893.

Ham. Soc. Rec.—*The Hammersmith Socialist Record.*

History of the Fabians—Edward R. Pease, *The History of the Fabian Society* (2nd ed.; London, 1925).

Hopes and Fears—William Morris, *Hopes and Fears for Art* (London, 1882, 2nd ed. 1883, 3rd ed. 1883; Boston, 1882; London and New York, 1896, reprinted 1898, 1901, 1903, 1905, 1908, 1911). German translation, Leipzig, 1902. Longmans Pocket Library, 1919, reprinted 1921.

Journal for 1881—B.M. Add. Ms. 45407.

Journal for 1887—B.M. Add. Ms. 45408.

Journal for 1893—B.M. Add. Ms. 45409.

Journal for 1895—B.M. Add. Ms. 45410.

Journal for 1896—B.M. Add. Ms. 45411.

Lee—Francis Watt Lee, ed., *William Morris, Poet, Artist, Socialist* (New York, 1891).

Letters—The Letters of William Morris to his Family and Friends, ed. Philip Henderson (London, 1950).

*Mackail—*J. W. Mackail, *The Life of William Morris* (London, 1901; first published 1899).

*Man and Myth—*R. Page Arnot, *William Morris: The Man and the Myth* (London, 1964).

*Massé—*H. J. L. J. Massé, *The Art Workers' Guild 1884–1934* (Oxford, 1935).

NED—A New English Dictionary on Historical Principles.

*Nettlau Coll.—*The Nettlau Collection, SL Archives, The International Institute of Social History (Amsterdam).

*On Art and Socialism—*Holbrook Jackson, ed., *William Morris on Art and Socialism* (London, 1947).

*Penguin Edition—*Asa Briggs, ed., *William Morris: Selected Writings and Designs* (Harmondsworth, 1962).

PMG—The Pall Mall Gazette.

*Romantic to Revolutionary—*Edward P. Thompson, *William Morris: Romantic to Revolutionary* (London, 1955).

*Russian Edition—*U. I. Shvedor, ed., *Selections from William Morris* (Moscow, 1959).

*Selected Writings—*G. D. H. Cole, ed., *William Morris: Selected Writings* (London, 1934; reprinted 1944).

*Signs of Change—*William Morris, *Signs of Change: Seven Lectures Delivered on Various Occasions* (London, 1888), German translation, Leipzig, 1902.

*Socialist Diary—*B.M. Add. Ms. 45335.

SPAB. Reports—Annual Report of the Committee (London, 1878–1967).

*Tamiment—*The Tamiment Collection, New York University Libraries.

*Texas—*The Miriam Lutcher Stark Library, University of Texas.

*Trans. Biblio. Soc.—*Transactions of the Bibliographical Society.

*V & A MS—*The manuscript collection of the William Morris letters at the Victoria and Albert Museum.

*Walth. MS—*The manuscript collection of the William Morris Gallery, Walthamstow.

CHRONOLOGY OF THE PRINCIPAL EVENTS IN MORRIS'S LIFE

1834   Born at Elm House, Walthamstow on March 24.

1848–51   Attends Marlborough College, a preparatory school.

1853–56   Studies at Exeter College, Oxford and receives a "pass" B.A. degree. In these years Morris meets Burne-Jones, Rossetti, and several other Pre-Raphaelites.

1856   Signs articles to study architecture under G. E. Street, a prominent architect. In August, Burne-Jones moves with Morris to rooms on Red Lion Square, London. From January to December of this year Morris finances and writes for *The Oxford and Cambridge Magazine*.

1858   Publishes his first volume of verse, *The Defence of Guenevere*, in March.

1859   Marries Jane Burden of Oxford on April 26.

1859–60   Collaborates with Philip Webb in designing, building, and furnishing the Red House, Upton. This effort together with the formation of Morris, Marshall, Faulkner and Company—a decorative-art firm—signals a new beginning for English domestic architecture.

1867   Publishes *The Life and Death of Jason* in June.

1868   Volume I of *The Earthly Paradise appears*, with volumes II, III, and IV following in 1869 and 1870. As he completes Volume I, Morris begins intensive studies of

	Icelandic language and literature with the help of Eirikr Magnússon, an Oxford Don.
1869	Publishes his first translation from the Icelandic, *The Saga of Gunnlaug Worm-Tongue*, in January.
1871	In the spring Morris takes joint tenancy with Rossetti of Kelmscott Manor, Lechlade. He makes his first journey to Iceland this summer.
1872	Publishes *Love Is Enough*, a modern morality play.
1873	Journeys a second time to Iceland in the summer.
1875	Re-organizes the firm in March. Morris himself becomes sole proprietor, and the name is shortened to Morris and Company.
1876	Publishes *Sigurd the Volsung*, an epic, which Morris believed to be his greatest achievement in poetry.
1877	Forms the Society for the Protection of Ancient Buildings in March. In December he delivers his first public lecture and his first political speech.
1882	Publishes the first collection of his lectures, *Hopes and Fears for Art*.
1883	Accepts an honorary fellowship from Exeter College early in January. In the same month he joins the Democratic Federation and declares for socialism.
1884	With Belfort Bax, Eleanor Marx, and others breaks with the Federation late in this year.
1885	The break-away group forms the Socialist League in January and begins publication of *The Commonweal*, organ of the League.
1886–87	Publishes *The Dream of John Ball* as a serial in *Commonweal*.
1887	November 13, "Bloody Sunday," dampens his hopes for a speedy socialist revolution.
1888	Publishes his second volume of lectures, *Signs of Change*, in May.
1889	Represents the English Socialist Movement at the International Conference of Socialists in Paris. *The Roots of the Mountains*, first of the late prose romances, appears in November.
1890	*News from Nowhere* appears serially in *Commonweal*.

In December Morris leaves the Socialist League to form the Hammersmith Socialist Society.

1891   Publishes *The Story of the Glittering Plain,* first production of his Kelmscott Press. In October the Press issues a collection of his later verse, *Poems by the Way.*

1893   Joins H. M. Hyndman and G. B. Shaw to write *A Joint Manifesto of English Socialists.*

1896   Gives his last public speech on January 31. He dies on October 3.

INTRODUCTION

From 1877 to 1896, the years of his public life, William Morris prepared and delivered about one hundred speeches and lectures, most of which he read from long foolscap pages covered with his own graceful calligrapher's hand. Early in his speaking career especially, he was unsure of his oratorical powers; and his meticulous composition was a way of making sure he could be understood. George Bernard Shaw once wrote, "how he found time to write so many, even when he was reviving the lost art of fine printing in his spare time, I cannot imagine."[1] Considered simply in terms of their number and the care Morris gave to them, his lectures have always indicated clearly, if that were necessary, his energy and his deep commitment to social reconstruction and to popular art. Only today are we at last becoming aware that—though written usually for immediate purposes and with no conscious reference to any later audience—his lectures are the solid basis for a complete revaluation of his worth. Raymond Williams has made this point most effectively:

> I would willingly lose *The Dream of John Ball* and the romantic socialists songs and even *News from Nowhere* . . . if to do so

---

[1] "Editor's Note" to *Communism: a Lecture by William Morris,* Fabian Tract No. 113 (London, 1903), p. 4.

were the price of retaining and getting people to read such smaller things as *How we Live and How we Might Live, The Aims of Art, Useful Work versus Useless Toil,* and *A Factory as It Might Be.* The change of emphasis would involve a change in Morris's status as a writer, but such a change is critically inevitable. There is more life in the lectures, where one feels that the whole man is engaged in the writing, than in any of the prose and verse romances. . . . Morris is a fine political writer, in the broadest sense, and it is on that, finally, that his reputation will rest.[2]

The critical attention that will accomplish this change in status is slow in coming. But all the texts have not been available, and even the available texts often exist in biographical and bibliographical confusion. This edition provides texts of the more important unpublished lectures and, as appendices, a calendar and bibliography of the entire lecture production. These texts should help focus critical attention on the lectures and encourage a reassessment. As he developed from Pre-Raphaelite to Marxist— and both these stages need some re-interpretation—Morris involved himself increasingly in an attempt "to set the crooked straight," to teach a new social ethic. Obviously, to explain this entire development is the proper function of a full-length study, and that project is now under way. But these public utterances, now for the first time available in complete form, illuminate several of the deepest concerns of the most mature Morris.

For the greater part of his public life—say, his last fifteen years —Morris was probably unaware that his difficult new art had any importance beyond the immediate moment. True, in the pre-socialist years when he often lectured in the full-dress Victorian fashion, he attempted to write and speak definitively. Five of these careful, formal pieces were collected and published in 1882 as *Hopes and Fears for Art.* On August 10, 1880, he wrote Georgiana Burne-Jones:

I will be as serious as I can over them and when I have these last two done ["Some Hints on House Decoration" and "The Prospects of Architecture in Civilization"], I think of making a

---

[2] *Culture and Society, 1780–1950* (New York, 1958), pp. 155–56.

book of the lot, as it will be about what I have to say on the subject, which still seems to me the most serious one that a man can think of; for 'tis no less than the chances of a calm, dignified, and therefore happy life for the mass of mankind. (*Letters*, p. 134)[3]

But as he went on to deeper involvements, Morris lost all traces of "The Grand Manner" and all consciousness of any audience but the one in front of him. To become an agitator, a Marxist revolutionary, he gradually changed all aspects of his public effort—even when his message carried strong echoes of earlier ideas. He learned that when the object is to move people, to convince them, one must give up the luxury of final statements.

As a revolutionary agitator, he wrote many more lectures and gave much more time to speaking than before. Publication, however, became only another function of his propaganda, useful now and then but not inevitable, and certainly not the goal he looked toward during his painstaking composition. When his audiences became more often and more exclusively working-class, book publication began to seem less desirable, generally, than separate publication of individual lectures in penny-pamphlet form. Of the agricultural labourers of Buscott Village, to whom he spoke about the Bloody Sunday disturbances in 1887, he later suggested, "a good distribution of leaflets would be fruitful among such men: although many of them cannot read, they would get them read to them."[4] Obviously, this new audience could seldom afford books even if able to read them. At the same time, Morris became aware of a very real difference between a socialist lecture as given in the lecture hall and as read in the library. In the Preface to *Signs of Change* (1888)—the second and last collection he made—he touches on this difference:

> These pieces are all of them simply Socialist lectures written for *viva voce* delivery; if any excuse be needed for their publication, as may well be, the one I have to offer is, that I have often been asked by persons among my audiences to publish them, and I would fain hope that what interested those persons may also

---

[3] This and all later abbreviations in the text and notes are expanded in the List of Abbreviations.

[4] *Commonweal*, December 10, 1887, p. 393.

interest others who may first come across them in a book instead of in a lecture-room. (*Collected Works*, XXIII, 1)

Never fully conscious of the advantages in his new prose form, Morris nevertheless keenly felt one major difficulty when his socialist lectures were collected and published as a volume of essays:

> I must ask the reader's indulgence for the repetitions which occur in these pieces. Socialist lecturers speak almost always to mixed audiences, and hope on every occasion that amongst those who listen to them there may be some to whom Socialism is only a name. . . . Therefore they [the lecturers] can scarcely omit in any lecture the statement of certain elementary propositions— such, e.g. as the necessity for the abolition of monopoly in the means of production. (*Collected Works*, XXIII, 1)

It is not without reason that he adopted an apologetic attitude toward his lectures when they were to be read as essays by a more literate audience. But it is clearer now than it was to Morris that, struggling for simplicity, he produced his most powerful writing when he addressed himself to those working-class audiences who seemed to him so different from himself.

He published only the two small collections already mentioned, collections that brought together only twelve of his lectures. All the others that were printed during his lifetime were done individually as pamphlets or periodical articles, the forms best suited to reach his special audiences. When he died in 1896 he left many complete manuscript lectures, some that he had delivered many times, some that he clearly thought to be good, some that he had been requested to publish by others.[5] But he had seen only a very small proportion of them into print in anything like a permanent form.

The subsequent history of the lectures has a special interest both because of what it tells of the realities of publishing and because of what it tells of the Morris books themselves; but parts of that history are difficult to reconstruct since the correspond-

---

[5] See Morris's comments in *Man and Myth*, pp. 97–98. In a report to *Commonweal* ("The Art Congress," Nov. 16, 1889, p. 364), Morris tells of one occasion when he had such requests to publish "Of the Origins of Ornamental Art."

ence and records of Longmans, Green & Co., chosen by Morris as
his publishers in the last year of his life,[6] were destroyed during
the World War II bombing of London. The published books
themselves yield something to examination, however; and a considerable amount of what descriptive bibliographers call "collat-
eral evidence" has recently been made available in the diaries
and letters of several of the people most directly concerned,
especially Robert Proctor and, the most important of Morris's
executors, Sir Sydney Cockerell.[7] It is mainly through these unpublished sources that the story, or most of it at least, can now be
told.

As one might expect, there have been many selections from
Morris's lectures printed since his death, and many more reprints
of individual lectures in anthologies and as separate items. But
there have been few attempts to gather together lectures still
scattered in obscure periodicals or rare pamphlets. Moreover,
only one of these collections, May Morris's *William Morris: Artist,
Writer, Socialist* (2 vols.; Oxford, 1936), introduces new material
from those many unpublished manuscripts left by Morris.

The first two collections contain no identification of their makers. Sydney (later Sir Sydney) Cockerell edited the first, a series
of five thin quarto volumes, including six lectures and an essay
on Westminster Abbey, all from printed sources. Set in the
Golden Type of the Kelmscott Press and bound in blue boards
much like those used in the Leighton bindery to bind many
Kelmscott Press books, these beautifully-printed volumes had a
ready acceptance.[8] In September, 1900, when Cockerell was half-

---

[6] See the Diary of Sydney C. Cockerell, entry for Dec. 23, 1895: "went up to town
with W. M. to see Mr. C. J. Longman about a transfer of the publishing of the
books, Reeves being now too old" (*Cockerell Papers*).

[7] Proctor's diaries are now deposited in the British Museum Manuscript Room,
catalogued as B.M. Add. MSS. 50190–50195. They cover the period from January
1, 1899, to Proctor's death in early September, 1903; but volume III, from July 16,
1901 to August 29, 1902, is missing. Cockerell's diaries and correspondence were
deposited in the British Museum in 1965 (see the List of Abbreviations).

[8] F. S. Ellis, trustee of the Morris estate, with Cockerell and Mrs. Morris, wrote to
tell the editor that, "there are few pieces of literary work so cheaply done as your
editing of these lectures at 2–2 [each] . . ." (letter of Oct. 7, 1900; *Cockerell
Papers*). For further background to this edition, see Cockerell's letter to Mrs.
Morris, March 9, 1898.

way through this project, Longmans proposed to print all the Morris books that had not been done at the Kelmscott Press in the same Golden Type.[9] Cockerell's friend Robert Proctor, the first great incunabulist of the British Museum and an admirer of Morris and his work (he was to replace Ellis as trustee after the publisher's death in 1901), agreed to take a share of editorial responsibilities.[10] Between January 28, 1901 and June 23, 1902, eight large quarto volumes, also bound in blue boards, issued from the printing works of the Chiswick Press, two devoted to Morris's late prose romances, two to Icelandic saga translations, two to translations of Homer and Vergil, and two to lectures. With the first of the two lecture volumes a "Note" was loosely inserted:

> It has been found advantageous to make one volume instead of two of "Hopes and Fears for Art" and "Signs of Change," and to unite the extra lectures, which were originally intended to form a part of volume vii and viii, in volume viii, with the title "Architecture, Industry and Wealth," which will complete the series."[11]

In the same year that this luxurious Golden Type first edition appeared, 1902, Longmans produced a popular edition.

When May Morris came to edit her father's lectures for the

---

[9] See Ellis's letter to Cockerell, Sept. 6, 1900.

[10] For their services, which included preparing texts for the press (and in some cases maps, notes, and indices) and reading proofs, each editor received forty pounds (see the diaries of Robert Proctor, B.M. Add. MS. 50191, entries for Oct. 11, 1900, and Sept. 4, 1902). Though his name is very well known among bibliographers, Proctor's services to the study of Morris have never been properly recognized. He was the first to recognize the 1858 "printing" of *Sir Galahad, a Christmas Mystery* as a forgery. The standard biographical treatment of Proctor was written by his British Museum colleague, Alfred W. Pollard, and published in *The Library,* N.S. Vol. V (Jan., 1904), pp. 1–34. His diaries have been described by J. V. Scholderer, *The Private Diary of Robert Proctor* (London, 1951), but this account gives little indication of Proctor's notes on his collecting and editing of Morris.

[11] Proctor sent a working paper for this new volume to Cockerell on April 28, 1902. It is a list of lectures, in Proctor's hand, divided into parts "A" and "B" and indicating next to the title (there are many more than were actually used) the number of words in each lecture and the pages, calculated at the rate of "500 words to a page of Golden Type." The volume title as finally adopted appears at the bottom in Cockerell's hand (*Cockerell Papers*).

Collected Works (24 vols.; London, 1910–15), she had the entire lecture production to choose from: the four published collections described above, the many single lectures still in pamphlets or articles only, and the unpublished manuscripts. But she published only two volumes of lectures (vols. XXII and XXIII), including only the four collections and five published but uncollected pieces, those being two essays and the three lectures, "True and False Society," "Monopoly," and "Communism." To omit so much from an edition designed to be standard is odd, and it has prompted one scholar, R. P. Arnot, to suggest a measure of political bias in the publishers, exercised under the mask of excluding "much that did not appear to possess 'literary merit,' " (*Man and Myth*, p. 109). But other more practical considerations (however mistaken they may have been) can now be advanced as having influenced the decisions of May Morris, the trustees, and the publisher. Bias there may have been, still. But it could not have been very apparent at the time because of the gravity of the reasons proposed.

May Morris was fired with enthusiasm for her father's work and devoted to his principles. As his editor, she wrote in her preface to volume XXIII that, "it was originally intended to include most of the unpublished manuscripts, arranging all lectures and papers in chronological order, so that those interested in following my father's ideas could do so fully in these pages." Despite those redundancies which Morris himself had recognized, she was convinced that the manuscript material should be printed:

> There is bound to be repetition in some of the papers and addresses, but the questions are generally presented at a different angle, and in none of them, whether in those which deal with the various aspects of the political situation of the day, or those which enlarge upon the welfare of humanity in the future, is the diction languid or dull, as may well be imagined. (*Collected Works*, XXIII, xii)

The contrast between these intentions and the contents of the lecture volumes suggests strongly that despite her readiness to accept responsibility for editorial decisions—as editor of the *Collected Works*, May Morris did not always have her own way. Her judgment was subject to pressures from her more experienced advisors, some of whom had legal authority to grant or deny permission to publish. Neither Mrs. Morris nor St. John Hornby, who succeeded Proctor as executor,[12] have recorded their opinion on this matter, if they had any. But neither of the other two people involved, J. W. Mackail and Sydney Cockerell, were in sympathy with Morris's political and social opinions, and both felt bound to protect the poet's "reputation," that is to say, the image that they, both scholars and bookmen, felt was the essenial Morris. J. W. Mackail was the official biographer, often consulted where matters of literary judgment were concerned. And after looking at Mackail's work on Morris's life most carefully, E. P. Thompson concluded that he had a "hostility to revolutionary Socialism . . . so great that he was not above mild tampering with quotations, when it suited him" (*Romantic to Revolutionary*, pp. 736–37). Both he and Cockerell felt that the publication of new Morris material should depend on whether it met their own standards of literary excellence.[13]

But Cockerell's was almost certainly the decisive influence. Mackail, significantly, expected him to exercise final authority since legally it was vested in him and the other trustees. Cockerell was, moreover, the most active of the executors, conducting negotiations with the publisher, finding and nominating new trustees when necessary, acting as the channel through which all

---

[12] Hornby was the originator and proprietor of the Ashendene Press, but his main functions as executor seem to have been damping down May Morris's "extravagance" over the building of a William Morris Memorial Hall at Kelmscott, and keeping the Trustees' books (see the Cockerell correspondence with C. H. St. John Hornby).

[13] Mackail wrote to Cockerell on July 3, 1910: "I had a long talk with May last Sunday over her work. She is doing it, it is clear, very carefully and conscientiously: the only thing I am afraid of is her judgment as regards unpublished work. I expressed myself very strongly against what she is evidently eager to do, that is to print the fragmentary Scenes from the Fall of Troy. I am quite certain that this would be a disastrous mistake. But I greatly fear that she will do it unless she is stopped: if she does, it will I am sure give occasion to the adversary to blaspheme" (*Cockerell Papers*). The poems were printed and there is no reason to think now, half a century later, that they have had any effect one way or another on estimates of Morris. Cockerell, liberal about permissions to reprint but certainly not about his mission to protect the image of Morris, states his principles in a letter to Theodore Watts-Dunton in *The Best of Friends* (London, 1956), p. 18.

payments from "trustee stocks" and royalties went to the heirs, and exercising final authority generally; all this is obvious from the voluminous correspondence on trust matters. When his views collided with May Morris's over the lecture volumes, he wrote a carefully phrased letter to her (Aug. 25, 1913), which is nonetheless quite unequivocal in tone:

> My view about these volumes is that much of your father's writing in his later years was hasty and was intended to be ephemeral and that the three existing volumes of lectures contain the greater part of what he wished to stand as his message on art and socialism.

He not only judges with an undefined excellence as his standard, he also calls Morris as witness to his judgment by virtue of his failure to collect or publish the later, socialist work, assuming that Morris used similar standards when selecting from this material for publication. Cockerell concludes:

> I do not think his reputation will gain by a gathering together of everything by him that can be collected. The bulk of his writings being already very large. Of course I do not wish to dictate in any way, but merely to put my views before you—for your friendly consideration. (*Cockerell Papers*)

But despite Cockerell's clever reminder of his legal power to dictate, May Morris seems not to have been greatly impressed with the argument. Subsequently, on September 2, Cockerell wrote her another, longer letter, one which deserves extensive quotation here both for its account of the history of the unpublished manuscripts and for its economic argument for curtailing the edition:

> With regard to the lectures, as I think you know, after your father's death it was contemplated that Lethaby should edit a volume on art, and Shaw one on Socialism. I think they both came to the conclusion that the best lectures had already been selected for publication by your father and that most of those that remained would need a certain amount of editing to avoid repetitions and anyhow—they never did what we hoped they would do—and then Proctor and I got out the Architecture, etc. vol. of lectures (besides the five 2/6 vols.) which added a good deal to the lectures by your father previously accessible in book form.

The point is essentially the same as before, with Shaw and Lethaby's inaction (dangerously negative evidence, this) as well as Morris's to give it weight. In addition, Cockerell implies, plenty of that sort of thing is available already.

But May Morris was a woman of considerable strength of will in some things and especially about her father's work; and she saw excellence in much of this remaining work, viewing it as she did from a rather different social and political angle. So Cockerell concluded with what must have been the deciding point to a faithful daughter who knew very well indeed that royalty payments made a real difference, much more in the lives of her semi-invalid mother and epileptic sister than in her own. Cockerell had to concede that she was:

> very likely to find some other splendid lectures in MS and I can understand the temptation to print every syllable—but there is a danger in bulk, as the collected edition of Ruskin has shown (now greatly fallen in value) and I believe you will be wise to add only what is so markedly first rate that it would be folly and wickedness to leave it out. (*Cockerell Papers*)

There is irony, as well as practical significance, in the reference to the Cook and Wedderburn edition of John Ruskin (39 vols.; London, 1903–1912) which is often acclaimed as a monumental example of scholarly care and completeness and, naturally, is much sought after.

Longmans' original proposal, however, was for a thousand sets of "about 20 volumes," and it was the firm's opinion, according to Cockerell, that "the volumes will have to be issued . . . in rather rapid succession to keep the subscribers together, and it would involve some daily proof reading for about a year. . . ."[14] Longmans agreed to do "all financing except incidental expenses that would not arise but for Morris's not being present."[15] When Cockerell wrote these two letters to May Morris quoted above, the project was in its fourth year and was still three volumes from its eventual completion, that completion being four volumes more than Longmans had thought likely to require financing. As it

---

[14] Letter to Mrs. Morris, Sept. 1, 1909.
[15] Letter to Mrs. Morris, Sept. 31, 1909.

turned out, all copies printed and issued for sale were eventually sold, the last going in 1928; and considerable profit did accrue both to the estate and to the publishers.[16]

But the discussions on what to include were going on in the year following the completion of the Cook and Wedderburn edition of Ruskin. A slump in the demand for that book, representing a very large investment by another firm, must have been a sobering thought in that economically uncertain time just before World War I. It was this complicated set of interests, involving economics certainly and politics and taste to a degree not definitely determinable, that confined the lectures to two volumes in the *Collected Works* and the contents of those two volumes to already printed material. Twenty years later May Morris recalled that she had "much more material than it would have been possible to include in an edition already committed to a certain number of volumes" (*Artist, Writer, Socialist,* I, 373).

But after that project was finished and the *Collected Works* finding buyers at a quite steady pace,[17] May Morris continued to look for opportunities to display her father's remaining work in a proper setting; not surprisingly in light of the preceding correspondence, she got little encouragement. Cockerell, evidently responding to her queries, wrote to say:

> Your father's lectures, like the best of Ruskin's, are far more compact of wisdom and insight than any that are given nowadays—but one has to face the fact that there is a strong reaction against these two mighty prophets and that the average young man and woman of intelligence cannot read them any more than we could read Wordsworth and Bryon . . . one has to realize that they have different eyes and understandings.[18]

Again, the names of Ruskin and Morris are linked, for good or ill, in a way that seems to leave out of the question all that side of

---

[16] See Cockerell's letters to May Morris, 15th Oct., 1920; 1st May, 1923; and 4th July, 1929.

[17] About twenty-five sets were sold each year after the first (Cockerell letter to May Morris, May 4, 1929).

[18] Letter of Nov. 22, 1916.

Morris's work that has most significance in a modern world, his revolutionary socialism.

But May Morris would not give up, and by the time he wrote to her in 1919, Cockerell had come around so far as to say, "With regard to the publication of the Socialist lectures, etc. my own view is that they should be open to all the world, having been written for that purpose. . . ."[19]

Another edition by May Morris went forward then, with much new material from manuscripts, off-prints from magazines, and pamphlets. An extensive narrative and autobiographical commentary by the editor links the essays, lectures, etc., of her father together. Published by Basil Blackwell's Shakespeare Head Press under the title, *William Morris: Artist, Writer, Socialist*, these two large volumes more than doubled the previously collected non-fictional prose. Again, however, despite their half-million words, they omit published and unpublished material that challenges comparison with that which was selected for inclusion.

The background of this edition is also an interesting one, though there are areas of it that remain vague and confused. In the glow of recollection that followed the 1934 Morris Centenary celebrations, May Morris found Basil Blackwell ready to venture the new edition, to be bound uniformly with the *Collected Works* and—to confirm its supplementary nature—ending with an index to the *Collected Works* as well as the two volumes.[20] In his essay, "Memories of May Morris,"[21] the publisher tells how this project was started, of offering to bring out the uncollected material and shortly thereafter being overwhelmed by a huge parcel of manuscripts, offprints, etc., that dropped on his desk. As the story goes, he then asked for some abridgements, but was forced to retire in some confusion before the implacable Miss Lobb, May Morris's

---

[19] Letter of Feb. 12, 1919.

[20] This is said to be the work of Mrs. Blackwell.

[21] Until recently unpublished, a copy of the original version of this, rendered in Sydney Cockerell's unmistakeable hand, is now in the Fales Collection, New York University Library. Portions have been printed as the "Introduction" to Bernard Shaw's *Morris As I Knew Him* (London, 1966), and in "More about Miss Lobb," *The Bookseller*, October 27, 1962, p. 1763.

companion and personal factotum, who took him aside and insisted that he publish everything and thus relieve May Morris of editorial duties that, at her age, would overtax her strength. Basil Blackwell then gave way, he says, and "completed the Morris canon" with the two-volume *Artist, Writer, Socialist*. Paradoxically, considering the story of Miss Lobb, May Morris did more editing in these volumes, in the sense of choosing, arranging, and introducing her father's work, than in any of the *Collected Works* volumes. What is much more difficult to explain is how this story can be reconciled with a letter Cockerell wrote to May Morris as early as July 13, 1932 (*Cockerell Papers*): "Walker told me about the rejection of the volumes on which you have spent so much labour. We could neither of us see how Longmans could have done otherwise in these days of meagre sales—but I quite understand your disappointment." From this it appears that the editing was finished and had been for more than two years before the proposal came to publish it at Blackwells.

There is much more certainty about the reasons for excluding the remaining unpublished lectures, speeches, etc., including those collected here, from the supplementary volumes put in the simplest terms. May Morris did not feel they were good enough. In her choice she used her own standard of excellence as a guide:

> In considering the publication of work left by a dead author there are always two difficulties to face: on the one hand one may run the risk of harming his reputation by printing immature or unfinished work; on the other hand one may be withholding writing of value and interest to the public. I have had these two difficulties constantly before me in making up these volumes, and I hope that nothing has found place there that is not of value in itself or that has not some special point of interest attached to it. (*Artist, Writer, Socialist*, I, 373)

At the end of her labors, she—now a trustee herself, with St. John Hornby and Cockerell, consigned all her father's remaining unpublished writing to archival darkness.

> The trustees of the family, having carefully considered these writing, in the growth and working out of an idea . . . they do or quoted in these volumes and in the *Collected Works*, they are only of value to students who are interested in the development

of the young man's poetical powers or, in the case of later
writing, in the growth and working out of an idea . . . they do
not wish these manuscripts to be printed. (*Artist, Writer, Socialist*, II, 607)

Obviously, the publication of the ten lectures included here
runs contrary to these wishes. Justification, final justification that
is, will depend on the extent to which these pieces stimulate
interest in Morris and illuminate further his position and his
talents. More immediate justification can be derived from the
certainty that these are not "immature or unfinished pieces," nor
can there rightly be any fear that their publication will "run the
risk of harming his reputation" (if that can ever be said to happen
in these circumstances). The first lecture in this volume [Art: a
Serious Thing], is one of the few pieces of evidence that remain
to tell us what Morris was thinking in the crucial months just
preceding his joining the SDF. Here his vividly expressed responses to natural beauty and to Jan van Eyck's painting, so
similar in basic feeling, leave an ineffaceable impression of integ-
rity. "Of the Origins of Ornamental Art," a later recasting of a
lecture first delivered at Eton College in 1883, Morris himself
called "a good lecture," with a "Socialist sting in his tail" (*Man
and Myth*, p. 97). The opening passages of it were almost certainly a reply to James McNeill Whistler's "Ten O'Clock."[22] "Early
England" is the first part of a trilogy of lectures on "England as it
was, is, and may be," of which the other two parts, "Medieval
England" and "Art and Industry in the Fourteenth Century,"
have been published.[23] Like "The Early Literature of the North
—Iceland," it represents an attempt unique in his work to express
in a direct, non-fictional frame his special feeling for a particular
historical time and place, his sympathy for that manifestation of
the human spirit he found there. [The Present Outlook in Poli-
tics], another lecture for which the title has been derived from
sources other than Morris himself, is Morris's assessment of the
political scene as it presented itself to him after the shocking,

---

[22] See E. LeMire, "Morris's Reply to Whistler," *The Journal of the William Morris
Society*, I (Summer, 1963), 3–10.
[23] See Appendix I, 12–12–86, 2–13–87, and 5–15–87.

violent events of Bloody Sunday, November 13, 1887. This lecture and [The Depression of Trade] are two of a comparatively
few public statements Morris made on contemporary politics
outside the pages of *Commonweal*. Both convey something of his
intensive and remarkably successful effort to understand the political and economic system he lived under and despised. The
others—containing Morris's treatment of The Gothic Revival, the
relation of art to labour, and the Socialist ideal—are devoted
exclusively to topics which he constantly refers to in lectures on
other subjects. Here these central topics are handled directly.

Indeed, the literary quality of several of these pieces, combined with their biographical and historical significance, raises
some doubt whether May Morris and her co-trustees were sufficiently aware of their importance. The books were closed on
further publication in 1936, by which time May Morris was in her
seventies. Never much concerned about the need for accurate
record keeping (being her father's daughter), by the 1930's she
could not always find her way with certainty through the laby-
rinth of published and unpublished, collected and uncollected
writing.[24] Several of these pieces lack titles on the manuscripts,
and the dates and places of their presentation are not established
in the usual sources—i.e. letters, diaries, *Commonweal*, etc. This
is not to imply that May Morris excluded them because she
feared making an error, but it is rather more than possible 1) that
she was not quite sure what had been published and what had
not, and 2) that without some specific information of their background it would have been much more difficult to weave several
of these pieces into the narrative fabric. The manuscripts of
"Early England" [Art: a Serious Thing], "Of the Origins of Ornamental Art," and "The Gothic Revival [I]" all have pencilled
marginalia in May Morris's and Cockerell's hands that bear witness to attempts, apparently unsuccessful, to identify and date
the work.

---

[24] Confused, for example, by a change in title, she reprinted "Architecture and
History" in her supplementary edition though she had herself already included it
in the *Collected Works*. Careful comparison of the Calendar and Bibliography
(see Appendices I and II) with her "Bibliographical Notes" to the *Collected
Works*, vols. XXII and XXIII will reveal other bibliographical confusions.

The reasons for bibliographical confusion are evident. As has been noted here, William Morris did not think his lectures important enough to anyone outside his immediate audience to give much attention to collecting them or seeing them through the press. He apparently gave no time after the original composition and delivery to arranging, dating, or identifying his manuscripts, some of which he read on several different occasions with changes in title to fit new audiences. On March 25, 1886, he wrote to J. L. Mahon about a coming series of talks at Leeds:

> As to subjects there is my lecture called now "Socialism" and which I am to deliver substantially at Dublin as the dawn of a new epoch; I can touch it up and make it serve your turn I think and you may call it the present and future of the working class. (*Man and Myth*, p. 59)

May Morris, for many years her father's only editor, was no scholar. And she did not turn her attention seriously to editing a large part of his writing until forty years after his death, when she was herself at an advanced age. Nearly all the Morris papers, excepting some manuscripts of published works and many letters, eventually found their way into the British Museum, but they were in a rather confused state, with many unpublished manuscripts, fragmentary and complete, that had not been properly arranged, identified, or dated. May Morris died in 1938, and Dr. Robert Steele, her executor, deposited the papers in the Museum the following year.[25] This coincidence of the deposition with the beginning of World War II may explain why nothing was done then to correct the jumbled state of the manuscripts and why, apart from Philip Henderson's selected edition of the *Letters* (1950), no scholarly use of the papers was made until Edward Thompson's study, *William Morris: Romantic to Revolutionary* (1955).

If the unpublished lectures have been obscured by this confu-

---

[25] Shortly thereafter they were described in an article by R. Flower, "The William Morris Manuscripts," *British Museum Quarterly*, XIV (1939–40), 8–12. The new printed catalogue of MSS, which is in galleys now, clarifies matters considerably. The MSS themselves now are much more carefully arranged and bound in volumes.

sion, the canon of the published ones was not much clearer until recently. None but the most knowledgeable scholars could read even the published texts in their proper sequence and with a true sense of the place each occupied in Morris's career. Now, however, the reader can consult R. C. H. Briggs's *Handlist of the Public Addresses of William Morris to Be Found in Generally Accessible Publications* (London, 1961). Going considerably farther, but in the same direction, the Calendar and Bibliography appended to this volume are intended to give as complete a picture as possible of Morris's lecturing activity and the publication of his texts.

On balance—this must in fairness be said—there is little cause for quarrel and much for praise in May Morris's editorial work. While much substance and precision have been added since her time to our knowledge of her father's work, later scholarship owes a great deal to her. Her *Collected Works of William Morris* will remain the standard edition in all likelihood. While she omitted some work from the supplementary volumes, she—as has already been noted—more than doubled there the previously available amount of Morris's non-fictional prose, some of this new material being of the greatest importance to the understanding of her father's public life. The texts and notes of the 1936 volumes are indispensable sources for later discussions of Morris as a thinker and an artist.

So imposing is her editorial accomplishment that there has been little effort since to go back to the sources, to get behind May Morris and grapple with remaining problems arising from her father's texts. Other editors—G. D. H. Cole, Holbrook Jackson, U. I. Shvedor, Asa Briggs, to name only a few[26]—have generally been content to reprint from the *Collected Works* or *William Morris: Artist, Writer, Socialist,* making no attempt to add new material, to correct errors, or to explain and arrange what remains obscure or confused. True, they were presenting popular editions for the general reader, not scholarly tools. But the very existence

---

[26] Details of these editions are included in the List of Abbreviations. G. D. H. Cole, who included "Gothic Architecture" in his collection, is the only editor to reach past May Morris's volumes.

of the wide general interest they serve underlines the need now to see this side of Morris's activity whole, to clarify the question of what he wrote and when, and to edit the remaining unpublished texts. It is long since time that all the evidence be assembled and arranged.

This volume supplements May Morris's editions of the lectures by making available ten of the most important remaining unpublished texts and by providing a chronological list of his speaking engagements and a bibliography of his published texts. A thorough bibliographical study of Morris is still to be done, but when it is, this part will be among the most important.

The texts printed here are all taken directly from manuscripts in the British Museum Collection. Comparison of these manuscripts with contemporary newspaper accounts of their deliveries establishes that these are the lectures in the final form in which Morris read them. In each case authorship is established by the provenance and handwriting of the manuscripts.[27] All but one are unpublished, that is, they have not previously been available to the public either as complete texts or in portions so extensive and central as to express sufficiently the lecturer's theme. Brief quotation in a published work to illustrate points peripheral to the lecture itself has not been considered publication. "The Gothic Revival [I]," "Early England," and "The Early Literature of the North—Iceland," for example are all included even though quotations from them appear in May Morris's background notes.[28] But in each case the quotations illustrate her points, not necessarily Morris's, and all are without proper titles or dates. The one lecture in this volume that has been printed is "Of the Origins of

---

[27] For further details on the manuscripts and the newspaper accounts, see the first footnote to each lecture and the appropriate Calendar entries.

One Bodleian manuscript, "The Man v. the State" (MS. Eng. misc. c. 143) had been catalogued as a Morris holograph, but with the helpful suggestions of E. P. Thompson and some collation by Philip Long of the Bodleian, this has been traced to its true author, Morris's friend, C. J. Faulkner, for many years the bursar of University College, Oxford.

[28] For "The Gothic Revival [I]" see *Artist, Writer, Socialist,* II, 630–31; for "Early England" see *Collected Works,* XVIII, xv–xix; for "The Early Literature of the North—Iceland" see *Artist, Writer, Socialist,* I, 449–453.

Ornamental Art," a nearly complete text having appeared in the *Manchester Guardian* (Sept. 27, 1886) when Morris first read it. But few files of the *Guardian* go back that far, and the importance of this text made its greater accessibility the primary consideration.

The Calendar and Bibliography appended here show where all the lectures fit as parts of a single major esthetic and intellectual effort. From 1877 to 1896 Morris spoke so many times (over six hundred occasions are listed in the Calendar, and it is surely incomplete), before so many different groups, on such a variety of topics, usually reading from fully prepared texts, but sometimes depending on notes and sometimes later in his career speaking wholly extemporé, that this portion of his bibliography became a maze. Only the more obvious parts of it were charted by Morris's two posthumous bibliographers.[29] An accurate view of his entire work has been the more difficult because no one knew how many lectures he wrote or even which ones were available. The Calendar and Bibliography were built up from a study of published and unpublished Morris materials in Great Britain, Holland, and the United States; from a review of those periodicals—*Commonweal, Justice, The Architect,* etc.—that normally reported his activities; from a correlation of letters, diaries, and biographies with information in contemporary periodicals; and from clues in the lectures themselves. The result is an extensive and, I believe, accurate chronology and handlist of Morris's public speaking. Both of these are tools that should be useful for research even as they are being augmented and corrected by researchers.

---

[29] See H. Buxton Forman, *The Books of William Morris Described . . .* (London, 1897), and "Temple Scott" (i.e. J. H. Isaacs), *A Bibliography of the Works of William Morris* (London, 1897).

EDITOR'S NOTE

Reproducing Morris's lectures in print involves a special problem. Traditionally interpreted, the editorial function is to render the author's words exactly as he intended them to be *read;* but there is no indication that Morris ever intended these lectures to be read in their present state by anyone other than himself. His practice, therefore, in writing them did not always adhere to the conventions of written language. He knew perfectly well what he meant, and certainly no one in his audiences would have noticed a missing comma, hyphen, or question mark. Though we read them now as essays, it should be remembered that they were not written as such.

The editorial problem arises from differences between lecture and essay. If the writing of the holographs differed from conventional essay writing only in an expeditious omission of normal punctuation, it would be comparatively easy to correct it by inserting the missing marks. But punctuation in the MSS varies from usual practice—or even usual nineteenth-century practice—in three ways. First, there are those omissions mentioned above, evidently made possible by the author's knowledge of his text. Question marks are often omitted because other signals in the sentence indicate clearly how it should be read; for the same reason, Morris did not always separate items in series by commas.

Second, there are omissions at the ends of lines or paragraphs in the MSS—usually periods or question marks—where necessary pauses are supplied by the ends of the lines. Third—and most important—commas, dashes, colons, and semi-colons are inserted or left out in a fashion consistent only with Morris's own unconventional view of convention. Within this class of variations are included his peculiar use of colons between independent clauses and his almost wholly rhetorical, illogical distribution of commas (sometimes, though rarely, resulting in what freshman composition handbooks call "comma fault" or "run-on sentences"). Examples of these practices abound both in the MSS and in the lectures Morris edited himself (in *Hopes and Fears, Signs of Change,* and *Commonweal*). He once said to George Wardle (B.M. Add. MS. 45350): "punctuation is made for man, not man for punctuation." Acting on this conviction, he departed from established rules, attempting to make even his pointing a part of his art.

How well he succeeded can only be seen in an essentially unchanged text. Certainly the temptation to "correct" is sometimes strong, but—as with the restoration of ancient buildings—once started, how does one know where to stop? Carried to any extent, changes soon affect the structure itself.

To avoid this possibility on the one hand, and the equally repugnant one of facsimile reproduction on the other, the following rules, sketching the limits of editorial manipulation, have been followed throughout. The text that results may sometimes bring the reader to a momentary halt, but there is no passage so obscure that a moment's reflection will not clarify it. Moreover, such occasional difficulties seem a small enough price to pay for authenticity.

1. Omitted question marks and periods are inserted only when the context indicates careless or "short-hand" omission, as, for example, at the end of paragraphs. Commas, colons, semicolons, and dashes are unaltered, except for the silent insertion of commas between items in series. This was a consistent practice in the lectures Morris himself prepared for publication. Quotation marks are inserted only in the case of omitted close quotes, and then only when the position is obvious.

2. Capitalization is exactly as in the MS, except where inserted silently at the beginning of sentences.

3. Spelling has been regularized—that is, made consistent with late nineteenth-century practice. It has not been modernized or, of course, Americanized. The *NED* was the authority in all these matters.

4. Hyphens and apostrophes are considered matters of spelling and inserted or deleted silently.

5. All abbreviations are completed in brackets, but ampersands are written out silently.

6. Obviously inadvertent repetition is corrected silently, but omitted words or letters are supplied in brackets. Errors in grammar are corrected and the original versions given in footnotes.

7. Morris's revisions or deletions are given in footnotes whenever they throw further light on the text or when the version adopted is a reconstruction of an obscure passage. Deleted structure words—prepositions, articles, conjunctions—are not footnoted.

8. All marginal notes by the author—directions for delivery, notations on organization, or reminders of specific illustrations—are reproduced in the notes.

9. Quotations and allusions are identified in footnotes.

[ART: A SERIOUS THING]¹

Some six weeks ago I had occasion to go from London to a place not far from here (called Manchester if you must know),² we left London about 9 in the morning I think on rather a cold morning, with a white frost on the grass and a thickish mist piled above it some feet into the air, though it was visibly not a foul-weather day; well we went on so till we got to the foot of those chalk hills near Tring, the Chilterns I suppose, there we ran into a tunnel, and coming out on the other side were off the clay; being off the clay we were also out of the mist, and into the bright morning sun: it was an almost magical change,

---

¹ The text of this lecture is taken from B.M. Add. MS. 45332(3), which is entirely in Morris's hand. It was, apparently, delivered only once, on Dec. 12, 1882, before the Leek School of Art on the occasion of the annual distribution of prizes to the students of that school. This lecture represents one of Morris's first appearances under the auspices of the national program of art education then known as "The South Kensington System" (see Appendix I, 12–12–82, and Appendix II, item 34). This title is written in pencil at the head of the first MS folio, but it is not in Morris's hand. It may have been added by W. R. Lethaby who once was to edit the unpublished lectures on art. Comparison of this title with samples of Lethaby's hand tends to confirm this.

² Six weeks before (see Appendix I, 10–20–82) Morris had addressed the promoters of the Manchester Fine Arts and Industrial Exhibition at a banquet celebrating the exhibition's opening.

instead of the white thick mist through which one could barely see the ghost of a tree here and there, the bright hill-sides lay before us with the pleasant homesteads lying at their feet surrounded by the autumn elm-trees, and the sky above was clear blue though pale, while the only sign of the mist that had hidden meadows, houses, and all while we were on the clay, was a wreath or two of white vapour dragging along some of the hollows halfway up the hill: indeed it was all very beautiful, and I settled myself down to enjoy myself, knowing how little there is amusing to look at on the L.[ondon] and N.[orth] W.[estern] railway till you have got clear of the pottery towns: but I had scarcely got my eyes well focussed on it when—crick—my neighbour opposite found the sun was in his eyes and pulled down the blind. I was so vexed that I was really inclined to be uncivil to the good man, who for the rest didn't look very ruffianly; like a business man I should say, his countenance bearing no particular expression of any sort; just that look of mingled boredom and anxiety which [is] the usual expression of the modern Anglo-Saxon face: I suppose I ought to have suggested a change of seats to him, but I was too shy, so I just flounced off angrily to the other side, the unsunny side, of the carriage, and looked out of the window, which was also the dull and flat side as well as the unsunny; however there was something to be looked at, and my anger gradually faded away, while something in the sunny glimpse I had had reminded me of a window which was opened to me last year in the midst of Paris, and this is what I saw from that window:[3]

---

[3] It seems unquestionable that the picture Morris describes here is "The Madonna with the Chancellor Rolin" by Jan van Eyck, which was painted c. 1434–5. There are however certain inaccuracies in Morris's description that indicate that he depended wholly on memory for his facts. There is no indication that the "woman" Morris mentions is sitting for her portrait; she is in fact the Virgin, and she sits with the Christ Child in her lap. The "painter . . . serious of face" is the Chancellor Rolin, who kneels in the left foreground with what appears to be a book of hours before him. Finally, the islet seen through the arches is on the far rather than the near side of the bridge. In all other details, including the placing of the picture at the Louvre, Morris is correct. For reproductions of the painting and a discussion of its dating, see Ludwig Baldass, *Jan Van Eyck* (London, 1952), pp. 55–57, plates 116–119 and frontispiece.

In the foreground I saw a sort of corridor or cloister of lovely and delicate round-arched architecture in which sat a slim serious-visaged woman dressed in a gown of deep blue; she was sitting for her portrait, and the painter who was taking it was serious of face also with a look of staid but refined enthusiasm, and was dressed in rich but sober stuffs: the cloister was in half-tone almost, but the sun shone widely abroad without, serene but not glittering: a quaint flowery garden I saw stretching down from the cloister pillars, 2 peacocks strutting about the path: the garden ended in a terraced battlemented wall over which leaned two burgher-like persons dressed in red and blue cloth of antique cut and looked at the landscape beyond: indeed they might well look for even what I could see of it was fair enough: we were in some house, an Abbey I think, but certainly high up on a hill out into terraces, and below the garden wall I could see a river running through a rich country of meadow and hill slopes; an islet split the river some way up and beyond it was a bridge guarded at both ends and the middle by ashlar-built towers: past this I could see the river coming down from hills that grew higher and higher till at last they grew into mountains and rose higher yet till their snow-capped summits cut the clear pale sky so far and far away.

That was the window I looked out in the gallery of the Louvre at Paris, and I thought I had not come all the way from London for nothing since I had seen all that, which I shall never any more forget.

Now he who opened that window to me and keeps it open for whomever will cross the narrow seas, has been dead near 500 years ago;[4] when he was alive he was a citizen of a city which he called in his country tongue the bridges, but which we today call Bruges, and his name was John Van Eyck, the brother of Hubert and Margaret; all three of them had wondrous skill of hand, which however would have served them but little as window-openers but for the eyes they had and the diligent use they made of them; now that kind of use of the senses which nature has

---

[4] Jan Van Eyck's " 'burial fees' were entered in the registers of the church of St. Donatian at Bruges" on July 9, 1441 (*ibid.*, p. 22).

given us and joined in a strange way to that other part of us which we call the mind and soul is what I wish to recommend to all who are here present, not only to those who use their hands in trying to tell us what they think they see, and who are called artists, but also to other reasonable people, as a means for curing that bored and anxious expression of the Anglo-Saxon countenance, which, give me leave to say, is a ridiculous mask to put on our faces in a world which has or ought to have so much to interest a reasonable man as ours has or ought to have.

In passing I may say that my window-shutting fellow traveller turned out to be good-natured enough and not unintelligent, but it was quite clear that he never used his eyes for looking at anything that his business or his bodily wants didn't compel him to look: his landscape was bounded by his ledger and his mutton chop.

Here is a contrast to that long-dead citizen of Bruges to whom I owe such gratitude, I and many another; for indeed you need not cross the narrow seas to look through his eyes, for in no prettier or cleaner place than Trafalgar Sq.[5] in London you can see a chamber in Bruges city, and a man and his wife standing hand in hand amidst their household goods just as they stood 500 years ago, and to make it clear to all that he really did see it, the citizen of Bruges above-named wrote on the wall in gold letters, 'Ego Johannes de Eyk fuit hic': 'I John Van Eyck was here.'

I say that is a great contrast, which however is only worth noticing because the man who snuffed out the sunlit Chilterns for me was no monster of stupidity, but the type of a class, and that class comprises the most of people nowadays; and once more I say no wonder that such people look bored and anxious.

Further the remedy to this strange perversity which I commend to all reasonable people is to use their eyes to wit. I am bound chief of all to commend to such of you as are definitely studying art, as we call it, to those of you whose special business it is to see yourselves and to make others see what there is in the

---

[5] In the National Gallery, which fronts on Trafalgar Square, is displayed Jan Van Eyck's "Wedding Portrait of Giovanni Arnolfini," dated 1434 (*ibid.*, pp. 55, 72–76, plates 137–40).

world: by which indeed you will gain some insight both into what has been and what will be in it: with you it lies to get people in general to use their eyesight, for you can give them examples of the benefit of doing so: there is, or perhaps I may hopefully say, there was an idea abroad that the artist was a lazy, loafing sort of fellow, who if he were born of well-to-do people became an artist for the same sort of reason that his brother went into the army or the church, in order namely that he might escape hard work; or if he were an artisan work pretty hard at high wages 2 days a week so that he might be lazy and probably drunk the other 4 days: I say that was the idea of [the] result of a man being born with some artistic gift, if he were so ill-advised as to let the said gift have any scope and carry him into a fatal course of life.

Well, the amount of truth that may be at the bottom of this theory, I can dimly discern, but so dimly, that it is not worth while to try to put it into words for you: because practically and as far as dealing with the actualities of life, from a business point of view, let me say there is *no* truth in the theory.

I have the honour and advantage of knowing several artists of the higher kind, and nothing about their way of working is more noteworthy than the pains they take: they will not allow anything to come easy to them, for they are forever intent in making the very best of their talent, and when they have got the mastery over one point, they don't rest and be thankful, but go on to master another: they don't hug themselves on the work that they have done; hope which lit their path till that work was turned out of hand, has died out of it now, and is shining on the work which they have to do: nothing can be ever done well enough for them. Pray is this likely to be a lazy, loafing kind of life?

I don't want to find fault anywhere if I can help it, but you must pardon me for saying that if our law-makers and law-administrators, our practical common sense men of business, who can be trusted worked half as hard, and single-heartedly as our real artists do—why England would be quite a decent place to live in.

Mind I say our real artists, and I don't profess to think there are many of them: there are plenty of pretenders to the title, as there are in all occupations, who are criminal nuisances nothing short of it: so please to remember all you that are studying art that you have a heavy responsibility on your shoulders: if you are less than honest in your work, and you may judge by what I have just been saying what my standard of honesty is, if you are less than honest I say, every act of your artistic life is a nail in the coffin of art, or in plain words of civilization, or in plainer words still, of the hope of mankind to live a decent life fit for men.

Indeed I suppose that the fact of your having made up your minds to study art shows that you have some gifts in that direction: but pray don't play with the matter, but find out through any failures if it must be so what your gifts are: then the worst that can happen will be that you will find out that you have no gifts for art, in which case, out with the knife—cut it all away, and betake yourselves to some other occupation, and you will at any rate have saved yourselves loss of time, and self-respect.

But the worst case will not be common: most men have still some gifts towards the arts which can be brought to light if they have opportunities for developing them; that last sentence shows you the meaning of the schools of art which have been established to teach people to use their eyes, and to eschew drawing down blinds on sunlit landscapes.

These opportunities for developing your talents, will if you use them properly show you infallibly what you can attempt, and what you had better leave alone: in the first place I believe that nearly as many people can be taught to draw anything that will stand still, as can be taught to write: well, well, I do assure you that many people are incapable of learning writing, even distinguished ones: I think the ghost of Dean Stanley[6] for instance will forgive me for saying that he was one of them.

Now, though a man may draw well in a sense, and still not be an artist in any sense, still the acquirement of the art will be useful to him even then, and I think it ought to be taught more widely and more systematically than it is, even looking at it from that point of view. But if you can learn to draw not only mechani-

---

[6] Arthur Penrhyn Stanley, Dean of Westminster and a fairly voluminous writer (*The Life of Dr. Arnold* was perhaps his best-known work) had died in July, 1881. See R. E. Prothero, *The Life and Correspondence of Stanley, Late Dean of Westminster.* 2 vols. (London, 1893.)

cally, but artistically also, that is to say, in such a way that it is
obvious to those who can use their eyes that you have had
pleasure in the drawing, and a hope of carrying on your art
further, if this be the case, then you can lay claim to be an artist
of some sort: in striving to find out of what sort, to what rank of
artist you belong you will doubtless have difficulties and disap-
pointments, but it will all come right in the end, so long as you
are honest in your work: nor, as long as there is any real appreciation of art, need any man quarrel with himself because his rank as
an artist is humble; everyone comes to the end of his tether step
by step whether he be great or small; and let me tell you, that
though every real artist aspires to do his best, and ever to better
it, yet every real artist has also in him a fund of content, or if you
please so to call it of humility: withal I repeat that whenever art
is at all approximately in the state that it should be there is room
for artists of all capacities from the greatest to the least: to be a
pretender, a bungler, that is to be not a humble artist, but none at
all; and the distance between the humblest man who can do a
thing, and the showiest pretender who can *not* is not to be
measured at all, it is infinite, the difference between nothing and
something.

I think sometimes that there have been ages in the world's
history of which ours is one, that have thought over much of the
glories of great men, and not enough of the welfare of common
men; such ages have had a tendency to carry due hero-worship,
which is a proper and necessary thing, into superstition; by which
they not only injure their great men, flattering them like flunkies
instead of honouring them like men and their very fellows, but
also are easily led astray into taking pretentious men for great
ones, not remembering that the foundation of all greatness is
humility; you must be a man first before you are a great man.
Now all artists cannot be Michael Angelos, but all can be worthy
fellows and helpmates for him: and he will be the first to ac-
knowledge this, the first to feel the want of such helpmates and
fellows, if unhappily the time does not breed them for him: be
sure that every great artist will do full justice to any piece of
artistic work which is good and sound of its kind, and will not
despise it because it does not profess to solve 'the riddle of the

painful earth' in a hurry: indeed he need do justice to it, for it will show him that there is at least someone who can sympathize with his troubles and triumphs; he can no more do without an audience than can any other interpreter between nature and man; and I will go bail for it if he is a man of any note, he has had enough of the kind of worshipper who will stand before his easel, and say "charming!" looking out of the window at nothing all the time.

But remember this great man who will be sympathetic, indulgent even, for all genuine work will have nothing but justice for all empty pretence: the slap-dash and the vague they will send back to their grammar, and bid them learn before they try to teach.

I say remember this, and don't be too mild in judging yourselves, however kind you are to others: and as to how you are to judge yourselves, I must say again use your eyes: your *own* eyes, you understand, in one way or other, and not other people's: for I have noticed that one is often rather anxious for the favourable opinion of others on a piece of work which in one's own heart one has condemned already.

Now as to the standard of comparison by which you are to judge your work, apart from the works of the great master, nature, I would have you take a high standard; nor be discouraged at the apparent difference between your attempts and this exemplary accomplishment: it is part of the great gifts of all thoroughly good work, and finely illustrates the fellowship of all genuine workmen little and great which I have been speaking of, that such work does not discourage the learner, but encourages him: I suppose the reason for this is that the great natural principles on which it was done shine through the workmanship, and are, tacitly or not, understood by those who are honestly aspiring to do good work: while on the contrary coming across a bad and pretentious piece of work, does not exhilarate a successful artist with a sense of superiority but depresses him with a feeling of doubt as to the value of his own work: so immeasurable is the difference between bad and good in the arts, so unceasing the evil that falseness gives birth to.

Now again as to your standard of excellence though I do not

wish to be considered a pedant or even a mere antiquarian, I do think you will judge yourselves better by comparison with work that has stood the test of ages, and is still accounted excellent, than if you used contemporary work to test yourselves by: to say, I can do as well as or better than my fellows, people who are in the same hobble as ourselves, that is apt to lower our standard, I think, and reduces what ought to be calm and cool judgment of our own work by ourselves to a mere piece of competition, and competition which is apt to be decided by reference to conventional standards applied by people who do not thoroughly know us.

Well, I have caught myself for some little time past advising you that are art students here; caught myself, I say because I feel shy of doing this to an audience I am not thoroughly acquainted with, and who are taught by competent teachers on a definite and well-considered plan:[7] all I can say in excuse is that it rather leads up to what I am going to say to you, and which I would say to any audience, whatever their calling might be.

A while ago I was speaking of what I considered the erroneous estimate that was and perhaps still is made by people of the effect of the study and practice of art on the lives of the artists: quite conventionally made, let me add, for the people who hold that view know nothing whatever of artists' lives or the difficulties of their work: In trying to confute this erroneous impression which people have or had of art, I spoke almost entirely of the kind of workman whom we today call an *artist:* that is to say a man whose work is demanded entirely by the necessities of the mind; but there is another kind of workman whose work is demanded partly by the necessities of the body: him we call by various names, which I am ashamed to say do in most people's minds imply inferiority: artisan for instance, or operative: as these names are certainly not English, and to my mind there is a smack of insult about them, as withal their etymological meaning is vague, I shall by your leave use an English word in their stead;

---

[7] The "plan" referred to here is the national program of art education then known as the South Kensington System.

a word full of meaning, and to all reasonable people implying honour and not reproach: I shall use the word handicraftsman.

Please excuse a word or two etymological, which also will have a serious bearing on our general subject of the arts; and let me remind you that the word craft and its adjective crafty have been degraded and misapplied in modern English very unfortunately as I think: they are used to express trickiness or dishonesty, where we ought to use the words guile or guileful: oddly enough by the way our kinsmen on the other side of the herring-pond have served the word clever in the same way, while they use the word 'cunning' in its true sense, 'knowing' viz. Well, the right meaning of the word craft is simply *power:* so that a handicrafts-man signifies a man who exercises a power by means of his hands, and doubtless when it was first used was intended to signify that he exercised a certain kind of power; to wit, a readiness of mind and deftness of hand which had been acquired through many ages, handed down from father to son and increased generation by generation: surely a class of men who possess such a power is a class to be honoured and thanked rather than nicknamed by foolish outlandish words.

Well anyhow this kind of man is or ought to be the other kind of artist who is or was conventionally considered to be a 'loose fish' by prescriptive right: but I should call that opinion a libel on him if I had not heard it said that 'twas a maxim of law, the greater the truth the greater the libel: so the first syllable of the word *libel* must answer my purpose: for my own part I know by experience that ever so little of the artist added to the handi-craftsman makes him a more profitable man to employ, to say nothing of the effect of art on himself, as giving some additional pleasure and interest to his life.

Thus much I have been saying of the artist and the handicrafts-man as if they were naturally two distinct classes of workers: I suppose it is almost the universally received opinion not only that it is so, which is obvious, but also that it is natural and right that it should be so.

But if that be so, I will ask in the first place, what is intended to be done by all the schools of art and the like, which have been established under the superintendence of the Depart[ment] of Sci[ence] and Art?[8] Are they intended to turn out any number of artists? and if so what kind of artists, and how are they going to live: my impression is that there is a pretty sharp struggle for subsistence in what may be called the lower ranks of those we call artists.

The fact is these schools were not intended to turn out what are conventionally termed artists, they were intended first for general artistic education, and second for the special education of those who design for industrial arts. As for the result of the second of these purposes, I have some doubts if it has quite answered the expectations formed, as for that of the first I suppose it has not been disappointing on the whole; at all events from whencesoever it comes there is more interest felt in art than there used to be; and moreover there was assuredly an idea in those who founded these places of education that some tincture would not spoil the handicraftsman but would improve him; in short that it is not natural and right that the artist should be wholly dissociated from the handicraftsman.

Meantime however, the wide distinction remains as wide as ever; the only difference made by the spread of artistic education is that there are more, and I hope better artists than there were; if a handicraftsman shows any decidedly artistic talents, instead of remaining in his craft, and illuminating it, so to say by his talents, he climbs up out of it into the class of artists, the craft that really needed his talent has lost it; the profession that did not specially want it has gained it, and probably smothered it into invisibility: surely there is waste of power here, waste of craftsmanship.

Well now I can understand some of you saying; but are you a crusted old Tory? would you prevent a clever man from rising in the world? because whereas when he was a handicraftsman he was not a *gentleman,* now he is one, since he is an artist, and so he has risen a step even if he hasn't bettered his income; would you we say prevent the man from rising?

Indeed I mustn't say what I am, but I suppose I may go as far as to say what I am not, and that is a crusted old Tory: so in any

---

[8] This is the official title of the South Kensington System.

case I am glad if a clever man rises, and know well that in order to rise he must do as I have been saying as things are—more's the pity! more's the waste! and to be plain with you, you won't better the matter on this side till you have got rid of all that folly of calling a man a gentleman or denying him the title according as he works in this or that way; all that quaint heraldic jargon with the mismanagement of forces and unfairness that goes with it.

Now don't misunderstand me, I don't want a mere confusion of the different grades of artists for I have said before that such grades must exist; but there must be no sharp distinction if we are to have art worth the trouble, widespread and 'understanded of the people': if we are to have popular art.

If things are to go on as they are now what will art amount to when we clear our eyes and look into the matter without fear of making ourselves disagreeable: in fact without hypocrisy? To my mind it will amount to this:

There will be on the one hand a great body of artists so-called turning out most of them unsatisfactory work not for lack of talent, but because their talent will be misapplied; they will be compelled to be gentlemen and more or less useless because they are more talented than their fellows, and so are to be set to supply the demand for *fine art* as 'tis called, and not really being artists *enough* for that demand will have to supply a substitute for it, which will receive very languid attention from the public in general, yet more attention than it will deserve: above the heads of these will be a very few man of genius, who at the expense of great toil and suffering will have acquired real mastery over their art, and will produce works of art of a high quality, but which will not in the least be 'understanded of the people' partly from their fault or rather misfortune, partly from the fault or misfortune of the people.

All this will supply the languid demand for the more intellectual side of art: the fine arts: but there is still a demand for the less intellectual side of the arts to wit the ornament of the industrial arts, that side of it which should be done by handicraftsmen. How is that to be supplied if things are to go on as they are? Well, the handicraftsmen can't supply it, if the article is to be genuine, for they are not taught to be artists, nay are not allowed to be, are in fact turned into 'operatives' which I take it is another name for machines.

Now the machines some of which will be of steel and brass and some of flesh and bone will not turn out art, for a machine cannot do it, but they will turn out a substitute for it, which will be sold very cheap, but will not be worth the money it costs, for it will be worth nothing.

So that will be the art produced by the wasteful system of forcing men to do what they are unfit to do simply because we have fallen into a groove and will not get out of it: let us look at it clearly and see what it means.

First at the top of the tree will come very scanty however precious fruit, the art done by great men struggling under great disadvantages, the worst of which will be that the public in general will have little sympathy for them.

Then lower down the fruit will be tolerably plenteous, but unripe of little use as it is: the art of a good number of men of fair talents, but undisciplined, and striving to do what they have no chance to do really well: such art will be plausible pretension, but unsatisfying: nobody will care much about it because it will not have the root of the matter in it.

Last and lowest will come a very strange fruit indeed, which nobody will want, and nobody will be willing to pay for, but which will go on being produced from a sort of habit: that will be the position of ornamental art so-called; to be allowed to exist when it does not get in the way of the machine which is to be used for producing riches that nobody will be able to use.

Well, there is one comfort about it, that such a state of things cannot last very long: civilized man will either say, 'let us have an end of this folly called art and live like decent beasts—' or what else will happen?

Indeed I should hope that man, even when he is so civilized as to be forced to live in Burslem or Widnes or Manchester[9] will still

---

[9] All three of these cities are primarily important as manufacturing centers. Burslem is a great pottery-manufacturing town; Widnes produces huge quantities of soap; and Manchester—by far the largest of the three—is the center of the textile industry.

have some longing for beauty left him, enough at all events to feel discontented with the sweet spots I have just named, and that he will cast about to see if something cannot be done to get him as large a share of it as a red-skin or a Zulu gets for himself, and if by some means art cannot be begun again; in which case what ideal will he look up to beyond the humble present endeavours to bring art to a healthy new birth again? What ideas will he have as to what art has to do for him, and what kind of sacrifices will he be bound to make for it?

Surely, first of all he will remember that no pyramid can stand on its apex, but must stand on its base: he will know that before anything worthy to be called art can exist, it must be longed for by the whole people, and he will look forward to the day when no one save a few curious exceptions, men of more or less diseased minds, will fail to understand art and to demand his due share of it: in that day though there will be gradations of art from the humblest to the most exalted, there will [be] no sham art, nor even any bungling, because everyone who works with his hands will find out his real and proper place, and will do his best in it: and between all handicraftsmen will be mutual help and sympathy; they will all keep touch, as the drill sergeants call it: the great artist will think it a matter of course that his house and the goods in it should be made beautiful and interesting by the hearty thought and happy deftness of his humbler guild-brother, who in his turn will not find that the great master speaks to him in an unknown tongue: moreover it will be a consequence of this that civilized man will no longer seem (as he does now) to be the enemy of nature, to shame her and befoul her, and turn her rest and order and beauty into feverish ragged squalor: the house shall be like a natural growth of the meadow, and the city a necessary fulfillment of the valley. Nor is that all, nor the most of it: for this outward order and beauty will be but a token of fair and orderly life, of days made up of unwearisome work, and of leisure restful but not vacant: of a life in which year by year the land of his fathers shall grow dearer and fairer to a man as he gets to know it better and better, although his times be cast in a place where nature wears her everyday clothes, no queen but a thrifty housewife: so that when he goes into other lands richer of startling beauty and wild romance, he will fare not as a man driven by dullness that nothing can brighten, by weariness that no idleness can soothe, but as a pilgrim who has left his home a while that he may come back stored with new pictures and tales of the life of other men. A steadfast home that he shall never weary of, work that he shall never turn from in disgust, neighbours that never shame him with faces soured by injustice and hopelessness; these are the surroundings that he shall look to art to find for him, and if it be the art of his ideal, it will not fail him: would not such things as these be worth buying at a heavy price? or what price could buy them?

Indeed if ever such art as I am thinking of be gained by men once more when they look back on anything which they have had to sacrifice for it, they will think it little enough: but, to us looking forward, and, many of us, thinking of art vaguely, looking upon it as a pretty ornament which our lives may wear or not as they think fit, and be none the worse if they refuse it: to us I say who do not rightly know what art means, or have had [no] leisure or opportunity to think what a dull blank the total loss of it would make in all men's lives, the necessary sacrifices to be made before art can be born again might seem great and overgreat if we could see them rightly all at once.

But let me say for myself, that I have now followed art for a good many years and through all that time have more and more directly set my face toward that ideal of art which I have been speaking of, till it seems to me that I have gained some inkling of what sacrifices must be made before art can become healthy and progressive again.

My views if I stated them fully would seem to many here too wild and eccentric to be even listened to, yet something I must at least hint at, since it seems to me that the first sacrifice to be made in favour of art is the pleasure of prophesying smooth things to one's friends and neighbours whose kindness one would fain forebear to try by differing from them even a little.

I have said already that I durst not ask a man born to earning weekly wages to sacrifice his ambition to rise out of his class: what can I ask men to do who have little money and little leisure to spare for any cause that does not seem very clear indeed to them? Yet surely among such men the hope is not lacking nor the effort to raise their whole class as a class, and by such efforts is art more helped if we artists did but know it than by anything else that is done in our days.

I have taken note of many strikes, and I must needs say without circumlocution that with many of these I have heartily sympathized: but when the day comes that there is a serious strike of workmen against the poisoning of the air with smoke or the waters with filth, I shall think that art is getting on indeed, and that the schools of art have had a noble success: meanwhile I fancy most of you will agree with me in thinking it a hopeful token that all classes show signs of uniting to prevent the robbery of commons which till quite lately has gone on unchecked in England:[10] the more individuals are kept in due order by the public, the more public rights are respected the nearer grows our chance of the new birth of popular art.

For the rest I might I know preach a sermon to my brethren of the working classes on the benefit of thrift and sobriety and the rest of it, but I am thinking that art and the love of art will one day preach that sermon clearly enough to them so I had rather say a few words to finish with to those of my own class, to the rich and well-to-do, and the rather because, and it is a woeful confession to have to make I know little of any class save my own.

Now then I will say what I have often said before, and shall go on saying till there is no more need to say it: what I mean by art, what I am really interested in, is not the prevalence of this or that style, not the laying on the public taste whether it will or not a law that such or such a thing must be done in art, not this interests me, and forces me to speak when I had far rather hold my peace; but rather a general love of beauty, partly for its own sake, and because it is natural and right for the dwellers on the beautiful earth to help and not to mar its beauty, and partly, yes

---

[10] Morris was quite active at this time in the Commons Preservation Society, of which George Shaw-Lefevre, M.P., was chairman. In the Society's *Reports of Proceedings, 1876–80*, Morris is listed on the General Committee.

At this point in the MS the words "or the heaping up of riches without regard to the way in" are deleted.

and chiefly, because that external beauty is a symbol of a decent and reasonable life, is above all the token of what chiefly makes life good and not evil, of joy in labour, in creation that is: and this joy in labour, this evidence of man helping in the work of creation, is I feel sure the thing which from the first all progress in civilization has been aiming at: feed this inspiration and you feed the flame of civilization throughout the world; extinguish it, and civilization will die also: material prosperity, as they call it, that is a thing, which according to our way of dealing with it will be either the helpful servant or the cruel tyrant of civilization: are you satisfied that it is still only our servant? If so bid it give back to England the green fields which it has wasted, bid it turn its terrible power to the task of giving us something worthy to supply the place of the stored-up loveliness of ten centuries of which it has robbed the homes of England: give it that command first, and see if it will obey you, for there will be tasks heavy enough for it when it has begun that.

And if you will find that it will not obey you, and that it is, as indeed I fear, our master now, and not our servant, what shall we do then? Two courses lie open to us; the first to sit down deed-less, and pretend that we believe all is well and better, to let our material prosperity drag us into deeds of injustice at home and abroad: to destroy the prosperity both material and spiritual of far-off countries in the name of civilization, while at home we weakly try to palliate with our left hand the miseries we have recklessly raised with our right: to sit still and feign content, though we know that for all men day by day is less and less leisure, more and more wearisome work unworthy of men; to gather if we be rich some share of material prosperity to us, making an island in the sea of squalor, and hoping at least that we shall be eaten last or one of the last.

That is the one course open to us when we know that we have become the slaves of the tyrant we have made for ourselves: and the other what is that? Daily and hourly resistance to our tyrant. Ceaseless plotting of rebellion against him, till one day it breaks out openly and reduces him to his old condition of servant again: a heavy task you may say, even those of you who have your eyes open, and know the monster which we have misnamed commerce for what he is.

Indeed it is no light task, but I do believe that the heaviest part of it lies in making up our minds that it has to be undertaken: some ease and comfort the rebels of commerce will have to sacrifice doubtless, and many things which men oftenest desire; but of those many, most, will be found when we have lost them, to have been but troublous hindrances to life.

Surely there are those who now desire money unreasonably and who distress themselves (and their neighbours) very much in the acquirement of it who strive for it for reasons which would no longer exist if civilization should get into the right road again: I know some of those reasons, of the nature of fencing oneself against the intrusion of barbarous ugliness, or the desire for the private possession of works of art. The time will come when no one will need money for such purposes for ugliness in the work of man's hands, which is now the rule will exist no longer; when there will be humble but satisfying art in private dwellings, and lofty soul-inspiring art in public places, in short nature here unspoiled, there helped in her loveliness about us on all hands.

Could any money buy that now? Still more could any money buy the deep content of which it will be at once a token and a cause, a content arising from a population employed in worthy work, which will bring pleasure and sympathy for the worker in him who uses it, pleasure and self-respect in him who makes it?

Compare that with the track of waste and squalor which the misnamed monster Commerce leaves behind him now, and join me I beg of you in hastening forward the day when the motto of our country and of all countries shall be 'one for all, and all for one.'

THE GOTHIC REVIVAL [I][1]

By this name I understand all those attempts to break down the slavery imposed on us first by the Italian Renaissance, which at first was but little felt; partly because the traditions of the free art of the Middle Ages were still influencing people's minds, and partly because of the great mass of individual talent and genius which existed in the artists, the painters, and the sculptors, of that exciting period, and which even yet dazzles our eyes so much by its splendour, that we are scarce able to look steadily enough at the condition of art and labour at the time and see what was really going on: I say the slavery which the days of the Renaissance brought on all labour was at first but little felt in the arts; but as time went on, the mediaeval traditions of work died out, and very speedily too, and the genius of the individual artists was buried in their graves, or flickered feebly in

[1] The text of this lecture is taken from B.M. Add. MS. 43331(10), which is entirely in Morris's hand. It was apparently delivered only once, on March 3, 1884 (see Appendix I, 3–3–84), to The Birmingham and Midland Institute in Birmingham. One week later (see Appendix I, 3–10–84) the second part of the two was delivered to the same audience.

Although a small portion of this lecture has been published in *Artist, Writer, Socialist* (II, 629–30), it seems proper for several reasons to include the entire text here (see Appendix II, items 44 and 45).

certain narrow circles, and all that was left us of that wonderful and much-behymned new birth was a *caput mortuum*[2] of academical pedantry, which, looking down on the world from the serene heights of cultivated stupidity, despised all genuine and sincere attempts at the expression of the thought of man by means of art, and above all despised the people, the true source of all art, as of all wealth, as base mechanical drudges, and brute beasts just good enough to wait upon their fellows for the hire of dog's wages.

It seems to me that any attack however feeble, from whatever side, of however little importance in itself, on such a monstrous and cowardly tyranny is worthy of our attention and sympathy: but I think that before I have done with my subject I shall be able to show that in spite of much ignorance and many fantastic errors, in spite also of being directed on a side of human thought which is somewhat at a discount at present, the intellectual Revolt known as the Gothic Revival was and is really connected with the general progress of the world, with those aspirations towards freedom, from which in truth no sincere art can ever be dissociated.

Now it was the very essence of the academical pedantry to which the Renaissance led, as its natural degradation, that it was ignorant of real history: for it history fell asleep some time about the death of Nero to awake in Italy in the days of Kaiser Maximilian: all that had gone before the days of Pericles was a vague, ill-understood, empty dream; all that took place after the first palmy days of the Roman empire was but a confused jostling of barbarous peoples not worth looking at or considering. But the intellectual revolt which I have to speak to you about was even in its first days founded on an appreciation of the value of history; that feeling grew as the revolt strengthened, until at last a new science grew up, almost a new sense one may say, and real living history became possible to us; not a dry string of annals, not a mere series of brilliant essays or comparisons between the past and the present; but a definite insight into the life of the bygone ages founded on a laborious and patient sifting of truth from

---

[2] The *NED* defines *caput mortuum* as ". . . a worthless residue."

hearsay; the story of the past I say became possible for us to read, and we began to see why we [are] placed as we are [at] present, and whitherward we are tending: and from thenceforward we have not ventured to divide history into what is worthy and worthless to know of; men we are, and all that men have done or been is worthy our thought and study; even though we may be the crown of all that has been hitherto, something will come after us as something has gone before us, we are but a link in the ever-moving chain of history that goes from the dusk into the dark.

Well it is this new feeling for history which is almost as it were a religion on which the Gothic Revival has from the first been founded, and which it has itself in its turn done much to foster, stimulating the research, and throwing new light on the discoveries of those who were more historians than artists: I shall perhaps before I finish be able to point out to you more than one way in which it has brought this about; but I must now definitely address myself to the special task of the first of the two lectures I have to deliver to you, which I think will chiefly be the sketching for you some presentment of what the Gothic Art was, and how it was related to the history of the world, before I can lay before you finally the results of the revolt against the academical stupidity of the 18th cent[ury]: and give you my poor opinion of what its chances are in the future, and whether or not we may have to dread for the 20th century a recurrence of that inane tyranny of the 18th which our own time has at least felt uneasy under.

But before I go further I must ask you to understand that in using the word Art, I am thinking of a wide subject and include not only the lesser or architectural arts or those allied to industrialism but also at least all that side of literature which is born of fancy and imagination.

Now I have used the word *Gothic* Revival, and *Gothic* Art without any hesitation; not only because the word has been for long conventionally used to express that side of art and is now generally understood, but also because though it was I suppose originally used in a kind of good-humoured contempt it really expresses something of the history of the art in question, and that too not its least important side: for whatever its origins were of which I must next speak, certain it is that that branch of the great Germanic family whose isolated descendants have left behind us at once the most romantic and the most dramatic record of its morals, religion, and aspirations did set its seal upon it at least, and that their spirit shows in it always, and makes it what it is. But its origins are far enough removed from those kindred tribes whose laws and manners, developed by their own necessities apart from those of the older civilizations, forced it to take the form which we now all know as Gothic: I will for the present set aside the literary part of its development, the lines of which became confused by pedantry even early in the Middle Ages at the time when our own tongue became confused and to my mind degraded as the result [of] our dealings in various ways with the Latinized countries of the continent leaving these islands nothing that had any unadulterated flavour of the soil save the fragmentary literature of Ireland and Wales, the oral tradition and ballads of Scotland and the northern border, and the fragments of songs of the early Germanic invaders among which towers majestic the noble poem of Beowulf, unsurpassed for simplicity and strength by any poem of our later tongue.

So now, as to the origins of Gothic art in its narrower sense, that is to say of its Architecture with the accompanying arts, it is of course obvious that it was born from that Roman architecture which included in it the remains of Greek art, dealing with it however in no sympathetic spirit; which Greek mask or outward, ill-understood semblance overlaid an internal body of art deduced from the tribes of Italy by some process of which we know nothing clearly; this body which, while Roman architecture still remained classical, was little more than a habit of building was the germ from which one side at least of Gothic architecture sprang: and the birth became visible just about the time when the religion whose real aim was the worship of the great city as the visible embodiment of irresistible authority, when the city-worship of old Rome was fading out: Diocletian's Palace at Spalato gave the first sign that a new epoch of art was dawning on the world far as anybody could have been from suspecting that the last luxurious home of the Imperial tax-gatherer would date the beginning of the freedom of art.

That I say was the first beginning the first glimmer of Gothic Art: but it needed another influence to give it any reproductive force; that influence had been preparing for ages past in Mesopotamia first, and then in Syria and Persia, and seems to have already acted in its earliest times, superficially perhaps, on the ornamental side of Greek Art: this art of Mesopotamian origin changed by various circumstances as I say in Syria, and more still in Persia where it was subjected to the influence of the ancient and long-enduring religion of Zoroastrianism, did at last meet the body of the Roman work set free from the subjection of Greek ornament, and hieratic custom, and so long years after the death of Diocletian, and when whatever there was of real power in the empire had left Rome for Constantinople, and Greek was the official language of the Roman empire—and so at Constantinople produced what is generally called Byzantine Art, but which I will call the first style of Gothic, because, then first was art set free from the fetters of the long centuries of pedantry that followed the crystallization of Greek art into the academical degradation of what was once so vigorous and in most essentials so free. Now you must understand that this Byzantine art as it is called which came to strangely sudden perfection in the days of Justinian, the builder of St. Sophia, had a reflex influence on the art of Italy, which also became Byzantine though with a difference: from the two centres of old and new Rome it is not very difficult to trace the stream of art by means of the architectural monuments still left us, aided by some remains of the lesser arts if so one must call them, pre-eminent among which must be named, the important one of calligraphy and painting in books, which has preserved for us so much of the design and ideas of the Middle Ages which would otherwise have been lost, I mean to say if we had had only to depend upon the remains of the wall-paintings which once covered the interior of nearly every building in Europe. Well, by these means we can note that the Art of Byzantium proper on the one hand much influenced by the kindred development of Persian Art spread all over the Mussulman East, producing everywhere an architecture of nearly complete unity of style which can in fact otherwise only be named from the countries or among the tribes where it is found, as Indian, Arab, and the like; for as to

Indian Art, outside the Brahman architecture which is a survival of early Arian work obviously even amidst its lack of beauty akin to that of Greece, and outside also Buddhist art, which takes the impress in some places of other families of man who fell under the sway of that great religion, there is no art peculiar to the peninsula. While as to Arab art, except that the race has impressed a sense of its turn for number, order, and repetition, a sort of poetry of arithmetic upon the Byzantine-Persian ornament, which shows in its elaborate geometrical interlacements and the like, except for this, there is no trace of any prepossession towards any form of art among the Arab people.

So one may say that the first and most obvious branch of the new Free Art is traceable in the Architecture of the Mussulman East. The next, to make a long stride in place, is the art which was taken, apparently directly from Byzantium, by the Germans of the early Middle Ages, and by them carried all over northern, non-Latin Europe, including England before the Norman Conquest, and the Scandinavian countries to a certain extent; although they were partly influenced by an older form of art, which was probably pre-Arian, and certainly knew nothing of either old or New Rome. This art has until touched by the Byzantine influence no capacity for the representation of natural form, and seemingly no aspirations towards it; it is found unmixed chiefly in Ireland, where in the elaborate pieces of calligraphy which the monks of that country carried out were wrought for us monuments of an art as alien to the general feeling of Gothic as the Arab interlacements: the patience and clearness of execution of them is wonderful, nor do they lack a certain beauty, to a great extent owing to the splendour and care of the actual writing: otherwise than in Ireland although this ornament has its influence not only in England, Scandinavia, and north Germany but even, as far as book ornamentation is concerned in France and Germany it is never found without a share of distinct Byzantine Art, which in the Scandinavian art mingles with it and changes it into a separate style, but in England and France is simply used side by side with it without blending. There is no doubt in my mind, by the way, that the restless trader-buccaneers of Scandinavia played a great part in spreading over North Europe the art of

Byzantium by direct transmission of wares; up to the time of the Crusades they were always coming and going between their northern home and Constantinople and gold coins have been found in their hoards not only of those struck in that great city but even by Mussulman Potentates: I may mention quite up to the beginning of the 18th century the style clung to Iceland, embroideries are found there of that period which reproduce literally the patterns of the 12th century, themselves little changed from those of Justinian's time. Even Germany was for long very conservative of the forms of Byzantine Art; in the buildings of the North of the country the style exists very little changed, except as it were involuntarily, it has gone clumsier and lost some of its grace and beauty, and gained a little invention and some fantasticism and that is all. Even at Cologne whose Latin name and traditions might seem to account for the prevalence of a round-arched style amidst developed pointed architecture (for some at least of the fine churches of that city are no earlier than its French Cathedral), even there the influence of actual Byzantine art is obvious enough I cannot help thinking in St. Gereon.[3] At any rate Germany as a whole shows the direct influence of Byzantium apart from that of old Rome, and it lasted much later there than in other countries, till in fact it was swept away by the flood of Medieval Gothic, whose advent in Germany at least it seems reasonable to connect with the rise and development of the craft guilds, which just about that time were carrying the day, and organizing all labour under them.

But if it fared thus with the stream of art that crept from Byzantium over the northern parts of Europe, [which][4] had felt but little the rule of old Rome, it was quite different with that other stream which coming from the Eternal City spread through Italy and thence into south and north France, and so across the Channel with the Latinized Northmen of Duke William and our An-

---

[3] St. Gereon in Cologne was completed in 1191. See Kenneth John Conant, *Carolingian and Romanesque Architecture* (Harmondsworth, Middlesex, 1959), p. 265.
[4] The MS here has "who."

gevin kings: this indeed was the true stream of Architectural art
(among Latinized peoples): let us look as briefly as possible at its
course and the other affluents that swelled it as Mediaeval Europe progressed towards the great change of the Renaissance. In
Italy itself it found itself in the South, in Sicily, in direct contact
with the Byzantine-Mussulman art, but never mingled with it; in
North Italy on the contrary it fell into the midst of an actual
Gothic people, and the spirit of the North at once seized on it and
gave it life, and working through the old Roman forms produced
some of the most beautiful buildings which the world has ever
seen: but as with this Lombard architecture Gothic architecture
in Italy waned I will just note the fact here; asking you, if you
doubt it, to compare the two churches at Verona, St. Zeno and St.
Anastasia:[5] the first is round-arched, the second pointed, and
therefore formally Gothic: nevertheless St. Zeno is undoubtedly
in all essential respects far more Gothic; St. Anastasia being really
a classical building masquerading in Gothic: the fact is that
except for this Lombard enthusiasm, the forms at least of the
actual classical Roman architecture were always in Italy ready to
spring up into life: before I leave the whole subject I hope to be
able to show you what the Renaissance of the 16th century was,
and I do not mean to say that this love for the old classical forms
was a strong motive power in bringing about the change which
was much deeper than that, but when the spirit of change was
ready and urged people towards taking up the past again the
forms already sympathetic to it lay ready to hand.

Well the Roman branch of the Byzantine stream spread as I
said through Italy and so into France, in the south of which
country was developed a very handsome, dignified style having
little in common with the elegance of the architecture which
flowed from Justinian's Constantinople: it was in fact almost
purely Roman, but Roman set free, you understand from the

---

[5] For a discussion and a picture of St. Zenone Maggiore (completed in 1123–35)
see Russell Sturgis, *A History of Architecture* (New York, 1909), II, 277–9. For a
picture of St. Anastasia (completed in 1261), see Banister Fletcher, *A History of
Architecture in the Comparative Method* (16th ed.; London, 1954), p. 566.

affectation of imitating Greek Art: many most stately buildings are left us of this South-French-Romanesque, but alas most commonly sadly damaged by restoration; in some cases pretty much destroyed by it.

In the north of France the direct Roman influence is still plain enough; but there comes in again I fancy some of the feeling imported by the Northmen whose art, what they had of it, was as I have said directly taken from Byzantium: anyhow there is no doubt that the Gothic style which both there and in this country we not very inaccurately call Norman can by no means be considered a pure development of the Roman architecture; it is certainly influenced by the actual Byzantine feeling as the Lombard work is, but probably adds to that some borrowings from that early pre-Arian art of which I said that in some forms there was direct importation into France from Ireland, but which also, I repeat, is to my mind due at least partially to those Northmen whose name the style bears.

It remains to state definitely of this early Gothic style, what I have already hinted, that this Norman, or Franco-Norse Romanesque architecture did after the Conquest of Duke William entirely supersede the native English Romanesque, which undoubtedly had been developed partly from sheer rude imitation by the English of the mingled Roman-Byzantine and the pure-Byzantine, and partly from art imported from Germany, where as aforesaid the Constantinopolitan style was in use simply.

Thus far therefore we have gone towards the development of Gothic architecture: at the time where we are now making a pause there is a round-arched style in use all over Europe in [some][6] countries developed from the Roman Byzantine influenced here and there by the Romanized civilization of the imperial provinces, partly by the barbarous art (I use the word in no derogatory sense) of the pre-Arian time or at least pre-Germanic time: in other countries the style is developed more directly from the actual Byzantine of New Rome, and is altered by nothing more than the rudeness of the imitators and a not very strong strain of the above-said early European art. This is the first stage

---

[6] The MS is illegible here.

of actual Gothic Art, the time of the supremacy of unmixed Feudalism.

But now when this Romanesque style was fully developed came another element of change and the Gothic art of Europe was acted on by the brilliant but less intellectual art of the East which like so much of Gothic had its origin chiefly in Justinian's Constantinople. The cause of this new element, the presence of which is undoubted, is generally supposed to be the Crusades: but I doubt that their direct influence has been exaggerated: you see besides the fact that as time went on the art of Constantinople and the Greek Empire generally was falling more and more under the influence of Eastern art; there were all this time two points of Europe where that art existed in its completeness, Spain and Sicily to wit. Now you must remember that grand as the building art was in many parts of Europe before the 12th century, the other industrial arts were in a rude state even as to matters of ornament: the art of figure-weaving in N[orthern] Europe for instance was confined to actual tapestry, and a rude kind of figured cloth which is still woven in the Abruzzi in Italy, and in Iceland: whereas in Greece, Syria, Sicily, Egypt, and Spain, the art of figure-weaving as we now mean the word was thoroughly well understood and skillfully practiced: the woven goods made in these countries especially in Sicily, were widely sold all over Europe, and must have done much to influence the general character of mediaeval ornament; which for the rest was easy to influence at this period; for at the time of which we are now speaking, the end of the 13th or beginning of the 14th century there was a remarkable unity in the styles of the whole civilized world: you can indeed easily tell where such and such a piece of work was done, in England, France, Italy, or Persia, but the resemblance, or rather the sympathy of ideas will strike you much more.

Thus we have reached the time of the fully developed Gothic art, which indeed seems by this time according to the natural law of growth to have gone so far from its originals as to have become another thing, but in which notwithstanding every germ of the older art is visible to the seeker. Now before we proceed to the somewhat melancholy task of considering its fall and change, I will ask [you] to consider the nature of this art, which wrapped in its folds all Europe and much of Asia creating such a body of beauty on the earth as has not been seen before or since.

Now the very essence of its beauty was that it was founded on reasons no one can doubt that, whatever was the quality of the civilization of those days, men in their buildings for instance built what they wanted, what that civilization called for: no circumstances were really adverse to this elastic, intelligent, and free art: on the contrary the circumstances were used whatever they were for the advantage of the art: once more consider the buildings of the complete period and note how they used their materials, driven as they were by the want of each communication to make the most of what came readiest to hand: granite, freestone, brick, rubble, wood, plaster, the style creeps round each and fits it like a glove: nor was it only in the building art that this law of reasonable liberty inspired the arts, this knowledge of necessity defined by a philosopher as being the only true liberty:[7] through all details down to the smallest it passes: take for instance the surface ornament of the Gothic times: no designers ever understood better the necessity of mystery in pattern designing; but this mystery they well understood was not to be attained at the expenses of clear and definite meaning; all growth must be capable of explanation logical and clear: all outlines must be clean and sharp; if you go wrong you will be found out at once; all colour must be bright and clean, it must be absolutely good, no negation of evil qualities will serve your turn.

Now of the causes of all this I will speak later on: at present I will but note that so it is, that the Gothic is above all other intelligent, reasonable, and free. Furthermore it was, as I have already hinted universal: I have said that the industrial arts were in a rude condition in N[orthern] Europe at the beginning of the period; of course comparatively to our times or times earlier than ours that was more or less the case all through the middle ages: nevertheless rude as the technique of some of the arts was (pottery for instance) there was nothing either coarse or careless about their artistic qualities: it is doubtless a fact that the furni-

---

[7] The "philosopher" was Friedrich Engels.

ture and appointments of a 14th century house were not up to our standard of luxury, their household goods were few and simple: some people consider this a disadvantage, and call it a state of barbarism; I do not—but—however let all that pass at present; the point to which I wish to draw your attention is this, that scanty as the furniture of a mediaeval house might have been, and rude as some of it may have been every piece of it was properly made and properly ornamented, that is, was beautiful.

I will ask you to consider this fact and contrast it with the present state of things when you have the arts in your mind as a matter of history; everything made by any common artificer was naturally and without effort beautiful, just as the works of nature are beautiful without effort and though you don't notice them, thinking they were made for the convenience of your table or bed or what not. I say just think of that, and what a different world it was then from what it is now.

Now further this Gothic art had another characteristic which I suppose always accompanies great art: it was progressive, confident, intolerant, though there was history in every atom of it, it was not conscious of it, was conscious only of exultation in the present and hope for the future; that was the spirit of it as far as the mere art was concerned; otherwise deep in its soul was the melancholy of the North and its sentiment; but what of regret for past times lay in it regarded [not][8] the art of past times, but the life of the former generations gone like the leaves of the autumn trees, and such lives they really figured to themselves as differing no ways from their own. Now as there was in it some melancholy and abundant sentiment, so also there was no stint of humour: that liberty or knowledge of necessity which was the mainspring of it insured that: rough but kindly humour is an essential part of all the Gothic of the N[orth] at least; a wish to scare nobody away by contempt or pride, a feeling as near as may [be] the opposite of that which is the motive feeling of the pedantic art of the Renaissance. Here then we have the characteristics of Gothic Art: It was common to the whole people; it was free, progressive, hopeful, full of human sentiment and humour: such as this it

---

[8] The MS here has "nothing."

lasted with some gains perhaps in certain directions, but with
more losses, till the end of the 15th century: but with the beginning of the 16th came the change. It was not only that the
popular art grew poorer, coarser, and more meagre, though that
happened and for very good reasons, I think, but on the top of
this coarsened and worsened popular art was thrust another art;
produced by men who had gained a little more knowledge than
the naif workmen of the 14th century, and with that had gained
some feeling for history: which feeling was united to overweening hopes of the speedy progress of the human race which had
taken hold on people's minds owing to events, talk about which I
must again defer till my sketch-story of the arts is done. The
knowledge and the hope together of these men of the Renaissance bred in them an absurd contempt of the just-past pure
mediaeval times, and in the arts the result of that contempt was
that for the first time since art began, men looked backward for
their ideal of beauty and fitness, and culled from past times what
they thought could by some means or another be united to the
life of the present and palliate more or less the regrettable barbarism of the work which they were still obliged to use in a mechanical way: thus as far as the arts were concerned and especially the
architectural arts they were no longer men living an eager and
hopeful life producing beauty to show their pleasure in that life;
but scholars sitting under the rod of a pedant, whose teaching
they but half understood as they wrought anxiously to carry out
his lightest precepts. Such I say were the men of the Renaissance,
and art which had been free for 800 years fell into slavery again, a
slavery far darker and less hopeful than that from which it escaped
at the period of the fall of the Roman Empire. It is true indeed
that this fall in art was quite hidden from men's eyes at the time,
nay they called it a new birth, not a death sickness as they should
have done: for at the head of the great impulse towards change
and knowledge was a mass of talent and genius composed of some
of the most gifted men the world has ever seen, the blossom of all
those centuries of free art which had gone before them: the work
of their strenuous individual genius was so brilliant and entrancing that it has quite hid from many of us even at the present day

the sickness of all that side of art which depended not on individual genius but on collective genius or tradition; all that great mass of art in short which we now justly call popular, or the art of the people: while those great men of the Renaissance lived this was not obvious partly as I say because the splendour of their talent hid it and partly because the degeneration was but beginning in their time: but when they passed away, they left behind them as far as the individualist arts are concerned a mere *caput mortuum* of academical whims and pretences, a so-called art which prided itself on being exclusive, narrow, and uninteresting: and as to the arts of the people, they had become in countries where art had flourished most, as in Italy, a kind of necessarily tolerated appendage to intellectual art, in short to make my meaning plain in few words the flunky of intellectual, or rather I should say of academical art: they had become upholstery. Meantime in less artistic, and cultivated countries all pretence even of intellectual art had disappeared, but though popular art had fallen very low, it did not altogether fall into upholstery though [in] the last half of the 16th and the first half of the 17th [century] social and economical causes had indeed deprived it of its dignity and thoughtfulness, but tradition still clung to it, and even mere ignorance and clumsiness aided it to shake off to a certain extent the fetters which academical art imported from Italy would have laid upon it: the result of all this was that mass of architecture of which a good deal is still left us in our own country under the name of Elizabethan and Jacobean which brightens and makes historical many a humble landscape in England, and which even behind the quaint affectation of stilted pomp and would-be learning which not seldom oppresses it has a homeliness and love of life which makes it pleasant and human and even in a sense beautiful: it will not bear criticism but it forces us to love it in spite of all defects. But you must always keep in mind that it is not its super-imposed defects that make it lovable but the tradition still lingering in it which has remained from the times of art which produced work at once logical and beautiful: it is not the Renaissance form which we love in it, but the Gothic spirit.

Think of the different way in which we look on a Renaissance
building in Italy and in England: compare one of our old War-
wickshire houses with an Italian building of the same style: the
latter is twenty times more carefully designed, has much more
pretension to be considered a work of art, and as to execution of
details, of course there is no comparison between the two: yet
you hate the Italian building and love the English; and really
because the first is academical, pedantic, the second human: the
faults of the English building come from mere ignorance and
lumpishness, but those of the Italian from malice prepense: and
all this difference I say means that some Gothic or human feeling
still remains hidden under all its stiff-necked follies in the English
building, so that it gives us at least abundant excuse for loving it.

Well, this semi-Gothic feeling lasted in pretty abundant measure with us till the middle of the 17th century, but in out-of-the-
way corners of the country [it] lingered much later. For the rest
the flood of civilization swept over us and steadily swamped what
was left of Gothic feeling even in England, and the 18th century
saw the final degradation of the arts as genuine spontaneous
expression of men's thoughts and pleasures. Thencefor[war]d
throughout the century decade after decade architecture grew
more pinched, miserable, and ungenerous till it sunk at last into
the box of bricks with the slated lid of the beginning of this
cent[ury] which was I fear only too typical a habitation for the
mercantile person who lived in it with his poor, limited, grovel-
ling life. The lesser arts went the same road, whatever was natural
or instinct with pleasure or intelligence faded out from them, and
ornament became the mere slave of fashion a foolish, indefensi-
ble, inexplicable habit. Meantime England was as to the intellectual arts now going on an equal footing with Italy and the
English school of painting must I suppose be considered the glory
of the 18th century in that line: well I am bound to admit the
cleverness, readiness and confidence of it, but I will admit no
further good qualities [in] it: I call upon you for instance to shake
off the bondage of sham admiration, and tell me what it is further
than these qualities of cleverness, readiness, and confidence that
you really like in the acres of canvas covered by Sir Joshua

Reynolds, and on which such floods of adulation have been and I fear will be lavished: I ask you to look at them with your own eyes and not through those of art critics and tell me what you see in them; in that regiment presentation of the dullest men ever born, and the plainest women the world has ever seen whom not even the flattery of the courtly painter could turn into anything else than the simpering, vulgar fine ladies that they were: and all this smoothed down with a commercial conventionality just fit for the period which was bringing to birth the final triumph of commerce and saw nothing beyond it, no glimmer of the change[9] which I fervently hope is now on the way.

Nor can I pass by quite unnoticed the literature of this period of slavery, all the more as the revolt against it was first felt in literature: of that we must say that it entirely lacks all imaginative qualities, has in it in fact nothing save that cleverness, readiness, and confidence which I have admitted to be possessed by the English 18th century school of painting: not only does poetry seem dead in the 18th century, but if you attempt to wade through the books of verses of the time which insult the name of poetry, you find that even the commonplace English of the time was too romantic to satisfy the writer's hatred of imagination and humanity, and that he has been obliged to invent a new language which can barely be understood without a dictionary by us of the 19th century.

Here we are landed then in that prim and dull country of the 18th century where we no longer dare to call our souls our own: where history is studied only for the purpose of insulting the religion and aspirations of those who went before us and of magnifying our own mean and hypocritical sham virtues: where poetry is come to mean copies of smooth verses with as little meaning as can be got into them and without any glimmer of passion or imagination, where art finally is on the one hand a pastime of dilettanti, and on the other foolish upholstery provided by despised drudges for vulgar luxury. We have gone a

---

[9] The word "vengeance" has been rejected in the MS for the word "change."

long and weary way certainly from Ely Cathedral to Gower St.,[10] from Giotto[11] to Joshua Reynolds, from Beowulf to the Rape of the Lock. That strange force which for lack of a better word I suppose we hapless mortals call civilization has played us a scurvy trick certainly leading us on with numberless hopes till as I say it has landed us at the end of the 18th century stripped of all art and poetry that is to say of all the pleasure of life: with history a despised desert behind us, with a blank prospect of mere utilitarianism before us.

Nevertheless out of the midst of this dreariness came that intellectual Rebellion, which I have ventured to call the Gothic Revival, and which in spite of all the follies and illogicalities that have clung to it, has it seems to me been founded on reality, and is in fact part of that great change from the mere commercial period to something better and higher, which is verily going on but which in its fulness is but rarely recognized as yet.

I will finish what I have to say tonight by laying before you a very brief sketch of the beginnings of this revolt, leaving for my next lecture an account of the results of it in the art of the present day together with my estimate of its real value as a factor in the hopes of raising the general standard of life which we of these days cannot fail to entertain.

Now I hope that you will not think that my protest against the

---

[10] Gower Street was often cited at this time by architectural critics as an example of the extreme lack of imagination in the design of contemporary buildings. Part of the present Borough of Holborn-St. Pancras, this street borders one side of the British Museum and separates the University College from the Medical School. In the late eighteenth and early nineteenth century it was the site of a number of building projects whose most significant characteristics were uniformity and plainness, all the houses being built with "stock brick facings, plain parapet and slate-covered mansard roofs. . . ." See J. R. Howard Roberts and Walter J. Godfrey (eds.), *Survey of London* (London, 1947), pp. 178–87, plates 28–32.

[11] Giotto di Bondone (1267?–1337) was, understandably enough, one of Morris's favorite pre-Raphaelite painters, not only because he was a pre-Raphaelite, but also because he combined in his work the mystical aura of his religious subject matter and the precise eye for composition and detail ordinarily associated with architecture. He was himself the official architect of Florence in the last years of his life, designing during that period the campanile and the façade of the Cathedral. See [Margaret O.] Oliphant, *The Makers of Florence* (London, 1876), pp. 103–23.

pride of pedantry which from the first was an essential part of the Renaissance and in the end made it merely contemptible indicates on my part any foolish hostility towards real knowledge, towards real science, all genuine professors of which must surely have a due share of humility if that is true, as I believe it is, which I have seen written that however science may progress, the amount of what is unknown will always be infinitely more than that which is known.

At any rate I am so little swayed by any disregard of science that I must assert as I hinted above that whatever stirring has been among the dry bones of the 18th century began from some inspiration of historical science: and first of all on the side of language: till the time of the great philologers of the end of the 18th century the impression on the minds of scholars was that whereas Greek and Latin were languages possessing definite grammar all other tongues spoken were but such arbitrary accidental jargons as might have been expected from the rude barbarians who spoke them: but the philological scholars I am thinking of found out that this was far from being the case, and discovered the true relations of one tongue to another, and so demonstrated the unity of man: in the course of which study they also discovered the literary merits of the non-classical poems and other literature; nor only so, but also learned from them much as to the history and social conditions of the earlier nations which could have been learned from no other source, so that even the earliest of our ancestors became visible to us no longer as esurient sword-wielding machines but men of like passions to ourselves, bound together by the ties of Society, living under laws which not even the mighty power of Rome could destroy, but which played their part in the formation of the Society of Medieval Europe, now seen to be a far different thing from the jarring of courts and kings, the hubbub of a set of violent men accidentally pitch-forked into positions of rule over their fellows.

All this was the beginning of the modern study of history by whose light we not only saw something of what our own ancestors were like, but also and more easily were able to put ourselves in the places of the great peoples of antiquity, and sympathize with their real feelings instead of ignorantly worshipping them from without as the Renaissance pedants had been content to do.

It is clear that imaginative literature could not sit quietly by while historical research was providing her with so large a mass of material; and accordingly from this time poetry to use the word in its largest sense, was born again, and the school of what for want of a better word I am compelled to call the Romantic writers arose. I have said it was a long and weary way between the ancient poets of our race and the elaborate trifler Pope; but Coleridge and Keats and Shelley and Byron claim brotherhood not only with Shakespeare and Spenser, nay not only with Chaucer or even William Langland, but yet more perhaps with that forgotten man who sang of the meeting of the fallow blades at Brunnanburg, or who told of the old hero's death in the lair of the gold-guarding dragon; or he who bewailed the ruin of the ancient city, or he who sang so touchingly of the friendless, lonely man the Wanderer.

And now as a last word for tonight, consider the attitude of three men of that time as showing that the revolt against the old pedantry was undoubted at the same time it was with some at least unconscious: consider then Byron, Keats, and Scott as an illustration: the first praising Pope making a god of him almost, and yet writing always in hot revolt among the Romancists; the second so completely cut off from what was left even then of the old pedantic twaddle, so condemned then (even by Byron by the way) so completely accepted now: and the third worth considering yet more as being so closely connected both with history and Gothic art: for he like Byron, still felt himself bound to affect enthusiasm for the false civilization of his own day, or even was really touched by it somewhat; is always excusing Gothic life and architecture for its barbarism though he was clear in his own mind that it was that which he really liked; so strong you see was even the Renaissance pride of pedantry that it fettered Byron's rebellious mind; made the sweetness and passion of Keats seem nought to his contemporaries, and befogged the strong, manly spirit of Scott.

Here then for tonight we will leave it.[12] It was the product at

---

[12] The following passage is deleted in the MS: ". . . no longer at any rate completely triumphant in its narrowness and primness, but tending towards mere

first of a strenuous and exciting epoch, it was agitated by the rise of commercialism, made eager by the discoveries of past history, and of rising science; but it joined to that life and eagerness a tyranny arising from the beginning of the strongest and completest rule of the weak over the strong that the world has yet seen the plutocracy namely of the middle classes: which tyranny it backed with an hypocrisy which made it ungenuine and unhuman: which in Catholic countries took the form of pure materialistic cynicism masquerading in priests' garments; and in protestant of a religion made for the rich which proclaimed competition for a good position in this world and the next as the real rule of conduct. Such was the Renaissance in its first days, splendid amidst its tyranny, hypocrisy, and lack of hope: but at the time I have now brought you to its splendour was long gone, of its tyranny was left only the narrowness and primness which was the due accompaniment to its ever-increasing hypocrisy, the favourite vice of the bourgeoisie grown moral whom it had now mainly to depend upon for its support: it only existed because there was nothing better to take its place: but surely it seemed as if that better thing was coming; for its dulness now began to be illuminated by flashes of genius as strong and real as that of the time before the first days of that tyrannous Renaissance.

What that better thing turned out to be; what may yet come from it; whether it is the glimmer of real daylight, or the false dawn of a cold moon—all this I will ask you to consider in my next lecture.

---

anarchy illumined by flashes of genius as genuine as that of the time before the Renaissance. As to what art has striven to rise out of that anarchy, and may yet arise from it, I will ask you to allow me to suggest considerations on that point at my next lecture."

THE GOTHIC REVIVAL [II]¹

I n my last lecture I gave you my ideas as [to] the origin of the art of medieval Europe and the ways by which it spread over the various countries; I told you what to my mind was the spirit of the art, and pointed out how the change befell which brought it to an end, and supplanted it by an art which was retrospective in spirit, and therefore narrow and cumbered with pedantic pride: I showed how after a brief period of brilliancy owing to the individual genius of those great men who were given to the world at the beginning of the Renaissance period, that Renaissance fell lower and lower till at the end of the 18th century the arts of civilization were as far as beauty, invention, and imagination are concerned at a standstill: I concluded by hinting at the rise of that revolt against pseudo-classical stupidity, which took place as I think first in literature rather than in the manual arts.

This was necessarily the natural course since even the most individual and intellectual of the latter depends of necessity on processes which are the result of tradition of some sort however

---

¹ The text of this lecture is taken from B.M. Add. MS. 45331(11), which is entirely in Morris's hand. For background information see footnote 1 to "The Gothic Revival [I]," p. 54.

blind it may be; and this tradition is very difficult to shake off and can scarcely be shaken off indeed in the lifetime of any one person. However, the feeling for history and the attraction more literary and sentimental than artistic and critical towards Gothic art did show itself side by side with the revival of literary romance, though its results were at first feeble and even ridiculous, being little more than the perpetration of certain buildings in that queer style of Carpenter's Gothic of which one yet stumbles across specimens now and then, amongst which however one must stop to note the almost miraculous phenomenon of a painter of that period who had a real and strange genius for the decorative or beautiful side of the art, Blake to wit, who visionary as he was understood not only the power of words in verse but also the power of form and colour to delight the eye at the same time that it exalts the mind. Of course the Carpenter's Gothic aforesaid was attempted long before anything approaching accurate knowledge of the styles was current; it was the time when all round-arched architecture was spoken of as Saxon, and all pointed lumped together as florid; which distinction was in itself however a considerable advance over the knowledge of the previous years, which generally affected to speak of the architecture of seven or eight centuries of European history by the not very inclusive or explanatory name of monkish. However real and careful antiquaries soon got to work on the history of Gothic art when interest in it was once awakened, and Rickman at last discriminated the styles of English Gothic architecture with remarkable clearness,[2] and from that time forward real knowledge of its details was gained: details by the way that appealed so little to the understanding of the 18th century that it is not very long before Rickman's time that the draughtsmen of architecture could give any idea of the general appearance of a Gothic building.

Now about the time when Gothic architecture began to be somewhat understood, as if to give some countenance to the queer name of "ecclesiastical" architecture by which the general

---

[2] See Thomas Rickman, *An Attempt to Discriminate the Styles of English Architecture from the Conquest to the Reformation* (2nd ed.; London, [1819]).

public used to know it until quite recently, there came as an ally to the study of the arts the movement in the English Church which has since got the name of ritualism, which I think on the whole one may put down as a part of the general tendency to protest against the blank stupidity of the 18th century, or if you will part of the general tendency towards mediaevalism: anyhow by the time that this movement was well under way Gothic art began to receive a great [deal] of attention, and to vindicate its title to ecclesiastical art, or Christian Art as Pugin[3] with little more logic used to call it, by getting itself used as an imitative style for the building of churches everywhere at least in England: till at last almost every church which was built had to be built in this style such as it was; people not seeing as they don't altogether see even today the queer incongruity of building their houses in one style and their churches in another. With this the first act of the Gothic revival looked at in its narrower sense may be said to have ended: it triumphed as an exotic ecclesiastical style; and by this time was fairly well understood in an archeological way by several of the leading architects. I must just mention here to return to it afterwards one very luckless result of this alliance of quasi-art with quasi-theology: a mishap expressed by the word restoration, and which I am inclined to think we might have partly at least escaped if one side of the newborn interest in mediaeval history had not been dominated by theology: as it was the most frightful ravages were wrought by this pest while yet people's ideas about I won't say the essence, but the mere differentia of Gothic were very crude indeed, and the worst of it is that this enthusiasm for thoroughly mediaevalising in the theatrical way a building already mediaeval in reality has formed a habit of restoration in the country clergy who for the most part have as yet not so much as heard that there is such a thing as popular art: a habit which the worthy guardians of our national architectural antiquities would seem to exercise almost

---

[3] Augustus Welby Pugin (1812–1852), perhaps the most famous of the architects of the Gothic Revival, was an associate of Sir Charles Barry in the designing of the present Houses of Parliament. He wrote, among other works, *An Apology for the Revival of Christian Architecture in England* (London, 1843).

unconsciously like the hebdomadal sermons, and by which they play into the hands of archeologically-minded architects, who find it difficult to resist the temptation of beginning to tamper with an ancient building: and when once they begin find that it is very difficult to know where to stop. All which would be laughable indeed if it were not so woefully tragic: there is something quite sickening to a lover of art to think that an ancient building, a lovely piece of art in itself, the growth of the very soil of the country; the outcome of many centuries of thought; the witness of a state of society and methods of handicraft long passed away, after having escaped so many dangers of change and violence and accident and mere lapse of time should be liable to sudden, wanton destruction brought on it by a whim arising in the head of a half-educated man, who has not even grasped the fact that the workmen of today are in a different position to those of the Middle Ages: I say that it is sickening that this should be the case and that the public should have no protection against the whim of an individual and no appeal to anything else save his ignorance and prejudice: as to the architects who are the other factor in this bad business, it must be said of them, that while some are most honourably distinguished both by their knowledge and their disinterestedness, it is a matter of course under the present unhappy arrangement of society that the greater number should look upon such schemes as business matters and treat them accordingly.

Well the first act of the Gothic Revival, brought us I say to imitation Gothic triumphant as an ecclesiastical style, to a fairly accurate archeological-architectural knowledge of the construction and details of mediaeval building, and most unhappily to restoration. In the next act the knowledge of the style has much increased, and it is even perceived that it is founded on principles, that there is a life and spirit in it: from which perception it followed as a matter of course that those who knew anything about it proclaimed its fitness not only for ecclesiastical buildings but for all buildings: this perception one may say in passing had been much helped about this time by the growing study of foreign and kindred styles especially the architecture of Italy, Professor Ruskin's unrivaled eloquence and wonderful ethical instinct leading the way in this branch of the study of art as in

many others.[4] It was a necessary consequence of this more intimate study of the spirit of Gothic art that men should find
themselves drawn specially towards its earlier periods: already in
the first act of the Revival archeologists had marked pretty
clearly the periods of birth, growth, maturity, and decrepitude,
but it was not till this time when the subject was considered
scientifically almost, that they formed the hope of founding a new
style of architecture on the vigorous organic period of Gothic: the
period when still bearing obvious traces of all the history which
had produced it, it looked forward ever to fresh progress and
continuous change into something still more desirable, the period
of its greatest hope when it looked forward confidently from past
struggles to future perfection.

Once again even from this reasonable study of the best and
most characteristic epoch of an art came in the hands of feeble
and illogical people confused by their little knowledge fresh
misfortune for us in the shape of the foe Restoration: for many of
the newly-made–wise archeologist–architects in their enthusiasm
for purity of style, could see nothing worth attention or preservation in the works of the ages that followed the period of purity;
genuine though they were and instinct with the history and
aspirations of the people of the later middle ages: and seeing
nothing worthy of preservation after the 14th century they did
(and do I am sorry to say) not attempt to preserve later work,
but on the contrary destroyed it, supplanting it by such feeble
copies of the purer work as they could compass in the present
day: with the result that we have been deprived of a great bulk
of art which no age of the world could have afforded to lose, and
which to this age ridden by the nightmare of commercial ugliness
has been a grievous loss indeed.

With the third act of the revival came greater and more intimate knowledge of the art of the Gothic period; and withal a
spread of the knowledge of the conditions of life at that time
without which knowledge indeed mere archeology, though useful, is only useful as building up storage for reference. And now it
did seem to many people that architecture and the arts which

---

[4] See, e.g., *The Stones of Venice,* 3 vols. (London, 1851–53).

went with it had a real chance of a second new birth: several talented architects quite broke with the mere pedantry of imitation and set themselves seriously to build as a mediaeval builder would have done with his principles and instinct if he had been a member of our present society: it now became obvious that the Middle Ages did not come to a sudden end in 1320 and that an abundance of excellent works had been wrought as late as two centuries after that: many good buildings were the result of this closer study; buildings which if they had depended wholly on the architects' design and superintendence would have been of very great excellence. I may also be allowed to mention that some time in this act some of us thought that the revival might be extended to the accessory arts, and made I assure you desperate efforts to revive them: in which process we have at least amused and instructed ourselves a good deal, and even done what is called "lived on" our efforts; in other words have extracted a good deal of money out of the public by them: allow me to excuse ourselves for that brigandage by saying that the public will have these accessory arts, or some pretence of them, and that if I am not quite blinded by vanity ours are at any rate prettier [than] those which went before them.

Before I go further I ought to note one part of the Gothic revival which most of you will I doubt not think of more importance than these spasmodic attempts to build a new style of architecture and decoration on the remains of the older styles: that part of it I mean which has to do with the art of picture-painting: in which I must be understood not to be speaking of landscape art which has I suppose only been affected by the revival so far as it has tended to make it more realistic and honest: as to imaginative painting it has been affected by it much as literature has been that is in point of fact it has been reborn from its influence as could hardly fail to be the case; since on the one side the revival found it the reality of passion and sentiment instead of the obvious imitation of them, and on the other hand it found it ornamental scope, or in other words the aim at beauty of form and colour which the old pedantry despised and was ignorant of.

And now out of this third act of the Revival we may be said to have passed into the fourth which has strengthened the hope of many people that a new style of art is forming which will be at once beautiful and at the same time fitting to the life of our own times: strange to say, though, amidst all this, there has been a sort of reaction against that very Gothic art which began the architectural revival and at one time seemed to be the end all and be all of it: this reaction seems to be the legitimate issue of that new-found knowledge that there is something admirable in mediaeval architecture after its highest point of purity had been attained: perhaps also some of the worthy people who started with regenerating the arts by imitating the 13th century have grown older and have more or less sunk their ideals and are prepared to put up with the quaint bourgeois trimness of a Queen Anne house as good enough to make us in this age of ugliness forget the poetry and beauty of a 14th century grange. In truth there is something to be said for the exchange of an almost as good as real Queen Anne house, instead of a very far from as good as real 14th century one. To step from a very well done outside of Chaucer's time into an interior of afternoon tea and the music of the future is certainly a very prodigious shock; more of a shock, it must be admitted than finding a Queen Anne house inhabited by school-board ladies or gentlemen enthusiastic on sanitary reform: the days of Prestonpans[5] are easier for us to understand than those of Crecy: and yet not easy, for after all Queen Anne is dead: and moreover imitating the whimsical ghost of a style of the 18th century has the special disadvantage of forcing us to spend time and sometimes talent in imitating whims which were absurd even in those days, imitating things which were not founded on any principle: it forces us in fact to affect an affectation. And to finish with this last freak of the Gothic revival, I must remind you again that whatever was admirable about the quaint old houses of the middle of the 18th century was simply a survival of the Gothic

---

[5] Prestonpans is a small town in East Lothian, Scotland, on the Firth of Forth, where the Battle of Prestonpans was fought on Sept. 21, 1745. In the battle the Scottish forces under Prince Charles Edward Stewart completely routed the English forces under Sir John Cope. See P. Hume Brown, *History of Scotland* (Cambridge, 1911), III, 235–38.

times; the rest was mere insanity, a mere token of a narrow, pinched bourgeoisdom.

So much on what may be called the external history of the architectural Gothic revival: which arising as a necessary consequence of the historical revival and allying itself to an ecclesiastical-historical movement has in its limited way attained such a success as to be now undergoing a reaction: you may think perhaps I have treated this stir in art somewhat lightly; and to say the truth if I did not feel it to be the sign of something deeper than itself, I should scarcely think it worth much attention; for it is confined within very narrow limits, and cannot even be said to have altered perceptibly the external appearance of our towns, where in spite of all the talk among Artistic people, the real style of the day, Victorian Architecture, is in full swing; or in other words miserable squalor and purse-proud, rampant vulgarity divide our Architecture between them. But if it is not of much importance in itself it is of some importance as a token of men's minds being turned toward the historic method of looking at life and the hopes for the future of mankind: for us as I have before hinted there is no longer a brief period of perfection dropped down into a world no one knows how or why, an island in a dark sea of before and after, in which alone a rational man can find anything worthy of his attention; all reason and order [inside of it] unreason and anarchy outside of it; one thing to be imitated always, nothing else to be even looked at. In spite of the trumpery little reaction I have been speaking of just now, we have done with all that for ever, and have grasped the idea of the unity and continuous life of man, in which change and growth are always present, so that although we dare pick out one period and say it is bad, or another and say it is good, we cannot say this is great and that is little, for it is all growth together—that is to say life. As soon as this is felt by men it must at once influence their aims and hopes in an art like architecture, and it has been this feeling I am sure and not a mere arbitrary liking for some special forms as the pointed-arch or what not which has produced the Gothic Revival: it was felt that the mere imitation of classical models itself once a genuine historical development, had gone as far as it could go and that we were face to face with a dead wall of pedantry: this imitation then had to be abandoned, and we were compelled to seek for a style which had in itself the elements of further growth, that could only be found in Gothic art which after the fall of the old classicism had become the universal style: at first we imitated the outward aspects of it without understanding its spirit much as the Renaissance artists had done with the old classical art, but without infusing any of the spirit of our own times into it as they had done so as to make a living style: even this however is now to a certain extent being attempted owing to the knowledge of history having spread among us till we are beginning to be conscious of that growth and unity of mankind of which I have just spoken.

This to my mind is the meaning of the Gothic revival; and so looked upon it becomes I think a movement of great importance and not a mere excrescence of dilettantism: so that we may well ask what practical use can be made of it in civilizing the sur-roundings of life, which I fancy we most of us here present are in grievous need of being civilized.

The question is then what hopes for the future of art lie in the present condition of the Gothic revival? It is a difficult question and to answer it fully I should have to deal with the most serious questions of the day, nor indeed will it be possible for me to avoid touching on them before I have done. As far as I can however I will keep that for the end of my discourse and will now try to point out to you certain shortcomings in our neo-Gothic buildings: only you will understand I shall be thinking of the best of them, not of the worst; of those where the architect to some extent understands his style, and would build Gothic if he could, and not of those which are a mere collocation of certain well-known forms put together in a thoroughly modern way; that is to say the Carpenters' Gothic of our day.

Well in considering these good specimens of the Gothic revival one thing is bound to strike us from the first—they are very florid. There is a determination in them to have a great deal of ornament —of some sort. Now you will hardly suspect me, an ornamentalist of underrating the pleasure which ornament can give us, but in this case I will go so far as to plagiarize on my friend W[illiam]

B[lake] R[ichmond][6] and say that as things are at present 'tis better to be chary of ornament: don't have any *cheap* ornament at all: for real ornament cannot be cheap: at present I say build big and solid and with an eye to strict utility: you will find that will be expressive work enough, and will by no means be utilitarian. But let us look into this matter of modern ornament, and see why you are to be chary of it, and why it is cheap—and nasty.[7]

Allow me to illustrate my views on the subject by means of an actual building which I have seen: some four years ago I went into a church (in the country) built by a friend of mine, an architect who knows Gothic architecture thoroughly, and I admired it very much: I think if I had gone into it in the dusk I should really have taken it for a genuine building of the 15th century. Well it was a costly building and there was lots of ornament in it especially in the chancel: the great ornament of which was a big reredos of carved stone all over the east wall, a mass of niches and imagery, and at first sight it looked very beautiful; but as I looked at it I began to get tired of it although I could find no fault with its design at all; and why was that? Well there were dozens of figures in the niches, which indeed filled their places: but when you looked at them you knew very well what they were; they were *carving* not sculpture. That is we have today to use two words which mean the same thing to indicate two different things: so I say they were *carving*, that is they were done by men who really had nothing to do with the design of them who cut them unfeelingly and mechanically without troubling their heads as to whom they represented, with no trace in

---

[6] W. B. Richmond, R.A., was the successor to John Ruskin in the Slade Professorship of Fine Art at Oxford. He was closely associated with Morris in many artistic and social endeavors, including the SPAB and the arts and crafts exhibitions of the eighties and nineties. On his friendship with Morris, which dates from the days immediately following Morris's Oxford career, see A. M. W. Stirling, *The Richmond Papers* (London, 1926), pp. 157, 164–65, 271, 314.

[7] "Cheap and Nasty," a phrase very popular among the pre-Raphaelites and other art reformers, was first popularized by Charles Kingsley in 1850 in a pamphlet entitled *Cheap Clothes and Nasty.* "Its title was the tailor's own slang for garments made under sweatshop conditions." Moreover, "much of *Alton Locke* is a dramatization of *Cheap Clothes and Nasty.* . . ." See Margaret Farrand Thorp, *Charles Kingsley, 1819–1875* (Princeton, 1937), pp. 67, 76.

them of my friend the architect's enthusiasm for the Middle Ages, by men who would just as soon have cut 18th century grave-stone cherubs, or apples and amoretti[8] in a new club house; in short they were just mechanical dolls nothing more.

Now just consider what they were taking the place of: as it is they were I must say positively worthless; but if that reredos had been filled with genuine imagery of the 15th century it would have been full of entrancing interest: it is likely that the figures would have been rudely cut, that they would have shown no great knowledge of anatomy, that the extremities would have been clumsy and ugly, the heads disproportionately big, the faces not of a high type, the pose of the figure not very graceful and so forth: in short doubtless they would have plenty of obvious faults, but that very fact to start with is comparatively in their favour, for it shows that you would have been compelled to notice them, to look at them: you couldn't look at the other stone dolls at all: with the genuine imagery there would have gone real thought and invention although the quality of it might have been rude and not to our taste: every figure would have had something characteristic about it, something which would have shown you at a glance that the carver had enjoyed his work and would not under any compulsion, nay could not, work out of his style: and I say that the difference between such work and that of the mechanical dolls above-mentioned is *infinite:* one is something and the other nothing.

Now though this may be an extreme case yet the illustration is applicable to every bit of ornament about a building: concerning which you must ask the question is it done by an artist or a machine—whether of flesh and blood or brass and steel matters nothing to our present purposes—if it is the latter have nothing to do with it: it will be worth [a] great [deal] less than nothing: if the former, well and good, only you must be very particular to see that it is done by an artist's hand, executed that is to say thoughtfully and with pleasure: in that case it will, I am sorry to say, be rare, and I imagine expensive, as things go now; only it will at all events be worth something. Such a principle will

---

[8] The *NED* defines "amoretti" as "cupids."

somewhat restrict the exuberance of ornament, and as I said you will have to put up with solid plain buildings that will by reason of their obvious utility have a certain amount of dignity about them; which will have a double advantage to us: first they will be good in themselves, that at no time to come will they bring shame upon us at least; and next that our very restraint and carefulness in the matter will set us longing for real ornament since the desire for it is natural to the properly developed human being; whereas at present being surfeited with the sham stuff which is so common, we begin to loathe the whole thing, and scarcely look on what is really good either of our time or past times.

This remark leads me to speaking of the other shortcoming of the careful architectural works of today, it is soon said: there are too few of them: there are as I said not enough to make any impression on the general mass of our modern towns, where the most of the houses rich as well as poor make no pretence to being anything more than utilitarian hutches within the case of the rich ones a certain amount of quite sham ornament laid on simply at the commands of Mrs. Grundy[9] without anybody but that impersonal Goddess even professing to be pleased by the transaction; so it comes to this as the shortcomings of the present learned and really architectural buildings, that as on the one hand their ornament when they have any is not genuine or spontaneous, so on the other they are not numerous enough to form a real style: which two objections to them taken together seem to me to point to the simple fact [that] though they are built in this century they are not of it: they are but exotics in fact: on which fact follows the question, are they likely to gain so much on the public as to be the prevailing style, in which case they might, I suppose compel the development of a due style of ornament exterior and interior? For my part I am compelled to answer that question in the negative: under the present conditions of life I cannot see the

---

[9] "Mrs. Grundy" had by the eighteen-eighties become for socialists of artistic temperament the personification of bourgeois morals and philistine art. "The creator of the original Mrs. Grundy died in 1838, the year after Queen Victoria's accession. He was Thomas Morton, the playwright, who invented the beldame in *Speed the Plough*, the most famous of his twenty-five dramas." See Osbert Burdett, *The Beardsley Period* (London, 1925), p. 41, note.

day when every little house, every small tradesman's shop, every farm building even shall be without effort duly built, architectural, in a word beautiful; and I assert very strongly that until such a change comes about there will be no real modern architectural style; so that we may see what further lies in the assertion, let us return to the matter of the ornament again, and try to find out why we cannot get it genuine except under very rare conditions, unless in fact it is done by a man having the name and position as an artist: why cannot we get it from workmen?

The starting point of the answer is obvious: it is because there is such a division of labour in our occupations nowadays that there is a trenchant line of demarcation between artists and workmen, even when the latter are engaged on what are considered in some sense works of art: the artist is at least independent [and] can take a job or leave it according as he thinks it will do him credit or not: the workman lives from hand to mouth and is not at all independent: it would be dangerous work for him to play with his jobs, to take this and refuse that; or if he has so much genius and spirit as to do this, he presently finds himself in such a position that he can lift himself out of his class and become a gentleman artist; nor can anyone expect him to abstain from using his advantage; but take notice how this one thing makes it impossible for workmen as a body to become artistic, for I repeat that the possession of genius joined to ordinary thrift and industry will deprive the class of workmen of a good craftsman, and add to the class of gentlemen probably a poorish artist: therefore this elimination of talent from the workmen always going on the cultured architect of today has to depend for the execution of his work not on the intelligent cooperation of brother artists, but on the grudging obedience of trained drudges, from whom it is absurd to expect any approach to that excellence, thoughtfulness, and delicacy which Mr. Richmond has told some of you in this city is necessary to any ornament which is worth having.

You see we do not expect a mere workman to have any sense of beauty; that is a luxury which is now confined to the well-to-do, to the classes of leisure: but even if the workman by some extraordinary accident has that sense of beauty, it is certain that he will have no opportunity of expressing it in his work: if there is to be any pretence of beauty in the work which is to pass through his hands it will have been arranged for him by some one else's mind, and all his mind will have to do with the execution of it will be to keep before him the fact that he has got to carry out his pattern neatly perhaps, but speedily certainly under the penalty of his livelihood being injured: any thought he gives us as he carries out his task will be so much dead loss to him. Under such conditions how can you expect architecture to flourish; architecture which is emphatically the harmonious expression of the sense of beauty inherent in the whole people? Under such conditions nothing is possible in architecture but jerry-built hovels for the masses and vulgar Victorian architecture for the well-to-do and rich.

Now since we are thinking of the changes in the future of the Gothic revival I must ask you to allow me to contrast this condition of things [to] the condition of the workmen of that Gothic period whose art we have been trying to revive.

In their time however labour was divided in[to] the occupations of men in general, and it was of course much less completely so than with us: in the crafts there was very little division of labour: every apprentice became a master as a matter of course, and when in the later Middle Ages the guilds had become less democratic, and contained a class of journeymen alongside of the privileged craftsmen, the journeyman was only below his master as to his privileges, not his skill; so that from beginning to end he had to know his craft and be master of it: furthermore at least before the end of the 14th century the workman was not working for a master but for himself and was therefore master of his time: and also his work being done there was little of the middleman's office to take away a share of his earnings from him: the transaction between him and the public was simple: a piece of work was wanted, he did it and pocketed the price himself. So he could not be a machine in the first place; he was forced to think about his work or he could never have done it; in the second place he had leisure to do it as he pleased, and possession of creative skill and leisure are sure to make work pleasurable, and as in the third place he had but to deal with his customer as the user of his wares and there was no profit-squeezing middleman between

them he could afford to show his pleasure in the work of orna-
menting it: which ornament springing from deliberate work and
ample leisure showed manlike invention and imagination in it,
controlled indeed by intercourse with his fellow men then alive,
and by tradition, that is by the thoughts of those who had gone
before him but not controlled by the sordid necessity of working
to a pattern prescribed by an irresponsible master.

Now if you have followed me you will take note that these are
the conditions under which artists work; and in fact the craftsmen[10] of the middle ages *were* all artists, and art or the creation of
beauty was a habit to them which they could not forego if they
would; and hence happened then which I have said was necessary to a real style of beautiful architecture that all building was
beautiful; which beauty if we now want we have at least to pay
extra for, if indeed we get it by paying extra which is doubtful: it
was once a free gift like the air of heaven; it is now a marketable
article, and like all other marketable articles is much
adulterated.

Here then I want you to understand once for all that the
Gothic art which we have tried to revive was the work of free
craftsmen working for no master or profit-grinder, and capable of
expressing their own thoughts by means of their work, which was
no mere burden to them but was blended with pleasure; that art
or beauty was a necessary incident to all handicraft and was not
paid for as a distinct article but was given in over and above just
as the colour in an apple or the lovely drawing in a wheat ear is.
On the contrary in reviving Gothic art the cultivated men who
are striving to bring in a rational and popular style of architecture
and decoration are condemned to see their work carried out by
workmen who are working for a master who has to grind a profit
out of them and so can afford them neither leisure nor thought in
their work, and who are in consequence incapable of expressing
their thoughts through their work; which is accordingly a mere
burden to them unmingled with pleasure: from which it comes
that so far from beauty being a necessary incident to all handi-

---

[10] Here the word "workmen" is rejected for "craftsmen" in the MS.

work, it is always absent from it unless it is bargained for as a special separate article having its own market value.

This then is the real bar to the success of the Gothic revival which aimed at bringing back reasonable, logical beauty to the life of man in civilized countries: it is not as some have supposed the difference in life otherwise, except so far as the stupid luxury of the rich and idle is founded on the oppression of the workers: it is the subjection of all labour to the necessities of the competitive market which stands in the way of the Gothic revival, as it was the beginnings of that subjection which brought about the degradation of art in the 16th century, and the development of the same tyranny which completed that degradation in the 18th.

And lest you should think as some men now seem to do that this Gothic revival or the revolt against tyranny in the arts is a light matter, and that it will henceforth be a sufficient compromise for our architects and us to make with the natural love of beauty, if from henceforward we agree to copy with as much delicacy of detail as we can the work of a period which does not profess to appeal to our feelings in any way, to copy some skillfully-designed but dull building—lest you should think that this will make a school of architecture or be an expression of our sense of beauty worthy of civilized times, lest you should think in a word that such a proceeding was worth doing at all, let me put before you the ideal of a school of architecture a school of popular art,[11] an ideal which once approached fulfilment amid all the turmoil and superstition of the middle ages, and which should surely be[12] easier of fulfilment now unless our boasts of civilization should turn out to be as I fear they may merely futile and empty words meaning nothing.

I beg you to consider those mighty and beautiful buildings raised by our forefathers in a land then scantily populated by a people without the mechanical appliances which we have gained since then, and to ask yourselves what gave to short-lived men

---

[11] Here the words "such as once did exist" are deleted in the MS.
[12] Here the words "completely fulfilled" are deleted in the MS.

the hope to begin and the courage and patience to carry out to an end from father to son such works as these. Was it fear of the jealous Gods and the hope of appeasing their wrath? Was it pride in the glory and mastery of a great nation? Do not think it: such motives might perhaps urge on a Pharaoh to build himself a Pyramid-tomb by means of slave-labour, but the teeming eventfulness and solemn mass of a Gothic Cathedral sprang from worthier thought than this: there have been nay are other means of satisfying such futile and disastrous passions as superstition and false patriotism which have used up men's lives in crueler ways than the production of works of art. Surely the root cause for making whatever is noble and beautiful must always be the strong desire for the production of beauty; and these glorious works which were of necessity the creation of the whole people were created by the people's aspirations towards nobility and beauty.

They are the outcome of corporate and social feeling, the work not of individual but collective genius; the expression of a great body of men conscious of their union: if their builders had striven for beauty mechanically, artifically, if they had been coaxed out of the people by the bribes of the rich or the tyranny of the powerful they would on the face of them have borne tokens of that corruption and oppression: they would have lacked the life which we all consciously or unconsciously feel which they possess and the love with which we have surrounded that life: they would by this time have become to us dead toys of time past, not living memorials of it: it was the art of the people which created them to live.

Now aspiration towards beauty, the hope of giving a lasting gift to the world, this of itself might you would think, be motive sufficient for the fashioning of a great work of collective art: but there was more motive power behind the workers than that and more direct power also: for it is of the essence of such works, of such gifts, that the labour necessary for their production should not be wasted in any way. It goes without saying that no work which can give lasting pleasure to the world shall be the work of slaves; now it is true that any enthusiasm of giving a work of art to posterity would take the workers on it out of the category of slaves: for if they sacrificed their lives and their ease to their work they would be doing so of their own free will: but, and this is most important to remember, even this free-will sacrifice is not asked for by art: for art cannot endure waste, and all sacrifice means waste, or the loss of some joy which we have a right to claim: free men don't ask for martyrs: every martyr implies some thousands of sneaks.

In collective art therefore is no martyrdom: the men who build it up not only give their gift of free will, but give it joyfully day by day, and take as they give, to the extinction of moody pride, to the fostering of hearty goodwill: not martyrs—but friends and good fellows.

Take now some one great work of collective or popular art, and in some such way as follows I think it will have been done: the hope and desire for it moving in people's minds stir up some master mind to plan it; but he is not puffed up with individual pride by finding himself ready for this creation; for he knows well that he could not even have thought of it without the help of those who have gone before him, and that it must remain a mere unsubstantial dream without the help of his fellows alive now and to live hereafter: it is the thoughts and hopes of men passed away from the world which, alive within his brain, make his plan take form; and all the details of that plan are guided, will he or will he not, by what we call tradition, which is the hoarded skill of man handed down from generation to generation. But, as he belongs to the past and is a part of it, so also he belongs to the present and the future: his plan must be carried out by other men living and to live, who share his thoughts, his memories of bygone times, and the guidance of tradition: through these men he must work, men it may be of lesser talent than himself; that is as it may be and matters not, but at any rate men of divers aptitudes, one doing this work, one that, but all harmoniously and intelligently: in which work each knows that his success or failure will exalt or mar the whole; so that each man feels responsible for the whole; of which there is no part unimportant, nor any office degrading: every pair of hands is moved by a mind which is in concert with other minds, but freely, and in such a way that no individual intelligence is crushed or wasted: and in such work, while the work grows the workers' minds grow also: they work not like ants or live machines, or slaves to a machine—but like men.

So that every night when a man is reviewing his day's work he has not got to say: I have been weary, over-burdened, vexed, pained; I have lost forever some part of my vital force, some part of my intelligence, my memory, my hope in short; but I can bear it, for the world is the wealthier for my day's grief and loss. He has not got to say that, but this rather: I have worked today; I have been dealing with difficulties, but have conquered them: I have been troubled but am merry: I have given and taken, and gained something; I am more of a man than I was yesterday: the world has been made wealthier by my gain.

That is the way a free man works; Society uses him and keeps him; does not use him and throw him away: he is I say it again, not a martyr among a world of sneaks, but a friend amidst friends.

Now be sure of this; that Gothic Revival or revolt against pedantry and narrow-mindedness needs just such workmen as this, and that is its only need: for myself I think that amidst all the paltriness and blindness which has oppressed it, it has been seeking for this necessary aid: it has indeed failed to find it because it has been for the most part hitherto merely an aspiration of cultivated men seeking art through art instead of seeking it through the life of the people: if it can do no more than that it will pass like a pleasant dream of what might have been without making any impression on the life of men in the present, or their memory in the future.

Those who care for it or hope anything from it, that is to say those who expect to see a living school of art amongst us must make up their minds to one thing, that their cultivation will not help it forward one whit unless it is shared by all men. And if they think that that will be an easy thing to bring about they are wrong. For the division into the cultivated and the uncultivated classes, or to put the matter plainer into the civilized and uncivilized, is founded on the system of labour which sustains our commercial system: upper and lower classes, rich and poor, you needn't trouble yourselves about any other divisions, are absolutely necessary to the existence of that system: that division into upper and lower, rich and poor is *necessary* for the existence of the present commercial capitalist system; can never be done away with while it lasts, while at the same time it entirely forbids that universal cultivation, ease, and leisure which alone can produce popular art: but if art is not popular, if it is not of the people, it is an idle and worthless toy. Therefore the progress, nay the very existence of art depends on the supplanting of the present capitalist system by something better, depends on changing the basis of society.

Is art a little thing then, something which can be done without? It is not a little thing, for it means the pleasure of life: I am no prophet, so I will not say it cannot be done without, but at what expense! How can we forego the pleasure of life? It is not a little question to ask ourselves are we to have art or not? It is a question between barbarism and civilization, nay between progress and corruption—between humanity and brutality—nay I am wrong there; for the brutes are at least happy—but men without art will be unhappy.

ART AND LABOUR[1]

I must first tell you what I mean by the words Art and Labour; and first, by art I mean something wider than is usually meant by the word, something which I fear it is not
very easy to explain to some of you born and bred in this great
manufacturing city,[2] and living under conditions which I will say
would have made art impossible to be if men had always lived
so.

Well you must understand that by art, I do not mean *only*
pictures and sculpture, nor only these and architecture, that is
beautiful building properly ornamented; these are only a portion
of art, which comprises, as I understand the word a great deal
more; beauty produced by the labour of man both mental and
bodily, the expression of the interest man takes in the life of man

---

[1] The text of this lecture is taken from B.M. Add. MS. 45334(2), which is entirely
in Morris's hand, although there are some penciled corrections and marginalia in
another hand. It was first delivered before the Leeds Philosophical and Literary
Society on April 1, 1884 (see Appendix I, 4–1–84, and Appendix II, item 46), and
it was repeated several times thereafter.
[2] In 1884 this lecture was delivered before audiences in Leicester, London,
Manchester, Newcastle, Preston, and Glasgow as well as Leeds (see note 1
above). Each of these places could fittingly be described as a "great manufacturing city."

upon the earth with all its surroundings, in other words the human pleasure of life is what I mean by art.

This clearly is a serious subject to consider, and should by no means be treated as though no one but a professional artist could understand it or deal with it: we are all interested in it whether we know it or not: because unless we have this peculiarly human pleasure of life we cannot be happy as men: and men cannot be happy as beasts, which would be the next best thing to being happy as men: they can only have such happiness as incomplete men can have; incomplete that is to say degraded men; which happiness arising as it does from mere ignorance and habit is at best ignoble and scarce to be desired.

So much by what I mean by the word art; now as to the word Labour without which art could not exist: understand then that the labour I am thinking of is the labour that produces things the labour of the classes called the working-classes; I am not thinking of what one might call accidental labour, that for example of the soldier, the thief, or the stockjobber, but I say of the maker of things: I would say of goods but I am sorry to say I cannot say that just at present since the question whether or not goods are always the result of this labour of the workman is just what I have to deal with.

Now you must know the questions I have to ask and try to answer tonight are these: what are the relations of the Labour of man on the earth the labour which produces all the means of human life to Art which is the pleasure of man living on the earth? or rather I must expand that question and say what have been, what are, and what should be the relations of Art to Labour?

Now further in order to let you know at once in what spirit I am speaking to you, and, to avoid anything like mystification I may as well say from the first that I in common with a good many others of the educated class am quite discontented with the condition of the Arts under the present system of labour, and that this discontent is what brings me before you tonight. But I differ from some of those who are as discontented with the present state of the arts in one important point: namely that they think that the matter is past hope and beyond remedy, whereas I

believe that there is a remedy for that state of the arts which so
arouses my discontent, and that the remedy lies in improving the
condition of those who produce or ought to produce art, or the
pleasure of life, that is to say of the people, as those who actually
work with their hands are most properly and accurately called:
let me repeat this statement of my hope, the remedy for that
sickness of the arts which I in common with many others feel so
deeply must be the giving of a new life to the people.[3]

Now in answering the question what were the relations of art
to labour, I must of necessity turn back to past times, and even
times a very long while passed; and you must believe that I do so
with the distinct purpose of showing you where lies the hope for
the future, and not in mere empty regret for the days which can
never come again. Let us then as briefly as we can glance at the
history of art and labour in very early days. Yet we will not go
back further than a time when art was in a very flourishing and
highly developed state, the days of the classical civilization of
Greece. From that time until now the labour of the people has
been exercised under three conditions; chattel slavery, serfdom,
and wage-earning. The two first conditions have passed away
from civilized communities, the third wage-earning remains still
in force.

In the days when the art of ancient Greece was flourishing, all
society was founded on chattel slavery: agriculture and the industrial arts were carried on by men who were bought and sold
like beasts of burden, and as a consequence all handicrafts were
looked down on with contempt, and what of art went with them
was kept in the strictest subjection to the intellectual arts, which
were the work of the free citizens in other words of a privileged
oligarchy: in most times this would have been a fatal obstacle to
the healthy development of art taken as a whole: but in those
days the world of civilization was young: the Greek race was
beautiful, vigorous, and highly gifted; and had an intense thirst
for the knowledge of facts; furthermore the climate was genial,
and did not call on men to provide elaborate shelter for them-

---

[3] A parenthetical organization note appears here in the MS: "what were what are
what should be."

selves, or tempt them into effeminacy or luxury,[4] ever the worst of all the foes of art; lastly though as I have said there was a world of slaves below that oligarchy of the free citizens, those citizens were free from the petty individual and family selfishness which in modern times habit has made a second nature to most of us; their lives and hopes were to them but a part of the life and hope of the city or community to which they belonged, and they reverenced it with a true religious devotion.

From this beauty, simplicity of life, and greatness and unity of aim sprang up that glorious art of Greece whose influence all civilization feels yet, and will feel for ever; and yet I must ask you to remember that though under these circumstances it was the rule rather than the exception for the free citizen to love and understand the higher forms of intellectual art, there was scarce any art of the people: the slavish handicrafts of the time produced things which were certainly not ugly, nay, which may in a sense be considered beautiful; but there was no delight of life in them, they were treated as works of the lower arts wrought by the lower classes, in those days called slaves.

Meantime to the cultivated Greek citizen there seemed nothing wrong or burdensome in chattel slavery, and all that it gave birth to: to him it was part of the natural order of things and the greatest minds of the day could see no possibility of its ever ceasing.

I can imagine what a free citizen of the time of Pericles, a cultivated Athenian gentleman would have said, if the question had been pressed on him of the right or wrong of keeping his fellow-man in subjection to the supposed necessities of a few: he would have formed an answer readily enough to extinguish any tendency towards revolutionary ideas, and to strengthen his conviction that the order of things under which he lived was eternal: I think he might have said: "In the first place it is impossible to do away with chattel slavery which is obviously founded on the moral nature of man: but apart from that, a society founded on the equality of freedom would be poor in all the elements of

---

[4] The words "any great elaboration/intricacy" are rejected in the MS for "effeminacy or luxury."

change and interest which make life worth living: such a change
would injure art and destroy individuality of character by taking
away the due stimulus to exertion; at best in a State where all
were free, there would be nothing but a dull level of
mediocrity."

So might our citizen have argued, not without the agreement of
many cultivated men of the present day, who, I observe, do think,
and not unnaturally that the cultivated gentleman of Greece or
England is such a precious and finished fruit of civilization, that
he is worth any amount of suffering, injustice, or brutality in the
mass of mankind below him.

But also I must say that our Greek gentleman might sustain his
argument in favour of chattel slavery in a manner rather embarrassing to us of these days of progress and wide-spread political
rights. For he might say: "Are you so sure that you will better the
condition of the slave by freeing him? at present it is the interest
of the owner to feed him and keep him in health: nay if the
owner be a benevolent or good-tempered man he will even do his
best towards making his slaves happy for his own pleasure: but I
can conceive of your state of free labour as leaving the greater
part of your citizens free indeed—free to starve: I can imagine a
state of things in which the sour faces of underfed and over-
worked wretches, would have no chance of making their masters,
the rich, uncomfortable since the rich would do their best to
forget their very existence and at least would steadily deny the
fact of their misery. "Nay believe me," our gentleman would say,
"you had better trust for the amelioration of Society to the hu-
manizing influence of the philosophical simplicity of the noble
and free citizen of our glorious state, which, as you well know, in
spite of all the tales of the poets, is the real God which we
worship, and which we may well hope may prove to be
immortal."

Thus might our Greek gentleman have argued, mixing up
things true and false, reasonable and unreasonable, into a seda-
tive to his conscience: thus might he have gone to work to elevate
the rules of successful tyranny into irrevocable laws of nature.

But what followed? This; the worship of the city found its due
expression at last in the growth and domination of Rome, the

mightiest of cities, whose iron hand crushed out the bickerings of ambitious clans and individuals, and cast over the world of civilization the chains of enforced federation under the rule of the tax gatherer: at last this system took the form of an inflexible central authority idealized into a religion and symbolized in the person of the emperor, the master of the world enthroned in an Italian city; such was the outcome of the worship of the city, that first took form in so-called free Greece.

Under this Roman tyranny chattel slavery still made good its claim to be considered the effect of eternally natural laws for some time to come; although the condition of the slaves, now largely working for the profit of the great Roman landowners was more dangerous to the state than it had been under Greek civilization.

But time passed, and the so-called eternal order of things changed again: the hideous greed of the capitalist landowners of Rome, whose slaves were in a worse condition than even the agricultural labourers of Great Britain are today, discounted the fertility of Italy: the huge, half-starved population of the city of Rome itself depended on supplies of foreign corn for their bare subsistence, and the enervating influence of rich men, had sapped all public virtue even to the extent of destroying military qualities so that foreign war made the foreign supply of food precarious; Rome was at last in an obviously dangerous condition; and at last the change came again; this time a tremendous one, and involving a change in the conditions of labour.

The huge crowd of starving slaves in whose minds a 'revolutionary Eastern Creed' was fast planting ideas quite foreign to classical civilization were by no means bound by the religion of city-worship, which had once put such irresistible might into the hands of the Roman legionaries: on all sides they recruited the bands of brigands and pirates whose exploits became so familiar to the civilization of later imperial Rome: and they were always present as an element of disorder ready to the hand of the foreign invader. Thus hunger, the child of class greed, did its work within the empire, while without it hunger in another form pressed on the tribes of so-called barbarians that surrounded the empire and so allied itself as a destroyer to the corruption of its

internal society: the tribes of the north and the east fell upon
Rome, and found no serious resistance since as aforesaid the gross
individualism of a corrupt society had eaten out all public
spirit.

Thus attacked on all sides by slaves, Christians, and barbarians
classical civilization fell, and to the eyes of all people then, and of
most historians since mere confusion took its place, from which as
people used to think grew up in a haphazard way the collection
of independent states which form modern Europe.

But the new order of things was really forming under this
confusion; the manner of its formation has become very obscure,
and in fact little emerges from that obscurity save the relics of the
art which was produced at the time, and which bears with it
evidence of a change in the condition of labour which can be
read by the light of the wider knowledge which we have of the
art and labour of later days. I must ask you to allow me to say a
few words about that art, which perhaps may be difficult for
some of you to follow who are not familiar with the art of past
ages; but which I will at least clear from all mere technicalities.

When Rome became mistress of the civilized world, she
adopted as far as she could the arts of conquered Greece: but
those arts had by that time already fallen from their best days,
nor was the adoption of them by a people far from sympathetic
with them likely to inspire new life into them: the tendency
therefore of the purely intellectual arts, those taken by Rome
from Greece, was ever downward: but influences, whose origin is
most obscure, were at work in Italy which produced forms of art
on the less intellectual side which had little or nothing to do with
Greece: from these sprang the architecture of the civilized world:
now in the earlier part of the decline of Rome that architecture
shared the general sickness of the arts and changed indeed, but
ever into something worse than before; its changes seemed at any
rate to be towards death and not life: it still however retained a
certain majesty of form if any new spirit could have breathed life
into its form.

Now that new spirit came to it in the midst of the confusion
and disgrace I have been speaking of, and its origin partakes of
the obscurity that veils most things worthy of consideration in the

period that followed the degradation of Rome; the period during which Constantinople took the semblance of the domination which Rome once really had.

But the spirit which was to breathe new life into the dead classical forms and [which] produced the new art which almost suddenly blossoms in the days of the Byzantine emperors, and bears with it something which the old classical art never had; that something is the very breath of life to it: and that something is nothing less than the first signs of freedom: this art neither expresses the exclusive, rigid, rational intellect of Greek art, nor the exclusive, academical pedantry of Roman art, but it has another quality which makes us forgive it all its rudeness, timidity, and unreason, that quality is its wide sympathy: it has become popular art, the art of the people.

Now I feel sure that whatever obscurity may enwrap the origins of this Byzantine art, this mother of Gothic art, this quality is really a token of the labour which produced it, having thrown off some of its chains at least; and I believe that what follows in history bears me out in this view. It seems to me that this new art was the token and effect of the rise of that condition of labour which may be briefly described as serfdom struggling towards freedom by means of cooperation for the protection of trade and handicraft.

Serfdom is the condition of labour in the Early Middle Ages, as chattel slavery was that of the Classical period: the chattel-slave, who was absolutely the property of his master was fed by him and kept by him in just such a condition of comfort as suited the convenience of the master. Sometimes as in the days of the huge Roman farms or Latifundia, the master hoping for exorbitant profit, fed the slaves so low that he was obliged to allow them to supplement their short commons by the additional industry of brigandage; but generally the master would find it better to keep his slaves in fair condition.

So much for the slave; now the serf on the other hand had to perform certain definite services for his feudal lord, generally to give him so many days work in the year, and for the rest of his time was free to work for himself and feed himself.

So doing he was living in harmony with the general arrangement of Society in the Middle Ages, a time in which every man had legal, definite, personal duties to perform to his superior, and could in turn claim certain degrees of help and protection from him.

This was the idea of the hierarchical Society of the Middle Ages; which was founded on a priori views of divine government, and under which every man had his due place which, theoretically, he could not alter or step out of: personal duties for all, personal rights for all according to their divinely appointed station was the theory of Society of the Middle Ages, which took the place of that of classical times in which indeed all the citizens were equally parts of the supreme city and lived in her and for her, but were served by men turned into mere beasts of burden.

Now it seems to me quite natural that this Mediaeval or hierarchical system should have been looked upon as eternal and inevitable with at least as much confidence as that which preceded it.

But revolution was in store for it no less than for the classical system. For as the half-starved slave of the Roman latifundia was driven to strive to better himself by brigandage first and then by service with the invaders; so the mediaeval serf was driven by the compulsion of labouring to feed himself after his compulsory work was done, into trying to better his condition altogether: he began at last to try to slip his neck out of his lord's collar and become a free man: and this struggle resulted in combination for freedom among the workers.

Apart from the religious houses, which in a way afforded protection to labour, and even gave working-men a chance of rising out of their caste on condition of their accepting the ecclesiastical yoke; apart from these combinations of ecclesiastics, there arose in the Middle Ages other bodies which grew to be powerful and far-reaching: these bodies are called the guilds.

The tendency of the Germanic tribes towards cooperation and community of life, a survival probably from former days, began to show itself quite early in the Middle Ages. In England even before the Norman conquest this tendency began to draw the workmen and traders into definite association: the guilds which were thus formed were at first of the nature of benefit societies:[5] from this they grew into what are called the Merchant Guilds, bodies that is formed for mutual protection in trading; and lastly these developed the craft-guilds or associations for the protection and regulation of handicrafts.

All these guilds aimed at freeing the individual from the domination and protection of the feudal lord, and substituting for that domination the authority and mutual protection of the associated guild-brethren; or to put it in another way the object was to free labour from the power of individual members of the feudal hierarchy, and to supplant their authority by that of corporations, which should themselves be recognized as members of that hierarchy, out of which indeed the mediaeval mind could not step.

Of course all this took a long time, and was by no means carried out without very rough work; as the merchant guilds resisted tooth and nail, especially in Germany, the changes which gave the craft-guilds their position. In the process of the struggle the merchant guilds became for the most part in England at least the corporations of the towns, and the craft-guilds fully took their place as to the organization of labour: by the beginning of the 14th century the change was complete, and the craft guilds were the masters of all handicrafts: all workmen were forced to belong to the guild of the craft they followed.

For a time, only too short a time, the constitution of these guilds was thoroughly democratic: every worker apprenticed to a craft was sure if he could satisfy the due standard of excellence to become a master; there were no mere journeymen.

This state of things however did not last long: for as the population of the towns grew because of the freeing of the serf field-labourers, these latter began to crowd into the craft guilds, and the masters who at first were simple, complete workmen helped by their apprentices or incomplete workmen now began

---

[5] The *NED* defines a benefit-society as ". . . an association whose members, by the regular payment of small sums, are entitled to pecuniary help in time of age or sickness." The reference is probably to the frith-guild or "peace-club" mentioned in J. R. Green's *Short History of the English People*, IV, 190. Morris did not believe that the merchant guilds developed from the frith-guilds. See *Socialism: Its Growth and Outcome* (London, 1893), pp. 68–69.

to be employers of labour. They were privileged members of the guild and besides their privileged apprentices employed journeymen, who though forced to affiliation with the guild did not become masters or privileged in it.

Now this, which was the first appearance of the so-called freeworkman, or wage-earner in modern Europe was at the time felt as a trouble: some attempt was made by the journeymen themselves to form guilds of journeymen beneath the craft-guilds just as the latter had done beneath the merchant-guilds: in this revolt against privilege they were unsuccessful, and the craft guilds went on getting more and more aristocratic so to speak, although at first the power of their privileged members over the journeymen was limited by laws made in favour of the latter.[6]

The labour of the Middle Ages therefore was carried on amidst a struggle, partly an unconscious one, for freedom from the arbitrary rule of aristocratic privileges: before looking at the results of this struggle, let us briefly consider the relations of art to labour during this period of the fully-developed Middle Ages.

From all we can learn of the condition of labour in England during this time, and the materials are ample, we are driven to the conclusion, that however rude the general conditions of life may have been; the struggle for livelihood among the workers was far less hard than it is at present; considering the prices of necessaries at the time the earnings both of labourers and skilled artisans were far higher than they are now:[7] I repeat that for the workers life was easier, though general life was rougher than it is in our days:[8] that is there was more approach to real equality of

---

[6] A note appears here in the MS, evidently added at a later date, though still in Morris's hand. It reads, "employers not capitalists strictly."

[7] Morris knew Professor Thorold Rogers and his *Six Centuries of Work and Wages* (see Thompson, *Romantic to Revolutionary*, pp. 245, 255, 456). Of that compendious work the section on the middle ages was published in 1866, the complete edition being issued in 1884, the year of this lecture. One of the major themes of Rogers' research was that the workman of the middle ages was in a better economic position than his counterpart in the seventeenth and eighteenth centuries. See *A History of Agriculture and Prices in England, from the year after the Oxford Parliament (1239) to the Commencement of the Continental War* (6 vols. Oxford, 1866) and *Six Centuries of Work and Wages* (2 vols.; London, 1884).

[8] For a more detailed statement by Morris on this question, see the chapter on

condition in spite of the arbitrary distinctions of noble and gentle: churl and villein.

But further as the distribution of wealth in general was more equal than now so in particular was that of art or the pleasure of life; all craftsmen had some share in it to begin with: this is illustrated by the fact that the pay of those who superintended labour, such persons as we should now call builders, architects, and the like, was very little higher than that of the workmen under them: nor were those who were doing what we should now call more intellectual work, artists we should now call them, paid more than ordinary craftsmen; the knowledge of art, and the practice of producing it were assumed to be the rule among craftsmen, and really were so.[9]

The system of exchange also was simple: there was little competition in the market, goods were made equal to the demand which was easy to ascertain: there was no work for mere middlemen; people worked in the main for livelihood and not for profit: so that the worker had but one master, the public, and he had full control over his own material, tools, and time; in other words he was an artist.

Now it was this condition of labour which produced the art of the Middle Ages, and nothing else could have produced it: people have sometimes supposed that the motive power for it was religious enthusiasm, or the spirit of chivalry, whatever that may be, but such theories are now exploded: history has been illuminated since then by careful research: we have counted our forefathers' pots and kettles and chairs and pictures, we know what their clothes and their houses were; we have read not only their books, but their family letters, their bills and their contracts, in short we have followed them from the church, the battlefield, and the palace to their houses and workshops and tilled fields,[10] and

---

"The Rough Side of the Middle Ages" in *Socialism: Its Growth and Outcome,* pp. 76–84.

[9] Another apparently later note in Morris's hand appears here: *"Exchange of Equivalents."*

[10] Among the advances in English historical studies in the nineteenth century—besides the interpretive work of such men as Stubbs, Freeman, Green, Lecky, and Gardiner—a number of very important primary sources were made available for

we find that these men of the same blood as ourselves, speaking the same tongue, connected with us by an apparently unbroken chain of laws, traditions, and customs, were yet amazingly different from ourselves, far more so than any religion, any spirit of chivalry, romance, or what not could have made them.

And I am sorry to say that one of the main differences between us is that whereas when goods are made now they are always made ugly unless they are specially paid for as things containing beauty, in which case they are not uncommonly uglier still, in the Middle Ages everything that man made was beautiful, just as everything that nature makes is always beautiful; and I must again impress upon you the fact that this was because they were made mainly for use, instead of mainly to be bought and sold as is now the case. The beauty of the handicrafts of the Middle Ages came from this, that the workman had control over his material, tools, and time.

I must now go back to the condition of the workman as we left it at the period when the guilds were beginning to be corrupted by the beginnings of capitalism at the end of the 14th century: I must say first that you must remember however that the distinction between the privileged guildsmen and their journeymen was after all an arbitrary one; the master craftsmen all worked: there were no such people as 'manufacturers' then [or] 'organizers of labour'; that is people paid very heavily to do nothing but look on while other people work: nor was there any division of labour in the workshop. Throughout the 15th century also the condition of labour remained much the same as in the 14th indeed wages rose on the whole throughout that century.

But somewhat early in the 16th century things began to change seriously; the Middle Ages were coming to an end: the body of men available for journeymen or 'free workmen,' working for the profit of a master increased greatly and suddenly.

---

the first time. The two-volume *Letters and Papers of the Reigns of Richard III and Henry VII* was issued in the years 1861–63; Gardiner's edition of *The Paston Letters* emerged from 1872 to 1875; and the entire monumental Rolls Series of the texts of English chronicles and memorials was published between 1857 and 1896. The State Papers of Henry VIII (11 vols., 1830–52) was one of the first great modern accomplishments in the editing of historical documents. For a full list of these more important nineteenth-century publications are Charles Gross, *The Sources and Literature of English History* (London, 1915).

Commerce was spreading all over Europe which was shaking off the roughness and ignorance of the Middle Ages: America had been discovered also, and Commerce was tending ever westward; Europe was the master now and Asia and the East the servant. In these islands the bonds of personal feudal service had been much shaken by the wholesale slaughter of gentlemen in the Wars of the Roses, and the landlords impoverished by that long struggle saw before them a chance of recovering their position by throwing themselves into the market of new-born Commerce.

Then began in England the great change, the death of the Middle Ages and Feudalism: hitherto men had produced for livelihood, they now began to produce for profit; in England the raising of raw material was the first step towards this profit-grinding, and it led as a matter of course to depriving the yeomen and workmen of the land; it was more profitable to raise wool for the foreign market than grain for home consumption, sheep were more profitable animals than men.

It was not difficult even at the time to see the danger of this step; in Henry VII's time legislation tried to check it, but the impulse toward Commerce was too strong: force and fraud applied without scruple soon did their work, and England from being a country of tillage interspersed with common land for the pasturage of the people's livestock, became a great grazing country raising sheep for the production of wool for a profit.

Two representative Englishmen have left in their writings full tokens of how bitterly this spoliation of the people was felt: Sir Thomas More, one of the most high-minded and cultivated gentlemen of his period, a Catholic and a martyr to his honesty in that cause was one: Hugh Latimer, a yeoman's son, the very type of rough English honesty, a protestant, and a martyr to his honesty in that cause was another: both say much the same thing and in words which leave the deepest impression on those who have read them, give a terrible picture of the results of Commercial greed in their days:[11] it is no idle word to say that such men never die; and now once more it seems as though the axe of More and

---

[11] The descriptions referred to are contained in Thomas More's *Utopia*, Book I, and Hugh Latimer's "Sermon on the Plow," ed. S. E. Corrie (2 vols.; London, 1844–45).

the faggot of Latimer had still left their spirits with us to produce fruit which they in their life-time, no not even More himself could ever dream would come to pass.

Henceforth Commerce went merrily on her destructive way: the direct spoliation of the people by driving them off the land was followed by their indirect spoliation in the form of the seizure of the lands of the religious houses: the pretext being (if any was thought necessary) that they no longer performed the public function for which they were held, and so were incapable of being used for any public function, and therefore had better be stolen by private persons.

This fresh robbery of the people apart from the hideous brutality with which it was carried out had on more than one side woeful enough immediate results; but as to our subject the thing to be noted about it is that it added to the army of mere have-nothings already produced by the driving off the people from the land.

So that in one way or other there had been created a vast body of people who had no property except the power of labour in their own bodies, which in consequence they were obliged to sell to anybody who would buy on the terms of keeping them alive to work. Thus was established the class of free labourers, of whom our Athenian friend warned us, men who were (and are) free— to starve.

Well this was the material ready for the use of the plague of profit-mongering politely called Commerce, then newly let loose on the world: at first the material was rather embarrassing by its abundance, and was hanged out of the way by the thousand by Mr. Froude's pious hero Henry VIII[12] and other law makers of the time. However things shook down again at last, and the market for labour, that is men's bodies and souls, adjusted itself: in Elizabeth's reign a poor law was enacted to take the place of the

---

[12] James Anthony Froude (1818–94), younger brother of the Tractarian Richard H. Froude, had reacted violently from the orthodoxies of the Oxford Movement and extended political liberalism into religion and history. The first four volumes of his *History of England from the Fall of Wolsey to the Defeat of the Spanish Armada* (London, 1873) were devoted to a justification of Henry VIII and the Reformation.

almsgiving of the monasteries, and the new order of things was established founded on Commerce, and tending ever more and more toward complete freedom of competition in the markets of the world, among the various manufacturers, now so called and their slaves the free workmen.

Thus had the struggles of labour to free itself from feudal arbitrariness succeeded: feudalism was overthrown, and commercialism was taking the empty place in its old throne.

The worker had entered into his kingdom then? all was straightforward justice and a good life for him from henceforth?

Strange to say not at all; the worker was the worker still, starved, despised, oppressed: a new class had been formed, that was all: it had grown up out of those elements of freed serf, corporate trader, privileged guild-craftsman, and yeoman and become a *middle-class*, which grew speedily in wealth and power, being fed by the very misery created by the dawn of the age of profit-grinding, which also produced the middle-class itself.

Well certainly they were a stout and vigourous set of men, those early middle-class people, their lives interesting enough, dear to the romance writer and the poet. Keen scholars, excellent poets, not bad musicians, the bravest pirates and among the greatest liars whom the world has ever seen: rough-handed and unscrupulous they pushed on against privilege with all the old traditions behind them of men who were struggling under different circumstances and with different aims, and probably were no wise conscious of that difference of aim: so they struggled and at last towards the middle of the 17th century they began to aim at supremacy in the state and not merely freedom for Commerce.

As to the condition of the free workers that had grown up under them it was poor enough, and the very character of the labour they did was changing: here and there indeed the form of the old individual work of the middle ages survived, though not for the benefit of the worker; but generally division of labour had begun under the rule of the capitalist masters: the men were collected into large workshops, their simple machines such as the loom, the lathe, and the potter's wheel though not altered in principle were lightened and improved: the employment of labour for profit necessarily stimulated the organization of the division of labour, which reached at last such a pitch that an intelligent man who once would have schemed and carried out a piece of work from first to last, was now forced to concentrate his skill and strength on a very small portion of that work; he was turned into a machine for the cheapening of market-wares.

As to the art which was produced in the early period of commercialism a very few words will suffice: in places where goods were turned out in a kind of domestic manner popular art lingered in a rude form, but was a mere survival of mediaevalism; elsewhere under the direct grip of profit-mongering it kept on sinking, and subsisted almost wholly on attempts to perpetuate the products of the great minds of the specially individualist artists of the beginning of the [16th] century:[13] division of labour extinguished even this poor remnant as it advanced step by step, and as more and more those who produced anything with a claim to beauty were divided into workmen who were not artists, and artists who were not workmen.

The 18th century saw the perfection of the division of labour system which was begun in the 17th[14] and therewith for a time at least the end of all art worth considering: all goods now were made primarily for the market, and all so-called ornamental art had become a mere incident of these market wares, something which was to help to force people to buy them, a thing which

---

[13] The MS reads, "15th century."

[14] In the lecture *Architecture and History*, delivered at the annual meeting of the SPAB on July 1, 1884, just three months after the first delivery of *Art and Labour*, Morris commented on the source of his concepts of eighteenth-century economics: "The exigencies of my own work have driven me to dig pretty deeply into the strata of the eighteenth-century workshop system, and I could clearly see how very different it is from the factory system of to-day, with which it is commonly confounded; therefore it was with a ready sympathy that I read the full explanation of the change and its tendencies in the writings of a man, I will say a great man, whom, I suppose, I ought not to name in this company, and who cleared my mind on several points (also unmentionable here) relating to this subject of labour and its products" (*Collected Works*, XXII, 311). It seems unquestionable, as E. P. Thompson has pointed out (*Romantic to Revolutionary*, pp. 276–77), that the "great man" referred to is Karl Marx and that the "writings" are *Das Kapital*.

would be bestowed or withheld according to the exigencies of profit: whereas once the beauty which went with all men's handiwork was bestowed as ungrudgingly as nature bestows her beauty; the workman could not choose but give it, his withholding it would have meant his depriving himself of a pleasure. But now you see he had no voice in settling whether he should have any pleasure in his work; he had become a 'free-workman,' and therefore it seems a machine at the beck and call of the master who was grinding a profit out of him.

So much for popular art, that is of real art: there was a sort of gentleman's art left, done entirely by 'artists' so-called and showing sometimes in the best of the pictures painted at the period a certain flippant cleverness as to invention and an amount of low manual dexterity in the execution which made the said pictures quite good enough for their purpose, the amusement namely of idle fine gentlemen and ladies.

As to this artists' art you may expect me to say something of its exploits and its prospects today; but I won't say much: I can't help thinking that it does produce something worthier than was turned out in the 18th century; but I know that if it does, it is because of the revolutionary spirit working in the brains of men, who at least will not accept conventional lies in anything with which they are busied: and whatever it is I fear it produces little effect on the mass of the people, who at present, since popular art lies crushed under money bags, have no share in the pleasure of life either in their work or their play.

Now if I shared the opinion of those who think that art is a thing which can be produced by the conscious efforts of a few cultivated men apart from the work of the great mass of men, if I thought it was a thing that could be shuffled on and off according to convenience like Sunday religion and family morality, if this were my view of the matter I should not have another word to say; but as I think pretty much the contrary of this I must trouble you with a few more words.

As far as history has gone we have come to the end of art properly speaking, but for labour there was another change in store. The Division of labour system as perfected in the 18th century produced an enormous amount of goods for the markets, but the markets kept on growing beneath the adventurous spirit of profit-making, and mere machine workmen could not work fast enough to satisfy their demands; it became necessary to supplement their labour by the invention of machines, which did not fail to take place and labour once more entered into a new phase: for all the greater industries the workshop with its groups of workmen was turned into the factory which is one huge group, one machine in fact of which each individual workman is only an inconsiderable part, and in which the skill of the individual even his subdivided skill as a division-of-labour workman is supplanted by the social organization of the whole group.

This last great revolution in labour was effected in the most reckless manner, and consequently entailed terrible sufferings on the workers. Before it though England had had her share in the general increase of commerce, she was still in the main a quiet agricultural country; 50 years passed and she became what she is now, or at least what she has been till quite lately, the workshop of the world.

How do we stand now as regards the present and the future? is the question we have to ask ourselves, and I plead with you to ask yourselves the question in a wide and generous spirit, and not to be contented with an answer which will put an aim before you scarce worth aiming at. There are some who will tell you that we are going on very well now on our present lines, and that the condition of the people has much improved during the last fifty years; and they imply by this that the progress will be steady and uninterrupted on its present lines. Now remember that 50 years will carry us back to the time when the utter confusion caused by the revolution of the great machine industries had scarcely begun even to settle down: shall we then make it a matter of exultation that we have improved a little on the very darkest period of the history of labour in England? Is the improvement, I say, from that welter of misery of which the Chartist revolt was a token to be made a standard of our future hopes; and on the other hand can we venture to hope in the face of all that is going on in all our great centres of labour today that this improvement will be steady and permanent unless some real change from the root upwards is made in Society? I say no with all the emphasis I can.

Do not let us fix our standard of endeavour by the misery which has been but rather by the happiness that might be: do not let us suppose that labour has seen its last revolution: if it has I do not quite know what to say in favour of civilization but I know something to say against it; this namely that for the mass of mankind it has destroyed art, or the pleasure of life.

I have been trying to show you how owing to the rise of producing for profit the workman has been robbed of one pleasure which as long as he is a *work*man is perhaps his most important one: pleasure in his daily work: he is now only a part of a machine, and has indeed little more than his weariness at the end of his day's work to show him that he has worked at all in the day. Beauty, the pleasure of life then has nothing to do with his work: has he not some compensatory pleasure in his life outside his work? Where does it lie then? In his home? Why in these manufacturing districts not even a rich man can have a decent dwelling, much less a poor one, since it has been thought a little thing to turn the rivers into filth and put out the sun, and make the earth squalid with the bricken encampments, I won't call them houses, in which those who make our wealth live such lives as they can live: yet I have heard that even your hovels in the manufacturing districts are better than our London ones, where a nation of the poor dwells beside a nation of the rich, and both are supposed to call each other fellow countrymen.

Or does leisure compensate the workman for his dreary toil? not what I should call leisure, though for a middle-class man I work pretty hard; not sufficient and unanxious leisure; such leisure as he has, the workman has pretty much to steal; he knows that competition will punish him and his wife and children for every hour's holiday he takes.

Or high wages? if indeed they could be any good to a man condemned to live all his days in a toiling hell. No, his wages can't be high; as long as profit has to be made out of his labour they must be kept down to the point which a long series of struggles has made him think just necessary to live on; and mind you in spite of all past struggles he can't depend on keeping his wages up even to their present level.[15]

Shall he be recompensed by education then? Some people think he can be: I do not. I wish him educated indeed in order that he may be discontented; more education than that he cannot have as things go—why education means reasonable, pleasant work, and beautiful surroundings, and unanxious leisure, these are essential parts of it.

Quite plainly therefore I say that the modern workman, the poor man can have no art that is none of the beauty of life: his work will not produce it, and he has neither money to buy it with or leisure and education, that is to say refinement to relish it.

I fear that there are some people who will say that all this doesn't matter at all: they think, the man is well enough fed, housed, clothed, educated to make him a good workman—for making profits for other people, and he is contented with his lot—as yet. After all I don't care what such people think so long as I can get the workman himself to think that it does matter to him whether he is robbed of the pleasure of life: it is to him therefore to the workman, that I turn and tell him what I think he ought to claim for himself.

Well first he must claim to live in a pleasant house and a pleasant place; a claim which I daresay many people would be inclined to allow for him—till they found out wh[at] he meant by it, and how impossible it would be to satisfy it under the profit-grinding system: until for example we consider what time, money, and trouble it would take to turn Glasgow into a pleasant place.

---

[15] Morris here comes as close as he ever does to an expression of "the iron law of wages," a proposition very popular among early English and continental socialists. According to this theory the worker's wage is kept at a bare subsistence level by the superfluity of the workers themselves, who multiply by Malthusian progression and thereby offset any advantages won by increased productivity, etc. Frederick Engels, in a letter to August Bebel (March, 1875) indicates that the idea originated with Ferdinand Lassalle, the great German socialist, and that it does not square with Marxian principles. See *Karl Marx and Frederick Engels: Selected Correspondence* (London, 1956), p. 355. It is doubtful, however, that Morris ever fully accepted the "iron law" since the Malthusian theory was never acceptable to him in other contexts.

Second the workman must be well-educated: again all people at least pretend to agree with this claim till they understand what I mean by it; namely that all should be educated according to their capacity, and not according to the amount of money which their parents happen to possess: less education [than][16] this means class education which is a monstrous oppression of the poor by the rich.

Third the workman must have due leisure; which claim I know numberless benevolent men agree to till they know what it involves; namely the prevention at any cost of overwork for profit; which further implies that there must be no idlers, and that the duration of the day's work must be legally limited.[17]

You will see I daresay that what these three claims really mean is refinement of life for all; what is called the life of a gentleman for all; a preposterous claim doubtless to make for a workman; but one which they will get satisfied when they seriously claim it; and if they don't claim it and get it, surely the hopes which this last period of the world began with the revolutionary hopes of the last hundred years will fade out: and then conceive what the worker's life will be when he has no longer any lurking hope of revolution.

So far I have been speaking of the conditions under which the workman should work, I must say an express word or two on the work itself, though I have indeed implied it before.

There must be no useless work done, which follows as a matter of course on the claim to limitation of the day's work: but of course few well-to-do people can agree with doing away with useless work, as in one way or other almost all of the richer classes live upon it.

All useless work being abolished whatever of irksome work is left should be done by machines used not as now to grind out

---

[16] The MS reads, "that."

[17] In the years 1884, 1885, and 1886, the SDF and various radical groups engaged in strenuous agitation for a legal limitation of the working day to eight hours. Morris seems to have jettisoned this idea along with what he later called "palliatives" when he left SDF. In the "Notes" he wrote for *Commonweal* in 1885 and 1886 he often pointed out that the benefits to be derived from such a limit were merely illusory.

profit, but to save labour really: this I know involves what to some will seem the monstrous proposition that machines should be our servants and not our masters: nevertheless I make it without blushing.

No useless work being done and all irksome labour saved as much as possible by machines made our servants instead of our masters, it would follow that whatever other work was done would be accompanied by pleasure in the doing, and would receive praise when done if it were worthy, and it is most true that all work done with pleasure and worthy of praise produces art, that is to say an essential part of the pleasure of life.

Now I must remind you that I have said that the work of all handicrafts in the Middle Ages produced beauty as a necessary part of the goods, so that some approximation to the ideal above stated was realized then; I have also said that the workman produced this beauty because he was in his work master of his material, tools, and time, in fact of his work: therefore you will not be astonished to hear me say that in order to produce art once again the workman must once more be master of his material, tools, and time: only I must explain that I do not mean that we should turn back to the system of the middle ages, but that the workmen should own these things that is the means of labour collectively, and should regulate labour in their own interests; also you must bear in mind that I have already said that all must work therefore the workmen means the whole of society; there should be no society outside those who work to sustain society.

Now I know well enough that this means altering the basis of society, putting Socialism, that is universal cooperation, in place of competition or universal war: but if that startles you I can only say that I am quite sure that those claims for the well-being of the workers which I have made are necessary to be carried out, and that it is simply impossible to carry them out in a condition of universal war, which I repeat is in truth the condition under which we are living: our present state of sham peace and real war is the outcome of many centuries of the war of classes, in which the oppressed class was ever striving to raise itself at the expense of the oppressing class: always in the process of this strug-

gle at every stage of it the issue has been wider and wider: I have
said a few words about that stage of it which produced the
present middle classes of civilization whose struggle was crowned
at last with success by the French Revolution and the years of
triumphant Commerce which have succeeded it: but the very
triumph of the commercial middle-class has strengthened and
solidified the working-class, has collected them into factories and
great towns, has forced them to act together to a certain extent
by the trades unions, and has given them a certain amount of
political power: what they need now to enter on the last stage of
the modern revolution of labour is that they should understand
their true position, which is in short that they are the real necessary part of Society, and that the middle and upper classes which
now rule them are but hangers-on, who have been forced into
usurpation of the governing power of the community; they must
understand that the division into classes which for so many
hundred years has been a curse and a burden to the earth is a
system which is wearing out, and that the sign of its approaching
end is to be found in the fact that the division is sharper and
simpler than it has ever been; that it is no longer consecrated by
religion and sentiment, but stands out in its naked hideousness
dependent on nothing more sacred than the possession of money.
On the one side are the rich: on the other the poor: and the rich
possess not only more wealth than they themselves can use, but
also the power of allowing or forbidding the other class, the poor,
to earn themselves a livelihood; since they possess all the means
whereby labour can be made fruitful and the poor possess nothing but the power of labour inherent in their bodies: now I say
that when the working-classes once understand this, and that it
[is] necessary for their happiness nay for avoiding their degradation into the condition of brutes that they should assert their true
position of being themselves society, when they understand that
they themselves can regulate labour, and by being absolute masters of their material, tools, and time they can win for themselves
all that is possible to be won from nature without deduction or
taxation paid to classes that have no purpose or reason for existence; when this is understood, the workers will find themselves

compelled to combine together to change the basis of Society and to realize that Socialism the rumour of whose approach is all about us.

What resistance may be offered to this combination by the present dominant classes who can say? but I know that it must be futile: I address one last word to my middle-class hearers who are really interested in the condition of the people, who are amazed and grieved at the corruption and misery which civilization founded on a Society of classes has brought us to.

You are not bound by your class to the futile resistance which your class as long as it remains a class must oppose to the advance of Socialism; with your leisure and opportunities it ought to be easy to you to study this question which it is now obvious cannot be suppressed. When you have gone into the matter, and have found, as you must do, that there are but two camps, that of the people and that of their masters, and that you must take your choice between them, will you hesitate then? To shut your eyes against reason then, and to join the camp of the masters is to brand yourself as an oppressor and a thief: you did not mean to be either before you knew what Socialism was; you meant to be just and benevolent; be no worse now when you know what Socialism is, and what it asks of you and throw in your lot with the workers at every stage of the struggle.

So doing you will be part of a great army which must triumph, and be helping to bring about the day when the words rich and poor, that have so long cursed the world, shall have no meaning, when we shall all be friends and good fellows united in that communion of happy, reasonable, honoured labour which alone can produce genuine art, or the Pleasure of Life.

[THE DEPRESSION OF TRADE][1]

hat is the essence of the society which took the place of feudalism: free competition—that is in other words a desperate war in which every man fights for his own hand; the aim of the struggle being to live free from labour at the expense of those that labour. This struggle results necessarily in the formation of two great classes, the successful and the unsuccessful, which in spite of minor divisions among them, have now taken the place of all the elaborate castes of feudality: the struggle therefore proposed for everyone born into the world of civilization is the getting, or the keeping of a place in the class which lives on the labour of others: the getting or the keeping; because there are some who are born privileged to be useless, and others who win that privilege by industry, talent, good-luck, and unscrupulousness: accordingly one solemn duty is recognized tacitly by all people who live under our present system of commercialism the formation of a family who shall become a group in the class of

---

[1] The text of this lecture is taken from B.M. Add. MS. 45334(5), which is entirely in Morris's hand. Contemporary newspaper accounts and the references to Lancashire (p. 221) and Oldham (p. 225) establish that Morris first delivered this lecture under the title indicated above on July 12, 1885. Later in the same year he read it before a London audience (see Appendix I, 7–12–85, 9–9–85, and Appendix II, item 68).

the non-producers: observe once more how entirely the necessities of the system which rules us flies in the face of the morals which, we, whatever our creed profess to believe: in all codes of morals it is thought wrong to take away from an unwilling fellow-man the means of subsistence or enjoyment; this is commonly called stealing; and when practiced by an individual in an unorganized manner if we catch him we think ourselves justified in torturing him in various ways in order to frighten others off from the like courses: for we call him a thief and his unorganized interference with other people's livelihood and pleasure we call stealing: nevertheless there is no man in any of the creeds so pious, there is none in any of the philosophies of such rigid morality that he does not with the approbation of all men do his very best to raise (as we call it) himself or at least his children into the class of non-producers, that is to say of those who by force or fraud take away from their unwilling fellows the means of livelihood or pleasure: it [is] only the commonness and the organization of it that prevents this class from being called the class of thieves; so you see in spite of all our religion and all our morality we consider it a sacred duty to put those whom we love best, ourselves and our children into the position of thieves.

However [if] it were only a matter of a conflict between our professions of morality and our practice of it it would be no great matter perhaps; we should, as men always have done, make our morality square with our necessity; that we have not systematically done so no doubt points to the very transitory character of our present system, so that even almost as soon as it has been developed fully it begins to show signs of disruption: and no wonder for it is clear that the greater part of men cannot belong to the successful classes: obviously every one person who refuses to do his share of production must have attached to him at least one person who does his share of work; at least one; but as a matter of fact he has many more, because since he does no work and is served by others he considers himself a superior person above those who keep him by their labour, and claims successfully to live at a higher rate than they do; he eats and drinks, is clad and housed more expensively than they; although they do something and he does nothing: he keeps them toiling at making wares which they have no chance of using, if they cared to use them, their labour is forced from them to amuse and beguile the stupidity of his idleness: the result of all which is that many thousand of skilled and should-be useful hands and lives are utterly wasted and all the time the work that is absolutely necessary for sustaining the lives of men has inexorably to be done, and so both the burden of it falls on few people comparatively, also it is much worse done than it should be: indeed many matters that reasonable people would think of the first utility, to be done before anything else were attempted are never even set about at all: as for instance while I speak to you London is practically undrained; a huge mass of sewage, which should be used for fertilizing the fields of Kent and Essex now and especially the latter actually passing out of cultivation, a wall of filth is accumulating at the mouth of the Thames garnering up for us who knows what seeds of pestilence and death.[2] While here in Lancashire you have allowed yourselves to be so hoodwinked and enslaved that you are forced to live amidst squalor and wretchedness which men of an earlier age could scarcely have conceived of in order that you may make wares of whose sale you are now beginning to have doubts, while at the same time you don't know what to do, what to turn your hands to save making ever-fresh relays of unsaleable wares: like the miserable debtors that one has heard of who have no resource for staving off importunate creditors than ordering more luxuries which cannot be paid for.[3] Or take a last instance; with all the lines of competing railways

---

[2] Adequate drainage is still a difficulty in London, due largely to the sluggish tidal currents of the Thames estuary, that do not move the sewage out to sea rapidly enough. In the late nineteenth century this problem was acute. Edward Walford, in *Old and New London* (London, [1927]), Vol. V, 238, speaks of the sewers of the time as channels through which "rolled the refuse of London, in a black, murky flood, here and there changing its temperature and colour, as chemical dye-works, sugar-bakers, tallow-melters, and slaughterers added their streams to the pestiferous rolling river. About 31,650,000,000 gallons of this liquid was poured yearly into the Thames, in its course through London. . . . The river of filth struggling through its dark channel sometimes rose to a height of five feet, but generally from two to three." It is doubtful however that any modern health official would sanction Morris's idea of using city sewage for fertilizer.

[3] This is Becky Sharp's stratagem in Thackeray's *Vanity Fair* (New York, 1950), pp. 218–19.

that score the land like crackling on a leg of pork tons upon tons of fish wholesome, nay dainty food, if it could only be brought to the consumer are scattered for manure over the fields of Suffolk and Norfolk while people in the East End of London are becoming scarcely human for lack of decent food, and the fishermen of East Anglia risk their lives in cockle shells of boats on the sea living roughly and precariously for the noble reward of 12/0 a week: or yet again one last instance of the folly of slaves and slave-owners. Did you ever hear of the Irish famine?[4] that found 8 millions of human beings in Ireland and left 5 millions there? a famine we call it: but what is a famine? a great scarcity of food: now do you know that while all those people were dying of starvation, were clemming[5] in Ireland quantities of food—butter, eggs, and bacon were being transported to England to be sold at a profit there. And what came between those starving people of Ireland and the food which their labour had produced? remember every one of those Irishmen that died, or went across the sea bearing with him a bitter load of hatred against those who to him represented the system of the civilization of the 19th century, was capable of producing more than he needed for his own subsistence if he had only been allowed to work on his own land and to have for himself the produce of his own labour: what came between him and the victuals he and his had produced and so slew him or drove him from home? the class system, the system of landlord and tenant, of capitalist and workman; in other words the system which has for one pillar a propertied, non-producing class and for the other a property-less, producing class, which as a class has no hope save revolution, which same revolution is staved off only so long as the members of the working-class can buoy themselves up with the hope of rising from the class of the employed into that of employers: this of course only a few of

---

[4] Although much of Morris's argument from the Irish Famine was in general usage among the socialist propagandists of the eighties, it is probable that both he and his colleagues were indebted to Karl Marx for their facts and many of their inferences. See Karl Marx, *Capital*, tr. by Samuel Moore and Edward Aveling, ed. by Frederick Engels (10th ed.; London, 1904), pp. 719–35.

[5] The *NED* defines "clemming" as ". . . to pinch as hunger or fasting does; to waste with hunger, starve."

them can do even at the best, leaving behind them the great mass
of hopeless labour, which has no choice or chance save to work
tomorrow as today at a task which is a mere burden, and so
always regarded, and the reward for which is precarious; subject
at the best and in the epochs when trade is briskest to those
periodical stagnations which mean diminished profit to the employer and diminished necessities to the employed: but in a
period like the present when all trade is chronically stagnant
what can we say of the worker's hope if he can see no futher than
a continuance of the present relations of employer and employed;
if the system of capital and wage-earning is to go on? That system
means, as I have been trying to show, a wasting of the worker's
labour-power, his only possession, in the free competition or war
which has for its object the securing a position of deedless ease
for a lucky few—if indeed they can be called lucky. Let us for a
few minutes see how that war is waged. In the first place this war
is the chief, almost the only occupation of the possessing classes:
just as the slave-owners of Greece and Rome used the leisure
which the possession of slaves gave them to fight endlessly for the
aggrandizement of their tribe or city, just as the ownership of
lands tilled by serfs gave the Mediaeval baron leisure to fight
ceaselessly for honour (and more land and serfs) so does the
possession of capital, or the power of compelling unwilling labour
from poor men, enable the modern monied man to fight ceaselessly in the markets of the world for his share of the *profits*
wrung by his class from the labour-class; and this I say is almost
his only occupation—his other ones being various forms of the
less harmful occupation of obvious busy idling—amusements—
such as yachting, travelling, shooting, or electioneering and legislation. Now in this war as in others the weakest goes to the wall,
so that each combatant must of necessity be quite unsparing of all
kinds of waste or else he will be beaten: understand that when I
was speaking just now of the waste of the class system I was
thinking chiefly of the waste of wealth consumed in the idle life
of the rich, and not so much of the waste caused by the war for
profits, that is the waste caused by the necessity of the capitalist
to make money breed money: this necessity of course makes him
quite careless of what kind of goods he gets produced; it is

enough that there be a market for them; and a market he mostly
ensures by means of cheapness: this cheapness he uses as a
weapon against his fellow competitors and also he uses it as a
petard, a charge of dynamite if you will, to open to him the
markets of the world: now you will often have people preaching
to you the beauty of this cheapness, and how easy it is to live
because of it now-a-days especially if working men will only be
'thrifty,' as the said preachers call it, meaning thereby pinching
and niggardly: well well thrift is often not a difficult virtue for
the poor to exercise if it means, as it should not, the living on a
little: but let that pass: for as to this cheapness there is another
way to look at it than that of the enthusiastic praisers of the
present system: for you see after all cheap goods as far as the
workers are concerned means cheap labour—and do you like
cheap labour? more about that presently, suffice it now to say
that the capitalist can by means of the aforesaid cheapness force
populations both at home and abroad to live a certain kind of life,
the life namely which suits the profit-maker best: dare I venture
to say in Oldham that there are places in the world that buy our
cotton cloth, not because they want it but because they can't help
it: of course you all know that there are some places where we
have done this—well rather coarsely: I mean we have said "buy
this or—take a bayonet in your belly!"[6] That is undoubtedly part
of the process, and is getting now-a-days to be nearly indispensable if commerce is to be kept alive: Mr. Goschen and the Pall
Mall Gazette[7] will tell you all about that; and they chuckle not
without some reason at the conversion of the once peaceful 'Man-

[6] In 1885 Britain was involved in a succession of crises in Egypt, the Soudan, and
Afghanistan. The socialists argued that the exercise of British arms in those areas
was really a method of forcing British goods on the natives. Outside the movement,
this argument usually elicited highly unsympathetic responses, particularly after
the massacre of General Gordon's forces at Khartoum in 1885. See one such
reaction in *The Edinburgh Evening News*, April 27, 1885.

[7] George Joachim Goschen (1831–1907), later Viscount Goschen, became Chancellor of the Exchequer under Salisbury in 1886. In 1885, the year Morris wrote
this lecture, Goschen was busily explaining in his campaign speeches how a
Liberal-Unionist might justify colonial expansion. All of his speeches were given
detailed coverage in the *PMG*, perhaps partly because Goschen's secretary was
also on the staff of that paper (see Arthur D. Elliot, *The Life of George Joachim
Goschen*, London, 1911, p. 289).

chester School'[8] to the doctrines of 'your money or your life!'
which to them seem so eminently sensible and patriotic at one
and the same time: but this coarser part of the process I will not
say much of at present, because even without Lord Wolseley[9] and
his machine he can manage to force our wares on the natives of
the countries we long to benefit by means of the weapon cheapness: people don't want the goods we offer them, but they are
poor and have to buy something which [will] serve their turn
anyhow, so they accept cheap and nasty,[10] grumbling; their own
goods made slowly and at greater cost are driven out of the
market, and the metamorphosis begins which ends in turning
fairly happy barbarians into very miserable half-civilized people
surrounded by a fringe of exploiters and middle-men varied in
nation but of one religion 'Take care of number one.' Well, you
may say "we are really sorry for them but we must sell our goods
somewhere or we shouldn't get work and therefore we shouldn't
be able to live." Truly if you don't raise your own victuals you
must make something which people will take in exchange for
victuals: but wait a bit we haven't done with this cheapness, the
sword of commerce, yet; and the case of our workers at home as
far as their conquest by the capitalists is concerned is much
nearer to that of the Arab or Zulu or South Sea islander than

---

[8] The "Manchester School" of economists was most influential in the formation of
British economic policy in the third quarter of the nineteenth century. Its leaders,
Richard Cobden and John Bright, consistently opposed foreign military adventure
and supported Gladstone's program of "Peace, Retrenchment, and Reform"—until
the election of 1880. After Gladstone was made Prime Minister, however, the
legacy of foreign involvement inherited from the preceding Disraeli ministry made
retreat impossible. Thus the Liberal Party and the Manchester School were carried
along in the wake of conquest through South Africa, the Soudan, Afghanistan, and
Egypt. And as markets in these places became more and more important to
English industry, the Manchester School came more and more to accept the
inevitability of imperialism. For Morris's view of the situation, see "A New Party,"
Commonweal Supplement, Sept., 1885.
[9] Viscount Garnet Wolseley (1833–1913) was the commander of the British forces
sent to relieve General Gordon at Khartoum. His brilliant operations against Arabi
Pasha in 1882 established British supremacy in Egypt. Shortly before the first
delivery of this lecture Queen Victoria had raised him to a Viscountcy as a reward
for his unsuccessful attempt to rescue the garrison at Khartoum (see George
Arthur, *The Life of Lord Wolseley*, London, 1924), p. 219.
[10] See footnote 7 to "The Gothic Revival [II]," p. 83.

seems at first. You also British workmen are forced by cheapness into a certain manner of life: for look you, the capitalist must needs sell as cheap as he can or as I said he succumbs; a fraction of a penny more of price in a yard or a pound will ruin him, will land a district in a crisis: now in order to turn out goods at their cheapest he must have the newest and best machinery and the most perfect organization in his great machine, the factory; and he must make himself as independent as he can of that part of his machinery which gets hungry twice or thrice every 24 hours; skilled work must get less and less necessary to him; women and children and labourers must replace the skilled workman: in short he must by all means reduce the expense of his *wages,* as compared with his other expenses. As you know his capital, the money which breeds money for him is expended first in raw material, machinery, rent, and the like and secondly in the labour or power of labour supplied by the bodies and minds of working people; I don't know whether I need tell you that the first part of this capital is always increasing at the expense of the latter half as manufacture gets more complex and capital rolls up into bigger balls, but so it is: and all this time the war goes on, and the capitalist has to provide for sudden emergencies of great bursts of trade and for that end must have ready to his hand more power of labour, men, women, and children that is, than can be employed in average times, let alone bad times; if he had not when the big orders came he would be out of the game which would be played out by his foreign competitors: for here I will say once for all that besides the war between the capitalists of our community there is also a constant war going on between country and country which sometimes takes the shot and gunpowder form: for please to understand that all wars now waged have at bottom a commercial cause: nor forget that in this struggle of nations for commercial supremacy natural circumstances and historic also complicate matters: for instance in some nations the workers are much thriftier than in others, or say can for various reasons live upon less, a circumstance much to the benefit of the capitalists of that nation because it gives them an advantage in the race for cheapness, but not at all for the workers who have their wages lowered and their hours lengthened exactly in proportion to their thriftiness and industry.[11]

Well now I have been trying to show you how hard and consequently wasteful the battle is between the employers for their share of *profit;* and this battle they are able to keep up because there is another one going on between the workmen for their share of wages, of livelihood: and these things I have just been mentioning: the proportionate increase of plant and machinery as compared with wages; the increased productiveness of the unskilled labourer; the increased frequency of crises in trade, its increased precariousness, the huge reserve [of labourers] and lastly the continuous development of foreign countries containing populations hardy, industrious, and thrifty, combined with the *international* character of capital which will seek for employment wherever it can best be found all these things the civilized world over and especially among ourselves have made the competition of the workmen keener and bitterer than ever.

Now you may say is it not the office of Trades Unions and strikes or threats of strikes to deal with this competition and modify it in the interest of the workers? In answer I cheerfully admit that Trades Unions and strikes have done much in this direction; but that was under different conditions to those now existing: Let us look at the matter, it is pretty simple: England has been especially the country of Trades Unions, and why? Because she had some forty years ago and up to some 10 years ago the decided pre-eminence in trade, a pre-eminence unchallenged: that means that the capitalists were making large profits, and sooner than lose them or lose a month of them they would give way and consent to the terms of the workman: whereby the

---

[11] The position Morris assumes here on the question of the forces that determine wage levels bears a distinct resemblance to Ferdinand Lassalle's Iron Law of Wages (see footnote 15 to "Art and Labour," p. 114). In his "Letter from the Pacific Coast" (*Commonweal,* Feb., 1886), Morris makes a more detailed statement of his position on the question of the importation of foreign labor, and it is plain that for him the responsibility for economic hardship belongs to the competitive system itself rather than to any inherited racial characteristics among various groups of workers.

standard of life was raised for a certain part of the workers, notably for the factory hands: which they have not yet lost: but that is now a thing of the past: large profits are no longer made: if capitalists get rich it is because of the great aggregation of money and the great scale of the dealings; there is no longer a margin to give up to the demands of the workmen: the Trade Union revolt which in England has been during the years of prosperity the expression of that contest of classes which has existed all through the Commercial period has come to an end defeated by its own success: as all attacks of the workmen on capital must in the long run be defeated that are not international in their character.

For do not deceive yourselves: the Depression in Trade in this country is not accidental or transitory, nor is its cause hard to find: the overweening hopes of our capitalists 30 years ago were founded on the assumption that England was to be for ever the one serious manufacturing country in the world, supplying all other countries with manufactured goods and receiving from them raw materials for the non-human machines and food for the human ones to be constantly worked up into fresh goods: the market was to be unlimited, the expansion of production unchecked; changes had happened in the constitution of society before but could never happen again: the heaven of the well-to-do middle class was realized here in England.

You cannot need to be told at length how that hope has been deceived? a hope I will frankly say as base as any set of men ever held: other nations have as I said developed their resources for production, and England has to contend with them in the world-market on something like equal terms, to the terror of the more forseeing of our rich middle-class, we are howling for fresh markets through the trumpet of patriotism, and are trying to persuade themselves that Australia and Canada will consider themselves one country with each other and with England so as to give weight to any attempts at Burglary which it may be convenient for us to make.[12]

---

[12] The Imperial Federation League was formed in 1884 to promote mutual defense and trade ties between the colonies and Britain. "W. E. Forster [was] its first

I cannot express better the desperate condition of those who see nothing before us but ever fresh development of our capitalist system than by quoting the words of the great Socialist economist F[rederick] Engels from the March [1885] number of the Commonweal: "Here is the vulnerable place, the heel of Achilles for capitalist production: its very basis is the necessity for constant expansion, and this constant expansion is now become impossible. It ends in a deadlock; every year England is brought nearer face to face with the question; either the country must go to pieces, or capitalist production must: which is it to be?"[13]

Which indeed, for my part I think England, meaning by that much abused word the men and women of this community instinct with all the history of their fathers who have gone before them, will before long find out what the whole trick means and will refuse to sacrifice themselves to so base an end as the upholding of the idleness of the non-producers.

For it is of the nature of a system founded on mere war, which is always destructive, to wear itself out, to perish through its own endeavours to keep itself alive; and there are signs of this approaching end visible not only in England but all over the civilized world: I say the commercial system itself will kill itself: for instance, it could never have reached its present state of perfection in the organization of labour for the purpose of making a profit out of it without bringing the workers together in great masses, and making them feel that they are a class with interests of their own as a class: the necessities of capitalism have consolidated the workers and so fashioned a force which will do away with capitalism itself by taking its place; furthermore its necessities have compelled it to the invention of almost automatic machines which, though they are now wasted on the grinding of profits for individuals, will when the worker-class, the proletariat, is full-grown be the instrument which will make Socialism possible by making possible the equalization of labour as applied to

---

head; Lord Rosebery, W. H. Smith, Froude, J. R. Seeley, and James Bryce were among its supporters; and it enrolled some of the best-known colonial statesmen. But its members could never agree on a positive policy; and in 1893 it broke up" (R. C. K. Ensor, *England, 1870–1914;* Oxford, 1936, p. 178).

[13] The quotation is from an article titled "England in 1845 and in 1885."

the necessities of life, and will thereby leave open to men the higher field of intellectual effort full of opportunities for individual excellence and generous emulation. And this indeed it is on which the hopes of all reasonable revolutionists are founded; the certainty, for it is no less, that the process of evolution is building up with one hand while it pulls down with the other, so that revolution does always mean reconstruction.

It is this reconstruction which Socialism aims at, which we believe firmly is coming either with our help or without it. I have hinted at the present constitution of society—it is composed of two classes propertied-non-producers, and propertyless producers; and its motive power towards industrial production is competition or the struggle of each individual to get more than his share of what is produced, that is to say to advance himself at the expense of his neighbour: to put the matter shortly I should say of modern society that its aim is robbery and its instrument is war.

That is the firm belief of us Socialists: are you astonished that a body of men who hold that belief should turn their thoughts toward revolution, which as I have told you implies reconstruction? Will you blame them since this is their belief that they find themselves compelled to work actively towards a change in the basis of that society which they believe is founded on robbery and war? will you find it strange that they are willing to sacrifice their ease, their time, their money, their lives in short for that hope of revolution which shines before them like a candle in the dark? You must I am sure say no to all these questions.

And further remember how practical this question is: it is no matter of abstract rights, of speculative belief, of titles, of imaginary possession of things which do not exist: it might perhaps gall me sometimes that I were unable to vote on a question which [I] could understand as well as other people; but after all I could if I felt strongly about a subject find some other way of making my opinion felt besides voting for a member of parliament: it might annoy me to be scolded and denied access to heaven because I can't believe the literal truth of certain legends and historical documents; but I could live well and do my duty in spite of scolding and curses: and lastly I might in moments of ill temper resent being called plain Mister, while people no better than myself are called my lord, your grace, or your majesty; yet if that were all it doesn't matter, so long as I am as well educated as my lord is, and can satisfy all my reasonable requirements bodily and mental.[14] But it is another matter if I am really of a different class: if I have no leisure while my lord has too much, if he is refined and I am degraded; if whatever my chances of heaven may be earth at any rate is to be a hell for me: if though I have a vote I tremble lest I may lack bread for myself and my children. I say then it is quite another matter, and I must see to it myself and try to amend the state of things, or brand myself as a helpless slave.

In short what I want you to understand is that it is not as some people think, and as some people who know better say, that Socialists envy rich men because they are rich and live in enjoyment: if a man could be rich and do no harm with his riches it wouldn't matter: nay even if he had stolen his riches once for all we could put up with it and pass him by with no more active feeling than contempt: but unhappily riches always do do harm because they go on stealing day by day: riches on one side imply poverty on the other: the rich man has taken from the poor, and daily takes from him in order to be rich; what he gains we lose: therefore he is our enemy and cannot help being so in spite of any personal good will he has towards us or some of us; nor while the present system lasts can we relieve him of his false position: the rich man like the King never dies; another takes his place at once, and we can only change the tyrant and not the tyranny as long as the system of capital and wages lasts: it is the class, understand, that is our enemy and not the individual; although most unhappily these class divisions do create and cannot help creating vices in the individuals composing them which we cannot help noticing.

This class division therefore is what Socialism attacks; and mind you the individuals of the rich class will not really suffer from its realization; we don't want to ruin and render unhappy a

---

[14] The three great shibboleths of Radical reform in the nineteenth century—universal suffrage, disestablishment of the Church, and abolition of the House of Lords—are embodied here.

group amongst this class, though to my mind some of the semi-so-
cialistic remedies now proposed would have that effect: what we
want is that the rich, who as things go now are not necessarily
happy should melt into the great community of labour and take
their fair chance of happiness which Socialism would ensure to
everyone: could they possibly complain of this as an injustice?

'Tis said that a man named Saul of Tarsus once said 'If a man
will not work neither should he eat.'[15] This saying has been
preserved in a book considered holy by many, and it will do to
start with as a motto for Socialism: only you must remember that
there is work and work; some work is destructive, other, and if
you will believe me a great deal, useless: now you know saying
that work is destructive or useless is another way of saying that
nature won't reward such work: and if nature won't neither can
we: the man who works uselessly must be fed, clothed, and
housed by others who are working usefully: so we will extend
Saul of Tarsus' motto and say 'If a man will not work *usefully*
neither should he eat.' Because in that case he can only live by
stealing the wealth produced by others.

So you see what we socialists want to bring about is a state of
society in which as all must consume wealth so all shall produce
wealth: that I am sure cannot seem unreasonable to you, and it is
only by carrying out this principle that we can avoid the Depression of Trade into the causes of which Lord Salisbury and his
mates is going to enquire so diligently and—I hope—so successfully.[16] Nevertheless reasonable as that proposition is, it will
usually be considered a dangerous one, as indeed it is, since all
reason must be dangerous to a Society founded on an unreasonable basis: and I freely admit that the realization of this Socialist
hope can only be brought about by a change in the basis of

---

[15] 2 *Thess.*, III, 10: "Forever when we were with you, this we commanded you,
that if any man would not work, neither should he eat."
[16] The depression of the years 1883–1886 led ultimately to the Black Monday
unemployed riots late in 1886. Lord Salisbury's Royal Commission on the Depression in Trade and Industry set out in 1885 to investigate the cause of the business
decline. The Commission flirted with fair-trade doctrine for a while and, blocked
in that direction by Joseph Chamberlain, finally "buried itself under the pile of its
own blue-books" (Ensor, *England, 1870–1914,* p. 111).

society. Dangerous as it is it is surely a fair proposition, and mind it is the only condition of things under which we can have *peace:* because clearly men in general will only work for their own advantage unless they are compelled to work by other men: therefore it is that under the Commercial system constant war is necessary to keep the machine going: a war in which even quakers are compelled to take a part. But in a condition of things where all produce as all consume peace is possible, and war would at least be the exception and not the rule and only in a condition of peace can we make the most of the gifts of nature, instead of wasting them as we do now.

Now what must we do in order to realize this condition of things, a steady flow of wealth resulting from the labour of each and all, in the advantages of which each and all should share? We have been competing, we must combine—that is the revolution: we have been making war with each other: we must make peace —that is the revolution.

The labour of every man properly directed and helped by the inventions of centuries will more than supply him and his family not yet come to working age, or past it with all the necessaries of life: it is on this undeniable fact that all industrial society is based: and yet you see in all civilized countries a vast proportion of the population supplied with nothing more than the barest necessaries of life, and all except a few comparatively supplied with little more than those necessaries: as long as this lasts you cannot have peace: nay you ought not to: peace under such circumstances means the denial of the very nature of man, for it means unhappiness for most men, and all men must of their very nature strive for happiness.

Therefore when I bid you combine I know well that the first act of combination must be that of a class, when I bid you make peace I know that the first peace made must be between the individuals and the groups of a class; and that that combination and that [peace][17] will seem to many people like the beginning of war and not the ending of it as it really will be.

I say I bid you to class combination—but what class: the class

---

[17] The MS here has "war."

of labour all over the world, the class which is the only necessary element of Society: if that class combines and combines for justice and reason, and for nothing else can it combine, who can resist it? The monopolists who now live on the labour of the rest of mankind could never have sustained their position by their own mere force: Divide to Govern has been their rule: they have always by means of the instinctive cunning of an organism resisting destruction pitted one section of the workers against another, and so have held on precariously, depending always on the continued ignorance of those that they ruled over.

But the time for the end of this ignorance is drawing near: the workers have seen the wonderful effects of combination in increasing the productivity of labour, it remains for them only to shake off a few superstitions about the necessity of their retaining masters of a higher class of beings than themselves, and then they, the workers, will stand out as what they are—society itself —the old masters of society will also be recognized as what they are, mere useless hangers-on and clogs to life and the progress of humanity: and what will they, what can they do then to uphold their separate existence as a class? It is possible that they may attempt resistance to the inevitable and by no means hard fate of their forming a part, on terms of absolute equality, of a happy and mutually helpful community; but remember if they do they can only do so as supporters of a conscious injustice; and when it comes to that and they feel the conscience of the world against them, it will avail them little that they have the resources of civilization on their side; arms, armies, and long-standing organization will turn to nothing in their hands before the irresistible force of opinion, and the last act of the revolution which is now preparing will have come.

Even now that opinion is growing and gathering: you shall now hardly meet a thoughtful and unprejudiced man who will not accept the indictment which we socialists bring against society as it now exists: how prodigious the change of opinion is from what it has been some of you are scarce old enough to know: but I have lived through and noted the most degrading epoch of public opinion that ever happened in England and have seen the triumphant rule of the swindler in private and public life, the rule of hypocrisy and so-called respectability begin to shake and totter; I can see the existence of the miserable millions of the poor forcing itself on the conscience and fears of the rich, and I know that the song of triumph of almighty Commerce over the perfection of a civilization in which so many thousands of men of the same blood as ourselves live a life of mere starvation and hopelessness has even in the last few years sunk quavering into a trembling silence and a hope that it will last our time at least.

Yet Friends, it is no time to be sluggish and hope to let the last dregs of the old system trickle out of themselves: true the change is inevitable: true the old political parties are breaking up and are striking out wildly on the empty air: yet all we who are thoughtful and kindly and orderly have a part to play, lest mere violence and disorder be the only remedy for hypocrisy and tyranny: the new order of things has to grow up from the disrupted elements of the old, and every reasonable man's help will be needed that we may get out of the troubled waters speedily and with as little suffering to humanity as may be: therefore I call upon you all to look into these matters and judge of them without fear or favour, in the firm belief that when you have once learned and understood what the present system of Society is, and have considered what the power of man in dealing with nature for his benefit may be you, the intelligence of labour, must one and all become Socialists and revolutionists: and then I repeat who and what can resist you: you will see to it that every man in this vast community shall have a fair chance [of] gaining ease and happiness, which, believe me is the birthright of every man, only to be taken from him as long as men are blinded by tyranny and slavery.

OF THE ORIGINS OF ORNAMENTAL ART[1]

erhaps it may at first sight seem to some of you that orna-mental art is no very important subject, and that it is no great matter what its origins were: but I hope to show you before I have done that it is a subject of very great importance, and that it is well worth while to consider what its origins were, since it may lead us to finding out what its aims are, or should be; which in its turn may lead us to thinking of matters of the deepest importance.

First of all I must say that though the phrase is generally accepted it is not a good or descriptive one; for all art should be ornamental, and when it is not ornamental, and in the degree in which it is not, it fails of a part of its purpose: however, the phrase is used, and understood to mean a certain kind of art other than pictures or sculptures which tell a definite story and are

---

[1] The text of this lecture is taken from B.M. Add. MS. 45332(1), which is entirely in Morris's hand. The first recorded delivery of this version was at Kelmscott House on 5–19–86. Part of this text has been taken over from an earlier lecture given at Eton College on Nov. 24, 1883, as is suggested by a reference to Windsor and to St. George's chapel. Comparison with the published reports indicates that Morris recast it thoroughly, making extensive changes in the first half especially, sometime in 1886. Morris repeated this lecture on Oct. 30, 1887, and Nov. 2, 1889 (see Appendix I, 9–26–86, and Appendix II, item 87).

meant to represent according to some standard or another certain facts of external nature.

What then is this body of art which is something different from what we nowadays call pictures and sculpture?

It is the art of the people: the art produced by the daily labour of all kinds of men for the daily use of all kinds of men: surely therefore we may at the outset suppose that it is of importance to the race of man, since on all sides it surrounds our life and our work.

What is the end and aim of human labour? Is it not first the continuance, and next the elevation of the human race? If therefore it has gone astray at any time from its due aim, and no one surely will be so rash as to say that it never has, it has erred in turning its force to the production of things which are not useful either for the continuance or the elevation of the race of man.

Let us consider then what things human labour produces for the service of the world. Broadly speaking they may be divided into two kinds first those which serve the needs of the body, and second those which serve the needs of the mind: such things as food, raiment, and shelter, and the tools for obtaining these on the one hand, and on the other, poetry, music, the stored-up knowledge of the fashion of the universe which we call science, and of the deeds of men on the earth which we call history, and also the pictured representations of that history however wrought.

These two kinds of productions, between them make up the wealth of the world; the things that are made to satisfy the necessities of a healthy body and a healthy mind.

But furthermore the wealth made for the service of the body can again definitely be divided into those things which perish at once in the using, as food and fuel and the like, and those which are made to last some time and serve our needs day after day or year after year, as raiment and houses and so forth.

Here then you see between the rude arts, whose end is the production of mere food and raw material, and the exalted arts, which should satisfy the cravings of our minds, lies a mass of wealth-producing labour of a special character, which is that side of human labour to which I wish specially to draw your attention tonight; this labour is called in what I should almost venture to name our modern jargon the Industrial Arts.

Now all the things produced by these arts or crafts might be made without any reference to anything but their first obvious use: the house might have been just so many walls and so much roof: so much stone and timber, uncarved, unmoulded, unpainted (except for weather-defense); the cup might have taken the first[2] convenient form it would from the potter's hand; the cloth might have remained undyed, unfigured, and in all this men's bodies would have felt no lack; while their minds would have been free to exercise themselves with music and poetry and pictured images of the past, or with the gathering of the knowledge of what is and what has been.

But men would not have it so; from the very first they have striven to make their household and personal goods beautiful as well as useful; the rudest savage no sooner learns how to make anything than he learns also how to ornament it: before the earliest dawn of history this instinct for ornament existed as clearly as it did in the palmy days of Italian art: as you know implements exist of men who dwelt in Europe ages before any of the races we name now, on which were carved, with no little skill, the forms of the beasts of the forests they wandered in, and in which life must have been so hard and beset with so many dangers that we may well wonder that they had time or courage to think about art: so divine a thing is the spark of human intelligence.

What does all this mean? why did they do it and take all this trouble? Who taught them?

Indeed their teacher is not far to seek: whatever lived or grew about them: nay the mountains, the rocks themselves, the 'bones of the earth' as the Northmen called them, had something about them which they must have dimly known for beauty; the things which were useful to them for food and fuel and clothes were ornamented: the day and the night, sunrise and sunset which showed to their dim minds as beings of passions like themselves; the serpent whose lurking malice and swift wrath they feared,

---

[2] Morris here deletes the word "ugly" from the MS.

and whom they worshipped lest he should slay them: all these had been fashioned fair and lovely by forces of which they knew nothing: and they, the latest-born and maybe the most terrible force of nature, how could they choose but take up the links of the chain and work as nature worked about them: many things she compelled them to, and this also.

This then was the birth of popular or ornamental art, the birth of man's intelligence.

Now the works of art I have just been alluding to belong to times of whose history they alone give us any glimpse, and we can have but a faint idea of anything that might have gone on between those days and the dawn of history, the dawn of civilization: of that dawn itself we know but little indeed, yet are to a certain extent helped out by the consideration of the various backward peoples of our time, some of whom at least one cannot help thinking might have had a chance of developing gradually into a condition somewhat like our past civilization if it had been their doom to be born into the world at a time when civilization has taken the form which it has now; the commercial form, under which all Society rests on a gigantic system of usury, pitiless and implacable, which is prepared to crush out of existence all peoples and communities that cannot speedily adapt themselves to its laws.

However that may be we can learn something from these survivals, if so they be, from the earlier condition of the world joined to the few historical hints we have left of that earlier condition, of the dawn of history: the lesson they teach us as to the growth of popular art seems to me to be something like this: the period is that of a state of things when Society has begun, when every man has had to give up some of his individuality for the sake of the advancement of the whole community: in that community division of labour has begun, though there is none of it—or scarcely any—in each occupation: a man has no longer to be his own provider in everything; the strong and young fare afield to hunt or fish, or herd the beasts of the community, or dig and sow and harvest in the strip of communal tillage, while the weak, the women, and the cripples stay at home to labour at the loom or the wheel, or the stithy. So far at least has the division of labour gone. Now, rough as the hunter's life may be, he will have his joys however fierce and rude in his contention with wind and weather, his stealthy watching and final victory over the quarry: and the herdsman and tiller, although he has to take his share of rough torment from storm and frost and sun, yet has his eyes on beautiful things forever, and his ears often delighted by the multitudinous voice of nature as he goes to and fro through the changes of the year, nursing his hope of the harvest which is to be. With all such men, hunters, fishers, herdsmen, and husbandmen, it was well, and still may be, if they are not oppressed, but are allowed to have their due share of the goods which they have toiled to produce.

But how did it fare with their brethren, who sat within doors, paled by the lack of sun, down-hearted from want of air, with no excitement or promise of victory to stir their blood; surrounded by the blunders, the clumsiness, and the squalor of man instead of the order, deftness, and beauty of nature: hard indeed it seems it must be for them to forego all the brisk life and stir while they sit bowed over the loom and every minute's work is like that of every other minute, no change or hope but in finishing the web that they may begin another; or to keep for ever moulding the pot of ugly grey or brown clay, no one of which is better or worse than another (unless it be quite spoiled): or to have no aim before them as they begrime themselves in the stithy but to make a knife that will cut like everybody else's knife: it is hard that they should be unwilling martyrs to the comfort of the commonwealth while others were leading a merry life, that they alone should miss the glory of the tales of perils and daring by flood and field, or the shouts [of] laughter that welcome the happy end of the vintage or the harvest. Their case surely must be that they are the slaves of slaves and as they sit at their dull tasks what can they hope for save the night and sleep in which to dream that they have grown strong and warlike, and the masters of such as they are in their waking hours?

Nay it was not so bad as that: whatever burdens folly and tyranny laid upon mankind in those rough times, this burden of dull and wasteful labour, unrelieved by any thought of what might be good in the work itself; unrelieved by any hope of praise for the special excellence of the work, was not laid on the craftsman for many ages, except in the quasi-penal labour which was laid on hostile conquered tribes under the ancient civilizations of Egypt and Mesopotamia; for the most part very different was the tale from the full one I have been telling of: labour found out a solace and a glory for the handicraftsman from the earliest times.

For note, that the goods which the hunter and the husbandman conquered from nature mostly perished in the using, unless they were of the kind that demanded more labour on them to make them useful to man: the hunter despoiled nature of the goods she had already produced; the husbandman helped her or compelled her to yield more than she was willing to yield unhelped or uncompelled; but neither of them created anything and their gettings were consumed in the using, and the fame of them and joy in them died with them: but the craftsman by his labour fashioned something which without him would not have existed at all, and which was destined to last many years, nay for generations even: so that there needed to be no haste nor hurry in his work; he had time to think as he wrought at it, and to what should he entrust his thought for keeping and for communicating to other men rather than to the work which was growing beneath his hands, the thing he was making of whose life he was absolute master: where then was the dullness now? The flowers of the forest might glow in his web and its beast move over it: his imaginings of the tales of the priests and poets might be pictured on the dish or the pot he was fashioning; the sword hilt, the roof beam were no longer dead[3] bronze and wood, but part of his soul made alive forever: and now no day was like another to him: hope was with him when he left his work in the evening that he might mend the day's failure or carry on its success the next day: hope wooed him to his work in the morning and helped him through the day's weariness.

And with all this he was grown to be no longer a slave of slaves,

---

[3] Morris here rejects the word "iron" in favor of "bronze" in the MS.

but a master; a man looked upon as better and more useful than the hunter or the tiller of the soil, deserving of plentiful thanks from the community.

And these thanks, the glory for his creations were indeed often his on strange terms, for the type of craftsman was sometimes exalted to the rank of a god swaying the terrible forces of nature; forging the bolts of the world ruler, fashioning the furniture of the house of heaven; building the rampart which was to guard for ages the holy city of the younger Gods against the frost and fire giants of the North: but again and not without some countenance even from these older myths (note the lame and crafty Hephaestus)[4] the type falls to the half-malignant and altogether guileful mountain spirit, conquering rather by cunning than force the huge giant and mighty warrior and still fully possessing the gift of miraculous power and creation.[5]

Of course I do not mean to say that the primary intention was to make these craftsman-gods types of labour; Hephaestus, Thor, and Weland[6] had no doubt a wider and simpler origin than that; but they received the special characteristics of the literary myths from ideas of handicraft and craftsmen that had been long in men's minds.

Such then it seems to me was the first origin of ornament on wares: not merely an attempt to escape from the wearisomeness of labour, but rather an expression of pleasure in the hope and sense of power and usefulness which men felt in the making of things in the childhood of the world.

Now it has been said, and surely with truth, that those men are the best and usefullest who never altogether throw off their childlike qualities even when they are grown old: and that same maxim I would apply to the race of man as well as to the

---

[4] Morris probably drew much of his knowledge of Hephaestus, the Greek god of fire and patron of handicraftsmen, from the many allusions to him in Homer's *Iliad*. In Feb., 1886, Morris was reading this work with a view to doing a full translation, as he was then engaged in doing for *The Odyssey* (see *Letters*, p. 248).

[5] It is roughly from this pattern that Morris cut the character of Regin in Book II of *Sigurd the Volsung* (*Collected Works*, XII, 61–130).

[6] See another reference to Weland as "Wayland Smith" in "Early England," p. 160 and footnote 4.

individuals composing it; and if it were good that it should be so in other matters, and that the mirth and simplicity of earlier ages of the world should yet leave some reflection on our leisure, still more I think it is important that it should be preserved in our working time.

Nor indeed did that pleasure of labour fail man for many ages: I admit indeed that for a long time in the ancient world it was limited and indeed oppressed by the sternness of hieratic art; as notably for many centuries in Egypt, where the marvellous naturalism of its earlier days, in some branches at least, fell under the yoke of a stiff though far from ignoble conventionalism: but even in that period we have enough left us outside the more pompous ornamentation of temples and tombs to show that on many sides art was still free, and labour abundantly illuminated by fancy and invention: much the same may be said of that art which was passed on through the whole of the valleys of Tigris and Euphrates and even extended to Cyprus and other of the islands by the people or peoples of Babylonia, and of which happy accident has preserved so many specimens in ruin mounds of Assyria: the pleasure of the artists who wrought the bas-reliefs for Assur-bani-pal at Koycinjik is too obvious [in] the shapes of animals at least [for] it to need many words from me here.[7]

The freer peoples who formed what was then the northern and western hem of civilization were as a matter of course less oppressed in their art by hieratic conventionalism, though they were not, nor indeed needed to be, wholly free from it: under the classical peoples of antiquity popular art had to run another danger of slavery, which in truth it did not wholly escape.

In popular art the expression of man's thoughts by his hand does for the most part fall far short of thoughts themselves; and this always the more as the race is nobler and the thought more exalted; in short all the more as the art, as popular art, is more

---

[7] The reference here is to the sculptured slabs depicting the lion hunting of King Assur-banipal, King of Assyria, c. 668–630 B.C. They were deposited in the British Museum after their discovery among the ruins of Nineveh by R. Rassam in 1853–54. "Koycinjik" is Assyrian for "North Palace." For a discussion of the reliefs, see Georges Perrot and Charles Chipiez, *Histoire de l'Art dans l'Antiquite* (Paris, 1884), II, 44–49.

worth having, as there is more hope of continued life and progress in it: I mean that between the rough, speedily-penciled work on a piece of archaic Greek pottery, or the shorthand for a field of flowers of the Persian weaver, or the rough stone-cutting, half-pathetic, half-humorous, of the mediaeval mason, between these things and the highly finished and, in its way, perfect ingenuity of a piece of Japanese drawing or lacquer, there is a whole world of difference, the real worth being on the side of the clumsier expression of the historic workman.

Now for a long while among the Greek and kindred peoples, art was wholly in the condition of its thought being far greater than its expression, deft and graceful (as amongst early art) that expression was: then came a period when the technical excellence (of the truest kind) advanced with wonderful speed; the standard of excellence in expression grew very high, and the feeling of a people cultivated very highly within narrow limits began to forbid any attempt at expression of thought which did not approach within the limits prescribed something like perfection: no man must attempt to do anything which he cannot do in such a way that it is almost impossible to pick a hole in its technical qualities: thus art was in the palmy days of the classic times divided strictly into a great expressive art practiced only by those who had mastered the means of expression, and a very limited ornamental art which was but an adjunct to the higher kind and in which there was nothing to express but complete submission to certain limited and well-known rules of proportion: such a state of things among a less gifted people would have gone far towards destroying art altogether; but among the Greeks this aristocracy of art was so numerous as to give us an impression at this distance of time of a great popular art existing among them; and doubtless the rules of art must have been unconsciously so well understood among the population, that what is called nowadays bad taste did not exist among them at all; a condition of art the easier to be brought about because of the great simplicity of the life they led in which what we now call luxury made no part.

Nevertheless you must understand that perfect as their art was it was barbarously and oppressively limited in scope, going step by step indeed with their social conditions the foundation of which was mere chattel slavery: when all is said what a mass of expression of human thought, what a world of beauty that exclusiveness shut out from the light of day. Absolute perfection in art is a vain hope; the day will never come when the hand of man can thoroughly express the best of the thoughts of man.[8] Why then should we deprive ourselves therefore of all the fancy and imagination that lies in the aim of so many men of lesser capacity than that of great masters? Is it not better to say to all who have any genuine gifts however small, 'courage! it is enough for a work of art if it show real skill of hand, genuine instinct for beauty, and some touch of originality; cooperation will show you how your smaller gifts may be used along with the greater ones.'

Well the aristocratic exclusiveness of Greek art drew on it a heavy revenge enough: I have spoken of its first period during which the worth of its thought outwent its power of expression, and of its second, when the expression having reached a point approaching perfection, the exuberance of thought in it had to be repressed to satisfy the exclusive fastidiousness of the Greek mind: there remains yet a third period during which capacity of expression having reached its highest point could go no further, and when there was comparatively little to express by this perfected means, and the classical art was become academical and in fact all but dead.

By this time all domination had long passed away from the Greek name, and the Roman tax gatherer ruled the world of civilization; after a while more by the terror of the name of Rome than by any real power in the state: lower and lower fell the art which the Romans adopted from the Greeks, till at last it was redeemed from contempt only by the splendour, massiveness, and honest building of its great architectural and engineering works. In the meanwhile the great change drew near: the Roman landlords had turned all the people of civilization into their agricultural slaves, their hired servants and parasites, and the

---

[8] This may be taken as Morris's answer to Matthew Arnold's injunction to become conversant with "the best that has been thought and said." It seems to be Morris's conviction that the best that has been thought has not and never will be said. "Thought" means something more to Morris than cerebration, and his injunction is not to stop reading, but to start creating.

proletariat of the great cities who were fed on their bounty: before the operation was quite complete the state of things so brought about seemed likely to last for ever: for where was the foe to overturn it? But by the time it was complete the foe was at hand ready for its destruction: for the Roman had reckoned without his host: he had subdued all civilization and made it his private slave; and now he found that whatever was respectable and desired the preservation of society would not fight; whereas whatever was against him and the stability of society, the starving slaves, the Christians, the barbarians of the East and the North were valiant and aggressive and were ready at every point to push forward what he considered anarchy and the disruption of the world, but which was at the worst the Medea's caldron from which a new and vigorous Europe was to be born again: with that new birth of society, and faithfully following every stage of its fruitful death and change, a new art also was born: this art was at first clad in the body of the effete art which it took the place of; but yet was from the first startlingly different from it in soul and intention: as time went on it borrowed elements from the East and the North, and drew them together and moulded them into the Greco-Roman mass which was already revivified, and little by little the classical wrappings fell off from it, and left clear the strange and beautiful body of Byzantine art, the art of early Europe—of the time when feudality was shaping itself from the chaos of the ruins of old Rome.

From that city of New Rome it spread far and wide varying at first but little except as the materials in which it was wrought influenced it by their fineness or rudeness: in Sicily, Egypt, Spain, Persia it was modified by distinct eastern elements, all of them it seems referable to that art of the East which was carried wide about by the Arabs but was by no means Arab in origin but Persian rather: this influence abode with it and afterwards reacted strongly on the art of central and northern Europe which was born more directly of old or New Rome.

In the extreme North and Northwest of Europe it met with another modifying element in the shape of the Celtic or more probably pre-Celtic art, which existed pure in Ireland, somewhat changed in England and Scandinavia by Teutonic translation:

between this art, the representative of primitive ornamentation, and the elaborate fretwork of Eastern art there is a certain sort of relationship; so that it might be doubted whether the complete ornament of the Middle-Ages does not owe some of its forms to this probably pre-Aryan art of Europe: but I think in fact that except in Scandinavia in the modified form above-mentioned its influence on Mediaeval art was not abiding, the equally elaborate but more logical and measured forms of the East taking its place.

However this may be it is certain that the great and in the main homogeneous art of the Middle Ages was both in form and in spirit a simple and direct development of the new-born art which sprang from the corrupt though still beautiful remains of Greco-Roman art; and it is to my mind certain also that it owed the form of that new birth to the incoming of Eastern or Persian ideas and handiwork which acted on it in a way not easy to trace I admit: that mingled art as I have said was still more permeated in some parts by the Eastern element, and in that condition in the 12th century especially was very powerful in fashioning Mediaeval art into what it presently became: nevertheless I cannot help recognizing a certain fitness about the name Gothic for indicating the work of the Middle Ages, though at first it may seem an absurd misnomer born of the hasty glance the antiquaries of our grandfathers' time took of an art which they despised and were ignorant of.[9] For besides that the Goths were as it were the iron of the spear that slew the Roman Empire, and from the most righteous slaying sprang Gothic Art; there is obvious in it, nay the very soul of it is that spirit of the North which makes us what we are at the best: the wild imagination, the love of nature, the scorn of pedantry, and stilted pompousness; the genuine, unashamed sentiment, and all this tempered by plenteous good humour and a love of homely and familiar things; a courage in short which is not anxious to thrust anything which is human out of sight even in the most solemn times and places: these are the characteristics of

---

[9] The *NED*, defining the term "Gothic," quotes Cowper's *Table Talk* (1782) in a context that substantiates Morris's concept of the eighteenth-century usage of the term: "He sunk in Greece, in Italy he rose, and, tedious years of Gothic darkness past, Emerged all splendour in our isle at last."

Gothic art which pierce to the very heart of all those who are capable of feeling that manly love of man and his fair earthly home which is of all things that which most makes life worth living.

And now understand that that which makes Gothic art all this is its *freedom:* it was above all things the art of the people; the art of cooperation: no craftsman, who is a real one, is despised in it; there is room for every mind and every hand that belongs to a real man: something to express and some means of expressing it are all that is asked for: all the time this art lasts no handicraft lacks beauty for a moment, nor is anyone set to dull and slavish toil: things grow beautiful under the workman's hands without effort it would seem, and men do not know how to make an ugly thing: nowadays when we light on a piece of the household goods of this period we pay vast sums of money for it and treasure it up in a museum; for it teaches us—*us* who know everything else, this rough piece of handiwork done by an artisan who thought that the world was like a flat dish and that the sun went round the rim of it.

If this seems strange to you, let me remind you of one kind of work wrought by these craftsmen, which is both more accessible and more impressive than their moveable household goods: I mean the buildings which are [our] forefathers' and among some of which it is your rare good fortune to live: a good fortune which I hope will leave its impress in many an hour of sweet, indestructible pleasure on the future lives of every one of you.

Indeed they have had a hard time of it those ancient buildings of England raised once in such hope by the 'Famous men and the fathers that begat us':[10] pious and religious people battered and half destroyed them; not understanding that the spirit which raised them was the essence of all religions: those who fought for our liberties blindly looked upon them as the strongholds of slavery and gave over their precious stones, the work of valiant souls and free hands, to the titled thieves who stole the public lands of England: The pedant of the 18th century, anti-poetical, ignorant of history, supposing that no art could exist outside the

---

[10] The quotation is from *Ecclesiastes,* XLIV, 1.

middle of the classical period, despised them, botched them, degraded them: the pedant of today, self-sufficient, the slave of money, ignorant he also of that real history which is no dead thing, but the living bond of the hopes of the past, the present, and the future, believes that from his study or his office he can re-create past times, and without a word of sympathy or a day of education can get from the machine-driven workman of today work like that of the free craftsmaster of the Middle Ages: he while I speak is still busy in destroying the last remnants of our fathers' handicraft, and maybe he is the last as he is certainly the worst enemy they have had.

Yes even such a storm of folly and greed has swept continually over these glorious works into which was once builded the very soul of England: yet in spite of it all there they stand yet a token of the hope that was, and yet shall be of the freedom and honour of labour. Bare as they have been stripped, wounded and patched up as they have been can we even think of them without being moved at the energy of co-operative art which reared them in a rude age by the hands of a scanty population?

For I say that glorious as they are in themselves they do betoken something more glorious still: for remember they do but represent the kind of building which was used throughout the country: when your chapel rose in its splendour there was not a cottage or a shed even on the way between Windsor and London which did not share in its beauty, humble as it might be. Now think what this means; we are so used to houses being generally ugly that it is difficult to imagine, every house for instance in London or the suburbs more or less beautiful; not a chandler's shop at Hammersmith or Brixton but what was a work of art: there would be education for you: education which no books could give; amusement and happiness, to the builders as well as to the occupiers of such houses that no accumulation of wealth can now give to any richest man amongst us.

And I must tell you that if we have not this it is because we do not desire it: when we do desire it, and are ready to sacrifice greed and injustice for it we shall have this also as well as justice and goodwill between man and man.

Meanwhile you see I have taken you a long way from that first dawn of popular art: centuries we cannot count lie between the day when the cave-abider scratched his drawing of a mammoth on a mammoth's bone, and the day when the English masons and wood-carvers struck the last stroke before the Reformation at St. George's Chapel yonder.[11] During all those ages whenever we catch a glimpse of the life of the people we find the popular arts progressive on the whole, and seldom failing in their first aim of lightening the toil of man by giving him pleasure in his daily work.

A long lapse of years indeed, while from the time when Sir Tho[ma]s More wrote his eloquent attack on commercialism and land-grabbing[12] till now, the days are few, the time short: but what has happened to popular art in that short while? What has happened to the popular arts I say in those three hundred years of struggle, mostly successful, for religious and political liberty; in those centuries of miraculous progress, during which England has grown from a semi-barbarous island kingdom into a mighty empire, the master of the minds of men as well as of their bodies?

I can tell you in three words what has happened to those arts: they have disappeared.

That is a strange story indeed and you may well doubt its truth, the change is so tremendous: but my whole opinion is this; to have popular art, or the art of the people, it must be made by and for the people, which means as I have said that man's handiwork is universally beautiful to the eye and elevating to the mind. But such art as pretends to be popular nowadays, do the hands and minds of the people fashion it? Do the people use it? Is the people rejoiced with the making and the using of it?

So far is this from being the case, that the people does not even know that such art exists or ever has existed; what pretence there is of Decorative Art is little touched by the people's hands, and

---

[11] While there are many St. George's Chapels in England, it seems most likely that the one to which Morris refers is at Windsor. This church was finished in the reign of Henry VIII just before the Reformation, and it was well enough known in Morris's day to be recognized without further description than he gives it. See W. J. Loftie, "The Palace of Windsor," *The Art Journal,* XLIV (new series) (Feb., 1889), 47–51.

[12] The "attack" is contained in Book I of *Utopia.*

not at all by their minds: they work at it not knowing what they do; like all other toilers nowadays their work is a grievous burden to them which they would cast off if they could. We cannot help knowing that not another hour's work would be done on the Decorative Arts today if it were not that the workers feared death by starvation if they left their work.

I hope you do not suppose that on these terms of labour you can have an art which has any life in it: if you do you are dreaming and will have rude awakening some day: meantime you well know what vast sums of money rich people will spend to isolate themselves from the tokens of increasing population, from the hovels in short which are being raised with such frightful speed all over civilized countries; and I do not wonder; if I were rich I should do the same myself; I should try to escape from the consequences of the system which had made me rich.

For when it comes to explaining why the labour on which depends the well-being of the arts or in other words the pleasure of life is in its present condition of slavishness I must tell you that since the 15th century a great change has taken place in the social condition of the people at large, which some people ignore, and which more still are contented with as a positive gain, and which they believe has brought the world of civilization into a social state which will endure as long as the world itself.

It would be impossible within the limits of such a lecture as this to show by what gradual means this change took place; to show how the chattel slavery of the classical times melted into the serfdom of the early Feudal period; how from those serfs were gradually developed the burgesses or corporations of the mediaeval towns, the yeomen and labourers of the fields, and the craftsmen of the guilds, which classes together with the feudal lords formed the society of the later Middle Ages: it will be enough for our present purpose to state that throughout the middle ages although there was a sharp distinction between the feudal lord and his inferior that distinction was rather arbitrary than real; that difficult, and except by means of ecclesiastical preferment almost impossible as it was to pass from one grade of society to another, there was no class which was by virtue of its position refined, and none which was mentally degraded by the same virtue: at the same time although in the later middle ages this hierarchical system had reached the inside of the craft-guilds, and the craftsmen were divided into the privileged masters, with their privileged apprentices, and the journeymen who were unprivileged, there was no division of labour inside the guilds save that which arose from the learning of the craft: every full-instructed workman was master of his whole craft.

Neither outside the guilds was there any violent competition in buying and selling: the greater part of the goods made by the craftsmen were made for home consumption, and only the over-plus of this came into the market: it was necessary therefore for the very existence of the craftsman that he should be skillful, intelligent, and thoughtful; nor was he driven by the exigencies of the competitive market which might demand cheapness from him at the cost of other qualities to forego the leisurely way of working which alone can produce a work of art: the universal spread of art made people good judges of wares and keen marketers moreover and cheap and nasty[13] was in no demand.

Such I say was the condition of the artisan in the middle ages; it may be allowed that he was politically oppressed, superstitious, and ignorant—but he was an artist or free workman, using his brains for the pleasure and the solace of his working hours.

Passing over the gradual process which has changed him from what he was in the 15th century to what he is today let us look at the contrast of his position then and now, and glance at the state of Society which has produced it.

For in these days the system of hierarchical society has given place to a Society founded on what is called (miscalled I think) the system of free contract. Licence of competition almost complete has taken the place of the attempts to regulate life in accordance with a priori ideas of the duties men owe to one another. The distinctions between the classes [are] merged now into one distinction, that between rich and poor, or gentleman and non-gentleman: there is no insuperable bar to prevent a member of the poor or non-gentleman class rising into the rich or gentleman class: nay the thing is done every day, and in two

---

[13] See note 7 to "The Gothic Revival [II]," p. 83.

generations the offspring of the person who has climbed up that ladder between rich and poor may become the equal of the greatest families of the Feudal aristocracy, most of whom, to say the truth have very slender pretentions to representing the families whose titles they bear: moreover there is felt to be no difference in cultivation and refinement between the titled gentry and the rich capitalists or their hangers-on of the professional classes: they are all gentlemen together, even when the latter are scarcely as well-to-do as some of the best-off of the lower classes.

On the other hand there is the great class of working men, among whom there is certainly great diversity as regards their wages, some of them as aforesaid earning as much as or more than *when they are at work* the poorer gentlemen; but whatever their grades may be as regards their money fortune they are all non-gentlemen, and do differ really and not conventionally from the class of gentlemen: their education, their leisure, their refinement, their religion is weighed in a different balance from [that][14] of the gentleman, nay they do not even speak the same dialect of the mother-tongue as he does: they are in all respects the lower classes, really and not conventionally I say, so that a working man is not fit company for a gentleman, or a gentleman for a working man.

Now this class division of the 19th century as opposed to that of the 14th was brought about by the gradual development of the system of commerce which is now complete or nearly so; the system as I said of unlimited licence of competition which supplanted the mediaeval system under which life was regulated by a conception of the duties men owed to each other and to the unseen powers.

I will not tonight give you any direct opinion as to the operation on other sides of life of these two systems, but I am compelled by my subject to state to you that the effect of this change on popular or decorative art has been to destroy it.

This gulf between the rich and poor which is in fact a gulf between civilized and uncivilized people living in the same state and under laws nominally the same, this is the gulf which has

---

[14] The MS is illegible here.

swallowed up the popular arts; the art which raised our ancient buildings here and elsewhere, and under which every man's intelligence, were it great or small, was used and subordinated at once for the creation of a great work of art: whereas now it is accepted as a fact that whatever intelligence one of the non-gentleman class may possess is not and cannot be exercised during his working hours: in order to win that privilege he must raise himself out of his own class and become a gentleman.

Now the essence or soul of popular art is the due and worthy delight of each worker in his own handiwork, a delight which he feels he can communicate to other people, as it has been communicated to him by the thoughts of many generations of men under the name of Tradition.

If any of you care about art in any form I am sure you will allow that this reciprocal pleasure of communication is always present at the birth of a work of art: when you have been listening for instance to a beautiful piece of music could you possibly suppose that it was an irksome task to invent the sounds which were filling your whole soul with satisfaction or when you have been reading some beautiful passage of poetry, could you suppose that the strong and melodious words which were elevating your souls and opening new worlds to you, had been given forth from the writer's brain in a dull and pleasureless mood? Surely it is impossible that it should be so.

Yet remember, the artist's, the musician's, the poet's work is not easy, it is real labour enough unless he is a pretender: there are traps and pitfalls on the right hand and on the left into which his hope of creating a work of art may fall, and against which even the best man has to be laboriously on his guard: I say he is a workman or no artist: and on those grounds I claim some share of the divine pleasure of creation which accompanies it for all handicraftsmen, believing firmly that the making-good of this claim is a necessity for the world, if civilization is to be anything else than a name. For first, unless this claim is allowed and acted on, unless it is insisted upon as a necessary part of the organization of Society, it must be the *rule* that all things made by man for the use of his daily life will be ugly and base, will show wherever they are placed as mere blots on the beautiful face of the world.

And 2nd it will surely be but right and just that they should be ugly and base, for so done they will be but tokens of the enduring sorrow and slavery of the great mass of mankind: for all people not dishonest must work, and in one way or other their working hours must be the most important part of their lives: if therefore they have due hope, pleasure, and honour in their daily work their lives will on the whole be happy, if they lack that hope pleasure and honour their lives will be unhappy. It would therefore be unjust that art should come from the unhappy lives of the most of men: or in other words that the great mass of people should toil miserably for the pleasure of a few dishonest people.

Fortunately, you see, as far as the arts go that cannot be; it is a question of art and the happiness of the worker, or lack of art and his unhappiness.

In these days, then, in which man has obtained so much domination over the forces of nature, in which so much of what passes for wealth produced, in which Society taken as a whole either is or could be so rich: in these days what are the conditions of life for the working classes, that is to say for most men which would produce beauty and happiness for the world?

1st no honest or industrious man must be under Fear of poverty: the sordid troubles which this fear produces destroy imagination and intelligence, or turn them into other channels than the hope of giving *pleasure* to the world: every man therefore must be certain of earning a due livelihood, by which word I understand all things necessary for his mind as well as his body.

2nd all men must have due leisure: rest for body and mind; time for following according to their bent other occupations than the mere bread-winning one even if it be pleasant: and if their bread-winning work is of such a rough nature as of necessity to lack art or expression of pleasure in it, the daily hours of such labour must be *very* short.

3rd it follows from this last remark that all work in which art, or pleasure, is impossible should be done without as far as may be, that it should be looked on as a nuisance to be abated, a sickness of Society; as far as possible it should be done by machines: and machines should never be used for doing work in which men can take pleasure: whereas at present, as we all know

too well, men do the work of machines, and machines of men—
both disastrously.

4th those who are to produce beauty must live amidst beauty:
their homes and surroundings must be clean, orderly, and in a
word beautiful: this *should* be no hard matter to accomplish
since the whole world is beautiful save where man has made it
ugly.

5th all men should be educated, and have their due share in
the stored-up knowledge of the world, so vastly greater now than
in the days of art, but so much more unequally shared. All men I
say should be educated not down to their 'station in life' as
people call it, that is according to the amount of money their
parents may have, but according to their capacity.

6th when all these claims are allowed and acted on the last
claim I make for labour will come of itself: that is, that there
should be an end of class distinctions: that is to say that all crafts
should be honourable and honoured, and that every man should
be able to rise to eminence and fame by the exercise of his own
craft, the work he understands best; whereas at present he can
only rise to eminence by deserting his craft, by taking an undue
share of the wealth of the world as wages for doing lighter work
than his fellows; by becoming a capitalist as the phrase goes.

I will now sum up these conditions briefly: 1st extinction of
poverty; 2nd leisure; 3rd avoidance of wasteful work; 4th care of
the beauty of the earth; 5th education according to capacity, and
6th abolition of class distinctions, real, mind you, not formal.

To my mind these are the conditions of life for working men, or
really for all men, under which we can have in these days once
more popular art, or a happy life for most men. Is it worth while
to strive to bring about this happy life? If it be, can we say that
the price to be paid for it can be too high, whatever it may be?

You will have understood if you have followed my statement of
the due conditions of labour that in my belief that price is the
reconstruction of Society; for no mere palliatives of the evils of
the present system will bring about those conditions. Furthermore I admit that such a great change would involve the sacrifice
from many of us of things now much cherished: yet as I believe
that those who uphold the present conditions of labour on the

grounds of self-interest do so rather from stupidity than malice, so I think that their loss, or punishment, if you will, will be rather imaginary [than][15] real when the change comes: I think what we shall chiefly have to sacrifice will be the encumbrances, the troubles, the sorrows even which we now cherish as part of our wealth.

As to the means by which the Reconstruction is to be brought about, I must for more than one reason say nothing of them tonight; save this: that you yourselves in one way or other will as time goes on have offered to you opportunities of helping forward or of hindering that reconstruction; times when you will have to choose between the right hand and the left, and to range yourselves for or against the progress of the race of man: such chances are solemn times in the history of every man and it behooves us when we meet them to choose not influenced by our apparent self-interest but by our real sense of right and wrong: you may think that but a truism; yet I must tell you that in such matters it is the commonest thing to be said to anyone who thinks he ought to join some movement for the bettering of his fellows, 'what will *you* do if this change happens': to my mind it is manhood and not rashness to answer such an objection by saying, what shall I do? Why have my fair share like my fellows.

I believe the time is at hand when each one of us of the well-to-do and rich classes will have to choose whether he will strive to have the great mass of men his equals and friends, or to keep them down as his slaves: when that time comes may we all remember this, that wretched and shameful as is the condition of a slave, there is one condition more wretched and shameful still—that of slave-holder.

---

[15] The MS has "that."

EARLY ENGLAND[1]

I am no patriot as the word is generally used; and yet I am not ashamed to say that as for the face of the land we live in I love it with something of the passion of a lover: that is to say more than its beauty or interest in relation to other parts of the earth warrants. Perhaps that is because I am in the habit of looking at things that pass before my eyes; (which I think has now ceased to be a common habit) and connecting their present outward seeming with times gone by and times to come.

Again I will not say that the past history of our country is of interest so absorbing as to make us forget that of other countries: nay I know that there is a certain want of romance about it, compared with other stories of national life, and that as it goes on it tends ever more and more to the commonplace. But to us who are come of the actors of it and live amongst the scenes where it was enacted it has a special interest which consecrates it. Egotism you will say: well so it is, but under our present conditions and

---

[1] The text of this lecture is taken from B.M. Add. MS. 45332(4), which is entirely in Morris's hand. It was first delivered at the Hammersmith Branch, SL, on Dec. 12, 1886, as the first of a series of three historical lectures on *England as it was, is, and may be* (see Appendix I, 12–12–86, and Appendix II, item 97). This title appears, exactly as given above, at the top of p. 1 of the MS. It is crossed out and *Early England* is written above it.

perhaps for centuries to come an egotism which is natural, and if we only keep it in order by cultivating our sense of justice to other nations, and our insight and interest in the history of the whole world this affection for [our] own parish and the people of it may even [come] to [be] useful to us and others.

I make these excuses because, as you see by the title of my lecture I am going today to confine my story within the limits of our own island stowed away in an odd corner of the world. What I want to do is to give you a picture of what has been in England dwelling almost entirely on the most characteristic periods of its history, as those which lend themselves most to such a picture; to say a few words on its present condition so familiar to us all, so misunderstood by most, so sad to some; and to finish by hazarding some guesses at what it will be like in times to come: painting a picture in the air, this last will be I know: and I ask you to receive it as such.

Now I intend to say scarcely anything about the men of the earlier times before Caesar crossed the Thames up at Walton yonder, and his dark, short, close-knit soldiers plunged into the perilous woods of Middlesex on the other side.[2] Of those earlier days you may however remember that the records of them are chiefly to be found on the great chalk downs that run along and athwart southern England; this will help you to picture to yourselves, the lowlands covered with marsh and tangled forest, good only for hunting such beasts as could live there, badger, red deer, wild swine, wolf, squirrel, and the like; the untended rivers often spreading out in mere swamp and morass,[3] and the parts habitable by man the year round the downs, or the slopes of the hills on which sheep could pasture: there dwelt the earlier, not earliest, inhabitants of Britain, tribe fighting with tribe doubtless, and therefore raising earthworks on the brows of the hills in which the whole tribe could gather and drive their flocks and herds for safety: several races doubtless have used these rude but effective

---

[2] This reference is, of course, to the second invasion under Julius Caesar in 54 B.C. See Theodore Mommsen, *The History of Rome,* tr. W. P. Dickson (London, 1894), II, 64–5.

[3] See Charles Elton, *The Origins of English History* (London, 1882), pp. 106–8. Much of the factual matter in this lecture is taken from this source.

fortresses; as for instance the great earthwork, called Uffington Castle, which from the wall of the Wiltshire downs looks over the fair rich valley of the Thames: there along the ridge of the hill behind it runs a Roman road, while a furlong from it on the hill-ridge is the tomb of some chief of the earlier people, which to our Saxon forefathers, when they first came there, seemed so remote and mysterious that they named it by one of the earliest of their Gods, the Vulcan of the North, and called it the cave of Wayland the Smith.[4]

There also they raised holy places, concerning which endless guesses have been made, which probably must forever remain guesses; but at least one may say this of them that the earliest historical people that found them there seem little nearer to their builders than we do. Most impressive they are and also most instructive even amidst their history; the man must be hard to move indeed who is not moved who as he turns the corner of one of our commonplace English highways comes suddenly across that marvellous hedge of grey stones that our Saxon ancestors called Stonehenge: or looks from the great circular Earthwork of Avebury on the little old village that lies within it, where the cottages are cheek by jowl with the few remaining stones of the ancient temple there: lying close by the huge barrow of Silbury, the hills about all dotted with graves of the early chieftains; the mysterious Wansdjke[5] drawn across the downs at the back; wherein even now the horses are tethered when the yearly traditional horse fair takes place at 'Tan Hill.'[6] And lastly once more

---

[4] The cave Morris mentions was known locally as Wayland's Smithy, of which Elton (pp. 130–31, note 2) quotes the following legend: "At this place . . . lived formerly an invisible smith, and if a traveller's horse had lost a shoe upon the road, he had no more to do than to bring the horse to this place, with a piece of money, and leaving both there for some little time, he might come again and find the money gone, but the horse new shod." A marginal note here in the MS reads, "blowing stone."

[5] This "Wansdjke" may be the same, judging from its location, as the "Grimsdjkes" mentioned by Elton (p. 111) as representing the course of the old tribal boundaries. See also R. R. Darlington, "Anglo Saxon Wiltshire," in *A History of Wiltshire* ("The Victoria History of the Counties of England"; London, 1955), II, 10, and Map 15.

[6] "Tan Hill," better known as St. Annes or St. Anna Hill, is in the parish of All Cannings, Wiltshire. There, "The famous Tan Hill Fair [an exhibition of horses]

the Roman road running through it all towards Bath, just
swerved a little by the huge mass of Silbury: a familiar place to
my boyhood; yet a holy place indeed. There is a pretty story
current of Aubrey, the Wiltshire archaeologist of the 17th century,[7] that one day as he was out on the downs hunting or
coursing, he suddenly came across the Earthwork of Avebury and
the Stones of the Temple, then much more numerous than they
are now. He drew rein and sat there musing and at last turned
and rode home soberly, and from that day foreswore hawk and
hound and became a diligent and useful archaeologist.

Well, perhaps the life of these earlier peoples dwelling on the
high lands amidst their flocks and herds in a very elementary
society tending toward the tribal condition, and struggling slowly
into a more elaborate life and greater command over the powers
of nature, is easier to picture than the following periods, when
there were many peoples in Britain and many different conditions
of progress, the time when the Roman servitude first began:
many huge tracts of unsettled land [were] yet left; many of the
tribes were still in a savage state; but there were kingdoms,
probably Gaulish, on the East and Southeast which were not only
clear of the savage state but could scarcely perhaps be called
barbarian even; and tillage though interrupted by the wastes and
forests was widely spread; the population generally was ages past
the men of Avebury and Stonehenge. Into this population the
Romans brought 'the blessings of civilization,' and destroyed the
chances of the natural development of the British tribes, slowly
hammering to pieces all resistance, till they had established the
great taxgathering machine the Roman bureaucracy, the great
curse of the ancient world, as our commercial market-hunting
bureaucracy is the great curse of the modern world.

---

was held on Aug. 6, the Feast of St. Anne." See J. E. B. Gover, Allen Mower, and
F. M. Stenton, *The Place-Names of Wiltshire* ("Publications of the English
Place-Name Society," Vol. XVI; Cambridge, 1939), p. 312.

[7] The reference is to John Aubrey, F.R.S., whose own account of this incident
differs slightly from the popular legend related by Morris in that there is no
indication of a sudden conversion. Aubrey says that, after his meditations, he rode
back to the hunt, "cheered by the cry of the hounds." See John Britton, *Memoir of
John Aubrey, F.R.S.* (London, 1845), pp. 30–31.

On the miserable period of this Roman servitude I will not dwell: the one gift that the Imperial taxgatherers gave to the island was roads made through it for the safe-conduct of their bum-bailiffs, which to this day are useful both to thieves, lawyers, and honest men: for the rest it was a matter of course that they should deprive the unlucky people of all character and public spirit aɩɟd so make them an easy prey to the first comers who were necessitous and bold enough to take hold of the land which it was no one's business to defend.

The necessitous and bold newcomers were ready by this time: from the shores of the Baltic and the North Sea came the tribes of the English, the Jutes, and the Saxons coolly risking everything in their half-decked or undecked luggers,[8] the men who had long been a terror to the Roman provincials, who had learned to expect them on the coast when the weather was so bad that no civilized keel could keep the sea.[9]

These were the men that now fell upon our islands and made a new set of pictures for us to look on. And before I go further I should like to clear your minds of a misconception which some persons by a happy exercise of ignorance and cant have led us into. These men of the earlier world were rough, predatory, cruel, or at least of ungovernable passions which led them into cruelty; but there is no parallel between them and the offscourings of our commercial civilization as certain fifth-rate romanticists are apt to try to make us believe: the ruffians who are the quite worthy pioneers of American or English colonial civilization are to the backbone commercial; they are stockjobbers down on their luck, and only want a month or two of the ordinary varnish of civilization to become respectable members of Society; i.e. thieves under the protection and encouragement of the laws: and take note that their distinguishing characteristic is 'vulgarity' a quality which in

---

[8] The *NED* defines a "lugger" as ". . . a small vessel with . . . four-cornered cut sails, set fore and aft. . . ."

[9] A marginal note here reads, "The Count of the Saxon Shore," a reference to the officer selected by the Romans to govern " 'the maritime tract' and [who] provided for the defense of the fortresses which lined the South-Eastern coasts" (Elton, p. 337).

the full signification of the very modern word is a creation of this century.

Now if you ask me how I know that these terrible sea rovers who founded the English nation amidst rapine and bloodshed in these islands were free from this foulest of qualities I can tell you, first that they bore with them a literature, unwritten of course, but fragments of which having been afterwards written down are still left us: and doubtless these early poems at least, in which language is uncorrupted and has not yet learned to speak with the double tongue, reflect the mind of the people which produced them; the epic of Beowulf is worthy of a great people for its sincerity of language and beauty of expression, and nowhere lacks the epic quality of putting clear pictures before the readers' eyes; nor is there anything in it coarse, ignoble, or degrading; on the contrary it breathes the very spirit of courageous freedom: to live is good and to die is good if you are valiant and faithful and if you reckon great deeds and the fair fame that comes of them of more account than a few more short years of a trembler's life upon the earth. This is the simple ethic of our forefathers, and in these poems [it] is so set forth that it is clear they really believed it and that in consequence life amidst all its sufferings and hardships was a continuous poem to them. In later times it has become a commonplace and is no longer believed, therefore except for moments of spasmodic excitement life is dull shapeless, so that some in their foolish despair will ask, is it worth the living? Clearly it is not unless we can live fearlessly and confident of our immortality not as individuals but as a part of the great corporation of humanity; and that I say was the faith of our forefathers.

And this faith of which these glorious poems are the simple expression was itself bred of the conditions of life to which the race had attained: the hideous card-sharping border ruffians of America and the colonies are terrible to friend and foe alike, pure individualists, they have nothing to do with anything[10] except the immediate satisfaction of their own impulses; but the Teutonic tribes that followed the footsteps of the Roman taxgatherers were

---

[10] The words "anyone else's rights and wrongs" are rejected for "anything" in the MS.

corporate bodies of men united into artificial families for self-preservation and the satisfaction of the mutual needs of their members; and these families again were at the point of federating if they had not already federated into a bigger body 'the people' (þeoð). 'No rights without duties, no duties without rights' was in fact the principle which their constitution strove to *illustrate within the limits of the corporation of the family the gens and the þeoð:* so that within those limits it was to their foes rather than their friends that they were terrible. That limitation is necessary because outside their tribe or people it was war, and war brought prisoners sometimes and those prisoners became property and were called thralls. That is the blot on the constitution of our forefathers as it was of the ancient Greeks.

Now you must understand that the civilization of which the Roman Empire was a corruption was founded on the institution of the city: which means not the mere stones and mortar of the dwellings of the citizens, but the corporation of which they each formed a part, yet again the corporation fixed in a certain holy place: the city was the unit of civilization; outside it was nothing but confusion. The external aspect of this city-worship, for it was no less, the Roman domination had retained everywhere, even in such outlying spots as Britain. But the tribes who gradually supplanted the Roman Empire on the contrary had no idea of a city, this of the fixed abode for the gens or tribe or þeoð, the field amidst the forest rather is the idea of the dwelling of the germanic tribe. This of course meant a lower form of the development of Society; but into the Society of the City these tribes never developed, but their tribalism melted into the society of feudalism and the Church instead. And it was only where the influence of the Roman Empire was strong that any semblance of the ancient city life lasted into the Middle Ages:[11] in England for instance only those towns have any traces of it that were founded by the Romans: and it is interesting to note that if you come into any town which has many parishes such a town is almost certainly Roman in origin: e.g. Norwich, Yarmouth.

The Anglo-Saxons [who] then came to this country in the

---

[11] A marginal note here in the MS reads, "Italy House towns."

condition of barbarism [were] the most advanced toward that ancient civilization, which faded away altogether before they could develop into it. Their want of sympathy with the city life in the first years of their occupation was almost as marked as that of the gypsy or the Bedouin for house life. When they took one of the towns of the Romanized Britons they could not use it; they sacked it and burned it, and went back again to their own simpler habitations:[12] you must think of them then at first as dwelling in farm-steads along the rivers or the sea shore, or in clearings of the woods, in that field amid the forest of which I was speaking: thus sprung up those villages with English names all over the country, each one of which was the settlement of some family or other; and curiously enough sometimes their names used for constitutional divisions have outlasted the place itself (hundred of Ossulton—where is it?) nevertheless there was, if there is not now some stead which was founded by one Oswald and was therefore called his town. That very word [town] which we now use as the generic term for a collection of houses and a biggish one at that shows by change from its original meaning how far removed the first English were from city life: in Scotland the word is or lately was used to designate a farmstead merely or the house in it; while further north the word is still used in its original sense of the cultivated field around a dwelling as contrasted with the out-meadows or mere uncultured pasture lands.

Thus then did the tribes from the Baltic found the English nation in our island, and lived at first not so very differently from their fathers as they made their way through the great forests of mid-Europe: their history as read in the books is but a series of battles with the resisting Britons or chief with chief of their own blood; yet doubt it not that all the time their home life went on with something of dignity under the constitution of which I have hinted: in which every free man had to take his share of responsibility for carrying on the business of the Community. But as time passed and[13] the limits of the rule of the different Chieftains got

---

[12] This was the case, for example, with the Roman town of Anderida, which had been erected to defend the "Saxon Shore" (see Elton, pp. 384–5).
[13] The words "centralization grew" are deleted in the MS.

more defined, the tribal feeling waned: the Chiefs and Kings, also, as Mr. Elton says[14] began to inhabit the towns that the Romans had founded, and the aspect of the great building works of that most solid-building of peoples struck a chord of melancholy in the hearts of their poets: here are a few lines from a poem called The Ruin preserved in a volume written in Athelstane's time, the sentiment of which differs little from that of our own time—[15]

> Wondrous the wall-stone that Weird hath broken . . . the roof-tree riven, the grey gates despoiled. Often that wall withstood Raeghar and Readfah, chieftain after chieftain rising in storm. Bright was the burgh-place many the princely halls, and high was the roof of gold . . . And the court is dreary, and the crowned roof lies low in the shadow of the purple arch. Princes of old time joyous and gold-bright and splendidly-decked, proud and with wine elate, in war gear shone. They looked on their treasures, on silver and gems and on stones of price, and on this bright burgh of their broad realm. The stone court stands, the hot stream hath whelmed it, there where the bath was hot on the breast.[16]

To get done with this matter of the towns I may say also that other towns besides these Roman cities got founded, some as the surroundings of Burgs or strong places, some as merchant towns.

But now the Feudal system which was destined to embrace the customary law of the Germanic tribes and the remains of Roman authority, mingled here perhaps with some Easternism from New Rome, began to creep over the country: I tried to put before you some time ago the way in which feudality naturally developed from the customs of the tribes [that] conquered the kindred peoples of Scandinavia,[17] and much the same thing went on in

---

[14] See Elton, p. 384.

[15] The MS here contains a note "(quote) Elton 385," and omits the following passage. The quotation given here is taken directly from the reference cited by Morris.

[16] Elton (p. 385) identifies the quotation as follows: "The extracts are translated from the poems in the Exeter Book ascribed to 'Cynewulf.' Thorpe, Cod. Exon. p. 292, 476, 478."

[17] The reference here is undoubtedly to the lecture *The Birth of Feudalism in Scandinavia,* delivered at Kelmscott House, Hammersmith, on Oct. 3, 1886 (see Appendix I, 10–3–86).

England, so that by Athelstane's time there certainly was established a kind of feudality here; and from that time onward England was destined to be no longer isolated from the more Romanized nations of the Continent. Moreover from the time when Christianity first came amongst them some shades of Rome does as it were seem to hang over the Early English which the Scandinavian kingdoms were free from. As far as our early literature is concerned that was a great misfortune. The history and mythology of Scandinavia was enshrined in the rough casket of Iceland, and though at the time when it was written the people of that island had been converted to Christianity, yet except where the subject-matter positively demands it there is no sign of the new religion having made any practical impression on the writers, and though monks and priests took their part in this literature, works written in Latin are rare. But in England it was different; the literature was mostly in the hands of the monks, there are not many works left us in the vernacular, and of those several of the most important are paraphrases of bible stories or at least pieces founded on the Christian mythology of which we have so much in other forms. There are in Anglo-Saxon in short none of those pieces of local history told in a terse and amazingly realistic and dramatic style which bring back to us Iceland and Norway in the eleventh century: and what is still more unlucky we have lost the account of the mythology of the North from the Low German branch of the great Teutonic race: it is the feeblest and slenderest branch of the Goths that have been the story tellers of the race and not the Germans or the English: Odin we know in his goings out and comings in, but Wotan and Woden are but names to us. And it is a pity indeed; for what there is left of the poems of the ancient English (apart from Beowulf) show[s] tokens of the highest and most elevating capacities: no lyrics in the English language are more beautiful, and few indeed as full of feeling and true poetic passion as some of those preserved in that "Exeter book" I have already mentioned.

The turning of the rude kings and chieftains of an outlying island toward what was once the centre of the civilized world, and was still the centre of Christianity, has to the mere romanticist something striking and even pathetic about it: the stream of pilgrims daring the dangers that then beset the traveller through central Europe to reach the Eternal City; the kings and queens that laid their crowns at the feet of the holy father, and died in the odour of sanctity there:[18] an English Bishop (St. Boniface) the apostle of the heathen Wends[19] of Prussia and their martyr. And yet all that pomp of religion does not make up to me for the loss of the stories I might have had of how the folk of Middlesex ate and drank and loved and quarrelled and met their death in the 10th century.

But once more the time was coming when England was to be a part of Europe; and meantime it seems in spite of the stout men that dwelt here, she could not hold her own before the Furor Normanorum that stirred up all Europe that lay anywhere near the sea.[20] By the time the tribes were fairly settled and the development of the þeoð into a nation under a feudal king was going on, the Northmen had fallen on the island, and from that time till the Norman conquest gave it no rest except when the whole country was in their power: the English called them generically Danes but the first comers were from Norway a branch of the great stream that overran Europe: conquering Normandy, making yearly inroads right up into France, and North Germany: the men who carved Norse kingdoms out of Ireland, settled Iceland, and upheld the throne of the Emperor of the East. Against this energy, bred doubtless of necessity, the English could make but little head: the wide extent of sea-board with its numerous harbours beat them; and you must remember that they had to meet people who were born seamen while the English of that day and for centuries afterwards were not a seafaring people. So that for a time it seemed likely that the whole of society would be broken up by these bold strong-thieves. For the invasions of this early period were not for conquest but for pillage;

---

[18] See for example Morris and Magnusson's translation of *The Story of Grettir the Strong* (*Collected Works,* VII), which ends with just such a tale.

[19] The *NED* defines "Wend" as ". . . a member of the Slavonic race now in the east of Saxony, but formerly extending over Northern Germany. . . ."

[20] The following passage is deleted in the MS: "Edgar—the first successful over-king of this island—was in a sense the last successful one."

'lying out' was as regular a business with the northern landhold-
ers and yeomen as their ordinary field-work: it is told of an Earl
of the Orkneys that he had two regular viking cruises in the year;
the first after the seed was sown which he called his spring cruise,
the second after it was harvested, called his autumn cruise:[21]
some of the vikings went into partnership with the kings and
shared the proceeds both of peaceful chaffer and fighting: with
the most spirited, well-bred young men it was thought proper
that they should go through a viking cruise for one or two sum-
mers, such as our young gentlemen and noblemen used some 100
years ago to think it necessary to do the grand tour. Once again
you must not fall into the mistake of picturing the men who
partly lived on this woeful industry as being either like the
brigands of romance or the sordid pirates of more modern times
even Captain[s] Teach and Kidd, or like the chivalry of the later
Middle Ages:[22] the greater part of the men who harried England
were when they got back home respectable agriculturalists; yeomen, or at least landlords who were not ashamed to work with
their own hands: Gunnar, one warrior, is represented as sowing
his cornfield;[23] Arnkel a very great man in Iceland, mending his
own gate:[24] King Sigurd the father of King Harald the Terrible
who fell near York before our King Harald, is found in his hay-
field helping his men get in his hay harvest:[25] the warriors were
shipwrights, housebuilders and armourers, and almost every one
could [s]ettle a copy of verses on occasion. They lived under an
elaborate system of laws which later on were written out at
length, and doubtless had it not been for their narrow and barren
lands their fierce valour would have smouldered away amidst the

---

[21] This "Earl of the Orkneys" is Sweyn, Aslief's son. The description given here of
his "cruises" is contained in the account of the year 1171 in the *Orkneyinga Saga*.
See G. W. Dasent (tr.), *The Story of Burnt Njal* (Edinburgh, 1861), II, 370–71.
[22] G. W. Dasent (II, 369), whose translations of Icelandic materials Morris
certainly knew, parallels the Vikings with later pirates in a fashion most irritating
to Morris's anti-Renaissance prejudices: "Who is there on reading this stirring
story [*The Orkneyinga Saga*] that is not reminded of Drake, Hawkins, and
Cavendish, those sea-dogs of Elizabeth's reign."
[23] See "The Early Literature of the North—Iceland," footnote 11, p. 185.
[24] As above, footnote 9, p. 184.
[25] As above, footnote 8, p. 184.

peaceful occupations of the land: the sea that fed them drew them on to waylaying its watery roads.[26]

Well whatever they were at home they were a fearful visitation in the countries that they used as their hunting grounds: the first thing they did after landing on the coast was to throw themselves on any body of men that showed fight in order to get horses; for oddly enough they were as much horsemen as seamen: or they would row up the rivers, very much higher than we should expect them to have gone, and throw up an earthwork: you will read such entries in the Saxon Chronicle as 'This year the Host sailed up the Seine to Paris and sat a year there.' Another year they went up the Marne far beyond Paris. They rowed high up the Lea and entrenched themselves there against Alfred another time.[27] Sometimes a band would ally itself with the Welsh chieftains, sometimes with the Scots. In short the host of the Heathen was a ceaseless plague in the land and [as] I said seemed about to reduce it to a state of mere confusion when there appeared on the scene a man whose pure fame no amount of legend can obscure, and the interest in whom must always win one's heart however much his name has been hackneyed, the man born at Wantage in Berkshire, Alfred the son of Aethelwulf; of whom one must say that there was one other man of genius who has sat on the throne in England and that is Oliver Cromwell, and he betrayed the cause which he had in charge and was mourned by his friends rather before he died than when he died. But Alfred's fame was pure and stainless and both in his shortcomings and his successes he was human and sympathetic. Yes I think we must call him the one sole man of genius who ever held an official position among the English.

Well he began his contest with the Vikings with some hope of success, fought nine great battles in one year says the S[axon] Ch[ronicler]: one of them in which he and his brother Aethelred defeated the heathen and slew Baejsecg and Halfdan their kings,

---

[26] A marginal note here "(parallel)" is probably a reminder for the lecturer to compare these Norse warriors to the "brigands" of the Renaissance.

[27] A marginal note here reads, "in that year the Host which had sat down at Fulham went over sea to Ghent in France and sat there one year."

and was fought at Ashdown some mile from that Uffington Castle I have told you of, and as his men came back from the fight, they amused themselves by cutting away the turf from the slope of the chalk hill so that the white showed on the green in the figure of a white horse, the beast of their banner done so as to satisfy their imaginations of the thing: and from that day to this it has abided there unchanged: and one day this summer I sat on him and looked down on that fair plain of the Thames, changed enough in outward seeming from the days of Alfred but how much more in the ways of life of the people who dwell there![28]

The battle of Ashdown was pretty much the end of the first act of Alfred's struggle; the second was a time of defeat and disaster; but he struggled out of it, and again made head against the host, defeated it over and over again, made some sort of terms with the leaders, followed up all who resisted untiringly, and at last triumphed; the date of Ashdown is 871: in 886 the Chronicler writes "In this same year Alfred restored London; and all the Anglo-race turned to him that were not in the bondage of the Danish men." Much fighting there was afterwards, but in 897 the Chronicler could write as if the war was over: "Thanks be to God the Host had not utterly broken up the Anglo Race." So that England remained England, though the Danish kingdoms of Northumbria and East Anglia were still a thorn in its side. Successful kings followed Alfred, who however had plenty of fighting with the Danes,[29] till at last Edgar was acknowledged over-king of England, and received homage of the Welsh, Scotch, and Danish kings in England. It seems pretty clear that by his time that un-Romanized feudal system I have spoken of was fully established in the country. The king was no longer the head of a clan or even of a people or þeoð; but the master of the land giving fiefs to his earls and thanes, who in their turn gave them to their free men. Edgar (died 975) as he was the first over-king of England, was also the last successful one: the Northmen were again at war

---

[28] Morris amplified the thoughts he had on the occasion of his visit to Uffington in the essay "Under an Elm-Tree; or, Thoughts on the Countryside," first published in *Commonweal*, July, 1889. See *Artist, Writer, Socialist*, II, 507–12.
[29] A marginal note here reads, "Brunanburgh."

with the English regularly and not merely spasmodically: of the year 994 the Chronicler says—[30]

> In this year came Olaf (Anlaf) and Svein to London, on the Nativity of St. Mary (Sept. 8th), with ninety four ships, and then they were obstinately fighting against the town, and would have set it on fire. But they there sustained more harm and evil than they ever weaned that any townsmen could do to them. For the holy mother of God, on that day, manifested her mercy to the townsmen, and delivered them from their foes. And they then went thence, and wrought the greatest evil that ever any army could do, in burning, and harrying, and in man-slayings, as well by the sea-coast, as in Essex, and in Kent, and in Sussex, and in Hampshire. And at last they took them horses, and rode as far as they would, and were doing unspeakable evil. Then the king and his "witan" resolved that they should be sent to, and promised tribute and food, provided that they should cease from ravaging; and they then accepted that. And all the army then came to Southampton, and there took winter-quarters; and there they were fed from all the realm of the West Saxons, and they were paid sixteen thousand pounds of money. Then the king sent bishop Aelfeah and the aldorman Aethelweard after king Olaf; and the while hostages were given to the ships; and they then led Olaf with great worship to the king at Andover. And king Aethelred received him at the bishop's hand, and royally gifted him. And Olaf then promised him, as he also fulfilled, that he would never again come with hostility to England.

This Olaf was (afterwards, according to the sagas) King of Norway, and forced [Chris]tianity[31] on his unwilling people: his history is one of the most splendid and dramatic chapters of the old Norse king-stories; but the incident has more significance as regards his fellow king Swein who was king of Denmark: he opens a new chapter in the story of the Norse invasions; the earlier ones though not altogether mere pillaging raids, since the Vikings had their wives and children, aimed rather at settlements than conquering of the whole kingdom: indeed there was then no

---

[30] The MS here contains a note "(quote) (105)," and omits the quotation itself. The passage given here is taken from Benjamin Thorpe (ed. and tr.), *The Anglo-Saxon Chronicle* ("The Rolls Series"; London, 1861), pp. 105–6, which has the entry for the year 994 on the page cited by Morris. The complete entry for that year is quoted.

[31] The MS reads, "Xtianity."

kingdom to conquer, no centralized system of government, which as we have seen began to develop with Alfred: but now the struggle took the form of a definite attack by the Danish king on the English kingdom; which honey-combed by towns and settlements of his own blood was not hard to conquer: and also things to judge by the Chronicler were but in a poor way and the English tendency to muddle of which we have seen so much since was being well illustrated.[32]

> An. DCCCC. XCIX. In this year the army again came about into the Thames, and then went up along the Medway, and to Rochester. And then the Kentish forces came against them, and they stoutly engaged together, but alas! that they too quickly gave way and fled; because they had not the support which they should have had. And the Danish had possession of the place of carnage; and then took horses and rode withersoever they themselves would, and ruined and plundered almost all the West Kentish. Then the king with his "witen" resolved that they should be opposed with naval force, and also with a land force. But when the ships were ready, then they delayed from day to day, and harrassed the poor people who lay in the ships; and ever as it should be forwarder, so was it later, and from one time to another; and ever they let their foes' army increase, and ever they receded from the sea, and ever they went forth after them. And then in the end neither the naval force nor the land force was productive of anything but the people's distress, and a waste of money, and the emboldening of their foes.

The attempt at getting quit of the invaders by slaying all the Danes throughout England bettered matters little if at all: as the Chronicler laments they did not either pay or fight in time. In the year 1013 Swein had conquered England; and though he died soon after and his son Cnut had still a good deal of fighting to do, he soon became sole king of England.

So fell the country unto foreign kings; but the manners laws and language of the two peoples were so much alike, that, the fighting once over, the social condition of the people was little altered and all would have gone smoothly if things could have

---

[32] The MS here contains a note "(quote 109)," and omits the quotation itself. The passage quoted here is taken from Thorpe (p. 109). The entire passage for the year 999 is quoted.

remained thus. But England began more and more to be drawn
into the European whirlpool.

There had for long been a regular intercourse with Rome; there
was a School of the English there, and the Archbishop of Canterbury had to fetch his pallium thence i.e. his investiture by the
Pope. The art of the English also was necessarily under foreign
influence: it was they who wedded to the strange interlacing
ornament which the Irish developed from the natural growth of
the soil and which had no power of giving even hints at the
human form, the figure drawing deduced from the art of Byzantium, but which the English probably took from the Germans
who had an art which was an offshoot of the Byzantine style: of
the architecture of the English before the Conquest there are but
few specimens left: probably because their churches were small
for important places, and got rebuilt there in succeeding ages:
while in unimportant places they were built of timber as the
ordinary houses were and so perished by lapse of time where
they were not burned down or rebuilt. Scanty however as the
materials for judging of the architecture are they are enough to
tell us that the English had developed a style of their own quite
different from that which the Norman Conquest introduced: the
difference of the styles is the more marked as there is at least one
Norman church in England built before the Conquest, Waltham
Abbey, and one or two Saxon ones built after it. I should mention
that to my mind the Saxon[s] took their architecture from the
German version of the Byzantine style: all things thus tending
towards connecting England with the Continent, it was not long
before the great event came which made England merely a part
of the dominions of a French Duke.

Passing matters helped this forward: for Edward the Confessor
rested on the foreign element as a support against the power of
Earl Godwin and his sons; and gave a kind of a title to the
kingdom to Duke William: discontent grew; a riot at Dover made
by the French favourites was taken up by the Earl as an occasion
to appeal to the people against the King: he sailed up the Thames
to Southwark and lay there a tide, and shot the bridge with the
flood: the king's men were drawn up to receive him on the
Middlesex shore; and a great battle seemed imminent, but the

hearts of all men misgave them that they should fight Englishmen against Englishmen; truce was struck, the witan met, and Earl Godwin was reinstated in his lands and earldom with the good-will of all men; the evil customs and laws of the foreigners were done away with, and all looked hopeful.[33] I have mentioned this passage about Godwin to show that the Danish blood was by this time scarcely looked on as alien, since Godwin the popular hero and supporter of the English customs was in fact a Northman.

Well Edward died amidst these things, but a little after God-win and who but Godwin's son could be king after him; so Harald, called says one chronicler Harald the Hapless on his tombstone, became the last king of Early England. I have said that a[n] English History is apt to lack romance; yet the history of the great change for good and for evil which connected Eng-land forever with the continent could scarcely be more romantic. And here above all times does one regret that subjection of the native writers to monkish Latin, and longs for the story now never to be written which the English sagaman might have given us of that field of Hastings. And this all the more as one part of the story and that the least important part has been told dramatically enough by an Icelander.[34] For Tostig Harald's brother having quarrelled with him and being dispossessed in consequence, sailed away north and tried to get Swein the Dane-king to fall on England; and getting the cold shoulder from him went to Harald the Terrible, king of Norway, a redoubted war-rior, once captain of the guard of the Greek emperor, whom he enticed into the expedition: the story teller gives us all the usual preliminaries of a great tragedy in the tales of the north; pithy warnings of wise men; omens of seers, and the like; and dwells at length on the victories won by the Norse Harald before the English king caught him unawares, his army without their mail coats six miles from York: the fight that follows and the parley

---

[33] This passage about Godwin's near-battle with King Edward's forces follows very closely, though it is not a direct quote, the account given in Thorpe (pp. 148–50).

[34] The various details of the story as related by Morris leave no doubt that the "Icelander" he speaks of is the unknown author of the *Hemyng's Saga*. See G. W. Dasent (tr.), "The Story of Heming," in *Icelandic Sagas* ("Rolls Series"; London, 1894), III, 374–415.

before it are given in the usual dramatic and generous manner of the north, and makes one long that such a story teller should have told us what followed. The news of Duke William's landing on Michaelmas-day; the hasty march south of King Harald and his house-carls, and his muster of an army at the 'Hoar Apple-tree'; the wedge array drawn up round the king and his brothers round the Banner of the fighting-man: the oft repulsed charges of French Horsemen; the breaking up of the wedge-array in pursuit, and the battle lost but the men still fighting; the arrow shot at a venture and the death of Harald and his brethren and England lost and won once more. All this was worthy of being told in more words than the brief despair of the Chronicler, and in more life-like manner than the Latin scribbling Monk could compass.

So England fell, and it seems that the people of the country were not at first conscious of what had happened; but thought of it as they would of the last fight of Cnut with Edmund Ironside, which simply put a Danish king over them instead of an English one without changing their social condition: you must remember that though there was more national feeling then than later on under the Plantagenets still there was but little. The national patriotism we are so noisy about now was born much later when the Middle Ages were ending.

What had happened was serious enough: England had fallen into the hands of a Romanized landlord and from henceforth was a part of the great European Feudal System: its development as a pure branch of the Teutonic family was stopped forever; because the countries to whom it was now to be bound were, whatever their blood was, developed from Roman provincials, and had not even a language of their own, but were compelled to speak a dialect of Latin.

What might else have happened in the social and political development of England, if the Frenchmen had been driven out by Harald, who can say. For my part I doubt if the difference would have been great. In the next two hundred years the real popular history of Europe is comprised in that of the guilds, which after a long struggle established their control over all industry, yet in the end too late to prevent their falling in their turn under the double curse of bureaucracy and commercialism, which grew to be ruling powers as feudalism or the society of status waned into capitalism or the society of contract. In this history England took a fair share, and could hardly have done otherwise considering her position and importance, even had their been no Duke William and no Hastings; and in these matters England remained England at all events—with her art and literature it is different. She almost immediately received a new architecture, which developing slight differences nevertheless clung close to that of France, and produced such glorious and beautiful [buildings] that there is no room for regret left—literature also became Frenchified and here to its great misfortune as I think. The great works of the English poets ever since Chaucer's time have had to be written in what is little more than a dialect of French and I cannot help looking on that as a mishap. If we could only have preserved our language as the Germans have theirs, I think we with our mingled blood would have made the world richer than it is now—but these are vain regrets: it is all whistled down the wind with the last shout of the axes at Senlac: nor do I ask you to look on it now except as on a series of pictures of the past.

This was what the axes of Hastings resisted had they known it: but if they had, and whatever resistance had been attempted the result would have been the same. The day of centralization and bureaucracy had to be prepared for: the remains of the tribal custom of the English supported by a loose approximation to the Romanized feudality made our forefathers too weak to resist the shadow of Rome now rising again from the dead in the wrappings of feudality. Moreover stout-hearted and valiant as they were they seem to have had a good share of that stupid wastefulness of which many Englishmen are still proud: to burn the house down that our Sunday's beef may be cooked; to lose ten men in a battle where one would be enough; in fine to reduce ten counties to the condition of filthy cinder-heaps in order that ten thousand men may have ten thousand a year each (at other people's expense in all ways) this is the sort[35] of wastefulness which we have

---

[35] The MS reads, "these is the sort."

grown fools enough to be proud of, but which the old Saxon Chronicler lamented, not without reason: since surely it was one of the causes that made the brilliant victory at Stamford Bridge of no account; that broke the wedge-array at Hastings, and laid Harald the Hapless the last king of the English in a forgotten grave at Waltham Abbey amidst the streams of Lea River.

THE EARLY LITERATURE
OF THE NORTH—ICELAND[1]

I f you look at the map of Europe, you will see in its north-
western corner lying just under the Arctic circle a large
island considerably bigger than Ireland. If you were to take
ship and go there you would find it a country very remarkable in
aspect, little more than a desert, yet the most romantic of all
deserts even to look at: a huge volcanic mass still liable to erup-
tions of mud, ashes, and lava, and which in the middle of the
18th century was the scene of the most tremendous outpour of
lava that history records. Anyone travelling there I think would
be apt to hope, if he knew nothing of its history, that its terrific
and melancholy beauty might have once been illumined by a
history worthy of its strangeness: nor would he hope in vain: for
the island I am speaking of is called Iceland.

---

[1] The text of this lecture is taken from B.M. Add. MS. 45331(6), which is entirely
in Morris's hand on paper bearing an 1880 watermark.

Although Morris lectured on Icelandic literature as early as 1884 (see Appendix
I, 9–14–84), internal evidence and newspaper reports make it quite certain that
the text given here was first delivered in the lecture hall at Kelmscott House,
Hammersmith, on Oct. 9, 1887 (see Appendix I, 10–9–87 and Appendix II, item
113). It seems quite possible that Morris had considered publishing this lecture as
one of the Kelmscott Press works. The first page was actually printed off in the
Golden Type, but there is no indication that the rest of the lecture was ever done.
The first page is reproduced in *Collected Works*, XV, facing xvi.

It is a country of no account whatever commercially: the whole centre of the island being high above the level of the sea is a desert indeed, partly glacier, partly rough rock and black volcanic sand, the moraines I suppose of ancient glaciers across which the wind sweeps with a fury unknown in these islands forbidding any vegetation to rise above a few inches from the ground unless there is some special defense against it: here and there in favoured spots (I am speaking of these deserts) a little short grass grows, sweet on the hill slopes, on the low ground boggy and sour, dominated by that most grievously melancholy of all plants the cotton rush: elsewhere is nothing save moss, sea-pink, stone-crop (pretty flowers these last), and above all a dwarf willow which keeps on growing and dying, the bleached stems of the perished parts looking like white bones on the black soil (sprengi-sand). It is not a thirsty desert however; every valley almost has water in it and huge rivers rush toward the sea from the glaciers, turbid and white with the grinding of the ice, cleaving for themselves the most fantastic channels amid the blocks of lava and basalt. Awful looking are these Icelandic wastes, yet beautiful to a man with eyes and heart, and perhaps on the whole the healthiest spot in the world.

Round the sea coasts and along the rivers near it lives what population the island can support about 60,000: the grass sweet enough on the slopes there if they get any sun on them; sheep are bred everywhere, well-knit little beasts with a surprising power of jumping, and produce a fine, silky wool valuable enough if there were but more of them: cows also can be fed, but in many places not many, and also in some places, the chief wealth of the island sturdy little ponies, a good few of whom are natural pacers, and very agreeable beasts to ride: and consequently no Icelander walks a mile if he can help it. As you go down one of the long valleys, which always has a river through it you see on the hill-side a patch of emerald green and some low gabled sheds almost like grey tents rising from it: this is a homestead with its surrounding tún or home mead where the sheep are penned in the winter. I must not go into a description of modern Icelandic life, so I will only tell you that these homesteads are very populous, and more than one family commonly lives in each including possibly paupers, and (it used to be) sometimes criminals. Of the people there is little to be said save praise: they are kind, hospitable, and honest, and have no class of degradation at any rate, and don't take kindly to bullying: they are quick-witted, very talkative when they get over their first shyness, and mostly well-educated as things go: a friendly and refined people in short: implacably exploited by the Danish and Scotch dealers who sell them their necessaries and poor little comforts but otherwise, as I said a mere drop of water in the commercial ocean. But the interest in them which their hard life and the courage and good temper with which they take it cannot fail to awaken in every man of good will, is enormously increased when we bethink us of what these good-fellows really are: they are the representatives, a little mingled with Irish blood, of the Gothic family of the great Germanic race: their forefathers fled before 'the violence of kings and scoundrels,' as they worded it, to save their free tribal customs for a while in that romantic desert, and of their indomitable courage and strong individuality it befell that the rugged volcanic mass has become the casket which has preserved the records of the traditions and religion of the Gothic tribes, and collaterally of the Teutonic also; the instrument of this preservation is the language of their fathers, which is still current amongst them almost intact; the shepherd boy on the hill-side, the fisherman in the firth still chant the songs that preserve the religion of the Germanic race, and the most illiterate are absolutely familiar with the whole of the rich literature of their country, and know more of the Haralds and the Olafs of the tenth and eleventh centuries than most of our 'cultivated' persons know of Oliver Cromwell or William Pitt. Therefore I look upon these poor people with a peculiar affection and their country is to me a Holy Land.

I must tell you now briefly how these people cognate to our own dominant race got to their Isle of Refuge, and then say a little of the character of their literature, but really only as a kind of introduction to the subject.

I have said before in this room that a kind of native feudalism developed of itself in Norway as in England:[2] a certain number of

---

[2] The reference here is to the lecture *The Birth of Feudalism in Scandinavia*, which was scheduled for delivery at the lecture hall, Kelmscott House, Hammersmith, on Oct. 3, 1886 (see Appendix I, 10–3–86).

the old tribal chiefs yielded, generally very sullenly, to the claims of the overlord, but the bolder spirits could not stomach it and resisted King Harald Fairhair, with whom indeed history in the North begins, with all their might: this resistance culminated in a great battle of Hafrsfiorð (Goat-firth) on the Norway coast in which the king was triumphant, and the malcontent chiefs had to submit or seek their fortunes elsewhere: Russia, Normandy, England, Ireland, the islands of Scotland felt the effects for good and for evil of the emigration which followed: but where the Norsemen settled themselves amongst important populations whom their desperate courage had overcome, as notably in Normandy, they gradually mingled with the native population and soon lost their language and traditions. With the settlers in Iceland it was different: the land was uninhabited, they brought with them their tribal customs and traditions and kept them for long together with their language: this of course was the deliberate intention of the emigrants: the chief who fled before 'kings and scoundrels' as we are told the pillars of his high-seat on which Thor, the favourite God of the North was carved, and when they neared the land threw them overboard for the wind and tide to carry: then when he landed the chief went along the coast till he found the spot 'where Thor was come aland.' And there once more the home was founded, the chief claiming the land he needed by going around it with fire:[3] of course many adventurers came out who had no such pretensions to leadership as these besides the freemen and freedmen who went out with the chief and his thralls

---

[3] Commenting on the practice of throwing the pillars of the highseat overboard "to see where Thor was come aland," G. W. Dasent says in his introduction to *The Story of Burnt Njal* (I, 59–60): "See the Eyrbyggia Saga, where Thorolf Mostrarskegg tosses his pillars, on which the image of Thor was carved, over board, off Reykjaness, and follows them to Hofsvogr (Templevoe), in the Breibfijorbr (Broadfirth). It sometimes happened, that the pillars were not easily found; in that case a temporary abode was chosen, while the pillars were sought for. The search often lasted long; thus Ingolf, the first of all the settlers, only found his pillars after three whole years had passed; Lodmund again after three years; Hrollaugr in one; Thord Skeggi, not until he had hunted for them for ten or fifteen years." For a more detailed account of Ingolf's coming to Iceland, see Dasent's "The Norsemen in Iceland," in *Oxford Essays* (London, 1858), pp. 178–9. This essay (p. 180) also contains a detailed account of the practice of claiming land by riding around it with a burning brand.

many of whom he freed and gave land to on his coming to the new country; all these would form a kind of following to the chief, who presently on settling formed a priesthood as it was called and undertook the necessary religious rites and the care and guardianship of the thingstead, the place of meeting, over which he presided, and which was what would now be called the seat of government, the parliament, and the law court of the district: there about the middle of June all the freemen of the district met, and quarrels were prosecuted or arranged, fines imposed, and offenses taken note of and dealt with, all in the open air; no court being allowed to be held within doors or on cultivated ground (ne en akri nè engi).[4] All this sounds very systematic and orderly; and indeed in many of the sagas, whereof more hereafter, there is a great deal of law-quibbling of course always founded on custom and precedent. One thing you must remember however, that though our present Society is founded on a state of things very like this, this state of things was really so very different from ours in spite of our using the same words as our forefathers, that many people find it a difficulty even in conceiving of it. Political society was not yet founded; personal relations between men were what was considered and not territorial: when a priest or chief moved as sometimes happened, many of his thing-men accompanied him, there was no political territorial unit to which loyalty was exacted. Crime in our sense of the word was not taken cognizance of: violence was an offense not against a state but against a person: protection of person or goods had to be sought from the blood relations who were bound to proceed against the injurer: payment of the fines imposed by the courts [was][5] enforced by the relations, the gens, of the injured man, the offender having that protection formally withdrawn from him: he was made an outlaw as the phrase goes; that is those that held the feud against him could kill him without incurring any responsibility of fine or of having a legal feud raised against [them]. The morality of the time was enforced purely by public opinion, a shabby or

---

[4] The phrase translated means "neither in the plowed field nor the meadow." For Morris's imaginative re-creation of such a folkmote of an early Gothic tribe, see *The Roots of the Mountains* (*Collected Works*, XV, 273–92).

[5] The MS reads "were."

treacherous action was looked upon as something quite different from a legal offense, condemnation for which latter involving no kind of disgrace: and even when a man slew his enemy in a just quarrel he had to pay for him; though where the wrong was flagrant he could kill him at a less expense than otherwise (Gunnar).[6] All this you must understand was not mere private war and revenge and consequent confusion but simply a different system to our politico-territorial system, and was based as I said on the equal personal rights of all freedmen: you must remember that this society was an exact model of that which obtained in Norway and the rest of Scandinavia before the emigration; and also that the incomplete Feudality introduced by Harald Fairhair by no means entirely superseded it there.

As to the manners of these early settlers they were naturally exceedingly simple, yet not lacking in dignity: contrary to the absurd feeling of[7] the feudal or hierarchical period manual labour was far from being considered a disgrace: the mythical heroes have often nearly as much fame given them for their skill as weapon-smiths as for their fighting qualities; it was necessary of course for a northman to understand sailing a ship, and the sweeps on board their long-ships or fighting craft were not manned by slaves but by the fighting men themselves; all this is perhaps a matter of course, but in addition the greatest men lent a hand in ordinary field and house work, pretty much as they do in the Homeric poems: one chief is working in his hay-field at a crisis of his fortune;[8] another is mending a gate,[9] a third sowing

---

[6] The note "Gunnar" could refer either to a situation in the *Grettis Saga* (*Collected Works*, VII, 60–63) depicting the settlement made with King Svein for Grettir's slaying of a man named Gunnar, or to a similar settlement by Gunnar Hamundson in *The Story of Burnt Njal*. See Dasent, I, 210–13.

[7] A portion of the MS is illegible here.

[8] The reference is to King Sigurd Syr, whose story is told in the *Heimskringla*. See the translation by William Morris and Eiríkr Magnússon, *The Heimskringla*, 4 vols. ("The Saga Library"; London, 1893–1905).

[9] Arnkel Goþi, son of Thorolf Haltfoot, is the man who was "nailing together the boards of his outer door" when he was attacked by one of his enemies. The tale is told in the Eyrbyggia Saga, which was translated by Morris and Magnússon as *The Story of the Ere-Dwellers* ("The Sage Library"; London, 1892). The incident mentioned above is related in II, 94–5.

his corn, his cloak and sword laid by in a corner of the field:[10]
another is a great house builder, another a ship builder:[11] one
chief says to his brother one eventful morning: there's the calf to
be killed and the Viking to be fought. Which of us shall kill the
calf and which shall fight the Viking?[12]

The position of women was good in this society, the married
couple being pretty much on an equality: there are many stories
told of women divorcing themselves for some insult or offense, a
blow being considered enough excuse. I am bound to say too that
the women claimed and obtained immunity for responsibility of
their violence on the score of their being 'weak women' in a way
which would offend our comrade Bax seriously.[13]

Self-restraint was a virtue sure to be thought much of among a
people whose religion was practically courage: in all the stories of
the north failure is never reckoned as a disgrace, but it *is* reckoned a disgrace not to bear it with equanimity, and to wear one's
heart on one's sleeve is not well thought of. Tears are not common
in Northern stories though they sometimes come in curiously as in
the case of Slaying Glum, of whom it is told that when some one
of his exploits was at hand he was apt to have a sudden access of
weeping, the tears rattling on the floor like hailstones; this of
course was involuntary and purely physical.[14] For the rest I repeat self restraint of all kinds is a necessary virtue before a man
can claim any respect in the Northern stories. Grettir coming

---

[10] In *The Story of Burnt Njal,* Gunnar Hamundson was sowing his corn when
Otkell ran him down. See G. W. Dasent (tr.), *The Story of Burnt Njal,* I, 169–71.

[11] References to house-and-ship-building are so numerous in Icelandic literature
that it is difficult to identify the specific persons being referred to here. One
possibility for the ship-builder is Thorberg Shave-Hewer, spoken of in the
Heimskringla ("The Saga Library," I, 343).

[12] The source of this reference remains unknown.

[13] E. Belfort Bax was one of the mainstays of the Socialist League, having left the
Social Democratic Federation with Morris on the occasion of the split in 1884. A
philosopher of some note, his militant anti-feminist attitude led him into a number
of well-publicized verbal battles with such leading feminine socialists as Annie
Besant and Eleanor Marx-Aveling. For a digest of his views on the position of
women, see his *Reminiscences and Reflexions* (London, Ltd., 1918), pp. 163,
196–200, 269–74.

[14] See Gudbrand Vigfusson and York Powell (trs.), "The Story of Battle Glum," in
Origines Icelandicae (Oxford, 1905), II, 472.

home from abroad learns as soon as he sets foot on shore that his
father is dead, his eldest brother slain, and he himself outlawed,
and changes countenance in no wise.[15] Ingiald of the Wells when
he hears of the death of Njal falls down in a faint and the blood
gushes out of his ears and nose; when he comes to himself he
reproaches himself for behaving like a weak woman.[16] Another
chief after a battle sits down to have his breeches drawn off; the
thrall pulls and pulls and they won't come: truly says he you sons
of Snorri may well be thought great dandies if you wear your
breeches so tight. The chief bids him feel up his thigh, and lo
there is a broken arrow-shaft nailing his breeches to him, of
which he scorned to complain.[17] The tales of heroes very often
begin with the young man coming to a strange place and being
apparently loutish, stupid, and slothful, lying raking in the ashes,
the butt of everybody's scorn and especially of some loud-
mouthed braggart, till at last the time for action comes, the
cinder-raker rises like a God, the braggart's head spins off, and
the hero is made manifest by his deeds. 'Many a man lies hid
within himself,' says their proverb.[18]

Nevertheless a hard and grasping side to the character of the
heroes is not uncommon, and this especially in money matters,
which contrasts disagreeably enough with the heroes of Arab
romance: something at least may here be put down to the harsh-
ness of the northern climate and the hard fight for life there; and
after all a good deal to the love of realism which distinguishes the
tellers of the stories themselves. Yet there are plenty of examples
of generosity and magnanimity too; e.g. the dealings between the

---

[15] See *The Grettis Saga* (*Collected Works*, VII, 112).

[16] Morris is in error in ascribing this reaction to Ingeald of the Wells, who was
wounded by Flosi immediately after the burning of Njal. The situation described
by Morris is translated by Dasent (*The Story of Burnt Njal*, II, 195–6) as follows:
"Thorhall Asgrim's son was so startled when he was told that his foster-father Njal
was dead, and that he had been burnt in his house, that he swelled all over, and a
stream of blood burst out of both his ears, and could not be staunched, and he fell
into a swoon, and then it was staunched. After that he stood up, and said he had
behaved like a coward. . . ."

[17] This anecdote is told of Thorod Thorbrandsson, one of the personages in *The
Story of the Ere-Dwellers* ("The Saga Library," II, 128–9).

[18] See *The Grettis Saga* (*Collected Works*, VII, 170).

two friends Gunnar and Njal in the noble story of Burnt Njal are matchless for manly and farsighted friendliness in the midst of the most trying surroundings. The end of the same story recounts how Kari, wrecked on the coast near where his great enemy Flosi dwells, walks straight up to the house and into the hall where Flosi is sitting and greets him, Flosi returns the greeting of the unarmed, solitary man, embraces him, and the feud is at end.[19] Or take the story of Ingimund the Old the chief of Waterdale: Ingimund harbours an ill-conditioned scoundrel who is neither to hold or to bind: one day a messenger comes to tell him that this rascal is quarrelling with his sons down by the river: Ingimund who is blind as well as old rides down there led by a little lad, and upbraids the rascal who in turn throws his spear across the water and decamps: Ingimund turns away and home: as the boy helps him off his horse he thinks the old man slow to dismount and says to him 'you're stiff today, father.' Old men are used to be so, says Ingimund: the boy leads him into the hall and Ingimund sits down in the high seat; it begins to get dusk: the boy says shall we light up: no says Ingimund not yet: so there he sits till it gets quite dark, and at last the son comes in, and as he walks toward the high seat stumbles and saves himself with his hand, and feels that it is wet from the floor: he has a terrible inkling; cries out for a light, and when it comes to his hand is stained red, and there sits his father Ingimund dead in the high seat, the shaft of the scoundrel's spear hidden under his cloak: he had hidden his wound and died in the dark to keep the affair from his son until the scoundrel who slew him and whom he had heaped with benefits before should have time to escape pursuit.[20]

The sequel of the story is too tragic and not to be told: Ingimund had two freedmen to whom he had given land and when the news of his death came to one of them he drew his 'sax' or short sword and saying, if Ingimund is dead the world is not good for me, he stabbed himself mortally, and before he died pulled out the weapon and giving it to the messenger said take this to so

---

[19] See Dasent, *The Story of Burnt Njal*, II, 346–9.
[20] The story told here comes from the *Vatnsdaela Saga* (Vigfusson and Powell, trs., *Origines Icelandicae*, II, 275–314).

and so the other freedman, and tell him what you have seen: and so died; and when the messenger gave the sax to the other he followed his example at once.

Again it must be admitted that our Norsemen were not above using the weapons of deceit in their struggles for life and fortune: but when they do so it is as an act of war: compare the curious passage in the XIII book of the Odyssey where Athene, a Goddess, is delighted with Odysseus for telling her an intricate series of lies;[21] which indeed he is always doing, and cannot even resist the temptation of one last lie at the expense of his poor old father, which from my modern point of view I really think was too bad: again in book XIX Autolycus, Odysseus' mother's father, is spoken of as outdoing all men 'in thievery and skill in swearing,' clearly with approval,[22] of which cases again remember that in the Homeric literature and in the Norse it was peace within the gens or tribe and war always outside it; a lie or deceit therefore was like an ambush in war. Anyhow though the Northman would lie to his enemy like old Slaying Glum who, skillful in oaths like Autolycus, swore himself off in court by a grammatical quibble,[23] yet he would not lie to his friend and still less to himself—which latter is the modern method and the parent of all falseness. The Northman considered it disgraceful to brag, to make more than enough of a victory gained and still more to blacken the fame of a conquered enemy, which no doubt his instinct showed him was the stupidest of slanders, since if your enemy is an incompetent coward, the less is your glory if you beat him, and the more your shame if he beats you.

Icelandic literature as I have hinted has preserved for us the religious mythology which was largely common to all the Germanic tribes: it is really much akin to that of the classical peoples: but as was likely to be from the simplicity of the people the Gods are more obviously than in other mythologies the reflexion of their worshippers: good-tempered and placable though as fierce as you please, with no liking for or indeed endurance of servility

---

[21] See the *Collected Works*, XIII, 192–4.

[22] In his own published translation, Morris (*Collected Works*, XIII, 287) renders this passage as: "in thievish sleight, and shift of oaths. . . ."

[23] See *Origines Icelandicae*, II, 434–5.

and no complaisance for cowardice or yielding, kind to their
friends and hard to their foes, it must be said that the Norse Gods
are distinctly *good-fellows,* and really about the best that mankind has made. In one point they are very specially a reflex of the
men; that though [they] are long-lived they are not immortal, but
lie under the same fate as mankind. The day is to come when the
forces of evil that they have chained and repressed shall at last
break loose, and the good and evil of man's age and the Gods
who have ruled over it shall meet in mortal conflict at last, and
after fierce battle destroy each other. It is for this great battle
that all valiant men on earth are preparing, and when they leave
the earth, and go to the halls of Odin, they still as of old have to
go on with their training and fight and the semblance of fight is
still their business in Valhall, the Hall of the War-Slain, as it was
on earth. Before this great day of battle it will be evil days with
the world: as the Vala sings in the great mythological poem the
Vala's Foretelling:

> Then Brethren shall battle
> And be bane of each other
> And the sons of one sister
> Their kindred shall spill.
> Hard times in the world then
> And mighty the whoredom:
> An axe age a sword age
> The shields shall be cloven
> A wind age a wolf age
> Before the world waneth.[24]

Says the writer of the prose Edda

> The Fimbul winter the winter of horror, five winters with ne'er
> a summer between shall come before the Gloom of the Gods:
> men would have grown puny and weak-hearted all heroes and
> bold-hearts would have gone home to Odin to fight and to fall
> in the last battle of worldly good and evil. But man alive cannot
> conceive of his ending: a new world is to arise from the wrack
> of the old; the golden tables whereon Aesir played in the early
> days shall be found in the grass, the acres shall wax unsown, all

---

[24] For a complete text and translation see Vigfusson and Powell (eds. and trs.),
"Wolospa Reconstructed," in *Corpus Poeticum Boreale* (Oxford, 1883), II,
621–41.

bale shall be bettered; Balder the bright God of peace and
beauty, shall come back he who in the older days no weapon
would hurt, so that he would stand up in the Gods' Hall and let
all cast their spears at him unharmed, till at last the evil God
Loki put in the hand of the blind God Hod a twig of mistletoe
and the little crooked twig of the plant without root and without
fruit cast fatefully from the hands of a blind God slew the
pleasure and glory of God-home: he now shall come back and
his slayer Hod with him and they shall dwell in the Golden Hall
of Gimli and the world new-peopled shall be at peace.[25]

Of course all this can be explained in various ways by various
kinds of ingenuity: to some it even seems a mere reflex of Christianity: but it seems rather a paradox to maintain that one of the
most vigorous branches of the most progressive race in the world
could not have a mythology developed by themselves; and since
the songs on which the mythology is based were collected by the
men who had become Christians, the great collection even going
by the name of a Christian priest, one Saemund, it would seem
strange that if there were any Christianity in it there should be so
little. To my mind it seems rather to be derived from and coloured
by the same dualism which overlaid the ancient nature-worship
of the Persians, and formed the very long-lived religion still
maintained by the Parsees.

Anyhow it is very clearly the reflex of the lives and ethics of the
northern peoples whose real religion was the worship of Courage:
their morality is simple enough: strive to win fair fame is the one
precept: says Havamal.

> Waneth wealth, and fadeth friend
> And we ourselves shall die
> But fair fame dieth nevermore
> If well ye come thereby.[26]

Be it understood that this was not the worship of success; on the
contrary success that came without valour was somewhat despised: says the sagaman, e.g.: 'The Knigtlinga were very lucky

---

[25] For a modern translation of the Prose Edda, see Jean I. Young (tr.), *The Prose
Edda* (Cambridge, 1943).
[26] The passage quoted is strophe 76. For a modern text and translation see D. E.
Martin Clarke (ed. and tr.), *Havamal* (Cambridge, 1923).

men, but not very valorous."[27] Perhaps the serious consciousness of the final defeat of death made that mere success seem but poor to these men whereas the deeds done could no longer be touched by death. The practiced reader of a saga always knows when he is drawing near to the death of the hero; for the style heightens, the tale-teller remembers more poetry and a kind of halo seems to gild the presence of the man who is now about to make his fame safe forever.

I will now try briefly to give you an idea of what the Northern Literature consists of.

There are first the mythological songs preserved to us by the collectors of the 12th or 13th century of which the most complete is the Vala's Foretelling already mentioned besides which there are various poems containing stories of the Gods: The Lay of the Way-wearer telling in few but sublime words of Odin's journey to the underworld [to] bring back the slain Balder.[28] The Fetching of the Hammer telling of Thor's recovery of his wonderful Hammer from the giant land; a strange grotesque piece,[29] and others concerning the dealing of the Gods with the evil God Loki, and their final defeat of him till the day of the God's Gloom.[30] There is also a curious piece called the Lay of the High One, which is partly a mass of proverbial lore and partly a set of hints at magic.[31] The Rigsmal is a curious poem telling of the visit of Heimdal one of the Gods to earth and his coming across the classes of man Earl, Carl, and Thrall.[32]

These mythological poems form the first half of the songs of the Edda as the great collection of the early poems [is called] and I must say before I go further that a work the nominal scope of which is a treatise on poetic diction, attributed to Snorri Sturle-

---

[27] The "Knigtlinga" are "the sons of Cnut."

[28] The original title is *Baldrs Draumar*. For the full text and a translation, see *Corpus Poeticum Boreale*, I, 181–3.

[29] The original title is *Þrymskviða*. For the text and a translation, see ibid., I, 100–110.

[30] The original title is *Lokasenna*. For the text and a translation, see ibid., I, 100–110.

[31] The reference is to the *Havamal* (see footnote 26, above).

[32] The reference is to the *Rigsðula*. For a text and translation, see *Corpus Poeticum Boreale*, I, 234–42.

son the historian of the 13th century and known as the prose or Younger Edda, has preserved a good many of the legends of the Gods.[33] The second part of the poetic Edda may be called the Romantic part of it: and contains stories of the heroes mostly with a genealogical tendency. The great story of these is the Niblung Tale which to modern readers is better known through the ballad epic, so to call it of the German poets of the 14th century under the name of the Need of the Nibelungs; to my mind this splendid work is a literary deduction from the Norse Poems and is not founded on a special or German ancient tradition. However this story of the Nibelungs has grown, and following it up through all its fragmentary songs and variants I must unhesitatingly call it the noblest and in a sense the completest story yet made by man, embracing the highest range of tragedy; passion, love, duty, valour, honour, in strife with the blind force of fate, vanquished by it, but living again in death in the souls of all the generations according to the words which the Homeric poet puts into the mouth of King Alcinous: "But this thing the Gods have fashioned and have spun the Deathful Day For Men; that for men hereafter might be the tale and the lay."[34]

Again these Romantic early poems are supplemented by a mass of prose literature which gather[s] up the remembrance of other poems in the 13th and 14th centuries. The most important, though scarcely the most artistic of these is the book called the Volsunga Saga which has preserved in a quasi-connected form the glorious story of the Nibelungs aforesaid:[35] some record of the poems totally lost is preserved also in the dreary Latin of Saxo Gramm[aticus], a Danish Bishop of the 13th century,[36] and another writer or two notably Adam of Bremen:[37] one story in Saxo

---

[33] See footnote 25, above.

[34] See Book VIII of Morris's translation of *The Odyssey* (*Collected Works*, XIII, 117).

[35] See Morris and Magnússon's translation (*Collected Works*, VII, 283–396).

[36] The lost poems that have been reconstructed in the *Gesta Danorum* of Saxo Grammaticus include: *Haddings saga, Froða saga, Hapar saga, Eiriks saga málsðaka, Friðleifs saga, Ala saga fraekna,* and *þorkels saga aðalfara.* See Stefan Einarsson, *A History of Icelandic Literature* (New York, 1957), p. 158.

[37] Adam of Bremen wrote the *Gesta Hammaburgensis Ecclesiae Pontificum,* which reconstructs a number of the lost Icelandic poems. For a discussion of this work

most English-speaking people have heard of: it is about a chieftain who pretended to be mad in order to revenge his father; his name was *Amloji;* but you will know him better by the name of *Hamlet* a queer corruption which is due to weary old Saxo's dog-Latin in which he figures as Amlethus.

Leaving these romantic sagas for the present we now come to a very remarkable mass of literature, which is I think quite unparalleled, the historical sagas: these are wholly the work of the dwellers in that rugged desert isle of Iceland which I have told you of. They may be divided into the stories of Norway and incidentally of other parts of Scandinavia together with the Orkneys, the Faroes, and Greenland even on the one hand and on the other stories of various families and their feuds in Iceland itself: In order to account for the first of these, you must know that it was customary for Icelandic adventurers to take service especially in their younger years with the Scandinavian lords and kings on the mainland, including the Russian settlements and Gaeland and sometimes with the English kings, besides serving on occasion in the bodyguard of the Greek emperor at Constantinople (the Lions of Aegina).[38] From the memories of these men which they carried back to their kindred in Iceland, which were often enshrined in verses of various degrees of merit grew up historical traditions of the scenes in which they had played a part; these were collected in connected tales of the reigns of the Kings, the chief collection being attributed to Snorri Sturleson who wrote the Prose Edda, and being named after its first words the Heimskringla:[39] going through all the kings it begins with the confessedly mythical period and carries us down to the twelfth century. Snorri has been called the Herodotus of the North not inaptly as the history is told by way of anecdote as Herodotus tells his; but Snorri is far more personal and dramatic than the

---

and its relation to the history of Icelandic literature, see G. Turville-Petre, *The Origins of Icelandic Literature* (Oxford, 1953), pp. 72, 77, passim.

[38] G. W. Dasent (*The Story of Burnt Njal*, I, x) says, "Wherever he goes the Northman leaves his mark, and to this day the lions of the Acropolis are scored with the runes which tell of his triumph."

[39] See Morris and Magnússon's translation (footnote 8, above).

delightful old Ionian.[40] Every character that he tells us of lives and moves before us, nor does any particle of partiality obscure the clearness of the pictures that he shows us: how often have I lamented that our own history has lacked such a poet, for Snorri was no less than that. Froissart alone amongst the mediaeval chroniclers can be named along-side of him: but then Snorri tells in a dozen words what the Hainalter would take several hundred to tell, and that with a shrewdness and keen wit which pierces through the very bones and marrow of his subject.

I have said Snorri: but after all these once for all are the characteristics of the Icelandic prose stories; you may think that their subject matter is undignified or petty, but certainly whatever they have to tell of they can make it most vividly clear to us, they are in short the best tellers of tales that have ever lived, and stuffed full of the closest detail as their stories are they are never long-winded: they at least escape the reproach of the Lacedaemonians to the Ionian envoys; 'It is very pretty but since we have forgotten the beginning we don't know what the end is about.'

Besides these King-Stories as they are called we have as I said the tales of family events or feuds in Iceland itself: these are very naturally the literature that the modern Icelander loves the most: almost all those patches of emerald green on the grey hill-side that I told you about are still identified as the spots where the ancient chieftains lived and fought and died: nay the spots where such and such events happened are still pointed out to the traveller by people who believe firmly in them, and in the long winter nights while the others mend their harness and carve and shape horn spoons and the women spin and card the wool some one reads to them the deeds of their forefathers, it may be on the very spots where their houses once stood.

Amongst the longer works of these Parish histories there are three which are at once the most artistic and the most admired by the people of the country. The story of Burnt Njal,[41] The Story of

---

[40] The following words are deleted in the MS: "whose delightful book has filled our minds with the tales of the Greeks."

[41] See G. W. Dasent's translation (footnote 2, above).

Grettir the Strong,[42] and that of Egil the Son of Skallagrim:[43] Gisli the outlaw[44] and Gunnlaug the Wormtongue[45] bear off the bell, I think among the shorter tales: of all these I think Egil's Story is the most popular in Iceland: to us it would seem very rough and even ferocious in its manners; but it has the merit of containing three very fine poems traditionally the work of Egil himself: two out of the three are rhymed which is not usual in Icelandic poetry: they are in my opinion quite impossible to translate, so as to preserve any of their real merit. Another point of interest to us is that Egil's dealings were largely with England where he served King Aethelstane and was one of his Norse allies at the great battle of Brunanburgh. The Story of Grettir is intensely Icelandic; it is the tale of a valiant and physically strong man who was pursued by life-long ill-luck, and, being made an outlaw early in his career by the machinations of his enemies, sustained himself in those terrible wastes I was telling you of by dint of his indomitable courage and a kind of fierce generosity which makes him a very attractive character. But of all the domestic sagas that of Burnt Njal is certainly the finest: the characters amidst all their faults and even the crimes of some of them are on a high level of nobility and generosity quite unsurpassed in story: it perhaps adds to the interest of the tale that Njal himself the twin hero of the first part of the tale is not a warrior but plays the part throughout of the wise, kindly, and peacemaking neighbour: his warrior friend Gunnar is the darling of Icelandic history and so without more ado I will give you his portrait as drawn by the sagaman, which as far as his mental and moral qualities are concerned is fully borne out by the tale.[46]

---

[42] See Morris and Magnússon's translation (footnote 6, above).

[43] Egil Skalla-Grímsson (c. 910–990) has been called "by far the most important" of the Old Icelandic poets (see Einarsson, op. cit., pp. 57–60). Morris's reference is to the *Egils Saga*. For a modern translation see E. R. Eddison (tr.), *Egil's Saga* (Cambridge, 1930).

[44] The reference is to the *Gisla Saga*. See G. W. Dasent (tr.), *The Saga of Gisli the Outlaw* (London [1928]).

[45] See Morris and Magnússon's translation (*Collected Works*, X, 7–47).

[46] The MS here bears the notation "(quote)," omitting both the passage quoted and any indication of its source. The passage inserted is the description of Gunnar

There was a man whose name was Gunnar. He was one of Unna's kinsmen, and his mother's name was Rannveig. Gunnar's father was named Hamond. Gunnar Hamond's son dwelt in Lithend, in the Fleetlithe. He was a tall man in growth, and a strong man—best skilled in arms of all men. He could cut or thrust or shoot if he chose as well with his left as with his right hand, and he smote so swiftly with his sword, that three seemed to flash through the air at once. He was the best shot with the bow of all men, and never missed his mark. He could leap more than his own height, with all his war gear, and as far backwards as forwards. He could swim like a seal, and there was no game in which it was any good for any one to strive with him; and so it has been said that no man was his match. He was handsome of feature, and fair-skinned. His nose was straight, and a little turned up at the end. He was blue-eyed and bright-eyed, and ruddy-cheeked. His hair thick and of good hue, and hanging down in comely curls. The most courteous of men was he, of sturdy frame and strong will, bountiful and gentle, a fast friend, but hard to please when making them. He was wealthy in goods.

I am sorry to say that in this tale the women do not play an agreeable part, they are throughout the make-bates; and Hallgerð Long-Coat, Gunnar's wife and his ruin, has had many a curse laid on her grave down by the waters of the firth near to where the modern Reykjavik stands. Altogether I must say that the man who has read this tale and is not moved by it has no right to give an opinion on such matters.

The shorter story of Gunnlaug the Worm-Tongue is of much the same quality, but the passion of love plays an important part in it. Gisli the Outlaw is no worse except that it is shorter: its hero lives and falls much as Grettir.

There is another short story that of Howard the Halt which is wonderfully dramatic; it recounts the tale of an old man and the signal vengeance taken by him on a scoundrel who has murdered his son, a splendid and generous young man.[47] The Tale of the

---

in Dasent's translation (*The Story of Burnt Njal*, I, 59–60); this version was selected because it was the standard English translation in Morris's time and because, as has been seen before in these notes, Morris used it extensively.

[47] The original title is *Landnámabók*. See Morris and Magnússon's translation ("The Saga Library," I, 1–69).

Banded Men[48] is an exceedingly humorous account of another old man's triumph: this time by the exercise of his mother wit over a set of powerful but somewhat stupid chieftains who had got on the hip the gaffer's son, a man of the same quality as themselves. These are by no means the only sagas which show artistic qualities in the telling; but I think they are the best as to having a decided beginning, middle, and end.

The story of the dwellers at Ere is one of the most interesting of the pure chronicles.[49] The Lax-dalers' Story,[50] and that of Waterdalers[51] are also very interesting the former containing a very touching and beautiful tale, but it is not done justice to by the detail of the story. The detail of the Ere-dwellers' tale is as good as may be.

Besides these traditional-historical sagas there are a few called in contempt by the Icelanders Skrok sagas, that is nonsense-tales; in other words fictions: one at least of these, the story of Viglund the Fair is a very graceful and charming novelette.[52]

Besides all this and a good many lost sagas the names of which still remain the Icelanders did a certain amount of translation: one of the best histories of Thomas Beckett is in Icelandic:[53] the earliest form of the mediaeval tale of Tristram and Iseult is preserved in Icelandic:[54] and several mediaeval Romances were also rendered in that tongue. In ballad literature and purely oral tradition I don't think they are as rich as their kindred on the

---

[48] The original title is *Bandamanna Saga*. See Morris and Magnússon's translation (ibid., I, 73–121).

[49] The original title is *Eyrbyggia Saga*. See Morris and Magnússon's translation, entitled *The Story of the Ere-Dwellers* (ibid., II, 3–186).

[50] The original title is *Laxdaela Saga*. See Thorstein Veblen's translation, *The Laxdaela Saga* (New York, 1925). A poetic version of this saga, "The Lovers of Gudrun," was included by Morris in his *Earthly Paradise* (*Collected Works*, V, 251–395).

[51] The original title is *Vatnsdaela Saga*. See the translation by Vigfusson and Powell (note 20, above).

[52] See Morris and Magnússon's translation (*Collected Works*, X, 81–126).

[53] The original work, by Olafr Hvítaskáld, is entitled *Tómasardrápa* (See Einarsson, op. cit., p. 71).

[54] The reference here is to ". . . *Tristrams saga*, which was translated into Norwegian as early as 1226 for King Hákon," (ibid., p. 149).

mainland; but some very beautiful ballads remain: and there is a very interesting collection of oral stories published not many years ago. I should have mentioned the Song Chronicle of the Sturtings called sometimes the Great Saga which carries on the history of the country till it lost its old tribal liberties and fell into the clutch of the Norway kings in the 13th century.

After this there is little of literary excellence till quite modern times, though some volumes of annals, dry reading enough exist: a curious little vol[ume] called the Tyrkjàràns Saga gives an account of the descent of the Algerine pirates on the island about 1630 and forms an interesting commentary on the state of Europe at that time.[55]

I may finish by saying a word on the present condition of Iceland: they have suffered very much there from bad seasons of late:[56] but I cannot help thinking that in spite of that they could live there very comfortably if they were to extinguish individualism there: the simplest possible form of co-operative commonwealth would suit their needs, and ought not to be hard to establish; as there is no crime there, and no criminal class or class of degradation and education is universal: and unless by some special perversity should the question of politics stand in the way: the only persons who would be losers by it would be the present exploiters of this brave and kind people: and if these men were all shipped off to—well to Davy Jones, there would be many a dry eye at their departure. I speak of this from the sincere affection I have for the Icelandic people who treated me so kindly when I was among them, and who are the descendants, and no unworthy ones, of the bravest men and the best tale-tellers whom the world has ever bred.

---

[55] For further details on this saga, see ibid., pp. 196–9.
[56] Morris himself had been very active on the Committee of the Iceland Famine Relief Fund in 1882 (see *Mackail*, II, 77–79).

[THE PRESENT OUTLOOK
IN POLITICS][1]

It is] good to review the state of political parties from time to time and to try to get an idea of what our relations as socialists are to the general mass of political opinion, whether we are advancing, or retro[gressing], or standing still: in fact we cannot help speculating on the influence ordinary parties may have upon our movement and in what direction they are pushing us as to tactics in carrying on that movement: there are dangers as well as hopes for us in the welter of political life so that it behooves us to look at the prospect with as clear eyes as we can lest we fall into traps. Perhaps however some of you may say that unless to the eyes of an electioneering agent the prospect is so clear that it doesn't need thinking about or looking into closely: but then there will be more than one set of people who will think this, and the prospect will be very different to the

---

[1] The text of this lecture is taken from B.M. Add. MS. 45334(7), which is entirely in Morris's hand. Although the MS bears no title, references to "Bloody Sunday" indicate that it was written shortly after the Trafalgar Square riots of Nov. 13, 1887. This evidence combines with the reference to a socialist audience (p. 206) and detailed newspaper reports to definitely establish that the lecture was first delivered under the above title on Dec. 18, 1887 (see Appendix I, 12–18–87 and 1–8–88, and Appendix II, item 120).

different sets of people. The Gladstonian Liberal[2] e.g. thinks he can see quite clearly a speedy end of the present Tory Government,[3] and his own hero in power again, carrying with a triumphant majority a home rule bill without a flaw: Ireland contented and prosperous: trade recovering in England, those tiresome, worrying, pertinacious Socialists shut up not by police attacks (unless on the sly) but by the good sense of the political working men who clearly understand that they are only sustained by Tory money, which by the [bye] accounts for their being so overburdened with the latter commodity; and in short the Great Liberal Party united or not settling down, Irish matters being arranged, to doing—I'm sure *I* don't know what—looking about them I suppose from the official benches. Then there are the Chamberlainites; they also have a vision of success it seems: limited however, as far as I can note it, to the keeping of Gladstone out of office till he is good enough to die, and meanwhile to have the noble reward of plenteous flattery from their Tory allies for their patriotism and freedom from faction.[4] Again there are the definite Whigs belonging to the same party or semi-party, whose hopes are perhaps the clearest of all and the likeliest of fulfillment, for they hope and believe that parliament will do nothing at all in any direction whatever. Again there is the Irish parliamentary party who believe that they are within a measurable distance of a parliament (sham or otherwise) in Dublin. I wish I could hope that there were many of them who had any idea of what they can do in case they get the said parliament to utilize the steady

---

[2] After the famous parliamentary division of June 8, 1886, the Liberal Party was split into two camps: those who accepted Gladstone's leadership and the principle of Irish self-determination (hence the "Gladstonian Liberals"), and the opponents of home rule, who were led by Joseph Chamberlain under the banner of "Liberal Unionism" (see *Commonweal*, June 12, 1886).

[3] The rejection of Gladstone's Home Rule Bill (see footnote 2, above) toppled his government and necessitated a general election. In the Tory-Liberal Unionist victory that followed the election Lord Salisbury was asked to form a ministry, which he did in July, 1886. For Morris's immediate reaction to these political changes, see his "Political Notes," *Commonweal*, Aug. 7, 1886.

[4] After the general election the Liberal Unionists controlled 78 seats in the House of Commons. This made the Tory government of Salisbury dependent on their support to remain in power, and gave the Unionists a position of influence similar to that of the Parnellites in the previous ministry. See Ensor, op. cit., p. 172.

heroism of the Irish people. Then there is the great Tory party who seem to be quite as clear that all is going on well with them as the Gladstonites are of the contrary, although to their confusion there is arising a Torier-than-Tory party among them who have taken down the old banner of protection from the dusty, mouldy, chaff-littered cock-loft where it has lain so many years, and for their parts also are very clear that it will lead them to victory.[5]

It is clear that all these parties except the Irish are offering some bait to that part of the public which each one thinks is at once the post powerful, and the most easily influenced by their special dogma (if they have any). I say that this [is] clear because they are all of them so confident of success, or at least deem it politic to seem so. But of course the bait[s] offered by those parties which [have] any pretext to be considered as popular should be the clearest and biggest though I am not sure that they are. The Gladstonite party e.g. offers some relative extension of the franchise, in the hope that the new electors will vote for them, besides a half promise to disestablish the State Church as a bait to the nonconformists. The Unionists offer some vague hope of progressive measures if they can succeed in keeping the Tories in office. The fair traders offer the working men higher and steadier wages; nay the very Tories throw out hints about dishing the Liberals with more Liberal measures in order to catch votes from the working men discontented with the party they have mostly supported; and on the look-out for some opportunity of bettering themselves and serving-out their misleaders at one and the same time.

Of course this has always been more or less the state of things in a country nominally governed by a party majority in Parliament; so far there is nothing much to differentiate the present condition of parties from other times; all the more since though there is an extra number of groups, there are still as regards the game of Ins and Outs but two parties; the Salisbury Tories and the Gladstone Liberals: the group of blended Whigs and Cham-

---

[5] This was largely in reaction to foreign protectionist tariffs against English goods (ibid., pp. 275–6).

berlainites that call themselves Unionist Liberals whatever they
may call themselves will vote Tory till the crisis is over, and
mostly to the end of the chapter: and the protectionist Tories
have no intention of rebelling against their leaders who on these
fiscal matters have accepted the opinions of Cobden and Bright.[6]
For voting in Parliament and for parliamentary candidature there
are but two parties only I repeat, and if the great Liberal Party
ever comes together again, it will find that as far as numbers are
concerned the coming together will not help it much, as the
greater part of the dissentients will have declared themselves
Tories or will stand out as Whig allies of the Tories. However it is
probable that even this outward show of coming together will
never take place: because (if I may leave this formal word-chop-
ping about these contemptible factions for a minute) one must
remember that glibly as people talk of the settlement of the Irish
question it is not going to be settled by any Home Rule Bill big or
little that Mr. Gladstone may succeed in carrying through parliament: the two sections can only come together by the Gladstonites abandoning every rag of principle that they yet hold; I don't
say that it's impossible for them to do that: but then that will
complicate the matter by losing them their Irish support. So I say
there are the Ins and the Outs: and if you say, but this is only a
matter of the shifting groups of the M.P.s, I must remind you that
the political public, the ordinary voters, follow the lead of these
men with quite remarkable docility, and in fact they do represent
the political public whatever they do for the people at large in
that respect.

Now these Ins and Outs form two parties and no doubt the
struggle between them is exciting enough to those engaged in it
though somewhat dull to onlookers, but what real difference is
there between them? Well on ordinary occasions *none*. In matters
of administration *none;* in the leading of opinion, in the helping
of that lame dog the working public over the stile of livelihood
none. It is however necessary to find something or other which

---

[6] The reference here is to the great economists of the Liberal Party, Richard
Cobden and John Bright, who were the leaders of the "Manchester School" (see
footnote 8 to [The Depression of Trade], p. 125.

will serve as a bone of contention, and this function falls as a matter of course to the Liberal Party as progressists. It is their business to find something that can be fought over and which will not commit the progressive party too much if they carry the day; something also on which a compromise is possible and the fight over which will last long enough: such a subject has been found by the Gladstonites in the Irish question and in many respects the invention has been a useful one for parliamentary purposes: in the name of all patience it will last long enough: it needs not, to all appearance involve the Liberal party in revolutionary measures, and compromise was possible in the case of victory in the early stages at least, and that was enough since as you know no statesman ever looks six months ahead: so the Irish question was taken out of the "difference bag" and chosen as the bone to fight for, and I admit has not turned out well; being contrary to expectation too serious a subject to be played over by the two sides to the game. But we must not be too hard on Mr. Gladstone for this, or think that he acted recklessly: it would in fact have been a safe subject enough if it had not been for the growth of Socialism in some form or other in this island, and it would have been too much to expect of any statesman that he should have taken any account of an intellectual movement in an early stage. Besides he could not take anything else out of the difference-bag except the disestablishment of the Church, and after some hesitation he put that back; partly because he was afraid of his followers and of offending the respectability with which the establishment is so closely interwoven, and partly also I believe from a genuine personal love which he has (like Charles I) for that curious bundle of subterfuges and compromises the Anglican Communion. Also his last attempt at governing discontented Ireland was not a very happy one, and as of course he hoped to have a good long spell of office he did not want to start again on that tack: so in a way he was forced to make the battle over the Irish Question probably without foreseeing the serious split which followed, and which certainly was brought about by the Whigs and the more knowing of the advanced Liberals perceiving that the question was *not* a safe one but involved danger to property, threats against which were already in the air in other parts.

Of course the result of all this has been something which the English parliament never intended; it has been to land them in a real quarrel over Ireland; a quarrel too in which the Liberals are led by the Irish who are receiving real support from the democratic and socialist element in Great Britain. I don't mean to say that this latter element has done much if anything to further the matter in parliament, except so far as it has made the opposition to Home Rule more stubborn on the part of the Tories and their allies but it has certainly much embittered the reactionary feeling generally, of which more hereafter.

This then is the position in which we are landed as far as the parliamentary parties are concerned: the Ins and Outs game is being carried on as usual, though there has been a good deal of shuffling about of persons: but the cause of quarrel beyond the general agreement of both sides to fleece the people having been found has turned out to have a dangerous element of reality in it, partly because the Irish people is in deadly earnest to establish its practical independence, and partly because there is a gathering feeling towards revolution about which has been able to fix itself on the simple cases of exploitation by rack-rent going on in Ireland.

As a consequence of the Liberal party having stumbled on a revolutionary question it has weakened itself very much and has not only lost a great number of adherents but also great prestige, because under the grievous circumstances of its having to push forward a side of the popular cause it is compelled to fight soft and so encourage its foes and discourage its friends; and at present as far as ordinary parliamentary events go it is not easy to see anything which will unseat the present Tory majority.[7]

So far as ordinary parliamentary events go indeed; but outside of those there are events brewing which though they do not directly threaten the present Tory government, the Tories will yet have to reckon with. Although the putting forward of Home Rule has not answered the purpose of the Liberal party, it has served another purpose than merely consolidating the Tory party and winning it the open alliance of the Whigs. It has changed

---

[7] This Tory ministry did in fact remain in power for six years, 1886–1892.

and is changing the aspect of the Radicals and has given them
something to hope for beyond the narrow circle of a few reforms
scarcely any of which could be looked on as possible means to an
end very vaguely foreseen by the great mass of radicals; of course
it has acted on them as a solvent as it has on the Liberals and has
turned some of them into Whigs, but those of them that are left
are quite different from the radicals of a few years back; as they
will find out after the first measure of Home Rule is passed and
they are face to face with their old radical program of electoral
reform, peace, disestablishment, and what not. They will find all
that very dull after the Irish campaign, and will no longer be
content with it; for they have practically committed themselves
to the attack on property which has scared the Tories into acting
in their ancient manner, made the Liberals—well over-cautious
—and petrified the Whigs, if that were necessary. In fact the
spirit of the Radicals, where they remain Radicals, is getting to be
much more like that of the Chartists than what we have known
them; they have taken a step towards revolution, and consequently have pretty much lost all the importance they had, if ever
they had much, in parliament, and their old allies are preparing
to throw them off for good and all when they have squeezed the
last drop of use out of them. This is what they must always
expect: the constitutional or non-revolutionary game of play must
in a cons[titutional] country be fought out between the respectable Tory reactionaries and the moderate Liberals: the latter will
have nothing to do with the extreme progressive politicians except on the terms that they shall be their humble followers with
no will of their own. The Radicals as a parliamentary party can
never be strong, because at every advance in opinion the timid
ones of their party drop off from them, and the genuine ones who
have accepted the advances get further and further from anything that is likely to be put forward in parliament and as aforesaid become political outcasts: their true function we shall see
presently.

Well I have mentioned all the recognized groups of politicians,
if indeed the last group the extreme radicals or democrats can be
said to be recognized. Above this group all are engaged as aforesaid in playing the game of Ins and Outs; but this they only use

for a cat's paw now and then. There remains another party lower
even than the democrats, which party we are probably all of [us]
much interested in, I mean the Socialists. As to their position we
must all admit that it has much changed from what it was a few
years ago, when there were in England but a few remains of the
earlier school of Utopists,[8] a certain number of foreign refugees,[9]
and a very few English people who were intimate with them.
This made up what there was of socialism in England, and the
influence it had upon general thought and politics was almost nil.
I[t] was the common thing to say that in a country so advanced
in political freedom as England socialism had no standpoint: that
it was [the] disease of the absolutist countries where freedom of
speech was unknown, or one of the forms of Chartism which was
killed by the reform-bill and the repeal of the corn laws—And
now what is it? Feeble enough numerically you may say if you
count all the heads sheltered by the socialist organizations, but
then see how the phrases about it have altered. 'We are all
socialists now,'[10] is the common phrase today: or 'to a great extent
I agree with your criticism of existing institutions but—' and so
on and so on. In short socialism is permeating all society, and
consequently following the analogy of the political position of the
radicals stirring up furious enmity as well as attracting friendship
and curiosity. Let us for a little consider its relations to the
various groups of thought and political action, none of which

---

[8] These "Utopists" were the last survivors of Chartism and the co-operative
schemes of Robert Owen. With them may be grouped the few remaining followers
of Saint-Simon and Fourier in England (see *Romantic to Revolutionary*, pp. 315–7,
and William Morris and E. Belfort Bax, *Socialism, Its Growth and Outcome*,
London, 1893, pp. 206–17).

[9] These were the refugees "from the terror in Russia, from the Commune, from the
persecutions of the Austrian police, and—after 1878—from Bismarck's Anti-Social-
ist laws in Germany" (*Romantic to Revolutionary*, p. 317).

[10] This statement originally came from Sir William Harcourt, one of Gladstone's
most trusted lieutenants. About the same time as the composition of this lecture,
Morris sketched the circumstances of the remark: "The Government are taking
credit to themselves for their [Irish] Allotment Bill. . . . Sir William Harcourt has
nothing better to say about it than twit his political opponents with inconsistency,
reminding them that when a similar measure was talked of before, its furtherers
were called Socialists. 'But now,' says he, 'it seems we are all Socialists' "
(*Commonweal*, Aug. 20, 1887).

venture quite to ignore it. First there are the declared reactionists, the pure Tories. They you see are beginning to pay it the
compliment of persecution,[11] which means that they are growing
afraid of it; partly because they at last have begun to see that
they, once the old sham-feudal absolutist-bureaucratic party who
were attached to that expiring system, have tacked themselves on
to another system that is waning the commercial monopolist-bu-
reaucracy; that is the essential and enduring part of their fear;
the passing part of it is that unlucky business of Ireland which
Gladstone has lugged into the parliamentary arena, and with
which also they see that socialism is connected. So much for the
Tories we frighten them. Next come the Whigs pure and simple,
and perhaps one may have to withdraw the statement that no
group ignored socialism, and [say] that the Whigs pure and
simple do so. But then that's a way they have with everything
outside the four walls of Mr. Barry's Gothic hall at St. Stephens:[12]
that as far as discussion is concerned is their world.

Let us pass to the Liberals: if we frighten the Tories I think we
make the Liberals uneasy; for they note that the thing is spreading and wonder what the deuce it means, and are nervous lest
perhaps they may have to learn something new, and perhaps

---

[11] The "persecution" referred to here was the struggle between left-wing organizations and the government over the right of the former groups to speak in the
streets and other public places. At the climax of the struggle, Sir Charles Warren,
Commissioner of the London Police, prohibited a meeting that had been scheduled
by socialist and radical groups for November 13, 1887, later known as "Bloody
Sunday." When columns of marchers attempted to defy his order, he dispersed
them by repeated charges of mounted and foot police. Trafalgar Square, the
scheduled place of meeting, was kept clear, but a number of the demonstrators
were injured in the melee (see *Romantic to Revolutionary*, pp. 568–77, and *The
Times*, Nov. 14, 1887).

[12] Sir Charles Barry (1795–1860) was one of the leading architects of the Gothic
Revival. The "Gothic hall at St. Stephens" is Westminster Hall, erected on the site
of the cloisters and crypt of St. Stephen and incorporated into the Houses of
Parliament in Barry's design. Morris strongly opposed further restorations to the
hall in 1885 (see Appendix I, 3–11–85, and Appendix II, item 58). In this context
the reference might best be taken simply as an allusion to the Houses of
Parliament. On Sir Charles Barry's place in the history of English architecture, see
R. Furneaux Jordan, "Sir Charles Barry's Centenary: Skyline for a Monument,"
The Observer, May 8, 1960, and W. J. Loftie, "The Palace of Westminster," *The
Art Journal*, XLVI (Jan., 1889), 24–8.

have to shift their ground once more: I don't mean to say that they have begun to learn anything about it: Lord Roseberry[13] e.g. said the other day that Socialism meant sharing up all wealth, and that if it were shared up it would soon become unequally distributed again. A favourite theory with some of these bold politicians, whose watchword is for God's sake don't break up the party, is that Socialism is a faddist theory made use of by the Tories to injure the Liberals at elections: in short they seem to confound us with the Kelly and Peters lot:[14] and scent fair trade and sugar bounties in the wind when they pass by our meetings.

Then comes our relation to the true radicals: I think most of these will agree with me when I say that they are being very seriously permeated with Socialism; the old radicalism has become Whig-Liberalism, the new is fast becoming undecided socialism. When it becomes more decided the reactionists and the Whigs (stationaries) may perhaps cull a few more of the timider of the radicals, but there will be a democratic party instructed if not led by the socialists; indeed that is fast happening now, and perhaps it only needs a Liberal Bloody Sunday[15] to complement the Tory one for such a consolidation. Meantime our radical friends will I hope pardon me for looking upon them chiefly as affording a recruiting ground for socialists, since I believe that almost all the present genuine radicals will soon become socialists: yet as a party in spite of their parliamentary weakness they

---

[13] Lord Roseberry (1847–1929) was Foreign Secretary in the Gladstone ministry of 1886. Before that time Morris had worked with him on some occasions when both men were active in the Eastern Question Association and various public services, such as the Kyrle Society. See, for example, Appendix I, 1–27–81.

[14] The "Kelly and Peters lot" refers to the fair-trade movement among workingmen. T. M. Kelly and Samuel Peters were both on the committee of the central organization, the Workmen's National Association for the Abolition of Foreign Sugar Bounties, which Charles Bradlaugh had earlier attacked as a Tory front. Kelly and Peters gained a certain notoriety through their sponsorship of a meeting in Trafalgar Square on Feb. 8, 1886. When the meeting terminated in riots that embarrassed the Gladstone ministry, Bradlaugh claimed that it had been financed by Lord Salisbury and that Kelly and Peters had acted as Tory agents in the affair. See the account of the Peters vs. Bradlaugh suit in *The Times*, April 19, 1888.

[15] See footnote 11, above.

have another function viz. that of pushing forward measures which will help forward the disintegration of society, but which are not really socialistic in principle: again more of this hereafter.

But we have something else to deal with outside all these political parties, to wit all that very large part of the public that is not political in any sense: with the upper-class portion of it we need not concern ourselves much, since the greater part of these people only want to be let alone to thrive on the privilege of robbing labour and are willing instruments in the hands of the reactionists. However there are here and there a few who have not troubled themselves about politics because they have supposed the Gladstonite creed to be the ultimatum of progress, and have not seen in it anything like salvation to the human race from its realization, and who are really ready for the reception of socialism when they come across it. I say a few, because I fancy most of those who are worth anything have been touched by Ruskin's writings and converted into Socialists of some kind.

The other non-politicals belong to the working classes and must I fear be set down as the majority of them: and these again can be divided into people fairly well off for workmen yet so harassed by the struggle for life that they are consciously rather on the side of the masters who rob them and relieve them of responsibility, and those still more beaten down who are scarcely conscious of anything except that they are weary and hungry and cold: what can be done with these latter save feeding them in a miserable, hopeless way, before the social revolution comes to offer them useful work and due livelihood, makes men of them in short, I know not, nor does anybody else. But one thing I wish to say here that if you suppose you will find all the intelligence among the better-off workmen, and all the lack of it among the unemployed, the fringe of labour, you are deceived and that this is by no means the case: don't let anybody hug himself with the comforting notion that in the struggle for existence which the propertyless workman has to carry on, deftness, industry, thrift even ensure a man from falling into lack of employment and the lowest misery; that is by no means the case. Moreover it is quite as common to find that lack of intelligence which servile depend-ence on masters implies among the better-off workmen, and when you remember that even the Trades Unions are somewhat tarred with this stick (so far as they are not political) you must admit that this is a difficult element to deal with: in point of fact it is just this element which is what we mean when we speak of the apathy of the working-classes to their interests, and this slaves'-apathy really is analogous to the slave-holders' apathy among the well-to-do classes, and until it is thrown off it is little good abusing the latter for their apathy which is but an agreement with their comfortable position considering there are so many who acquiesce in their miserable position when they could alter it if they would but shake off their apathy. One cannot leave this subject without saying that amongst the most apathetic to their own interests are the workers who are usually assumed to be the most complete workmen, the *hands* in the great factory districts; it is easy to see why this should be; they are most under commercial drill, and are made to feel more than other workers that they are a mere part of the machinery of production for profit, and that if that machinery stops for a minute they are undone: therefore they refuse to take any responsibility on their own behoof further than helping the owners of the machinery not to strain the human part of it to the bursting-point or deprive it of fuel calculated according [to] the most economical scale: it is difficult to see any remedy for this slavishness until the workers find out that they are a part of the public as well as a part of the profit-grinding machine, and that the said machine is villainously ill-adapted to their welfare in the latter capacity.

Well now I will recapitulate as briefly as may be the way our movement looks at all these elements of the present political outlook: First the definite reactionaries, people who instinctively feel that it is their business to resist all progress and will only yield when they are forced to do so. Their political representative is parliament generally but especially the Whig-Tory party therein. Their intellectual representatives for strange to say they have such are the prig literateurs who once posed as advanced men, but are now shocked at the advance drawing near which they encouraged when it was a long way off: they are very superior persons.[16] Next there is the party of the moderates who call themselves Liberals in parliament who, blinder than the definite reactionists, believe that the advance will go just as far as them and stop there—perhaps forever; but at any rate as long as they live: these are wholly parliamentary and are (justly) much despised by the intellectual prigs, who indeed despise all things good and bad.

Next come the Democrats with whom we must class the Irish party who are their only representatives in parliament. These include the mass of politically-minded working-men.

Next comes the non-political, well-to-do, almost-entirely reactionaries. Lastly come the non-political working-men, mere slaves, and part of the profit-machine; whether they be 'intelligent working-men' or the unhappy drudges of the fringe of labour.

Of these the first two, the reactionaries or Whig-Tory and the sham-progressists or Liberals, are our declared enemies and there is not a pin to choose between them; we can get nothing from them except under the influence of fear of immediate consequences: add to this that we are wholly governed by them—by our enemies in short. The democrats on the other hand although we differ from them and though they sometimes through ignorance oppose us are our allies; they are working for us whenever they are not dragged along by the left wing of the enemy, the sham-progressists.

The non-political well-to-do are but a part of the reactionary party. The non-political working men are material for us and circumstances to work on.

Now what is going on amidst these various groups is that the revolution is preparing, a fact which we and the reactionaries know, and which the other groups ignore. It is a commonplace to say that the economical situation is the chief factor in this approaching change; but it is well to remember this if we feel

---

[16] It seems safe to assume that Morris would include James A. Froude, Matthew Arnold, and Henry George in this category (see footnote 12 to "Art and Labour," p. 108, and "Notes," *Commonweal*, Jan. 21, 1888).

discouraged at the stupid and unsympathetic attitude of the workmen of Lancashire e.g.[17] As time goes on the eyes of these men will be opened to the fact that they must accept their share of responsibility in the system of production and they will then have to admit that the system must be changed. Also it must be remembered that the disintegration of the old system will possibly be slow, and probably will be apparently interrupted by periods of "prosperity" and that during such periods the movement will have to depend on the face of it entirely on the intelligence of the workers and those who understand what 'society' really means.

Well at present the economical situation has had more obvious influence on the political than it has had for many years, since the Chartist times, say: and consequently, (to set aside for a little the direct efforts of the socialists) our enemies, our governors, are growing afraid on the one hand, and on the other our allies, the democrats, are learning that there is something beyond what is known as mere political freedom; they are learning to know the difference between the means and the end; and just in proportion to their learning of that lesson will they become formidable really although they may appear to be weaker than they were; because whereas when their demands were for "political" reforms they were really helping our governors to govern, but now as their demands are assimilating to ours they are asking what our governors cannot yield without compulsion, and are therefore embarrassing our governors in their governing. This is in short the explanation of the Tory reaction so much crowed over by the Tory newspapers; the Liberals are melting into mere reactionaries, the democrats are preparing to accept Socialism; so that the Tories are not really attacking their parliamentary opponents, or the Liberals defending political progress; but the former are attacking the great social change, and the latter are—letting them do so.[18]

---

[17] Attempts by League agitators to turn miners' strikes into a strong provincial socialist movement encountered several reversals at this time (see *Romantic to Revolutionary*, pp. 550–51).

[18] Bloody Sunday did not elicit any strong protest from the Liberals, nominally the champions of popular causes. Morris here refers to this silence of the parliamen-

As a result for the time the Tories are very strong and venture on proceedings which a few years ago they durst not have done. They know e.g. that if their conduct in London is called in question when Parliament meets that it will [be] a hollow affair; and that they will gain rather than lose votes by letting loose the police to attack peaceful citizens in the streets and imprisoning them afterwards for the crime of being blugeoned and ridden down.[19] Again as to the Irish question, although it is the fashion for speakers of either party to regret the waste of time that it causes, and though they both profess to be very anxious to get through it so as to deal with British matters: we all know that that is a most transparent piece of humbug, and that both parties will spread out the Irish question as far as it will go like scanty butter over sturdy bread, so as to prevent if possible any other question being dealt with, until the Liberals can pull out of that difference bag a good safe party question which will be of no importance at all to the general public.

The fact is that neither party knows what to do at present: the Liberals have reached the end of their tether, and the time has not yet come for the Tories to take their stand on mere commercial absolutism, although there are ominous signs that they will before long be able to do so: but that will mean the revolution (as people generally use the word) in full swing.

Meantime accidents may or rather will happen to confuse the logical development of events, which certainly does seem to point to the gradual building up of a great labour party. I have been only speaking about politics in Great Britain and Ireland, but continental Europe is not standing still to speak very mildly. It is possible that a system of oppression that depended wholly on armed force for its support might last as long as the world if you could shut out economical influences; but since you clearly can-

---

tary Liberals, who might well have used the occasion for a concerted attack on the Home Secretary and his appointee, Police Commissioner Sir Charles Warren (*Commonweal*, Jan. 7, 1888).

[19] R. B. Cunninghame Graham, M.P., and John Burns, among others, were arrested for their parts in the Bloody Sunday riots, and Cunninghame Graham was considerably beaten up in the process. For Morris's reaction to the arrests and subsequent sentencing, see "Notes on News," *Commonweal*, Jan. 28, 1888.

not, the time will come when even the German Army will not be able to ride rough-shod over all the necessities and desires of a huge population:[20] at the very worst when it has conquered all the world, all the world will conquer it. But to the worst we shall not come. Meantime in Germany at any rate reaction is going on merrily and it is a curious spectacle for civilization to see the most intelligent people in the world allowing themselves to be muzzled by one cynical old man. Well, you may be sure that the muzzle is clapped on because 'tis needed, and that when we need it we shall have it if an unlikely thing I admit we develop a Bismarck amongst us. The new Socialist law is no doubt a sign of progress;[21] and may be a sign of approaching European war, though I decline to be any longer moved by war scares which are probably got up by statesmen-thieves or stockjobbing d[itt]o:[22] however a European war is a possibility at any rate; and since England couldn't go to war unless at the last extremity such an event would no doubt make the Jingos[23] very bold, and also would

---

[20] Although Bismarck's Socialist Law of 1878 had been renewed periodically and was still in force when Morris wrote this lecture, it had not succeeded in slowing the growth of socialism in Germany. The German Reichstag elections in 1887 showed such an increase in socialist strength that Bismarck declared a "minor state of siege" in a number of German cities, including Berlin. "A large number of expulsions took place in 1887, and strict watch was continually kept upon Socialist movements . . ." (William Harbutt Dawson, *German Socialism and Ferdinand Lassalle*, London, 1888, p. 278).

[21] In October, 1887, the Socialist Law was extended for two years, but the inability of the government to add to the severity of its terms was considered a victory for the socialists (ibid., p. 279).

[22] Lord Salisbury's Conservative government viewed France and Russia as the potential aggressors of Europe and therefore leaned toward Germany in any quarrel that involved the European powers. Just at this time there was considerable talk of a coming war between France and Germany and of the possibility that England might be drawn into such a conflict on the German side. Morris's early experiences in the E.Q.A. had made him highly sceptical of war-scares, since he later concluded that Disraeli's bluster had been largely a matter of diplomatic tactics, that in fact he "never intended to go to war" ("Notes on News," *Commonweal*, Jan. 7, 1888).

[23] The term "Jingo" is a legacy of the Eastern Question crisis of 1877–1878, when the war party adopted a theme-song with the following verses:

> We don't want to fight, but, by jingo, if we do,
> We've got the ships, we've got the men; we've got the money too.

See *Artist, Writer, Socialist*, II, 51.

make for us a short period of factitious 'prosperity' by dint of drawing off more labour from production of utilities: both of which in turn would help to strengthen the temporary reaction.

In any case we have got to remember this, that neither war scares, nor war, nor the shabby oppression of cowardly shop-keepers,[24] nor the rigging of the markets, nor even the unconscious shifting of them under the influence of desperate competition for profits, will, or can get rid of the fact that the present system of production no longer suffices for the needs and aspiration of the present population. That in spite of growing cooperation for production, and growing mastery over the forces of nature, in spite of all the elaborate organization of commerce, we are poor when we ought to be wealthy, because labour is not organized and wealth not distributed in the interest of the whole public but in the interest of a privileged class, who not only produce nothing themselves, and tax the whole people to support their idle lives, but also waste the greater part of the labour of those whom they idly live upon. That is one side of the situation, and the other is that the knowledge of this stupidity can no longer be kept from those that suffer from it: you shall hear sometimes a reactionist saying that people are better off now than they were and more discontented and therefore all is well: you need not argue against his premises, because if it is so it is a sure sign that the change is at hand.

It is this that makes such a strange jumble of politics today; that makes refined and superior persons set mere brute force on a pedestal to be worshipped, so that we seem to be going back to the days of Peterloo;[25] and it is exactly this which we as socialists have to deal with: if we can but make it clear to the workers that

---

[24] Shopkeepers with places of business in the area of Trafalgar Square started a movement for its closure to public meetings early in 1887. The success of this movement in November, 1887, marked the beginning of the disturbance that culminated in Bloody Sunday (see *The Times*, Nov. 14, 1887).

[25] On August 16, 1819, at St. Peter's Field, Manchester, a crowd of some 60,000 people met to petition for parliamentary reform. Special constables and detachments of the Lancashire and Chesire Yeomanry attacked the crowd, killing 11 and wounding "about four hundred" according to one estimate. The incident later was known simply as "the Peterloo Massacre" (see E. L. Woodward, *The Age of Reform*, Oxford, 1938, p. 62).

they cannot live on comfortably as slaves even according to their present wretched standard, and that the first step that a slave must take in order to become a free man is to assume responsibility with all its attendant troubles, politics will have entered into a new phase: nothing will be allowed to pass current because it is 'necessary to the stability of society,' because it is 'not within the scope of practical politics,' and so on. We shall look our present system in the face and see what it is fit for, and shall not think it necessary to spend nine-pence on the mending of sixpence because it is called reform. It is certain that even now while we speak politics of the old kind, the shuffle of Ins and Outs, are waning away, and the new politics that are taking the place of the old mean a struggle against stupidity for the reconstruction of society on a tolerable instead of intolerable basis, so that at last we may be led into the happy days when society shall be what its name means, and politics will be no more.

WHAT SOCIALISTS WANT[1]

Socialists no more than other people believe that persons are naturally equal: there are amongst men all varieties of disposition, and desires, and degrees of capacity; nevertheless these differences and inequalities are very much increased by the circumstances amongst which a man lives and by those that surrounded the lives of his parents: and these circumstances are more or less under the control of society, that is of the ordered arrangement of persons among which we live. So I say first that granted that men are born with certain tendencies those tendencies can be developed for good and evil by the conditions of our lives, and those conditions are in our own hands to deal with, taking us nation by nation as a whole. If we are careful to be prudent and wise for ourselves and just towards other people those inequalities which are natural can be used for making life pleasanter and more varied:[2] but if we act stupidly and unjustly

---

[1] The text of this lecture is taken from B.M. Add. MS. 45333(6), which is entirely in Morris's hand. Contemporary reports indicate that it was first scheduled for delivery on Nov. 6, 1887; but the first delivery that was reported occurred on Feb. 5, 1888 (see Appendix I, 11–6–87 and 2–5–88, and Appendix II, item 115).

[2] In the MS the preceding clauses read, "Those inequalities which are natural and inevitable can if we are careful to be prudent and wise for ourselves and just towards other people can be used for making life pleasanter and more varied."

they become a source of misery to many, and of degradation to all.[3]

I have admitted that men are not naturally equal, yet all persons must admit that there are certain things which we all need; in that respect we are equal: we all need food, clothes, and shelter, and clearly if we need these things we need them in sufficiency, and of good quality, or else we have not really got them. Since then these needs are common to all, it follows that if anyone is not able to satisfy his needs in these respects there is something wrong somewhere, either with nature, or the man himself, or with the society of which he forms a part and which therefore dictates to him how he shall live.

But these things, food, clothes, and shelter, but these are our needs as animals only; as men and women we have other needs: however much we may vary we all of us need leisure and amusement and education of some sort or other for all men have the power of thinking, and that power may be repressed and may be developed, just as a plant may be starved or made fruitful by the quality of the soil it is planted in and cultivation it has. Again then I say that if a person has not leisure, pleasure, and education they fall short of human necessaries and there is something wrong somewhere.

So you see whatever inequality I admit among people, I claim this equality that everybody should have full enough food, clothes, and housing, and full enough leisure, pleasure, and education; and that everybody should have a certainty of these necessaries: in this case we should be equal as Socialists use the word: if we are not so equal, I assert that something is wrong either with nature, the individual man or the Society which tells him how to live.

There are, however, interlinear marks in the MS to indicate an alteration in syntax. While it is not possible to determine from them exactly how Morris intended the clauses to be read, the reading given here seems the most likely one. In this case one superfluous "can" has been omitted and capitalization changed to fit the new syntax.

[3] A more detailed discussion of human differences and their political consequences is contained in the lecture "Equality" (*Artist, Writer, Socialist,* II, 197–203). See also Glasier, pp. 118–21.

Now does this reasonable equality exist amongst us? There can be but one answer to that: it does *not:* this is the richest country in the world; there are numbers of clever and capable people in it, and numbers of hard-working people: nevertheless every year there are persons who are starved to death in it, and there are vast numbers of persons who have not enough food and enough clothing or good enough housing and who have no hope of obtaining these things: still more who have no leisure, except the dreadful leisure which lack of employment, that is starvation, gives them, no pleasure worthy of a man, nay far less than the beasts have, no education in the true sense of the word, no chance of developing the innate power of thought that lies in them, in a word in this the richest country that ever has been there are many poor.

Now consider, what is a rich person and what is a poor one? It is worth while asking you to consider that, because people sometimes tell us that poverty is no evil and that a poor person can be as happy as a rich one, and so forth: whether they expect the poor to believe them I do not know: they want to make the best of things I suppose which as they are well-to-do they don't find a difficult matter. Well let us see what is a rich and what a poor person: a rich man is sure of all those necessaries I spoke of bodily and mental, and other natural objects of desire he can reasonably hope to obtain: a poor man is scantily supplied with the bodily necessaries, has not got the mental ones, and risks losing even what he has, so that he lives in perpetual anxiety; as to the desire for superfluities, he has the desire indeed, but no hope of ever satisfying it: and I must say that all this seems to me as to all thoughtful persons a dreadful thing.

If therefore there are rich and poor in a rich country I am sure there must be something wrong: either with nature, or the individual persons, or with the system of Society under which such things happen.

Now I know that there are many people who say it is the fault of nature, and usually the same persons think it is also the fault of the poor people: in other words they think that certain persons are naturally incapable of earning their own livelihood, and that these people form the great mass whom we call the poor. I shall be able I hope to show you how greatly they are mistaken in this view.

There are others who think that it is the fault of the system of Society, and who try in various ways to alter that system, and all such people may fairly be called Socialists, though they don't all call themselves so, because they think it possible that a condition of things could be brought about in which these wrongs could be redressed and these gross inequalities made an end of: and it is cheering to think that the numbers of those who think this are increasing fast, and that many people are Socialists without knowing it; when they come to know it Socialism will be in a fair way to be realized.

Now then, let us look at that opinion which holds that it [is] necessary and natural that the poor should exist, that it is people's own fault that they are poor, and that nature has made them so.

It is a law of nature that mankind must labour in order to live, and men by means of their ever-increasing intelligence have striven to turn this law to their advantage by associating their labour and organizing it till in civilized countries they have brought it about that an ordinary average man can produce by his labour more than enough to keep himself (and his family) alive: that has been the case for a very long time; but in modern civilization the power of producing wealth has very much increased by the means of ever-improving organization of labour, and the invention of machinery: to give you an instance; it has been computed that in the great wheat-growing plains of Dakota the labour of one average man produces in a year 5500 bushels of wheat. However there is no need to go into elaborate figures and calculations on this point, because the very fact that there are rich and poor in the same community proves that the existence of the poor is not caused by natural laws but by artificial arrangements: for the poor do certainly labour, and by their labour produce the things on which men live and the luxuries which they enjoy, whereas on the other hand the rich either do not work at all, or if they do work do not produce wealth by their work: therefore the poor by their labour keep the rich: rich men are pensioners of poor ones, and if the poor were to withdraw their pensions the rich would either starve or have to work for their living. Do you doubt this by any chance? Then let us have an example. A man who owns a factory, and money which he does not need to spend on his own keep employs, say, a thousand men to work in that factory and by their labour they produce so much goods: why does he employ them? Clearly in order that he may get a certain advantage from them: what is that advantage? Well, he must pay these men something from out of that extra money he has, because if he didn't as they have nothing of their own except their bodies and minds and the power of labour in them they would starve to death; what does he pay them then? Does he let them have what they have produced by means of his factory after having made a fair deduction for the wear and tear of machinery the expenses of bringing the goods to market, the risks incidental to manufacture and trade and due payment for his superintendence, supposing him to be capable of superintending? If he did so he would have an advantage in employing them because he would be able to help them in their work by means of it, and so he would earn his livelihood along with them. Now that I think would be a fair bargain the details of which could be easily arranged among honest and reasonable men, and which would gradually tend to the perfecting of fairness between the associated workers. A fair bargain but if any workman ventures to propose it to his employer, he had better have another situation in the background lest he should get the sack for being a Socialist. For this fair bargain is, so far as the factory in question is concerned, a Socialistic one. As a matter of fact the advantages he proposes to gain from so employing men is very different from that: what he does is to pay wages to his men, that is to give them as little as they will take without revolting or striking, and to keep for himself, and make the most of, all that they produce over and above those wages. And if [he] does not get by this means more than will cover the wear and tear of machinery, the risks of business, the expenses of marketing, and payment for his superintendence if he superintends, he has failed in his object: he says he has made no profit and sooner or later he withdraws his capital, i.e. his extra money from the concern and embarks it in another which will produce him a profit. It will make this matter clearer to you if you think of the employer not as one man, who might take a part in the work done in the factory, but as a joint-stock-company, the members of which could not do so: you will then see that employers of labour are engaged in amusing themselves or in working or making a show of work elsewhere, while they are living on the labour of the men in the factory: from each one of those men they take a portion of what he produces and thereby make his life the poorer: thus they are the pensioners of the workers and evade the law of nature which bids men work in order to thrive; but since it *is* a law of nature they can only do so at other people's expense: unless all help to produce some will not thrive; that is certain: what we Socialists say, is let those who will not work be the ones who do not thrive: can anybody say that is unfair? Yet many and many a man has suffered poverty, imprisonment, loss of friends, the reproach of the public, yes and death on the gallows-tree for persisting in preaching that simple piece of justice.[4]

Now before I ask you to think if there is any good reason *why* all this should be, why strong, healthy, and capable people should be pensioners on others, let us try to *see* how it is; what the machinery is which enables such a joint-stock-company to live without producing: and let me say in passing that all that I have said about a factory and its machinery and capital applies equally to land: the land is also a factory, and its machinery is the fertility of it won by the labour of many generations of workers: the landlord is the pensioner of workmen past and present.

Now then this pension, this rent, or profit, which the landlord or the factory-owner live on is clearly not paid to the pensioners voluntarily or indeed consciously by the workers: they are compelled to pay it, and so cunningly that they do not understand the compulsion, though they feel it, and in an unconscious manner struggle against it. What enables the pensioners to force unwilling people to pay them a pension? This, that they are the owners

---

[4] The "death on the gallows-tree" of the Chicago anarchists—Albert Parsons, August Spies, Adolph Fischer, and George Engel—preceded by one day the riots of Bloody Sunday, Nov. 13, 1887. The entire sequence of trial, conviction, and execution and the effects of the proceedings on the English socialist agitation have been summarized by E. P. Thompson in *Romantic to Revolutionary*, pp. 591–5.

of the raw material and instruments of labour: they have a privilege to compel people to pay for the use of these things, a privilege which is supported by the whole power of the law; and indeed the maintenance [of this privilege] is the chief business of all law and government in this and all civilized countries.

Let me explain further: for the production of goods two things are necessary, the labour of men on the one hand, raw material together with the tools of labour on the other: the best workman in the world is useless without the wherewithal to work on, and in these days of the elaborate organization of labour if [he] is not also furnished with the most improved machinery he will fall far short of the workmen that are so furnished; the workmen of any country therefore must be able to have the use of the land of it, of the factories, machinery, railways, and lastly of the capital, i.e. the stored-up labour-power of past generations: if they cannot have these things they cannot work at all. Now the privileged classes, men like the joint-stock-company I have been speaking of, are quite willing that the workmen should work, that is necessary for the exercise of their privilege, if the workmen did not work, the idlers could not live idle: therefore they are allowed to use the raw material and tools of labour that the privileged own, but only on their paying a price for the use of them: now as for this price it cannot be more than would enable the workman to live and breed, and it cannot be less than would enable the property-owner to live on the labour of the workman; it varies between those two extremes; but the great mass of the workmen have to pay a price for leave to work little less than the highest price, or in other words their wages are little above what is necessary for them to live, work and breed on: because they are what is called unskilled workmen, that is they do work which requires no special aptitude or long training, and of this kind of labour the supply exceeds the demand, there are more workmen that is than the employers can employ at a profit to themselves.

So you see this is the reason why the manufacturer is not satisfied with that fair bargain of working amongst his workmen: the law gives him the power to force them to pay him for leave to work if by any means not illegal he has managed to acquire more wealth than he needs for his own use. Money as you well know can buy immunity from labour, but once again this means nothing more nor less than that the owner of it can force other people to work for him gratis after they have fed, clothed, and housed themselves poorly. So you see unless a man is well enough off to have at his command land at least if not machinery and capital he cannot work wholly for himself; some part of his time at least he must pay as a poll-tax for leave to work that is for leave to live; and as the owners of land and capital are comparatively few it follows that the smaller part of the population forces the larger part to pay this poll-tax. And what is this tax? It is no slight money charge which one man might easily pay to another and feel little the worse for it; we have seen already what it is: the price which the workers pay to the idlers for leave to live is the renunciation of all the comforts of life: in order that he may live the working man has to consent to live as an inferior being to the non-worker, and this he is forced to agree to, because certain persons are allowed to live not by producing wealth as the worker does but by *owning* it: by owning what is necessary for the worker to use, but which they the non-workers can only use as an instrument of compulsion to force the workers to work without being paid for a portion of their working.

Now then we can see surely that it is nonsense saying that [it] is natural for the great mass of people to be poor; it is unnatural: if nature bids us to work in order to live, and refuses to yield her treasure to anyone who does not work, it ought to follow on that, that those who work most should have the most, and those who do not work at all should get *nothing:* whereas under our present system exactly the contrary is the case: the great landowner, the rich shareholder, men who do not even pretend to do anything are at the one end of the scale and are most wealthy; the unskilled workman, the field labourer working day-in day-out their lives long, and ending with the workhouse are at the other end of it; and betwixt and between are various groups of whom in the main it is true that the harder and the usefuller their work is the less they get.

Now I say that this is a lamentable flying in the face of Nature, and the result *must* be the impoverishment of the larger part of mankind. I have said that this is a rich country, and yet perhaps that is a misuse of words; can a country be called rich that has so many poor in it?

So we see it is absurd to put down the inequalities of modern Society to the nature or necessity of the case. But the defenders of our present system, say it is the fault of the poor themselves that they are poor: that is quite as absurd; we have seen that the greater part of the workers are poor: is it possible that it can be their faults: its being their faults would mean that they do not work, that they are idle; but they do all the work that is done at any rate, and they do so much of it that they are not only enabled to live to work but they also have the honour (I won't call it a pleasure) of keeping those who do not work: so that is preposterous nonsense saying of the whole of this working class that they are poor through their idleness.

No we must I feel sure come to the conclusion that it is the system under which we live that brings about those terrible inequalities which most thoughtful men lament: and we ought to be very glad that we are driven to that conclusion: because if it were the work of nature we could not seriously amend it: or if [it] could be true that all useful people were idle, i.e. useless, what could we do then? But since it is the fault of a system, which has grown up to what it is by the carelessness and thoughtlessness of men, it both can be altered, and it will be, since it is of the very nature of all human systems to change into something else and to change in the direction of men's desires: and men's desires do now, and have for a long time tended towards equality, towards the extinction of classes, in a word towards the general happiness of the whole population. Ah my friends, it is a mournful thing to consider how hard and cruel men are to one another, not from malice or ill-nature but from ignorance and thoughtlessness when with a little courage, a little forethought, a little wisdom we could make such a different world of it, that we could make all the poor, rich or wealthy rather, without really injuring the rich one iota. Is it not worth while trying to do that? Well that is what Socialists want to do. And I say again that can be done, and will be done; but if people delay too long trying to do it the natural break-up of the system will bring about much misery and probably war and violence before the times better: which we might avoid by being wise in time, and thinking about what is to be done, trying our own selves to make the change from the bad old system to the better new come about with the consent of all thoughtful and well-wishing people: this is why I am speaking to you tonight trying to get you to agree with me that the position of working men can and should be altered and that altogether, not a little bettered merely; but quite changed; put on a new foundation.

I have shown you that the real reason for the poverty of the working-classes lay in the fact that some men wishing to live without working had managed to get into their hands those things which are necessary to the workmen to work with, and thus could compel them to keep them in idleness. Now this is the thing we Socialists want to alter: we say with St. Paul,[5] that no one who can work has a right to live unless he works; and we also say as I began by telling you that since every ordinarily healthy and capable man can produce more than he needs to keep himself every man who does a fair share of work ought to have a good livelihood.

I fear to some of you that may appear impossible; but you must remember what work now is, and what work should be: there is only a certain amount of labour-power in the country, and clearly if a great part of this labour-power is allowed to run to waste, the wealth of the country must be less than it should be. Now not only do a great many people refuse to work, but a great many others are set to do quite useless work by these idle rich men: if all the men who are doing nothing and all who are simply wasting their workers to work at making things which we want, which the whole community wants, and at distributing them in an unwasteful manner, we should as a community be abundantly wealthy: and if this wealth were shared justly we should be every one of us both healthy and wealthy: healthy I say without hesitation, because I am sure that all disease comes either from excess or from poverty.[6]

---

[5] 2 Thess., III, 10: "For even when we were with you, this we commanded you, that if any man would not work, neither should he eat."
[6] A parenthetical note here in the MS reads, "The Shakers," probably a reminder

Well then how are [we] to set to work about it? Perhaps you
may have been told that the Socialists want to share up all
wealth, and that the result of this would be that in a shorter or
longer time things would come back to the old condition of
inequality. Well of course they would if things remained otherwise as they are now. But then the Socialists do not want to share
up all wealth: they want all persons to enjoy what they have
fairly earned by their labour and what they can fairly *use;* and I
don't think that on consideration you can think that wrong. What
a man has and can use is his own; but what sense is there in his
calling a thing his own which he cannot use? Suppose you give a
child a sugar-plum and say that it is his but he mustn't eat it:
what will he do? Why he will be coming to you every hour of the
day and be saying "please may I eat that jumble *now?*" or else he
will show you practically what he thinks about property by eat-
ing it without asking you. So you see you do not injure a man by
taking away from him what he cannot use. But supposing he
abuses this property of his which he cannot *use* for doing a wrong
to someone else: are you injuring him by taking it away from him
then? for instance—if you see a man levelling a gun at another
man, are you injuring him by taking the gun away from him?
Certainly not; you are preventing him from committing a crime.
Well that is what we Socialists want to do: but further than that:
we would take from people that part of their property which they
cannot use and which they now abuse by wronging other people
by means of it; but we would not take it away to do nothing with

---

to Morris to mention the belief of that sect that all disease "is an offense to God,"
being the result of over-indulgence. As a Shaker rhyme put it,

> The glutton's a seat in which evil can work,
> And in hoggish nature diseases will lurk:
> By faith and good works we can all overcome,
> And starve the old glutton until he is done.
> But while he continues to guzzle and eat,
> All kinds of distempers will still find a seat—
> The plagues of old Egypt—the scab and the bile,
> At which wicked spirits and devils will smile.

(See Charles Nordhoff, *The Communistic Societies of the United States,* New
York, 1875, pp. 117–256).

it, we would *use* it and by using it would benefit the very people from whom we had taken it as well as other people. We fully admit the right of people to use property, we deny their right to abuse it: and I must tell you plainly that in doing so we are in direct opposition to the present laws of Society, the laws that keep you poor: their maxim is that a man has a right to use and *abuse* the wealth which he has legally acquired. This abuse of property we would put an end to at once.

You will of course ask me what we propose in this matter, how we propose to destroy the abuse of property: I cannot give you the details of such an arrangement; no man can at this stage of the question: but I think I can make the principles clear on which those details would be founded. In order to do that let me go back to that owner of a factory that I have been speaking to you about before, and who would be content to be paid by the workmen who use it for the wear and tear and risk involved in working it, and just consideration for his own personal work in it: I think such a man would only wish to call such a factory his own because if he gave it up he would be thrown out of work. I think he would be perfectly willing to surrender it to a body of men whom he could trust to use it duly and ensure him work in it at a fair remuneration; I think he would be quite contented if he could say not this factory is mine, but this factory is *ours:* whose? Why the men's who work in it including himself. That is cooperation you will say: yes so it is, and it is also Socialism, *if* (and the if is a great one) that is the condition of all factories throughout the country. But it can only be the condition of all factories if those factories cease to be owned by private persons and are owned by the people in general in some way or other. Therefore you see the only body to which our factory owner could surrender the property which is useless to himself unless the people ensure the proper use of it is the people at large: they are the only body which can own it without wronging someone. Well, when the people, the nation if you please, owned this property what would they do with it? They would allow the workmen who could use it for producing goods to use it on condition that they paid to the whole people for the wear and tear of their property, that they paid in short what was necessary to keep it a going concern, and that they dealt fairly in dividing amongst themselves what they earned by their work. This is what is called the Nationalization of the means of production, and I have dealt with the case of the factory first because if you will agree to that you will the more readily agree to the opinion that the land should be nationalized; although for my part I can see no serious difference between the position of the land and the other means of production. The land should be owned by no private person but by the people at large to be used by those who can use it: they will indeed have to pay rent to the people, because if they did not, the man who got hold of a piece of extra-productive land would have an unfair advantage over his neighbour: but this rent would [be] so apportioned that it would not begin till the cultivator had made a fair living out of the soil; and he then would not be paying a tax on his labour, but would be handing over to the people what he had not worked for, a fertility which was the work of accident and the labour of past generations. And of this which he would pay to the people he would have his share again as one of the people. The capital of the country i.e. the stored-up wealth to be used for further production would also be owned by the people; no one would be allowed to take interest on money in order to live idly without labour; the people would lend to those that needed it on the security of the labour-power of the borrower under due regulations: the railways and other means of transit like all machinery would be owned by the people to be used by everybody according to his convenience. Of course we should between us have to pay for the maintenance and renewal of these things, but we should find it more convenient to pay for them in the lump, and everybody to use them freely just as we do for our bridges and highways and our postal service.

Now this would mean a very great change: it would put Society on a new basis: everyone would have to work and everyone would be able to work according to his capacity: there would be no need for overwork, since everyone was working: labour would be free; workmen would not need to beg to be employed by a master, because they would be able to employ themselves, and the results of their labour would be all their own. Moreover the people would see that education was the same for everyone according to their capacity, and that the old, the infirm, and all who for natural reasons could not work should be properly taken care of; and since the standard of life for the worker would have been raised so much the standard of comfort for such people would you may be sure be of the same kind: the people also would undertake great works for public utility and pleasure as they might well do in a country where no labour was wasted; and probably having satisfied their ordinary wants on a generous scale, it would be to these public advantages that people would turn for whatever of luxury or splendour they desired.

You may have noticed that I have [been] saying 'the people' would take over such and such things, would do so and so: I have used this word as including all forms of administration bodies by which these changes would be carried out and the new Society maintained: I do not want to prejudge the question as to the exact form that such a Society would take. But in my opinion there would be far less centralization than there is at present, a board of officials, a parliament, or any such-like body should not attempt to administer the affairs of people living a long way off, whose conditions and surroundings they cannot thoroughly understand: surely it is always and everywhere good that people should do their own business, and in order that they may do it well, every citizen should have some share of it, and take on his own shoulders some part of the responsibility: true it is that this can only be done by free men, slaves can have no responsibility, and as long as the workers are the slaves of capital and have to work and live as it bids them, they must submit to what I should call professional officials, and have all public work ill-done at a huge cost.

Therefore to my mind in the new Society, we should form bodies like municipalities, county-boards, and parishes, and almost all practical public work would be done by these bodies, the members of whom would be working at and living by their ordinary work, and, as aforesaid everybody who had any capacity for such work would have to do his share of it: and you must remember that this is no new idea after all, but is the ancient constitution of the land, which [was] gradually corrupted and overlaid by officialism of one sort or other: of course these bodies would have to federate for national or international purposes: but no set of delegates would venture to consider itself the master of the public, it would be its servant rather.

To recapitulate. In the Society which we Socialists wish to see realized labour will be free: no man will have to find a master before he sets to work to produce wealth, a master who will not employ him unless he can take from him a portion of what he has produced: every man will be able to keep himself by his labour, and the combination of all these workers will supply those things which can only be used by the public, such as baths, libraries, schools, great public buildings, railways, roads, bridges, and the like. There will be no political parties squabbling incessantly as to who shall govern the country and doing nothing else; for the country will govern itself, and the village, municipal, and county councils will send delegates to meetings for dealing with matters common to all. The trades also will have councils which will organize each the labour which they understand and these again will meet when necessary to discuss matters common to all the trades: in short life and labour [will be organized] in the least wasteful manner, and the ordinary citizen will learn to understand at least some part of this organization.

Thus we shall learn to live reasonably. My own belief is that when we are once bound together by ties of honesty and mutual self-respect all this will tend to get simpler and simpler, until our business becomes very easy to transact. For instance I have been speaking as if there would still be some social inequalities, as if one man would earn more money than another, though none would earn less than enough to keep him comfortably: but I do not think that this would last long: we should find that when we ceased to fight with each other for livelihood and to rob each other that all ordinary necessaries and comforts would be so abundant and so cheap that they would be free for everybody to take as he needed: of course we should pay for them, but in the lump: let me give you an illustration: when a family that is comfortably-off sit down to a leg of mutton how do they act? do they bring in a pair of scales and weigh out to each one his share of the victuals? No that is done in a prison, but not in a family: in a family everybody has what he needs and no one grudges it:

Mary has one slice, Jack has two, and Bill has four: but Mary and Jack don't feel wronged, since they have had as much as they wanted: and the reason for this is that enough has been provided, and that the members of the family trust one another.[7]

My friends it is for you to choose whether you will live in a prison or a family: we Socialists beg you to choose the latter. But in order that you may do so you must understand and make others understand that the world can only be happy if [it] is honest, and it can only be honest by not allowing persons to live by making other men poor: all rich people do now live in that way and consequently the world is dishonest. Now you may think it is too difficult a task to convince rich people of this, or to convince poor people that it is their duty to *compel* the rich to be honest—i.e. to be rich no longer. It is a difficult task; but we Socialists do not despair of it because on the one hand the rich are not over-happy in their riches, and many of them are beginning to learn one thing, viz. that they have nothing to fear from a system which will destroy poverty as well as riches.[8] And on the other hand the poor are not so ignorant as they used to be, and they are beginning to learn that not only is it their interest not to allow themselves to be robbed, but that it is a necessity for them, or else ruin will overtake their masters along with themselves: everywhere employers make less and less profits; the big men are swallowing the small, the bigger the big, and the biggest the bigger: employment becomes yearly harder to get and harder to give. The old system is tumbling to pieces, and the workers must now come forward and show the way to the new, by claiming to be allowed to work for themselves, and thus form a Society where all will be workers: if they do not do this, consciously and speedily too, there will be a terrible state of things before the new system is born: we now living may yet see people dying by the dozen of starvation in our streets before full shops and crowded warehouses: or indeed people in their agony of necessity breaking through all restraints and sacking such shops and warehouses and destroying everything right and left in mad and ignorant

---

[7] A marginal note here in the MS reads, "poverty what we must end."
[8] A marginal note here in the MS reads, "precariousness."

riot: because they will not understand and cannot unless they are taught that it is not the day's stock of bread and beef or the year's stock of cloth that they need, but the raw material and instruments for making the bread, beef, and cloth, and the organization for employing these matters. This lesson is what we have to teach them, I am sure that if we who have learned it will but do our duty they will not be long in learning it; and when they have learned it they will claim their rights; their right to live free, and to use what they alone can use though others may abuse it, the raw material and instruments of labour. That claim cannot be resisted if [it] is made by the combined workers of the country.[9] The question is will they combine? I answer they must combine or starve.

But in order to combine in the best manner and to bring about the freedom of labour with least possible violence and misery, after they have learned what their position is and what it should be, they must cast aside all jealousy of one another, must understand thoroughly that they are not enemies to one another but all soldiers in one great army: they must be forebearing and slow to quarrel. . . .[10] and when they really feel this it will give them a courage which people can never have when they [are] acting in a selfish way each one for his own interests, a courage which will make them good men and true in all senses of the phrase: and then I repeat they will be irresistible: they will attract to them all that there is of intelligence in the working-classes, they will convince all those of the wealthy classes who are worthy and well-meaning, and the rest they will push aside to let them find out by experience that the life of a free man is better than that of either a slave or a slave-owner.

---

[9] Pencil marks in the MS indicate that most of the remaining portion of the lecture was deleted sometime after its composition. With the exception of the portion quoted in note 10, below, it is impossible to tell exactly which parts were to be deleted; therefore all doubtful deletions are included as part of the text.

[10] The following passage is deleted in the MS: ". . . and absolutely truthful and open with each other: all these virtues will give them the one thing needed that is courage. And indeed I think courage is the virtue of virtues for why are people false and thievish and shabby and suspicious but because they [are] afraid? And again when people have a great aim in view, when they are set on gaining something for the world which shall benefit the world at large"—the passage is not completed.

APPENDIX I:

A Calendar of William Morris's Platform Career

Since only those occasions that were public are included, ordinary business meetings of societies are omitted unless advertised as public or unless they had some exceptional significance. Cross-references to Appendix II after the heading "Text" appear only when some form of text exists; where there is no cross-reference it should be understood that no text remains. Titles are given as they appear in the reports listed under "Sources"; they are not necessarily Morris's final choice of title in printed versions. Where there is a difference of title, the one representing Morris's latest version is given in Appendix II. Dates are in numerical form with month first, then day and year. Asterisks after the dates indicate speeches that were scheduled but for which there are no subsequent reports of delivery. The direction "see above" after "Source" refers to the sources listed in the immediately preceding entry.

1877

3–2–77—Morris was chairman at a meeting held to form the SPAB at his firm's showroom, 22 Queen Square, Bloomsbury.
Source: *SPAB Report, 1934*, pp. 8–9 (Quotes minutes of the meeting).

12–4–77—"The Decorative Arts," delivered before the Trades Guild of Learning, probably in the Co-operative Hall, Castle St., Oxford St., London.
Sources: Letter to Mrs. Morris, Dec. 3, [1877], (B.M. Add. MS. 45338); Letter to Jane Alice Morris, Dec. 7, [1877], (*Letters*, p. 101); Letter from Philip Webb to Jane Alice, May, and Mrs. Morris, Dec. 5, 1877 (BM. Add. MS. 45342).
Text: see Appendix II, item 1.

12–19–77—A speech at an anti-war meeting sponsored by the EQA at the Lambeth Baths, Lambeth. Sir George Young was chairman.
Sources: Letter to Mrs. Morris, Dec. 20, [1877], (*Letters*, p. 103); *The Daily Chronicle*, Dec. 20, 1877, p. 6.

1878

1–7–78—"Address to English Liberals," delivered before the Chichester Liberal Association at Chichester.
> Source: Letter to Jane Alice Morris, Jan. 4, 1878 (*Letters*, p. 106).
> Text: see Appendix II, item 3.

1–16–78—A speech on the opening of the Dardanelles, delivered for the EQA at Willis's Rooms, King St., St. James's, London.
> Sources: Letter to Jane Alice Morris, Jan. 14, 1878 (*Artist, Writer, Socialist*, II, 570); Letter from Philip Webb to G. P. Boyce, Jan. 17, 1878 (B.M. Add. MS. 45354); *The Daily Chronicle*, Jan. 17, 1878, p. 5; *PMG*, Jan. 17, 19, 1878.

2–21–78—"Address at the Distribution of Prizes at the Cambridge School of Art," delivered at the Guildhall, Cambridge. Professor Sydney Colvin, Slade Professor of Fine Art at the University, was chairman.
> Sources: Letter to Mrs. Morris, Feb. 20, 1878 (*Letters*, p. 111); *The Cambridge Express*, Feb. 23, 1878.
> Text: see Appendix II, item 5.

6–21–78—Report at the First Annual Meeting, SPAB, delivered at Willis's Rooms, King St., St. James's, London. Earl Cowper was chairman.
> Sources: *SPAB Report, 1878*, p. 1; *The Times*, June 22, 1878, p. 7.
> Review: "The Anti-Restoration Movement," *The Architect*, July 13, 1878, pp. 17–18.
> Text: see Appendix II, item 6.

1879

2–19–79 (afternoon)—Chairman of the annual meeting of the subscribers to the Birmingham School of Art, of which Morris was President, at the Birmingham and Midlands Institute, Birmingham.
> Source: *The Birmingham Daily Post*, Feb. 20, 1879, p. 5.

2–19–79 (evening)—"The Art of the People," delivered as the annual Presidential Address before the Birmingham Society of Arts and the Birmingham School of Design at the annual distribution of prizes of the School of Design. The meeting was held at the Town Hall, Birmingham.
> Sources: Letter to May Morris, Feb. 25, 1878 (B.M. Add. MS. 45341); *The Architect*, Feb. 8, 1879, p. 88; *The Birmingham Daily Post*, Feb. 20, 1879, p. 5.
> Review: *The Architect*, Feb. 22, 1879, p. 112.
> Text: see Appendix II, item 7.

4–8–79—"The History of Pattern Design," delivered before the Trades Guild of Learning at the Co-operative Institute, Castle St., Oxford St., London. Mr. George C. Warr was chairman.
> Sources: Letter from Philip Webb to G. P. Boyce, April 7, 1879 (B.M. Add. MS. 45354); *The Daily Chronicle*, April 9, 1879, p. 5; *The Architect*, April 19, 1879, pp. 236–7.
> Text: see Appendix II, item 8.

6–28–79—Reading of the annual report of the SPAB at a meeting held at Willis's

Rooms, King St., St. James's, London. The Hon. Percy Wyndham, M.P., was chairman.

Sources: *SPAB Report, 1879,* p. 1; *The Architect,* July 5, 1879, p. 7.

Text: see Appendix II, item 9.

6–28–79 (same meeting as above)—A speech seconding a resolution against building restoration which "may obliterate" the historical significance of the buildings restored, delivered at the annual SPAB meeting at Willis's Rooms, King St., St. James's, London.

Source: *SPAB Report, 1879,* p. 30.

Text: see Appendix II, item 10.

11–6–79—A speech on the restoration of St. Mark's, Venice, at a meeting sponsored by the SPAB in the SPAB rooms, 9 Buckingham St., Strand, London. The Hon. Percy Wyndham, M.P., was chairman.

Source: *The Times,* Nov. 8, 1879, p. 11.

11–13–79—A speech at a meeting held in the theater of the Birmingham and Midlands Institute, Birmingham, to discuss "the desirability of memorialising the Italian Government on the subject of the proposed destruction of St. Mark's, Venice." Mayor R. Chamberlain was chairman.

Source: *The Birmingham Daily Post,* Nov. 14, 1879, p. 5.

11–15–79—A speech on the restoration of St. Mark's, Venice, for the SPAB at the Sheldonian Theatre, Oxford. The Dean of Christ Church was chairman.

Sources: *The Architect,* Nov. 22, 1879, pp. 298–9; *The Oxford and Cambridge Undergraduate's Journal,* Nov. 20, 1879, pp. 114–16; *The Times,* Nov. 17, 1879, p. 9; *Jackson's Oxford Journal,* Nov. 22, 1879, p. 7; *The Oxford Times,* Nov. 22, 1879, p. 6.

Review: "Oxford Letter," *The Cambridge Review,* Nov. 19, 1879, pp. 90–91.

1880

2–19–80—"Labour and Pleasure *versus* Labour and Sorrow," delivered before the Birmingham Society of Arts and the Birmingham School of Design on the occasion of the distribution of prizes of the latter group at the Town Hall, Birmingham.

Sources: Letter to Mrs. Morris, Feb. 16, 1880 (B.M. Add. MS. 45338); *The Architect,* XXIII (Feb. 28, 1880), 145.

Review: "Art among the Lowly," *The Architect,* March 6, 1880, pp. 159–60.

Text: see Appendix II, item 15.

5–31–80—A speech proposing an international committee for the preservation of St. Mark's, Venice. The SPAB convened the meeting at the Society of Arts, John St., Adelphi, and the Hon. Percy Wyndham, M.P., was chairman.

Source: *The Architect,* June 5, 1880, p. 392.

6–15–80—A speech seconding a resolution for Women's Rights, at the Annual Meeting of the Women's Protective and Provident League at the Society of Arts, John St., Adelphi. Prof. J. P. Bryce was chairman until toward the end of the meeting, when Morris took over in his place.

Source: *The Women's Union Journal,* V (July, 1880), 67.

Text: see Appendix II, item 18.

6–28–80—Reading of the annual report of the SPAB at a meeting held at the

Society of Arts, John St., Adelphi. Mr. Stanley Leighton, M.P., was chairman.
Source: *SPAB Report, 1880,* p. 1.
Text: see Appendix II, item 19.

11–13–80—"Some Hints on House Decoration," delivered before the Trades Guild of Learning in the lecture hall of the Society of Arts, John St., Adelphi. Professor Hale of King's College was chairman.
Sources: *The Artist,* I (Nov., 1880), 331; *Reynold's Newspaper,* Nov. 14, 1880, p. 8.
Reviews: see the entry for 12–8–80.
Text: see Appendix II, item 20.

12–8–80—"Some Hints on House Decoration," delivered before the Royal Society of Artists at Birmingham.
Sources: *The Architect,* Dec. 18, 1880, p. 384; *The Artist,* I (Nov., 1880), 331. *The Birmingham Daily Post,* Dec. 11, 1880, p. 8.
Reviews: "Mr. Morris on Domestic Architecture," *The Architect,* Dec. 25, 1880, pp. 397–8; "Mr. Morris on Flower Gardening," *The Artist,* II (Jan., 1881), 17; "Mr. Morris," *The Artist,* II (Feb., 1881), 38.
Text: see Appendix II, item 20.

1881

1–15–81—A speech delivered at a meeting called for the purpose of establishing The Radical Union, at No. 2, Regent Street, London. Mr. James Beal was chairman.
Sources: *Journal for 1881; The Daily Chronicle,* Jan. 17, 1881, p. 5.

1–27–81—A speech at the first public meeting of the Kyrle Society. The meeting was held at Kensington Vestry Hall, London, and Prince Leopold was chairman.
Source: *The Times,* Jan. 28, 1881, p. 10.
Text: see Appendix II, item 22.

3–10–81—"The Prospects of Architecture in Civilization," delivered before the London Institution, Finsbury Circus, London.
Source: Letter to Mrs. Burne-Jones, Aug. 10, 1880 (*Letters,* p. 134).
Text: see Appendix II, item 23.

3–16–81—A speech before the Nottingham Kyrle Society at "The Castle," Nottingham.
Sources: *Journal for 1881;* letter to Mrs. Morris, March 19 [1881], (*Letters,* p. 148).
Text: see Appendix II, item 24.

3–31–81*—A speech on the restoration of the Campo Santo, Florence, was planned for delivery before a meeting convened by the SPAB in London.
Sources: Letter to Mrs. Morris, March 31, 1881 (*Artist, Writer, Socialist,* II, 584); *Journal for 1881.*

6–24–81—Reading of the annual report of the SPAB at a meeting held at the Westminster Palace Hotel, London. James Russell Lowell, United States Ambassador to Great Britain, was chairman.
Sources: *The Architect,* July 2, 1881, p. 13; *The Times,* June 28, 1881, p. 7.
Text: see Appendix II, item 26.

10–13–81—"Art and the Beauty of the Earth," delivered before the Wedgewood

Institute at the Town Hall, Burslem. The Hon. H. T. Davenport, M.P., was chairman.

Source: *The Artist,* II (Nov., 1881), 325–27.

Text: see Appendix II, item 27.

12–10–81—"Some Hints on Pattern Designing," delivered before students of the Working Men's College at the College, Queen's Square, Bloomsbury. Thomas Woolner was chairman.

Sources: *Journal for 1881; The Artist,* III (Feb., 1882), 35.

Text: see Appendix II, item 28.

1882

1–23–82—"Some of the Minor Arts of Life," delivered before the Birmingham and Midlands Institute at the Institute, Birmingham, in support of the SPAB.

Sources: Letter to Mrs. Burne-Jones, Jan. 10, 1882 (*Letters,* p. 156); *The Birmingham Daily Post,* Jan. 24, 1882, p. 5.

Text: see Appendix II, item 29.

2–23–82—"The History of Pattern Designing," delivered as one of a series sponsored by the SPAB at the Kensington Vestry Hall, London.

Sources and Reviews: "A Group of Lectures," *The Architect,* March 4, 1882, pp. 128–9; *The Artist,* III (May, 1882), 129–30.

Text: see Appendix II, item 8.

3–17–82—Testimony before the Royal Commission on Technical Education at the South Kensington Museum. Mr. Bernhard Samuelson, M.P., F.R.S., was chairman.

Source: *Second Report of the Royal Commission on Technical Education,* (London, 1884), III, 150.

Text: see Appendix II, item 30.

6–9–82—Reading of the annual report of the SPAB at a meeting held in the lecture hall of the Society of Arts, John St., Adelphi. The Hon. J. Bryce, M.P., was chairman.

Sources: *The Architect,* June 17, 1882, pp. 272–3. *SPAB Report, 1882,* p. 1; *The Times,* June 10, 1882, p. 9.

Text: see Appendix II, item 31.

6–9–82—A speech delivered at the Fifth Annual Meeting of the SPAB seconding a motion for a vote of thanks to the chairman, the Hon. James Bryce, M.P.

Source: . . . *Fifth Annual Meeting of the Society. Report.* . . . (London, 1882), p. 46.

Text: see Appendix II, item 32.

10–20–82—"The Progress of Decorative Art in England," delivered at a banquet celebrating the opening of the Fine Art and Industrial Exhibition at St. James's Hall, Manchester. The Earl of Wilton was chairman.

Sources: *The Architect,* Oct. 28, 1882, pp. 262–3; *The Artist,* III (Nov., 1882), 330–32; *The Manchester Guardian,* Oct. 21, 1882, p. 5.

Reviews: "The Progress of Furniture Exhibitions," *The Architect,* Nov. 4, 1882, pp. 275–6; [Editorial], *The Manchester Guardian,* Oct. 21, 1882, p. 7.

Text: see Appendix II, item 33.

12–12–82—"[Art: a Serious Thing]," delivered at the annual distribution of Prizes of the Leek School of Art at the Temperance Hall, Leek.

Source: *The Architect*, Dec. 23, 1882, pp. 402–3.
Text: see Appendix II, item 34.

1883

3–6–83—"Art, Wealth, and Riches," delivered at the Manchester Royal Institution, Mosley St., before a joint *conversazione* of Manchester societies. Mr. George Milner, president of the Manchester Literary Club, was chairman.
Sources: Letter to Jane Alice Morris, Jan. 9, 1883 (B.M. Add. MS. 45339); Charles Rowley, *Fifty Years of Work Without Wages* (London, [1912]), pp. 130–31; *The Architect*, March 10, 1883, pp. 165–6; *The Manchester Guardian*, March 7, 1883.
Text: see Appendix II, item 35.

4–1–83—A lecture, delivered at a meeting in Hampstead, probably sponsored by the Hampstead Liberal Club.
Source: Letter to Jane Alice Morris, April 2, 1883 (*Letters*, p. 167).

4–15–83*—A lecture was scheduled for delivery before the Clerkenwell Branch, D.F., at the branch rooms, Clerkenwell.
Source: Letter to Jane Alice Morris, April 2, 1883 (*Letters*, p. 167).

5–3–83—A lecture, delivered at the Irish National League Rooms, Blackfriars Road, London.
Source: Letter to Jane Alice Morris, May 7, 1883 (*Artist, Writer, Socialist*, pp. 585–6).

6–6–83—Report at the Sixth Annual Meeting, SPAB, delivered at the Society of Arts, John-Street, Adelphi. Sir John Lubbock, M.P., was chairman.
Sources: *SPAB Reports, 1883* (London, 1883); *The Times*, June 7, 1883, p. 6.
Text: see Appendix II, item 37.

7–10–83—Speech at Islington.
Source: *The Journals of T. J. Cobden-Sanderson* (London, 1926), I, 96.

9–26–83—A speech in support of the D.F. program, delivered at a meeting held in the Temperance Hall, Temple St., Birmingham. Mr. H. G. Lane was chairman.
Sources: "The Social Agitation," *The Christian Socialist*, I (Nov., 1883), 92–3; *The Birmingham Daily Post*, Sept. 27, 1883, p. 8.

11–14–83—"Art under a Plutocracy," delivered before the Russell Club at University College Hall, Oxford. The Master of Balliol was chairman, and John Ruskin also spoke.
Sources: *The Architect*, Nov. 17, 1883, p. 314; letter to C. J. Faulkner, Oct. 23, 1883 (*Letters*, pp. 188–9); *The Times*, Nov. 15, 1883, p. 7, and Nov. 16, 1883, p. 7; *The Oxford and Cambridge Undergraduate's Journal*, Nov. 22, 1883, pp. 103, 115; letter from D. S. MacColl to Cockerell, Nov. 10, 1944 (*Cockerell Papers*); *The Oxford Magazine*, Nov. 21, 1883, pp. 384, 386–87.
Reviews: "Oxford Letter," *Cambridge Review*, Nov. 21, 1883, p. 93; *The Oxford Times*, Nov. 17, 1883, p. 8.
Text: see Appendix II, item 39.

11–16–83—"Art under the Rule of Commerce" delivered for the D.F., at the Lecture Hall, Wimbledon.
Sources: "The Social Agitation," *The Christian Socialist*, I (Dec., 1883), 109;

The Artist, V (Feb., 1884), 35–6; *The Times,* Nov. 19, 1883, p. 10, correspondence, *The Times,* Nov. 19, 1883, p. 3.

Text: see Appendix II, item 39.

11–24–83—"The Origin of Decorative Art," delivered at a meeting sponsored by the Eton College Literary Society in the Lecture Hall, Eton College, Windsor. H. E. Luxmoore was chairman.

Sources: *The Eton College Chronicle,* Nov. 30, 1883, p. 1493; letter from H. E. Luxmoore to Cockerell, "Epiphany," 1924 (*Cockerell Papers*).

Text: see Appendix II, item 40.

12–4–83—"Art under the Plutocracy," delivered before the Cambridge Union Society at the Cambridge Union.

Sources: *The Cambridge Review,* Dec. 5, 1883, p. 113, 122; *The Cambridge Chronicle and University Journal,* Dec. 7, 1883, p. 7.

Review: "The Social Agitation," *The Christian Socialist,* II (Jan., 1884), 125.

Text: see Appendix II, item 39.

1884

1–16–84—"Useful Work *versus* Useless Toil," delivered before the Hampstead Liberal Club at the Hollybush Assembly Rooms, Hampstead. Professor Henry Morley was chairman.

Sources: Letter to Jane Alice Morris, Jan. 16, 1884 (*Letters,* p. 193); *The Christian Socialist,* II (Feb., 1884), 131; *Justice,* Jan. 19, 1884, p. 6; *PMG,* Jan. 17, 1884, p. 7.

Review: "Passing Notes," *The Echo,* Jan. 17, 1884, p. 1.

Text: see Appendix II, item 41.

1–17–84*—A lecture was scheduled for delivery in Blackheath.

Source: Letter to Jane Alice Morris, Jan. 16, 1884 (*Letters,* p. 193).

1–21–84—"Useful Work *versus* Useless Toil," delivered before the Ancoats Brotherhood at the Churnett St. Hall, Manchester. Mr. Charles Rowley was chairman.

Sources: *Justice,* Jan. 26, 1884, pp. 6–7; letters to Jane Alice Morris, Jan. 16 and 26, 1884 (*Letters,* pp. 193–4); *The Manchester Guardian,* Jan. 22, 1884, p. 6.

Review: "Letters," *The Manchester Guardian,* Jan. 28, 1884, p. 7.

Text: see Appendix II, item 41.

1–22–84—"Art under Plutocracy," delivered at a meeting sponsored by the Ancoats Recreation Committee at the Memorial Hall, Manchester. Professor Munro was chairman.

Sources: *Justice,* Jan. 26, 1884, pp. 6–7; letters to Jane Alice Morris, Jan. 16 and 26, 1884 (*Letters,* pp. 193–4); *The Manchester Guardian,* Jan. 23, 1884, p. 6.

Text: see Appendix II, item 39.

1–23–84—"Art and Socialism," delivered before the Leicester Secular Society at the Secular Hall, Humberstone-gate, Leicester. Mr. T. Wright was chairman.

Sources: *The Midland Free Press,* Jan. 26, 1884, p. 7; *Justice,* Feb. 2, 1884, p. 7; letters to Jane Alice Morris, Jan. 16, 26, 1884 (*Letters,* pp. 193–4).

Text: see Appendix II, item 42.

1–27–84—A speech at a meeting sponsored by the Russell Club at the Clarendon

Assembly Rooms, Oxford. H. M. Hyndman delivered the major address.

Source: *The Church Reformer*, III (Feb., 1884), 46.

2–3–84°—"Art and Socialism" was scheduled for delivery to the LEL at 166 Bethnal Green Road, Bethnal Green.

Source: *Justice*, Jan. 26, 1884, p. 6.

Text: see Appendix II, item 42.

2–5–84—A debate on the proposition that socialism is the remedy for "the present anarchy," with Morris, Hyndman, and H. S. Lewis of St. John's taking the affirmative. The debate was held before the Cambridge Union Society.

Sources: *Cambridge Review*, Feb. 6, 1884, p. 161; *The Cambridge Chronicle and University Journal*, Feb. 8, 1884, p. 4.

Review: "Debate on Socialism at Cambridge," *Justice*, Feb. 23, 1884, p. 7, gives a résumé.

2–15–84°—A lecture was scheduled for the Merton Abbey Branch, SDF, at Merton Abbey.

Source: *Justice*, Feb. 15, 1884, p. 4.

2–17–84—"Useful Work *versus* Useless Toil," delivered at a meeting sponsored by the Bradford Sunday Recreation Committee at the Temperance Hall, Bradford. Mr. J. Hanson was chairman.

Source: *Justice*, Feb. 23, 1884, p. 7.

Text: see Appendix II, item 41.

2–22–84°—"Useful Work *versus* Useless Toil" was scheduled for delivery before the Invicta Club at the Club's rooms, William Street, Woolwich.

Source: *Justice*, Feb. 9, 1884, p. 7.

Text: see Appendix II, item 41.

2–25–84—"Art under Competitive Commerce," delivered at a meeting sponsored by the West Bromwich Institute at the Town Hall, West Bromwich.

Source: *The Architect*, March 1, 1884, p. 150.

Text: see Appendix II, item 39.

3–3–84—"The Gothic Revival I," delivered at the Birmingham and Midlands Institute, Birmingham.

Sources: *The Architect*, March 8, 1884, p. 160; *The Birmingham Daily Post*, March 5, 1884, p. 7.

Text: see this volume, pp. 57–73.

3–10–84—"The Gothic Revival II," delivered before the Birmingham and Midlands Institute, Birmingham.

Sources: *The Architect*, March 15, 1884, p. 179; *The Birmingham Daily Post*, March 12, 1884, p. 7.

Text: see this volume, pp. 74–94.

3–19–84—"Useful Work *versus* Useless Toil," delivered before the Edinburgh University Socialist Society at the Oddfellows' Hall, Edinburgh.

Sources: *Justice*, March 29, 1884, p. 7; letter to J. L. Mahon, March 13, 1884 (*Man and Myth*, p. 42).

Text: see Appendix II, item 41.

3–23–84°—"Useful Work *versus* Useless Toil" was scheduled for delivery, probably before the Fabian Society, at the South Place Institute, London.

Source: *Justice*, March 8, 1884, p. 7.

Text: see Appendix II, item 41.

4–1–84—"Art and Labour," delivered before the Leeds Philosophical and Literary

Society at the Philosophical Hall, Leeds.
Sources: *Justice,* March 29, 1884, p. 7; *The Architect,* Oct. 13, 1883, p. 232; *The Leeds Mercury,* April 3, 1884, p. 7.
Text: see this volume, pp. 94–118.

4–8–84—A speech at the opening of the Fourth Annual Loan Exhibition, sponsored by the Rev. Mr. Barnett at St. Jude's, Commercial St., Whitechapel.
Sources: *The Architect,* April 12, 1884, p. 232; *The Magazine of Art,* VII (1884), 345–7.
Review: Eleanor Marx, "International Popular Movement," *Today,* new series, I (May, 1884), 388.
Text: see Appendix II, item 47.

4–27–84—"Useful Work *versus* Useless Toil," delivered before the LEL at the Monarch Coffee House, 166 Bethnal Green Road, Bethnal Green.
Source: *Justice,* May 3, 1884, p. 7.
Text: see Appendix II, item 41.

5–18–84*—"Art and Labour" was scheduled for delivery before the Marylebone Branch, SDF, at 95 Hampstead Road, Hampstead.
Source: *Justice,* May 17, 1884, p. 7.
Text: see this volume, pp. 94–118.

7–1–84—Reading of a paper before the SPAB at the annual meeting, held at the Society of Arts, John St., Adelphi. The Hon. R. C. Grosvenor was chairman.
Sources: Letter from Philip Webb to G. P. Boyce, Aug. 9, 1884 (B.M. Add. MS. 45354); *SPAB Report, 1884,* p. 1.
Review: "Between the Past and the Future," *The Architect,* July 12, 1884, pp. 15–16.
Text: see Appendix II, item 48.

7–6–84—"Useful Work *versus* Useless Toil," delivered before the Hammersmith Branch, SDF, at Kelmscott House, Hammersmith.
Source: *Justice,* July 12, 1884, p. 6.
Text: see Appendix II, item 41.

7–11–84—"Textile Fabrics," delivered at the International Health Exhibition, South Kensington Museum, London.
Sources: *The Daily Chronicle,* July 11, 1884; *The Artist,* V (Aug., 1884), 256–7.
Text: see Appendix II, item 49.

8–17–84—"Art and Labour," delivered before the Hammersmith Branch, SDF, at Kelmscott House, Hammersmith.
Sources: Letter to Andreas Scheu, Aug. 20, 1884 (*Letters,* p. 212); *Justice,* Aug. 16, 1884, p. 7; "Art and Labour," *The Architect,* Aug. 30, 1884, pp. 135–6, gives a résumé.
Text: see this volume, pp. 94–118.

9–5–84*—"Useful Work *versus* Useless Toil" was scheduled for delivery before the Tottenham Branch, SDF, at Stone-Bridge Hall, London.
Source: *Justice,* Aug. 30, 1884, p. 7.
Text: see Appendix II, item 41.

9–8–84—"Misery and the Way out," delivered before the Borough of Southwark Branch, SDF, at the Queen's Bench Coffee Rooms, 23 Southwark Bridge Road, London.
Source: *Justice,* Sept. 13, 1884, p. 6.
Text: see Appendix II, item 50.

9-14-84 (afternoon)—"Iceland, Its Ancient Literature and Mythology," delivered before the Sheffield Secular Society in Sheffield.
Sources: *Justice*, Sept. 20, 1884, p. 7; letter to J. L. Mahon, Sept. 13, 1884 (*Man and Myth*, p. 49).
Text: see Appendix II, item 51.

9-14-84 (evening)—"Art and Labour," delivered before a meeting sponsored by the Sheffield Secular Society in Sheffield.
Sources: see above.
Text: see this volume, pp. 98-118.

9-20-84—"At a Picture Show, 1884," delivered at the opening of an Ancoats Recreation Committee art exhibition at New Islington Hall, Ancoats, Manchester. Mr. Charles Rowley was chairman.
Source: *The Manchester Guardian*, Sept. 22, 1884, pp. 4, 8.
Review: "Two Art Reformers," *The Architect*, Sept. 27, 1884, pp. 193-4.
Text: see Appendix II, item 52.

9-21-84—"Art and Labour," delivered at a meeting sponsored by the Ancoats Recreation Committee at New Islington Hall, Ancoats, Manchester. Mr. Charles Rowley was chairman.
Sources: *Justice*, Sept. 27, 1884, p. 7; *The Manchester Guardian*, Sept. 22, 1884, p. 8; *PMG*, Oct. 7, 1884, p. 8.
Reviews: "Two Art Reformers," *The Architect*, Sept. 27, 1884, 193-4; letters to the *The Manchester Guardian*, Sept. 25, 27, 1884.
Text: see this volume, pp. 94-118.

9-27-84*—"Misery and the Way out" was scheduled for delivery before the Progressive Association at Ye Old Mansion House, Essex Road, London.
Source: *Justice*, Sept. 27, 1884, p. 7.
Text: see Appendix II, item 50.

9-28-84*—"Misery and the Way out" was scheduled for delivery before the Bayswater and Paddington Branches, SDF, at St. John's Temperance Hall, Bell St., Edgware Road, London.
Source: see above.
Text: see Appendix II, item 50.

10-12-84*—"Useful Work *versus* Useless Toil" was scheduled for delivery before the Battersea Branch, SDF, at Henley Hall, Henley St., Battersea, London.
Source: *Justice*, Oct. 11, 1884, p. 7.
Text: see Appendix II, item 41.

10-19-84*—"Misery and the Way out" was scheduled for delivery before the Hammersmith Branch, SDF, at Kelmscott House, Hammersmith.
Source: *Justice*, Oct. 18, 1884, p. 7.
Text: see Appendix II, item 50.

10-22-84—"A Socialist's View of Art and Labour," delivered at a meeting sponsored by the Preston Eclectic Society at the Unitarian Chapel, Preston. The Rev. W. Sharman was chairman.
Sources: *Justice*, Nov. 1, 1884, pp. 6-7; *The Preston Guardian*, Oct. 25, 1884, p. 10.
Text: see this volume, pp. 94-118.

10-29-84—Chairman at a Limehouse meeting arranged by the SDF as part of a socialist drive in London's East End.

Source: *Justice,* Nov. 8, 1884, p. 7.

11–2–84—"Useful Work *versus* Useless Toil," delivered at a meeting sponsored by the Rotherhithe Branch, SDF, in the China Hall, Lower Road, Rotherhithe.
Source: *Justice,* November 8, 1884, p. 7.
Text: see Appendix II, item 41.

11–9–84—"Misery and the Way out," delivered before the Tower Hamlets Radical Club at 13 Redman's Road, Mile End.
Source: *Justice,* Nov. 15, 1884, p. 6.
Text: see Appendix II, item 50.

11–16–84—"Art and Labour," delivered at a meeting sponsored by the Newcastle Branch, SDF, in the Tyne Theatre, Newcastle. Dr. Spence Watson was chairman.
Sources: *Justice,* Nov. 29, 1884, p. 6; letter to J. L. Mahon, Nov. 20, 1884 (*Man and Myth,* p. 50).
Text: see this volume, pp. 94–118.

11–17–84—"Misery and the Way out" delivered at a meeting sponsored by the Edinburgh Branch, SLLL, at the large hall of the Literary Institute, Clark St., Edinburgh. Mr. Robert Buist was chairman.
Sources: *Justice,* Nov. 29, 1884, p. 6; *The Edinburgh Evening News,* Nov. 18, 1884.
Review: [Editorial] *The Edinburgh Evening News,* Nov. 18, 1884.
Text: see Appendix II, item 50.

11–21–84—Morris read his "The Passing of Brynhild" at an "Art Evening" sponsored by the SDF at Neumeyer Hall, Hart Street, Bloomsbury.
Sources: "Programme" published by the SDF (reproduced in *Letters,* p. 214); letter from F. Engels to Laura Lafargue, Nov. 23, 1884 (*Frederick Engels, Paul and Laura Lafargue: Correspondence,* Vol. I; Moscow, 1959, pp. 245–46).

11–23–84°—A lecture was scheduled to be delivered before the Glasgow Branch, SDF, in Glasgow.
Source: Letter to Andreas Scheu, Oct. 8, 1884 (*Letters,* p. 215).

11–30–84°—"How We Live and How We Might Live" was scheduled for delivery to the Hammersmith Branch, SDF, at Kelmscott House, Hammersmith.
Source: *Justice,* Nov. 29, 1884, p. 7.
Text: see Appendix II, item 53.

12–5–84—"Misery and the Way out" delivered before the Merton Abbey Branch, SDF, at the branch rooms, High St., Merton.
Source: *Justice,* Dec. 13, 1884, p. 6.
Text: see Appendix II, item 50.

12–7–84—"Misery and the Way out" delivered at a meeting sponsored by the West Central Branch, NSS, at the Athenaeum Hall, George St., London.
Source: *Justice,* Dec. 13, 1884, p. 7.
Text: see Appendix II, item 50.

12–11–84°—A lecture was scheduled for delivery before the Greenock Branch, LRL, at Greenock, Scotland.
Source: Letter to Andreas Scheu, Oct. 8, 1884 (*Letters,* p. 215).

12–13–84°—"How We Live and How We Might Live" was scheduled for delivery at a meeting sponsored by the Edinburgh Branch, SLLL, at Picardy Hall, Edinburgh.

Source: *Justice,* Nov. 22, 1884, p. 7.

Text: see Appendix II, item 53.

12-14-84 (morning)—An extemporé speech before the Glasgow Branch, SDF, at the branch rooms, Glasgow. W. J. Nairne was chairman.

Sources: *Justice,* Dec. 20, 1884, p. 6; *Glasier,* pp. 30–33.

12-14-84 (evening)—"Art and Labour," delivered before the Glasgow Sunday Society at St. Andrew's Hall, Glasgow.

Source: *The Glasgow News,* Dec. 15, 1884, p. 4.

Text: see this volume, pp. 94–118.

12-19-84*—"Misery and the Way out" was scheduled for delivery before the Working Men's Club, Crown Hill, Croydon.

Source: *Justice,* Dec. 13, 1884, p. 7.

Text: see Appendix II, item 50.

12-21-84*—Morris lent a lecture, "The Origin of Ornamental Art," to be read at a meeting sponsored by the Hammersmith Branch, SDF, at Kelmscott House, Hammersmith.

Source: *Ham. Min. Book.*

Text: see Appendix II, item 40.

12-26-84*—"How We Live and How We Might Live" was scheduled for delivery to the Working Men's Club at Crown Hill, Croydon.

Source: *Justice,* Dec. 20, 1884, p. 7.

Text: see Appendix II, item 53.

1885

1-4-85*—"Work, as It Is and as It Might Be" was scheduled for delivery at a meeting sponsored by the Hammersmith Branch, SDF, at Kelmscott House, Hammersmith.

Source: *Ham. Min. Book.*

1-11-85—"How We Live and How We Might Live," delivered at a meeting sponsored by the Bethnal Green Branch, LEL, at the Hoxton Academy Schools, Hoxton.

Source: *Justice,* Jan. 17, 1885, p. 7.

Text: see Appendix II, item 53.

1-25-85—A Lecture to the Woolwich Branch, SDF, in Woolwich.

Source: Letter from Robert Banner to J. L. Mahon, Jan. 30, 1885 (*Nettlau Coll.*).

1-30-85*—Morris was scheduled to read his poem, "All for the Cause," at a Socialist "Art Evening" at Ladbrooke Hall, London, for the benefit of Adam Weiler.

Source: [Program], *Art Evenings,* Berg Collection.

2-1-85*—"How We Live and How We Might Live" was scheduled for delivery at a combined meeting of Branch 23, SDF, and the Deutscher Club, LEL, at the latter club's rooms, Featherstone and Moorgate Streets, London, E.C.

Sources: *Commonweal,* Feb. 1885, p. 8; *Justice,* Jan. 31, 1885, p. 7.

Text: see Appendix II, item 53.

2-7-85*—A speech was scheduled for the opening session of Edward Aveling's lecture series on Karl Marx's *Kapital.* The series was conducted by the SL at the South Place Institute, Finsbury, London.

Source: *Commonweal,* Feb., 1885, p. 5.

2–8–85*—"How We Live and How We Might Live" was scheduled for delivery at the Hammersmith Radical Club.

Source: *Ham. Min. Book.*

Text: see Appendix II, item 53.

2–15–85—"Slaves and Slave Holders," delivered to the Hammersmith Branch, SL, at Kelmscott House, Hammersmith. Mr. E. T. Craig was chairman.

Sources: Letter to May Morris, Feb. 20, 1885 (*Letters,* p. 230); *Ham. Min. Book.*

2–22–85*—"Useful Work *versus* Useless Toil" was scheduled for delivery before the Southwark Branch, SL, at the Forester's Arms, 62 Blackman St., London.

Source: *Commonweal,* Feb., 1885, p. 3.

Text: see Appendix II, item 41.

2–25–85—An extemporé speech, delivered before a meeting sponsored by the Oxford Socialist Society at the Music Room, Holywell, Oxford. Professor C. J. Faulkner was chairman, but he found it impossible to keep order, and the meeting was finally dispersed by a stink-bomb set off by a student in the audience.

Sources: Letters to May Morris, Feb. 20, 1885 (*Letters,* p. 231); March 11, 1885 (*Letters,* pp. 232, 4); *Commonweal,* April, 1885, p. 24; "Oxford Letter," *Cambridge Review,* March 4, 1885, p. 249; Letter to Mrs. Burne-Jones, Feb., 1885 (*Letters,* pp. 231–2).

Text: see Appendix II, item 57.

3–3–85—"Art and Labour," delivered at a meeting sponsored by the Bristol Branch, SL, at the Bristol Museum and Library.

Sources: Letter to May Morris, March 11, 1885 (*Letters,* p. 234); *Bristol Mercury and Daily Post,* March 4, 1885, p. 3; *Western Daily Press,* March 4, 1885, p. 6; letter from H. H. Gose to J. L. Mahon, March 5, 1885 (*Nettlau Coll.*).

Reviews: *Bristol Mercury and Daily Post,* March 4, 1885, p. 5; *The Bristol Evening News,* March 5, 1885, p. [2].

Text: see this volume, pp. 94–118.

3–8–85—"Work, as It Is and as It Might Be," delivered before the Manchester Square Branch, SL, at the Westmoreland Arms, George St., London.

Sources: *Commonweal,* March, 1885, p. 16; letter from F. Lessner to SL Council, March 9, 1885 (*Nettlau Coll.*).

3–11–85—Testimony before the Parliamentary Committee on the Restoration of Westminster Hall. Mr. Shaw Lefevre, M.P., was chairman.

Sources: *The Architect,* Aug. 29, 1890, pp. 121–2; *The Architect,* March 14, 1885, p. 170.

Text: see Appendix II, item 58.

3–13–85*—A lecture was scheduled for delivery to the Merton Abbey Branch, SL, at Merton Abbey.

Sources: *Commonweal,* March, 1885, p. 16; letter to Wilfred Scawen Blunt, March 3, 1885 (*V & A MS*).

3–22–85—A speech in commemoration of the Paris Commune, delivered at the anniversary celebrations sponsored by the SL and combined London anarchist groups. The meeting was held at Neumeyer Hall, Hart St., Bloomsbury.

Sources: *Commonweal,* April, 1885, p. 24; letter to May Morris, April 1, 1885 (B.M. Add. MS. 45341).

3-27-85—"Commercial War," delivered before the Croydon Branch, SDF, at Crown Hill, Croydon.

Sources: *Justice,* April 4, 1885, p. 7; letter to May Morris, April 1, 1885 (B.M. Add. MS. 45341).

Text: see Appendix II, item 60.

3-29-85*—"Socialism" was scheduled for delivery before the Mile-End Branch, SL, at 110 Whitehorse St., Whitechapel.

Source: *Commonweal,* March 1885, p. 16.

Text: see Appendix II, item 61.

4-2-85—A speech moving a socialist rider to an anti-war resolution referring to the Soudan. The meeting, held at St. James's Hall, London, was sponsored and presided over by Mr. Charles Bradlaugh, M.P.

Sources: Letter to May Morris, April 1, 1885 (B.M. Add. MS. 45341); *Commonweal,* May, 1885, p. 36.

4-10-85*—A lecture was scheduled for delivery to the Merton Abbey Branch, SL, at Merton Abbey.

Source: *Commonweal,* April 1885, p. 23.

4-12-85*—"Commercial War" was scheduled for delivery before the local LEL at the Academy Schools, Hoxton St., Hoxton.

Source: *Commonweal,* April, 1885, p. 23.

Text: see Appendix II, item 60.

4-19-85*—"Commercial War" was scheduled for delivery before the Hammersmith Branch, SL, at Kelmscott House, Hammersmith.

Source: see above.

Text: see Appendix II, item 60.

4-23-85—Chairman of an Anti-Soudan-War meeting sponsored by the SL at South Place Institute, Finsbury, London.

Sources: Letters to May Morris, April 1, 14, 1885 (B.M. Add. MS. 45341); *Commonweal,* May, 1885, p. 38.

4-24-85—Poetry readings by Morris from his own works. This was in aid of the Glasgow Branch, SL, which sponsored the meeting at Pillar Hall, Queen's Rooms, Glasgow.

Sources: Letter to Jane Alice Morris, April 28, 1885 (B.M. Add. MS. 45339); *The [Glasgow] Evening News and Star,* April 23, 1885, p. 1, gives the programme.

Reviews: *The [Glasgow] Evening News and Star,* April 25, 1885, p. 1; "Mr. William Morris's Readings," *The Glasgow News,* April 25, 1885, p. 4.

4-25-85—"Work, as It Is and as It Might Be," delivered at a meeting sponsored by the Edinburgh Branch, SLLL, at the Free Tron Hall, Edinburgh. The Rev. John Glasse was chairman.

Sources: Letter to Jane Alice Morris, April 28, 1885 (B.M. Add. MS. 45339); *The Edinburgh Evening News,* April 27, 1885.

Review: [Editorial], *The Edinburgh Evening News,* April 27, 1885.

4-26-85—"How We Live and How We Might Live," delivered at a meeting sponsored by the Glasgow Branch, SL, at the Albion Hall, Glasgow.

Sources: *Commonweal,* April, 1885, p. 23; letter to Jane Alice Morris, April 28, 1885 (B.M. Add. MS. 45339); *The [Glasgow] Evening News and Star,* April 27, 1885, p. 2, gives a précis.

Reviews: *The [Glasgow] Evening News and Star,* April 27, 1885, p. 1; *The Edinburgh Evening News,* April 27, 1885.

Text: see Appendix II, item 53.

4–27–85—"Work, as It Is and as It Might Be," delivered before the Chesterfield and District Workingmen's Radical Association at the Stephenson Memorial Hall, Chesterfield. Mr. Edward Carpenter was chairman.

Sources: *Commonweal*, June, 1885, p. 48; *The Derbyshire Courier*, May 2, 1885, p. 5.

5–8–85°—"How Can We Help?" was scheduled for delivery to the Merton Abbey Branch, SL, at Merton Abbey.

Source: *Commonweal*, May, 1885, p. 36.

5–10–85—"How Can We Help?" delivered before the Hammersmith Branch, SL, at Kelmscott House, Hammersmith.

Source: *Commonweal*, June, 1885, p. 48.

5–24–85—"Work, as It Is and as It Might Be," delivered before the Mile-End Branch, SL, at 110 White Horse St., Stepney, London.

Sources: *Commonweal*, May, 1885, p. 36; letter to Mrs. Burne-Jones, May 27, 1885 (*Letters*, pp. 236–7).

5–30–85—A speech at a meeting called by the SPAB to protest against the "demolition of Churches of York." The Hon. R. C. Grosvenor was chairman, and the meeting was held at the Corn Exchange, York.

Sources: *The Architect*, June 6, 1885, pp. 338–40; *The [York] Evening Press*, June 1, 1885, p. 4.

Comment: [Editorial], *The [York] Evening Press*, June 1, 1885, p. 2.

6–4–85—The opening speech, as chairman, delivered at the annual SPAB meeting, held in the rooms of the Society of Arts, John St., Adelphi.

Sources: *The Architect*, June 13, 1885, p. 335; *The Artist*, VI (July, 1885), 218; *SPAB Report, 1885*, p. 1.

Text: see Appendix II, item 65.

6–9–85—"Socialism," delivered before the Oxford Branch, SL, and the Marx Club in Oxford.

Sources: *Commonweal*, July, 1885, p. 60; *Artist, Writer, Socialist*, II, 192.

Text: see Appendix II, item 66.

6–11–85—Reading of the poem "Socialists at Play," specially written by Morris for the social event celebrating the completion of Edward Aveling's lectures on Marx's *Kapital*. The soiree, sponsored by the SL, was held at the South Place Institute, Finsbury, London.

Source: *Commonweal*, July, 1885, p. 56.

6–14–85—"The Hopes of Civilization," delivered before the Hammersmith Branch, SL, at Kelmscott House, Hammersmith.

Source: *Commonweal*, July, 1885, p. 60.

Text: see Appendix II, item 67.

6–27–85°—An open-air speech was scheduled for the Hammersmith Branch, SL, at Weltje Rd., Hammersmith.

Source: *Ham. Min. Book*.

6–28–85 (morning)—"Socialism," delivered before the Northampton Branch, NSS, at Cow Meadow, Northampton. Mr. Edmund Powell was chairman.

Sources: *Commonweal*, June, 1885, p. 36; *Northampton Mercury Daily Reporter*, June 29, 1885, p. 2.

Text: see Appendix II, item 66.

6–28–85 (evening)—"How We Live and How We Might Live," delivered before the Northampton Branch, NSS, at the Secular Hall, Gold St., Northampton. Mr. R. Reid was chairman.

Sources: *Commonweal*, June, 1885, p. 48; *Northampton Mercury Daily Reporter*, June 29, 1885, p. 2.

Text: see Appendix II, item 53.

7–5–85—Chairman of the First Annual Conference of the SL at Farringdon Hall, 13 Farringdon Road, London.

Sources: *Commonweal*, July, 1885, p. 65–7; *Commonweal Supplement*, Aug., 1885, pp. 73–5.

7–11–85—"The Hopes of Civilization," delivered at a meeting sponsored by the Manchester Socialist Union at the Memorial Hall, Manchester.

Sources: *Commonweal*, Aug., 1885, p. 72; letter to Andreas Scheu, July 16, 1885 (*Letters*, p. 237); *The Manchester Guardian*, July 13, 1885, p. 5.

Text: see Appendix II, item 67.

7–12–85—"The Depression of Trade," delivered at a meeting sponsored by the Oldham Branch, SL, at the Large Hall, Cucumber Gardens, Royton (a suburb of Manchester).

Sources: *Commonweal*, Aug., 1885, p. 72; letter to Andreas Scheu, July 16, 1885 (*Letters*, p. 238).

Text: see this volume, pp. 119–35.

7–13–85—An open-air speech at Thomafields, Oldham (a suburb of Manchester). Morris spoke in favor of free speech, and members of the Manchester Socialist Union, which was then being harassed in its propaganda by the local police, supported him.

Source: *Commonweal*, Aug., 1885, p. 72.

7–14–85—Extemporé speech delivered in the New Hall, Desborough. Mrs. Walters was chairwoman.

Sources: *Commonweal*, Sept., 1885, p. 84; letter to Andreas Scheu, July 16, 1885 (*Letters*, p. 238); *The Kettering Guardian and North Northamptonshire Advertiser*, July 17, 1885, p. 5.

7–19–85—An open-air speech on the occasion of the "Revolutionists' Excursion" to Epping Forest, sponsored by the International Club of London.

Source: *Commonweal*, Aug., 1885, p. 68.

7–26–85—An open-air speech in Victoria Park for the SL.

Source: *Tom Mann's Memoirs* (London, 1967), pp. 48–9.

8–5–85—A speech on W. T. Stead's "recent disclosures" in *PMG* regarding London Prostitution. The meeting, held at Farringdon Hall, 13 Farringdon Road, was sponsored by the SL.

Source: *Commonweal*, Sept., 1885, p. 78.

8–8–85—An open-air speech for the Stratford Branch, SL, in Stratford.

Source: *Commonweal*, Sept., 1885, p. 84.

8–16–85—"Commercial Depression," delivered at a meeting sponsored by the Hoxton Branch, LEL, at the Exchange Coffee House, Pitfield St., Hoxton.

Source: see above.

Text: see this volume, pp. 119–35.

8–22–85*—An open-air speech was scheduled for delivery at the "Hyde Park Demonstration for the Protection of Girls."

Source: *PMG*, Aug. 19, 1885, p. 12.

8–23–85—"What's to Become of the Middle Classes?" delivered before the

Hammersmith Branch, SL, at Kelmscott House, Hammersmith.

Source: *Commonweal,* Oct., 1885, p. 92.

9–1–85*—"The Hopes of Civilization" was scheduled for delivery before the Mile-End Branch, SL, at Swaby's Coffee House, Mile-End.

Source: *Commonweal,* Sept., 1885, p. 84.

Text: see Appendix II, item 67.

9–9–85—"The Depression of Trade," delivered at a meeting sponsored by the North London Branch, SL, at Camden Hall, King St., Camden Town.

Source: *Commonweal,* Oct., 1885, p. 92.

Text: see this volume, pp. 119–35.

9–20–85*—"The Guilds of the Middle Ages" was scheduled for delivery before the Hammersmith Branch, SL, at Kelmscott House, Hammersmith.

Source: *Commonweal,* Sept., 1885, p. 84.

9–23–85*—Morris was scheduled for poetry readings at a public Entertainment sponsored by the Merton Abbey Branch, SL, at the Branch Rooms, High St., Merton.

Source: MS text for a handbill (*Nettlau Coll.*).

9–26–85 (afternoon)—A seconding speech to a free speech resolution at an open-air meeting sponsored by Manchester socialists in Albert Square, Manchester.

Sources: *Justice,* Oct. 3, 1885, p. 3; *Commonweal,* Nov., 1885, p. 100; *The Manchester Guardian,* Sept. 28, 1885.

9–26–85 (evening)—A lecture on Socialist tactics and organization at a meeting sponsored by the Manchester Socialist Union at the County Forum, Manchester.

Sources: *Justice,* Oct. 3, 1885, p. 3; letter from Raymond Unwin to H. H. Sparling, Sept. 30, 1885 (*Nettlau Coll.*).

9–27–85—A lecture for the Ancoats Recreation Committee Sunday meeting at New Islington Hall, Ancoats, Manchester.

Source: see above.

9–30–85*—"The Larger Hope" was scheduled for delivery before the central SL at the SL Hall, 13 Farringdon Road, London.

Source: *Commonweal,* Sept., 1885, p. 84.

10–10–85—"Socialism," delivered before the Working Men's College at the College, Great Ormond St., Bloomsbury. Mr. Lowes Dickinson was chairman.

Source: *The [London] Daily Chronicle,* Oct. 12, 1885, p. 2.

Text: see Appendix II, item 66.

10–11–85 (morning)—An open-air speech welcoming John Williams, a socialist who had just been released from prison. The meeting, sponsored by London socialists and radicals, was held at Victoria Park, London.

Sources: Letter to Andreas Scheu, Oct. 16, 1885 (*Letters,* pp. 239–40); *The Daily Telegraph,* Oct. 12, 1885, p. 3; *The Times,* Oct. 12, 1885, p. 6.

10–11–85 (evening)—A lecture, delivered before the Marylebone Branch, SL, at St. John's Temperance Hall, Bell St., London.

Source: *Commonweal,* Nov., 1885, p. 100.

10–15–85—A lecture, delivered at Preston for the local socialists.

Source: Letter to Andreas Scheu, Oct. 16, 1885 (*Letters,* p. 240).

10–18–85*—"The Depression of Trade" was scheduled for delivery before the Hammersmith Branch, SL, at Kelmscott House, Hammersmith.

Source: *Commonweal*, Oct., 1885, p. 72.

Text: see this volume, pp. 119–35.

10–29–85*—A lecture was scheduled for delivery at a meeting sponsored by the South London Branch, SL, at the Camberwell Radical Club, Gloucester Road, Peckham, London.

Source: *Commonweal*, Nov., 1885, p. 100.

11–10–85—"The Rise of a New Epoch," delivered at a meeting sponsored by the Oxford Branch, SL, at the Music Room, Holywell, Oxford. Professor C. J. Faulkner was chairman.

Sources: Letter to Jane Alice Morris, Nov. 11, 1885 (B.M. Add MS. 45339); *The Oxford Times*, Nov. 14, 1885, p. 5; letter from Morris to H. H. Sparling, Nov. 11, [1885], (*Nettlau Coll.*).

Text: as "The Dawn of a New Epoch," see Appendix II, item 78.

11–13–85*—"Socialism, the True Road to Individual Development" was scheduled for delivery before the Eglesfield Club of Queen's College, Oxford.

Source: Letter to C. J. Faulkner, Nov. 2, [1885] (*Walth. MS.* J-541).

11–15–85*—"Socialism," was scheduled for delivery before the Hammersmith Branch, SL, at Kelmscott House, Hammersmith. Sir Sydney Cockerell's biographer, Wilfrid Blunt, says that Morris was not present on this occasion, his daughter May reading his text for him.

Sources: *Commonweal*, Nov., 1885, p. 100; Wilfrid Blunt, *Cockerell* (London, 1964), p. 46.

Text: see Appendix II, item 66.

11–20–85*—"The Rise of a New Epoch" was scheduled for delivery before the Croydon Working Men's Club at Crown Hill, Croydon. Morris, however, was ill at this time and probably did not keep this appointment.

Sources: *Justice*, Nov. 14, 1885, p. 3; letter from Morris to H. H. Sparling [Nov. 14, 1885] (*Nettlau Coll.*).

Text: as "The Dawn of a New Epoch," see Appendix II, item 78.

11–26–85*—A lecture was scheduled for delivery before the Bloomsbury Branch, SL, at the Eagle and Child Coffee Tavern, 45 Old Compton St., Soho.

Source: *Commonweal*, Nov., 1885, p. 100.

1886

1–7–86*—"How We Live and How We Might Live" was scheduled for delivery at a meeting sponsored by the South London Branch, SL, at the Camberwell Radical Club, Gloucester Road, Peckham.

Source: *Commonweal*, Jan., 1886, p. 8.

Text: see Appendix II, item 53.

1–10–86*—"The Political Outlook" was scheduled for delivery before the Hammersmith Branch, SL, at Kelmscott House, Hammersmith.

Source: see above.

Text: see Appendix II, item 80.

1–12–86—"Socialism," delivered before the Peckham and Dulwich Radical Club at 144 Rye Lane, Peckham. G. B. Shaw spoke afterward on parliamentary measures.

Sources: *Commonweal*, Jan., 1886, p. 8; letter to J. L. Mahon, Jan. 15, 1886 (*Man and Myth*, p. 56).

Text: see Appendix II, item 66.

1–13–86*—"The Political Outlook" was scheduled for delivery at a meeting sponsored by the SL at the SL Hall, 13 Farringdon Road, London.
Source: Handbill (*Nettlau Coll.*).
Text: see Appendix II, item 80.

1–15–86—"How We Live and How We Might Live," delivered before the Working Men's Club and Youth's Institute in the Congregational Hall, Blenheim Road, London.
Source: *PMG,* Jan. 16, 1886, p. 7.
Text: see Appendix II, item 53.

1–24–86 (afternoon)—"Socialism," delivered at a combined meeting of the Hackney and Shoreditch Branches, SDF, at the Hackney Branch rooms, Goldsmith Row, Hackney Road, Hackney.
Sources: *Justice,* Jan. 30, 1886, p. 4; *Commonweal,* Jan., 1886, p. 8.
Text: see Appendix II, item 66.

1–24–86* (evening)—A lecture was scheduled for delivery at a meeting sponsored by the Hammersmith Branch, SL, at Kelmscott House, Hammersmith.
Source: *Ham. Min. Book.*

1–27–86*—"The Political Outlook" was scheduled for delivery before the Clerkenwell (Central) Branch, SL, at the SL Hall, 13 Farringdon Road, London.
Source: *Commonweal,* Jan., 1886, p. 8.
Text: see Appendix II, item 80.

2–2–86*—"The Political Outlook" was scheduled for delivery before the Mile-End Branch, SL, at the International Workingmen's Educational Club, 40 Berner St., Commercial Road, London.
Source: *Commonweal,* Feb., 1886, p. 16.
Text: see Appendix II, item 80.

2–10–86—"The Political Outlook," delivered at a meeting of the Hammersmith Liberal Club at the Club's rooms, Hammersmith.
Sources: *Commonweal,* Feb., 1886, p. 16; *PMG,* Feb. 10, 1886, p. 6.
Review: *PMG,* Feb. 11, 1886, p. 3.
Text: see Appendix II, item 80.

2–14–86*—"Socialism" was scheduled for delivery before the Patriotic Club in London.
Source: *Commonweal,* Feb., 1886, p. 16.
Text: see Appendix II, item 66.

2–23–86*—Morris's lecture "Misery and the Way out" was scheduled to be read from his manuscript by someone else at a meeting sponsored by the Bradford Branch, SL, at Laycock's Temperance Hotel, Bradford.
Source: Letter from Fred Pickles to H. H. Sparling, Jan. 21, 1886 (*Nettlau Coll.*).
Text: see Appendix II, item 50.

2–28–86 (afternoon)—A lecture, delivered at a meeting sponsored by Sheffield socialists at the Secular Hall, Sheffield.
Source: *Commonweal,* April, 1886, p. 30.

2–28–86 (evening)—A lecture, delivered at a meeting sponsored by Sheffield socialists at the Secular Hall, Sheffield.
Source: see above.

2–30–86*—Morris's lecture "Misery and the Way out" was scheduled to be read from his manuscript by someone else at a meeting sponsored by the Bradford Branch, SL, somewhere in the Bradford area.

Source: Letter from Fred Pickles to H. H. Sparling, Jan. 21, 1886 (*Nettlau Coll.*).

Text: see Appendix II, item 50.

3–2–86—"Socialism, in relation to the London Riots," delivered at a meeting sponsored by the Worker's Brotherhood at the Concert Hall, Lord Nelson St., Liverpool.

Sources: *Commonweal*, April, 1886, p. 30; *PMG*, March 3, 1886, p. 12; *The Liverpool Daily Post*, March 3, 1886, p. 6.

3–7–86*—Morris's lecture "Misery and the Way out" was scheduled to be read from his manuscript by someone else at a meeting sponsored by the Bradford Branch, SL, somewhere in the Bradford Area.

Source: Letter from Fred Pickles to H. H. Sparling, Jan. 21, 1886 (*Nettlau Coll.*).

Text: see Appendix II, item 50.

3–8–86—"Socialism," delivered at a meeting sponsored by the Norwich Branch, SL, at the Victoria Hall, Norwich. Mr. Charles Reynolds was chairman.

Sources: *Commonweal*, April 1886, p. 30; [*Norwich*] *Daylight Supplement*, March 13, 1886.

Review: [Editorial], *The Eastern Evening News*, March 9, 1886, p. 2.

Text: see Appendix II, item 66.

3–14–86—"The Aims of Art," delivered before the Hammersmith Branch, SL, at Kelmscott House, Hammersmith.

Source: *Commonweal*, March, 1886, p. 24.

Review: "Mr. William Morris at Home," *The Artist*, VII (April, 1886), 101–2.

Text: see Appendix II, item 82.

3–31–86—"The Aims of Art," delivered at a meeting of the Hammersmith Liberal Club in the Club rooms, Hammersmith.

Source: *PMG*, April 1, 1886, p. 3.

Text: see Appendix II, item 82.

4–9–86—"The Aims of Art," delivered at a meeting sponsored by the Dublin Branch, SL, at the Molesworth Hall, Dublin.

Source: *Commonweal*, May 8, 1886, p. 43.

Review: "A Socialist Poet on Art," *The* [*Dublin*] *Daily Express*, April 12, 1886, p. 3.

Text: see Appendix II, item 82.

4–10–86 (afternoon)—"The Political Outlook," delivered before the Dublin Branch, SL, in Dublin.

Source: *Commonweal*, May 8, 1886, p. 43.

Text: see Appendix II, item 80.

4–10–86—The initial speech at an open debate on "Socialism: What Is It?" The debate, which ended in a near riot when someone turned out the gas lights, was held under the auspices and at the rooms of the Saturday Club, Dublin.

Sources: *Commonweal*, May 8, 1886, p. 43; *The* [*Dublin*] *Evening Telegraph*, April 12, 1886, p. 2; *The* [*Dublin*] *Daily Express*, April 12, 1886, p. 7; letter from Morris to SL Council, [April, 1886], (*Nettlau Coll.*).

Reviews: [Editorial], *The* [*Dublin*] *Daily Express*, April 12, 1886, p. 4; [Editorial], *The Irish Times*, April 12, 1886, p. 5.

4–13–86—"Socialism," delivered at a meeting sponsored by the Dublin Branch, SL, at 30 Great Brunswick St., Dublin.

Source: *The [Dublin] Evening Telegraph,* April 14, 1886, p. 2.

Text: see Appendix II, item 66.

4–17–86—"The Political Outlook," delivered at a meeting sponsored by the Leeds and Bradford Branches, SL, at the Co-operative Hall, Shipley. Mr. W. P. Byles was chairman.

Sources: *Commonweal,* May 8, 1886, p. 43; *The Bradford Observer,* April 21, 1886, p. 3; letter to J. L. Mahon, March 25, 1886 (*Man and Myth,* pp. 59–60).

Text: see Appendix II, item 80.

4–18–86—"Socialism," delivered at a meeting sponsored by the Bradford Branch, SL, at the Temperance Hall, Bradford. Mr. James Hanson was chairman.

Sources: *Commonweal,* May 8, 1886, p. 43; *The Bradford Observer,* April 21, 1886, p. 3.

Text: see Appendix II, item 66.

4–19–86—"The Present and Future of the Working Classes," delivered at a meeting sponsored by the Leeds Branch, SL, at the Assembly Rooms, New Briggate, Leeds.

Sources: *Commonweal,* May 8, 1886, p. 43; *The Leeds Mercury,* April 20, 1886, p. 8; *The Leeds Daily News,* April 20, 1886, p. 4; letter to J. L. Mahon, March 25, 1886 (*Man and Myth,* pp. 59–60); placard in the Mattison Collection, Leeds University; letter from J. L. Mahon to H. H. Sparling, April 25, 1886 (*Nettlau Coll.*).

Text: no text remains under this title, but the letter to J. L. Mahon cited above makes it clear that Morris revised "The Dawn of a New Epoch" for this occasion. See Appendix II, item 78.

4–25–86—"Our Policy," delivered before the Hammersmith Branch, SL, at Kelmscott House, Hammersmith.

Sources: *Commonweal,* April, 1886, p. 32; letter from G. Porter to SL, April 27, 1886 (*Nettlau Coll.*).

Text: see Appendix II, item 85.

4–28–86*—"Competition," scheduled for delivery before the Clerkenwell (Central) Branch, SL, at Farringdon Hall, 13 Farringdon Road, London.

Source: *Commonweal,* April, 1886, p. 32.

5–2–86*—"Art and Labour" was scheduled for delivery before the Clerkenwell (Central) Branch, SL, at Farringdon Hall, 13 Farringdon Road, London.

Source: *Commonweal,* May 1, 1886, p. 40.

Text: see this volume, pp. 94–118.

5–12–86*—A lecture was scheduled for a meeting sponsored by the Woolwich Branch, SL, at Woolwich.

Source: Letter from Robert Banner to Henry H. Sparling, April 29, 1886 (*Nettlau Coll.*).

5–16–86 (morning)—"The Aims of Art," delivered at a meeting sponsored by the Birmingham Branch, SL, at the Baskerville Hall, The Crescent, Birmingham.

Source: *Commonweal,* May 22, 1886, p. 64.

Text: see Appendix II, item 82.

5–16–86 (evening)—"Socialism," delivered at a meeting sponsored by the Birmingham Branch, SL, at the Baskerville Hall, The Crescent, Birmingham. Mr D. Baker was chairman.

Sources: *Commonweal*, May 29, 1886, p. 72; *The Birmingham Daily Post*, May 17, 1886, p. 5.

Text: see Appendix II, item 66.

5–17–86—"The Political Outlook," delivered at a meeting sponsored by the Birmingham Branch, SL, at the Exchange Buildings, New St., Birmingham.

Sources: *Commonweal*, May 29, 1886, p. 72; *The Birmingham Daily Post*, May 18, 1886, p. 5.

Text: see Appendix II, item 80.

5–18–86*—"Misery and the Way out" was scheduled to be read from Morris's manuscript by M. Sollitt at a meeting sponsored by the Leeds Branch, SL, at the St. James's Cafe, Brigatte, Leeds.

Source: Handbill (*Nettlau Coll.*).

Text: see Appendix II, item 50.

5–19–86—"The Origins of the Ornamental Arts," delivered before the Hammersmith Branch, SL, at Kelmscott House, Hammersmith.

Sources: Letter to Jane Alice Morris, May 21, 1886 (*Letters*, p. 254); *Ham. Min. Book.*

Text: see this volume, pp. 136–57.

6–2–86*—A lecture was scheduled for delivery to the Merton Abbey Branch, SL, at Merton Abbey.

Source: Letter to Jane Alice Morris, June 2, 1886 (*Letters*, p. 255).

6–4–86—"Art and Socialism," delivered at a meeting sponsored by the Bloomsbury Branch, SL, at the Arlington Hall, Bloomsbury.

Source: *Commonweal*, June 12, 1886, p. 87.

Text: see Appendix II, item 42.

6–5–86—An open-air speech in support of the Stratford Branch, SL, in Stratford.

Sources: Letter to Jane Alice Morris, June 15, [1886], (*Letters*, p. 256); *Commonweal*, June 12, 1886, p. 87.

6–6–86*—"The Dawn of a New Epoch" was scheduled for delivery before the Notting Hill Debating Society at the Monarch Tavern, Manchester St., London.

Source: *Commonweal*, June 5, 1886, p. 80.

Text: see Appendix II, item 78.

6–8–86—A speech seconding a resolution to establish a fund for the repair of ancient buildings, delivered at the Annual Conference, SPAB, at the Society of Arts, John-Street, Adelphi. The Hon. R. C. Grosvenor was chairman.

Sources: *The Architect*, June 11, 1886, p. 357; *SPAB Report, 1886*, p. 1; *The Times*, June 9, 1886.

6–11–86—"Whigs, Democrats, and Socialists," delivered before Fabian and other socialists at the Fabian Conference on Political Action, held at South Place Institute, Finsbury. Mr. Keddell was chairman.

Sources: Letter to Jane Alice Morris, June 15, [1886] (B.M. Add. MS. 45339); *To-Day*, VI (July, 1886), 8–14.

Review: "The Fabian Conference," *The Christian Socialist*, IV (July, 1886), 16.

Text: see Appendix II, item 89.

6–12–86—Two open-air speeches, delivered for the Marylebone Branch, SL, in

Hyde Park, near the Marble Arch.

Source: Letter to Jane Alice Morris, June 15, [1886], (*Letters*, p. 257).

6–22–86—A lecture, delivered at a meeting sponsored by the Arbroath Lecture Committee, in Arbroath, Scotland.

Source: *Commonweal*, July 3, 1886, pp. 105–6.

6–23–86—"True and False Society," delivered at a meeting sponsored by the Industrial Remuneration Conference Executive Committee at the Oddfellows' Hall, Edinburgh.

Source: see above.

Text: see Appendix II, item 90.

6–24–86—"True and False Society," delivered at a meeting sponsored by the Industrial Remuneration Conference Executive Committee at the Waterloo Rooms, Glasgow.

Sources: *Commonweal*, July 3, 1886, pp. 105–6.

Text: see Appendix II, item 90.

6–25–86—"True and False Society," delivered at a meeting sponsored by the Industrial Remuneration Conference Executive Committee, in Dundee, Scotland.

Source: see above.

Text: see Appendix II, item 90.

6–27–86—"The Political Outlook," delivered at a meeting sponsored by the Glasgow Branch, SL, at the Waterloo Rooms, Glasgow.

Sources: *Commonweal*, July 10, 1886, p. 114; letter to J. Bruce Glasier, April 24, [1886], (*Letters*, p. 253).

Text: see Appendix II, item 80.

6–28–86—"Socialism" delivered at a meeting sponsored by the Glasgow Branch, SL, at the Temperance Institute, James St., Bridgeton, Scotland.

Sources: *Commonweal*, June 26 and July 10, 1886, pp. 104, 114.

Text: see Appendix II, item 66.

7–2–86—"The Aims of Art," delivered at a meeting sponsored by the Fabian Society at the South Place Institute, Finsbury. Mr. Walter Crane was chairman.

Sources: *Commonweal*, June 26, 1886, p. 104; *History of the Fabians*, p. 66; *Our Corner*, VIII (Aug., 1886), 124.

Review: "Mr. William Morris on the Aims of Art," *PMG*, July 3, 1886, p. 6.

Text: see Appendix II, item 82.

7–11–86—"Education," delivered before the Hoxton Branch, SL, in Hoxton.

Source: *Commonweal*, July 17, 1886, p. 128.

Text: see Appendix II, item 91.

7–18–86 (morning)—An open-air speech for the Marylebone Branch, SL, on Bell St., then an area of dispute between socialists and the London police.

Source: *Commonweal*, July 24, 1886, p. 138.

7–18–86 (evening)—"Education," delivered at a meeting sponsored by the Hammersmith Branch, SL, at Kelmscott House, Hammersmith. Branch minutes give this title as "My Education."

Sources: *Commonweal*, July 24, 1886, p. 136; *PMG*, July 21, 1886, p. 13; *Ham. Min. Book*.

Text: see Appendix II, item 91.

8–1–86—An open-air speech, delivered for the Marylebone Branch, SL, at Hyde Park.

Source: *Commonweal,* Aug. 7, 1886, p. 151.

8–2–86—Morris spoke at an open air meeting sponsored by the Hammersmith Branch, SL, at Beadon Road, Hammersmith.
Source: *Ham. Min. Book.*

8–8–86—An open-air speech, delivered for the Hackney Branch, SL, at Victoria Park.
Source: *Commonweal,* Aug. 14, 1886, p. 160.

8–9–86—An open-air speech, delivered at a meeting gathered by the Hammersmith Branch, SL, at Walham Green, opposite the railroad station.
Source: *Ham. Min. Book.*

8–15–86—An open-air speech, delivered at a meeting gathered by the Hammersmith Branch, SL, at Walham Green, opposite the railroad station.
Source: *Ham. Min. Book.*

8–22–86 (morning)—An open-air speech, delivered at a meeting gathered by the Hammersmith Branch, SL, in Walham Green, opposite the railroad station.
Sources: *Commonweal,* Aug. 21, 1886, p. 168; letter to Jane Alice Morris, Aug. 23, 1886 (B.M. Add. MS. 45339); letter to Andreas Scheu, Aug. 20, 1886 (*Letters,* p. 258); *Ham. Min. Book.*

8–22–86 (mid-morning)—An open-air speech, delivered for the Hammersmith Branch, SL, at Beadon Road, Hammersmith.
Sources: Letter to Jane Alice Morris, Aug. 23, 1886 (B.M. Add. MS. 45339); *Ham. Min. Book.*

8–22–86 (evening)—"Our Tactics," delivered before the Hammersmith Branch, SL, at Kelmscott House, Hammersmith. Mr. E. Belfort Bax was chairman. Branch minutes give this title as "Socialism."
Sources: see above, also *Commonweal,* Aug. 21, 1886, p. 168.

8–24–86—"The New Epoch," delivered at a meeting sponsored by the Mile-End Branch, SL, at Mile-End.
Source: *Commonweal,* Sept. 4, 1886, p. 184.
Text: as "The Dawn of a New Epoch," see Appendix II, item 78.

9–5–86—An open-air speech, delivered for the Hammersmith Branch, SL, at Beadon Road, Hammersmith.
Sources: *Commonweal,* Sept. 4, 1886, p. 184; *Ham. Min. Book.*

9–5–86—"The Labour Question," delivered at a meeting sponsored by the Hammersmith Branch, SL, at Kelmscott House, Hammersmith.
Source: *Ham. Min. Book.*
Text: as "True and False Society," see Appendix II, item 90.

9–15–86—"Education," delivered at a meeting sponsored by the Clerkenwell (Central) Branch, SL, at the SL Hall, 13 Farringdon Road, London.
Sources: *Commonweal,* Sept. 25, 1886, p. 207; *The Artist,* VII (Nov., 1886), 342–3.
Text: see Appendix II, item 91.

9–17–86—A speech "against the Party of [political] compromise," delivered at a meeting called by the Fabian Society. On this occasion, socialists representing various London societies gathered at Anderton's Hotel to discuss the formation of a British Socialist Party.
Sources: Letter to Jane Alice Morris, Sept. 17, [1886], (B.M. Add. MS. 45339); *The Christian Socialist,* IV (Oct., 1886), 52; *To-Day,* VI (Oct., 1886), 156.
Text: see Appendix II, item 93.

9–26–86—"Of the Origin of Decorative Art," delivered at a meeting sponsored by the Ancoats Recreation Committee at New Islington Hall, Ancoats, Manchester. Mr. Charles Rowley was chairman.

Sources: *Commonweal*, Oct. 9, 1886, p. 221; *The Manchester Examiner and Times*, Sept. 27, 1886, p. 6; *The Journal of Decorative Art*, VI (Nov., 1886), 988; *The Architect*, Oct. 1, 1886, pp. 197–8.

Text: see this volume, pp. 136–57.

9–27–86—"Socialism: the End and the Means," delivered at a meeting sponsored by the Manchester Branch, SL, at the Ardwick Temperance Hall, Pin Mill Brow, Aston Old Road, Manchester.

Sources: *Commonweal*, Oct. 9, 1886, p. 221; *The Manchester Examiner and Times*, Sept. 28, 1886, p. 6; *The Manchester Guardian*, Sept. 28, 1886, p. 6.

Text: see Appendix II, item 94.

9–28–86—"Socialism: the End and the Means," delivered at a meeting sponsored by Sheffield socialists at the Lower Albert Hall, Sheffield.

Source: *Commonweal*, Oct. 9, 1886, p. 224.

Text: see Appendix II, item 94.

10–1–86*—A lecture on pattern designing was scheduled to be delivered before the Art Workers' Guild, probably at the Century Club Rooms, London.

Sources: Letter from Walter Crane to Morris, Sept. 18, 1886 (B.M. Add. MS. 45345); *Massé*, p. 12.

10–3–86 (morning)—An open-air speech on education, delivered in support of the Merton and Mitcham Branches, SL, at Mitcham Fair Green.

Source: *Commonweal*, Oct. 9, 1886, p. 223.

10–3–86 (afternoon)—An open-air speech on education, delivered at a meeting sponsored by the Metropolitan Radical Association in Trafalgar Square.

Source: *Commonweal*, Oct. 9, 1886, p. 224.

10–3–86 (evening)—"The Birth of Feudalism in Scandinavia" delivered at a meeting sponsored by the Hammersmith Branch, SL, at Kelmscott House, Hammersmith.

Source: *Commonweal*, Oct. 2, 1886, p. 216.

Text: Though no text remains on this subject or with this title, there is little doubt that Morris delivered some such lecture at this time and place. See note 17 to "Early England."

10–11–86—"Socialism: the End and the Means," delivered at a meeting sponsored by the Norwich Branch, SL, at Victoria Hall, Norwich.

Sources: *Commonweal*, Oct. 16, 1886, p. 232; letter to Jane Alice Morris, Oct. 13, [1886], (*Letters*, p. 260).

Review: [*Norwich*] *Daylight*, Oct. 16, 1886, p. 5.

Text: see Appendix II, item 94.

10–13–86*—A lecture was delivered at a meeting sponsored by the South-West Ham Radical Association at the Congregational Schools, Swanscombe St., Barking Road, London.

Sources: *Commonweal*, Sept. 25, 1886, p. 208; letter from J. O'Shaughnessy to SL [Oct. ?], 1886, (*Nettlau Coll.*).

10–15–86—"Socialism: the End and the Means," delivered at a meeting sponsored by the North London Branch, SL, at Milton Hall, London.

Source: *Commonweal*, Oct. 23, 1886, p. 239.

Text: see Appendix II, item 94.

10–17–86 (morning)—An open-air speech for the Hammersmith Branch, SL, at Walham Green.

Source: *Ham. Min. Book.*

10–17–86 (evening)—"Socialism, the End and the Means," delivered at a meeting of the Hammersmith Branch, SL, at Kelmscott House, Hammersmith.

Source: *Ham. Min. Book.*

Text: see Appendix II, item 94.

10–18–86—"The Coming Epoch," delivered at a meeting of a radical debating club at The British Workman, Reading.

Source: *Commonweal*, Oct. 30, 1886, p. 248.

Text: as "The Dawn of a New Epoch," see Appendix II, item 78.

10–31–86—An open-air speech for the Hammersmith Branch, SL, at Beadon Road, Hammersmith.

Source: *Ham. Min. Book.*

11–2–86—"Socialism: the End and the Means," delivered at a meeting sponsored by Lancaster socialists at the Palatine Hall, Lancaster.

Sources: *Commonweal*, Nov. 13, 1886, p. 264; *The Lancaster Gazette*, Nov. 6, 1886, p. 7; *The Lancaster Observer and Morecambe Chronicle*, Nov. 5, 1886, p. 4; letter from Edw. Hall to J. L. Mahon, Oct. 23, 1886 (*Nettlau Coll.*).

Text: see Appendix II, item 94.

11–3–86—"The Dawn of a New Epoch," delivered at a meeting sponsored by the Preston Eclectic Society in the schoolroom of the Unitarian Chapel, Preston.

Sources: *Commonweal*, Nov. 13, 1886, p. 264; *The Preston Guardian*, Nov. 6, 1886, p. 10.

Text: see Appendix II, item 78.

11–10–86—An open-air speech for the Hackney Branch, SL, on the Broadway, London Fields, Hackney.

Source: *Commonweal*, Nov. 20, 1886, p. 272.

11–14–86—An open-air speech for the Hammersmith Branch, SL, at Beadon Road, Hammersmith.

Source: *Ham. Min. Book.*

11–21–86—"Socialism: the End and the Means," delivered at a meeting sponsored by the Croydon Branch, SL, at the Royal Coffee House, Croydon.

Source: *Commonweal*, Nov. 27, 1886, p. 280.

Text: see Appendix II, item 94.

11–27–86—"The Dawn of a New Epoch," delivered before the Bedford Park Club at the Club Rooms, Chiswick. The Rev. Mr. Horsley was chairman. At this meeting Morris became acquainted with Sydney Cockerell.

Sources: *Commonweal*, Dec. 4, 1886; *PMG*, Nov. 29, 1886; Sydney Cockerell, *Friends of a Lifetime*, edited by Violet Meynell (London, 1940), p. 22; Sydney Cockerell, "Introduction," to *The Life of William Morris* by J. W. Mackail; The World's Classics Edition (London, 1950), pp. ix–x.

Text: see Appendix II, item 78.

11–28–86 (morning)—An open-air speech, delivered in support of the Fulham Branch, SL, at Walham Green.

Sources: *Commonweal*, Dec. 4, 1886, p. 288; *Ham. Min. Book.*

11–28–86 (evening)—A lecture, delivered before the Pentonville Progressive Society, at Pentonville.

Source: see above.

12–1–86—"Socialism: Its Aims and Methods," delivered before the Clerkenwell (Central) Branch, SL, at the SL Hall, 13 Farringdon Road, London.
Source: *Commonweal,* Dec. 11, 1886, p. 296.
Text: as "Socialism: the End and the Means," see Appendix II, item 94.

12–5–86—An open-air speech for the Hammersmith Branch, SL, at Beadon Road, Hammersmith.
Source: *Ham. Min. Book.*

12–12–86—"Early England," delivered before the Hammersmith Branch, SL, at Kelmscott House, Hammersmith.
Sources: *Commonweal,* Dec. 18, 1886, p. 304; *PMG,* Dec. 13, 1886, p. 13; letter from Morris to the *PMG,* Dec. 15, 1886 (*Letters,* pp. 264–5).
Text: see this volume, pp. 158–78.

1887

1–1–87—"The Origins of Ornamental Art," delivered at a meeting sponsored by the Hammersmith Branch, SL, at Kelmscott House, Hammersmith.
Source: *Ham. Min. Book.*
Text: see this volume, pp. 136–57.

1–2–87° (afternoon)—"Early England" was scheduled for delivery at the South Place Institute, probably before the Fabian Society.
Source: *Journal for 1887.*
Text: see this volume, pp. 158–78.

1–2–87° (evening)—Morris was scheduled to be chairman for Mrs. Annie Besant's lecture to the Hammersmith Branch, SL, at Kelmscott House, Hammersmith.
Source: see above.

1–23–87 (afternoon)—"True and False Society," delivered at a meeting sponsored by the Merton Branch, SL, at 11 Merton Terrace, High Street, Merton.
Sources: *Commonweal,* Jan. 15, 1887, p. 24; *Socialist Diary,* p. 1; *Journal for 1887.*
Text: see Appendix II, item 90.

1–23–87° (evening)—"The End and the Means" was scheduled for delivery at the Cleveland Hall, Cleveland St., London.
Sources: *Commonweal,* Jan. 15, 1887, p. 24; Text for a Handbill (*Nettlau Coll.*).
Text: as "Socialism: the End and the Means," see Appendix II, item 94.

1–25–87°—"The Labour Question from the Socialist Standpoint" was scheduled for delivery before the Hammersmith Club, at the Club's rooms, Hammersmith.
Source: *Journal for 1887.*
Text: as "True and False Society," see Appendix II, item 90.

1–26–87—A speech, in protest against the eviction of the Scottish crofters of Glenbeigh, who were then fighting an anti-rent war. The Hammersmith Radical Club sponsored the protest meeting, in Hammersmith.
Source: *Socialist Diary,* p. 5.

2–1–87—Chairman at a debate between Mrs. Annie Besant, FS, and Mr. G. W. Foote, president of the NSS. The debate was sponsored by the NSS at the

Secular Hall, London.

Source: *Socialist Diary*, p. 7.

2–4–87—Debated the question of the class war at a meeting sponsored by the Chiswick Club, in Chiswick.

Sources: *Socialist Diary*, p. 12; *Ham. Min. Book*.

2–6–87—An open-air speech for the Hammersmith Branch, SL, at Beadon Road, Hammersmith.

Sources: Letter to Jane Alice Morris, Feb. 7, 1887 (B.M. Add. MS. 45339); *Socialist Diary*, p. 9; *Ham. Min. Book*.

2–8–87—Chairman of a meeting to protest against "the coming war" between Germany and France. Combined London socialist and anarchist groups sponsored the meeting at Cleveland Hall, Cleveland St., London.

Sources: *Commonweal*, Feb. 5, 1887, p. 48; *Socialist Diary*, pp. 9–10.

2–9–87—A lecture, delivered before a literary society at a schoolroom on Peckham High St., Peckham. Canon Ridley was chairman.

Sources: *Socialist Diary*, p. 12; *Journal for 1887*.

2–11–87—Continued the debate on the class war (see the entry for 2–4–87).

Source: *Socialist Diary*, p. 12.

2–13–87 (morning)—An open-air speech for the Hammersmith Branch, SL, at Walham Green.

Source: see above.

2–13–87 (evening)—"Mediaeval England," delivered at a meeting sponsored by the Hammersmith Branch, SL, at Kelmscott House, Hammersmith.

Sources: *Socialist Diary*, p. 31; *Journal for 1887;* letter to Jane Alice Morris, Feb. 18, [1887], (B.M. Add. MS. 45339); *PMG*, Feb. 14, 1887, p. 11.

Text: as "Feudal England," see Appendix II, item 101.

2–16–87—"Mediæval England," delivered before the Clerkenwell (Central) Branch, SL, at the SL Hall, 13 Farringdon Road, London.

Sources: *Commonweal*, Feb. 26, 1887, p. 71; *Socialist Diary*, pp. 15–16; letter to Jane Alice Morris, Feb. 18, [1887], (B.M. Add. MS. 45339).

Text: as "Feudal England," see Appendix II, item 101.

2–20–87—A speech on monopoly, delivered before the Mitcham Branch, SL, at the Branch club-room, corner of Merton Lane and Fountain Place, Mitcham.

Sources: *Commonweal*, Feb. 26, 1887, p. 71; *Socialist Diary*, p. 16; letter to Jane Alice Morris, Feb. 18, [1887], (B.M. Add. MS. 45339).

Text: see Appendix II, item 102.

2–27–87—An open-air speech, delivered for the Hammersmith Branch, SL, at Beadon Road, Hammersmith.

Source: *Socialist Diary*, p. 21.

3–6–87—"How We Live and How We Might Live," delivered before the Hoxton Branch, LEL, at 2 Crondel St., New North Road, Hoxton.

Sources: *Commonweal*, March 5, 1887, p. 80; *Socialist Diary*, p. 25; *Journal for 1887*.

Text: see Appendix II, item 53.

3–13–87—"Monopoly," delivered before the Hackney Branch, SL, at the Branch rooms, 23 Audrey St., Goldsmith Row, Hackney.

Sources: *Commonweal*, March 1, 1887, p. 95; *Socialist Diary*, p. 27; *Journal for 1887*.

Text: as "Monopoly; or, How Labour Is Robbed," see Appendix II, item 103.

3–14–87—"The End and the Means," delivered at a meeting sponsored by the Edinburgh Branch, SLLL, at the Lower Free Tron Hall, Edinburgh. The Rev. John Glasse was chairman.

Sources: *Commonweal*, March 12, 1887, p. 88; letters to Jane Alice Morris, March 9, 17, 1887 (B.M. Add. MS. 45339); *Socialist Diary*, pp. 27–8; *Journal for 1887; The Edinburgh Evening News*, March 15, 1887.

Text: as "Socialism: the End and the Means," see Appendix II, item 94.

3–17–87—A speech, delivered at the Paris Commune anniversary celebrations, sponsored by the combined London socialist groups at the South Place Institute, Finsbury, London.

Sources: *Commonweal*, March 26, 1887, p. 104; letter to Jane Alice Morris, March 17, 1887 (B.M. Add. MS. 45339); *Socialist Diary*, pp. 29–30; *The [London] Daily News*, March 18, 1887.

3–20–87—"Monopoly," delivered at a meeting sponsored by the Chiswick Club, at the Chiswick Hall, London.

Sources: *Socialist Diary*, p. 30; *Journal for 1887*.

Text: as "Monopoly; or, How Labour Is Robbed," see Appendix II, item 103.

3–22–87—"Mediæval England," delivered at a meeting sponsored by the Hammersmith Radical Club, at the Club's rooms, Hammersmith.

Sources: *Socialist Diary*, p. 31; *Journal for 1887*.

Text: as "Feudal England," see Appendix II, item 101.

3–27–87 (morning)—"Monopoly," delivered before the Borough of Hackney Club, in Haggerston, London.

Sources: *Socialist Diary*, p. 32; *Journal for 1887*.

Text: as "Monopoly; or How Labour Is Robbed," see Appendix II, item 103.

3–27–87 (afternoon)—An open-air speech, delivered at a free-speech demonstration sponsored by the Hackney Branch, SL, and other London socialists, at Victoria Park, London.

Sources: *Commonweal*, April 2, 1887, p. 111; *Socialist Diary*, p. 32.

4–3–87 (afternoon)—An open-air speech, delivered for the Glasgow Branch, SL, at Jail Square, Glasgow.

Sources: *Commonweal*, April 9, 1887, p. 120; letter to Jane Alice Morris, April 14, 1887 (*Letters*, pp. 269–71); *Socialist Diary*, p. 35.

4–3–87 (evening)—"True and False Society," delivered at a meeting sponsored by the Glasgow Branch, SL, at the Waterloo Hall, Glasgow. Mr. R. B. Cunninghame-Graham, M.P., was chairman.

Sources: see above.

Text: see Appendix II, item 90.

4–4–87—A lecture, from notes, delivered at a meeting sponsored by the Rev. David Macrea, in Dundee, Scotland.

Sources: Letter to Jane Alice Morris, April 14, 1887 (*Letters*, pp. 269–71); *Socialist Diary*, pp. 35–6.

4–5–87—"Monopoly," delivered at a meeting sponsored by the Edinburgh Branch, SLLL, at the Free Tron Hall, Edinburgh.

Sources: *Commonweal*, April 16, 1887, p. 125; letter to Jane Alice Morris, April 14, 1887 (*Letters*, pp. 269–71); *Socialist Diary*, p. 36; *The Edinburgh Evening News*, April 6, 1887.

Text: as "Monopoly; or, How Labour is Robbed," see Appendix II, item 103.

4–7–87—"Socialism and the Labour Struggle," delivered at a meeting sponsored by the Hamilton Branch, SL, at the Choral Hall, Hamilton. Mr. John Munn was chairman.

Sources: *Commonweal*, April 16, 1887, p. 125; *Socialist Diary*, pp. 36–7; *The Hamilton Advertiser*, April 9, 1887, p. 6; letter to Jane Alice Morris, April 14, 1887 (*Letters*, pp. 269–71).

4–8–87—"Socialism: The Way and the Means," delivered at a meeting sponsored by Paisley socialists, in the Good Templar Hall, Paisley. Provost (Mayor) Cochrane was chairman.

Sources: *Commonweal*, April 16, 1887, p. 125; letter to Jane Alice Morris, April 14, 1887 (*Letters*, pp. 269–71); *Socialist Diary*, p. 37; *The Paisley Daily Express*, April 9, 1887, p. 3.

Text: as "Socialism: the End and the Means," see Appendix II, item 94.

4–9–87—An open-air speech, delivered for the Glasgow Branch, SL, at The Cross, Coatbridge, Scotland.

Sources: *Commonweal*, April 16, 1887, p. 125; letter to Jane Alice Morris, April 14, 1887 (*Letters*, pp. 269–71); *Socialist Diary*, p. 37.

4–10–87—An open-air speech, delivered for the Glasgow Branch, SL, on Glasgow Green.

Sources: see above.

4–11–87 (morning)—An open-air speech, delivered for the SDF and SL sponsored Northumberland Miners' Demonstration, in the Blyth Market Place, Blyth.

Sources: *Commonweal*, April 16, 1887, p. 125; *Socialist Diary*, pp. 39–40.

4–11–87 (afternoon)—An open-air speech for the SDF and SL sponsored Northumberland Miners' Demonstration, in a field outside Horton. The audience on this occasion, as estimated in the *Commonweal* report, included "between nine and ten thousand people."

Sources: *Commonweal*, April 16, 1887, p. 125; *Socialist Diary*, p. 40; letter to Jane Alice Morris, April 23 [1887], (*Letters*, pp. 271–4); *The Newcastle Daily Chronicle*, April 12, 1887.

4–11–87 (evening)—An open-air speech, delivered as a part of the Northumberland Miners' Demonstration, at Ryton Willows.

Sources: *Commonweal*, April 16, 1887, p. 125; *Socialist Diary*, p. 41; *The Newcastle Daily Chronicle*, April 12, 1887.

4–13–87—A speech, delivered at a meeting called by the SL to protest against the "Latest Irish Coercion Bill." The Clerkenwell (Central) Branch, SL, sponsored the meeting at the SL Hall, 13 Farringdon Road, London.

Source: *Commonweal*, April 23, 1887, p. 136.

4–17–87 (morning)—An open-air speech, delivered for the Hammersmith Branch, SL, at Beadon Road, Hammersmith.

Source: *Socialist Diary*, p. 42.

4–17–87 (evening)—"True and False Society," delivered at a meeting sponsored by the Hammersmith Branch, SL, at Kelmscott House, Hammersmith.

Sources: *Commonweal*, April 16, 1887, p. 128; *Socialist Diary*, p. 42.

Text: see Appendix II, item 90.

4–24–87 (afternoon)—An open-air speech, delivered at the SL Northumberland Miners' Demonstration in Hyde Park, London.

Sources: *Commonweal*, April 30, 1887, pp. 137–8; *Socialist Diary*, p. 42.

4–24–87* (evening)—"Socialism: Its Aims and Methods" was scheduled for delivery at a meeting sponsored by the Hackney Branch, SL, at the Morley Coffee Tavern Lecture Hall, Triangle, Mare St., Hackney, London.

Source: *Commonweal*, April 21, 1887, p. 128.

Text: as "Socialism: the End and the Means," see Appendix II, item 94.

5–1–87—An open-air speech for the Hammersmith Branch, SL, at Beadon Road, Hammersmith.

Source: *Ham. Min. Book.*

5–4–87°—"True and False Society" was scheduled for delivery at a meeting sponsored by the Christian Socialist Society, at the Industrial Hall, Clark's Buildings, Bloomsbury.

Sources: *Journal for 1887; The Christian Socialist*, V (April, May, 1887), 61, 77.

Text: see Appendix II, item 90.

5–8–87—An open-air speech for the Hammersmith Branch, SL, at Walham Green, Fulham.

Source: *Ham. Min. Book.*

5–15–87 (morning)—An open-air speech for the Hammersmith Branch, SL, at Beadon Road, Hammersmith.

Source: *Ham. Min. Book.*

5–15–87 (evening)—"Art and Industry in the Fourteenth Century," delivered at a meeting sponsored by the Hammersmith Branch, SL, at Kelmscott House, Hammersmith.

Sources: *The Architect*, May 20, 1887, pp. 303–4; *PMG*, May 16, 1887, p. 11.

Text: as "Art and History in the 14th Century," see Appendix II, item 107.

5–21–87—An open-air speech, delivered at a demonstration protesting against Irish coercion by the British Government. The Anti-Coercion Demonstration Committee sponsored the meeting in Victoria Park, London.

Sources: *Commonweal*, May 28, 1887, p. 175; handbill (*Nettlau Coll.*).

5–22–87—An open-air speech, delivered for the North London and Marylebone Branches, SL, at Hyde Park.

Source: see above.

6–1–87—"True and False Society," delivered at a meeting sponsored by the Clerkenwell (Central) Branch, SL, at the SL Hall, 13 Farringdon Road, London.

Sources: *Commonweal*, June 11, 1887, p. 192; *Journal for 1887.*

Text: see Appendix II, item 90.

6–5–87—An open-air speech for the Hammersmith Branch, SL, at Beadon Road, Hammersmith.

Source: *Ham. Min. Book.*

6–8–87—Chairman at the annual meeting of the SPAB, in the Old Hall, Staple Inn, Chancery Lane, London.

Sources: *SPAB Report, 1887*, p. 1; *The Architect*, June 10, 1887, p. 346; *The Times*, June 9, 1887, p. 7.

6–8–87—Speech delivered at the Tenth Annual Meeting, SPAB in support of a motion to establish a fund for the repair of ancient buildings. The meeting was held in the Old Hall, Staple Inn, London.

Source: *SPAB Report, 1887*, p. 56.

Text: see Appendix II, item 109.

6–9–87—"True and False Society," delivered at a meeting sponsored by the

Battersea Branch, SDF, at the Sydney Hall, 36 York Road, Battersea.

Sources: *Justice*, June 18, 1887, p. 4.

Text: see Appendix II, item 90.

6–12–87 (morning)—An open-air speech for the Hammersmith Branch, SL, at Beadon Road, Hammersmith.

Source: *Ham. Min. Book.*

6–12–87* (evening)—"True and False Society" was scheduled for delivery before the Hackney Branch, SL, at the Branch rooms, 23 Audrey Street, Goldsmith Row, Hackney, London.

Source: *Commonweal*, June 11, 1887, p. 192.

Text: see Appendix II, item 90.

6–15–87*—A lecture was scheduled for delivery at 102 Brompton Road, London.

Source: *Journal for 1887.*

6–16–87—Speech at a debate sponsored by the Fabian Society at the South Place Institute, Finsbury.

Source: Letter to J. L. Mahon, June 17, 1887 (*Man and Myth*, pp. 68–69).

6–27–87—An open-air meeting for the Hammersmith Branch, SL, at Walham Green, Fulham.

Source: *Ham. Min. Book.*

6–27–87 (evening)—"Monopoly," delivered at a meeting sponsored by the Hammersmith Branch, SL, at Kelmscott House, Hammersmith.

Sources: *Commonweal*, June 25, 1887, p. 208; *Ham. Min. Book.*

Text: see Appendix II, item 103.

7–3–87 (morning)—An open-air speech for the Hammersmith Branch, SL, at Beadon Road, Hammersmith.

Source: *Ham. Min. Book.*

7–3–87* (afternoon)—An open-air speech was scheduled for delivery for the Hackney Branch, SL, at Broadway, London Fields, Hackney, London.

Source: *Commonweal*, July 2, 1887, p. 216.

7–13–87—An open-air speech, delivered for the Hackney Branch, SL, at London Fields, Hackney, London.

Source: *Commonweal*, July 13, 1887, p. 240.

7–17–87—An open-air speech for the Hammersmith Branch, SL, at Beadon Road, Hammersmith.

Source: *Ham. Min. Book.*

7–23–87—An open-air speech on monopoly and socialism, delivered for the Mile-End Branch, SL, at Victoria Park, London.

Source: *Commonweal*, July 30, 1887, p. 247.

7–24–87—An open-air speech for the Hammersmith Branch, SL, at Beadon Road, Hammersmith.

Source: *Ham. Min. Book.*

7–31–87—"The Policy of Abstention [from Parliamentary Action]," delivered at a meeting sponsored by the Hammersmith Branch, SL, at Kelmscott House, Hammersmith.

Sources: *Commonweal*, July 30, 1887, p. 248; *Ham. Min. Book.*

Text: see Appendix II, item 110.

8–7–87—An open-air speech for the Hammersmith Branch, SL, at Beadon Road, Hammersmith.

Source: *Ham. Min. Book.*

8–14–87—An open-air meeting for the Hammersmith Branch, SL, at Walham Green, Fulham.
Source: *Ham. Min. Book.*

8–21–87 (morning)—An open-air speech for the Hammersmith Branch, SL, at Walham Green, Fulham.
Source: *Ham. Min. Book.*

8–21–87 (afternoon)—An open-air speech for the Mile-End and Bethnal Green Branches, SL, at Victoria Park, London.
Source: *Commonweal,* Aug. 27, 1887, p. 279.

8–21–87 (evening)—"Monopoly," delivered at a meeting sponsored by the Hoxton Branch, LEL, at the Globe Coffee House, 227 High St., Hoxton.
Source: see above.
Text: see Appendix II, item 103.

8–24–87—"The Policy of Abstention from Parlimentary Action," delivered at a meeting sponsored by the Clerkenwell (Central) Branch, SL, at the SL Hall, 13 Farringdon Road, London.
Source: *Commonweal,* Sept. 3, 1887, p. 287.
Text: as "The Policy of Abstention," see Appendix II, item 110.

8–28–87—An open-air speech for the Hammersmith Branch, SL, at Beadon Road, Hammersmith.
Source: *Ham. Min. Book.*

9–5–87*—A speech was scheduled for the "Liberal and Radical Fete and Demonstration" at the Alexandra Palace.
Source: letter from James D. Digby, n.d. (*Nettlau Coll.*).

9–11–87 (morning)—An open-air speech for the Hammersmith Branch, SL, at Walham Green, Fulham.
Source: *Ham. Min. Book.*

9–11–87 (afternoon)—An open-air speech, delivered for the Mile-End and Bethnal Green Branches, SL, at Victoria Park, London,
Source: *Commonweal,* Sept. 17, 1887, p. 303.

9–25–87—A speech, delivered at a demonstration for free speech in Ireland. The meeting was sponsored by the Hoxton Branch, LEL, in Hoxton Church, London.
Source: *Commonweal,* Oct. 1, 1887, p. 319.

9–27–87*—An open-air speech was scheduled for delivery for the Mile-End Branch, SL, on Mile-End Waste, London.
Source: *Commonweal,* Sept. 24, 1887, p. 312.

10–2–87 (afternoon)—"Art and Industry in the Fourteenth Century," delivered at a meeting sponsored by the Ancoats Recreation Committee at New Islington Hall, Ancoats, Manchester.
Sources: *Journal for 1887; The Manchester Guardian,* Oct. 3, 1887, p. 6.
Text: as "Art and History in the 14th Century," see Appendix II, item 107.

10–2–87 (evening)—"Monopoly," delivered at a meeting sponsored by the Salford Branch, SDF, at the Ford St. Temperance Hall, Salford (a suburb of Manchester).
Source: *Justice,* Oct. 8, 1887, p. 4.
Text: see Appendix II, item 103.

10–6–87—A speech, delivered at a meeting called to protest against the impending execution of the Chicago anarchists. Combined London socialist and anarchist groups sponsored the meeting, held at the Communist Club, 49 Tottenham St., London.

Source: *Commonweal*, Oct. 15, 1887, p. 333.

10–9–87 (morning)—An open-air speech for the Fulham Branch, SL, at Walham Green, Fulham.

Source: *Ham. Min. Book.*

10–9–87 (evening)—"The Early Literature of the North," delivered at a meeting sponsored by the Hammersmith Branch, SL, at Kelmscott House, Hammersmith.

Sources: *Commonweal*, Oct. 15, 1887, p. 335; *PMG*, Oct. 10, 1887, p. 13; *Ham. Min. Book.*

Text: as "The Early Literature of the North—Iceland," see this volume, pp. 179–98.

10–11–87*—A lecture, from notes, was scheduled for delivery at The Swan, Lechlade.

Source: Letter to May Morris, Oct. 5, 1887 (*Letters*, p. 276).

10–14–87—A speech, delivered at a meeting called by combined London socialist and anarchist groups to protest the impending execution of the Chicago anarchists. The meeting was held at South Place Institute, London.

Sources: *Commonweal*, Oct. 22, 1887, p. 340; handbill (*Nettlau Coll.*).

10–16–87 (morning)—An open-air speech, delivered for the Fulham Branch, SL, at Walham Green, Fulham.

Sources: *Commonweal*, Oct. 22, 1887, p. 343; *Ham. Min. Book.*

10–16–87* (evening)—"Monopoly" was scheduled for delivery at a combined meeting of the Paddington Branch, SDF, and the West Marylebone Working Men's Club, at the Club's rooms, 123 Church St., Edgeware Road, London.

Sources: *Justice*, Oct. 22, 1887, p. 4; *Commonweal*, Oct. 15, 1887, p. 336.

Text: see Appendix II, item 103.

10–23–87—An open-air speech, delivered for the Fulham Branch, SL, at Walham Green, Fulham, London.

Sources: *Commonweal*, Oct. 29, 1887, p. 351; *Ham. Min. Book.*

10–30–87 (afternoon)—"The Origins of Ornamental Art," delivered at a meeting sponsored by the Nottingham Socialist Club, in the Secular Hall, Nottingham. The Rev. Prof. Symes was chairman.

Sources: *Commonweal*, Nov. 5, 1887, p. 360; *Nottinghamshire Weekly Express and Journal*, Nov. 4, 1887, p. 6; *The Nottingham Daily Guardian*, Oct. 31, 1887, p. 6; *The Nottingham Daily Express*, Oct. 31, 1887, p. 8.

Text: as "Of the Origins of Ornamental Art," see this volume, pp. 136–57.

10–30–87 (evening)—"Monopoly," delivered at a meeting sponsored by the Nottingham Socialist Club, in the Secular Hall, Nottingham. Mr. T. Procter was chairman.

Sources: see above.

Text: see Appendix II, item 103.

11–2–87*—A lecture was scheduled for delivery in Highgate, London.

Source: *Journal for 1887.*

11–6–87*—"What Socialists Want" was scheduled for delivery at a meeting sponsored by the Fulham Liberal Club in Fulham, London.

Sources: see above, also *Commonweal*, Nov. 5, 1887, p. 360.

Text: see this volume, pp. 217–34.

11–8–87—"Socialism," delivered at a meeting sponsored by Huddersfield socialists, at Victoria Hall, Buxton Road, Huddersfield. Mr. Ernest Woodhead was chairman.

Sources: *Journal for 1887; The Huddersfield Weekly News,* Nov. 12, 1887, p. 7.

Text: see Appendix II, item 66.

11–13–87 (Bloody Sunday)—An open-air speech, delivered at Clerkenwell, London, before the attempted march to Trafalgar Square. Morris instructed his contingent of marchers to keep their demonstration orderly and peaceful.

Source: *The Times,* Nov. 14, 1887.

11–13–87 (Bloody Sunday)—"The Future of Society," delivered at a meeting sponsored by the Hammersmith Branch, SL, at Kelmscott House, Hammersmith.

Sources: *Commonweal,* Nov. 12, 1887, p. 368; *Journal for 1887; Ham. Min. Book.*

Text: as "The Society of the Future," see Appendix II, item 117.

11–20–87 (morning)—An open-air speech, delivered for the Fulham Branch, SL, at Walham Green, Fulham.

Sources: *Commonweal,* Nov. 26, 1887, p. 384; *Ham. Min. Book.*

11–20–87 (afternoon)—"The Coming Society," delivered at a meeting sponsored by the Clerkenwell (Central) Branch, SL, at the SL Hall, 13 Farringdon Road, London.

Sources: see above, also *Journal for 1887.*

Text: as "The Society of the Future," see Appendix II, item 117.

11–23–87°—A lecture was scheduled for delivery in Preston.

Source: *Journal for 1887.*

12–1–87—"The Coming Society," delivered at a meeting sponsored by the Bloomsbury Branch, SL, at the Athenaeum Hall, Tottenham Court Road, Bloomsbury.

Source: *Commonweal,* Dec. 10, 1887, p. 399.

Text: as "The Society of the Future," see Appendix II, item 117.

12–2–87—A lecture on "Socialism and the London disturbances" of Bloody Sunday, delivered at a meeting sponsored by the Rev. Oswald Birchall, at the Buscott Rectory. Morris spoke in the rectory because the local gentry barred him from the schoolhouse, the intended place of meeting.

Sources: *Commonweal,* Dec. 10, 1887, p. 393; letters to Rev. Birchall, Oct. 22, Nov. 7, 10, 28, [1887], (B.M. Add. MS. 45347).

12–11–87°—A lecture, probably "Of the Origins of Ornamental Art," was scheduled for delivery to the Hammersmith Branch, SL, at Kelmscott House.

Sources: *Journal for 1887; Romantic to Revolutionary,* p. 547, note 1.

Text: see this volume, pp. 136–57.

12–18–87 (early evening)—An open-air speech, delivered at the funeral of Alfred Linnell, who died of injuries received in Trafalgar Square, Nov. 20, 1887. The SLLL made the funeral, in London's Bow Church Cemetery, the occasion for a mass demonstration.

Sources: *Commonweal,* Dec. 24, 1887, p. 413; *Justice,* Dec. 24, 1887, p. 3; *PMG,* Dec. 19, 1887, pp. 1–3.

12–18–87 (late evening)—"The Present Outlook in Politics," delivered at a meeting sponsored by the Hammersmith Branch, SL, at Kelmscott House, Hammersmith.

Sources: *Commonweal,* Dec. 17, 1887, p. 408; *Ham. Min. Book.*

Text: see this volume, pp. 199–216.

12–25–87°—An open-air speech was scheduled for delivery for the Fulham Branch, SL, at Walham Green, Fulham.

Source: *Ham. Min. Book.*

1888

1–1–88 (morning)—An open-air speech for the Fulham Branch, SL, at Walham Green, Fulham.

Source: *Ham. Min. Book.*

1–1–88 (evening)—"In the absence of Comrade Faulkner," Morris lectured on "The Origins of Ornamental Art," at a meeting sponsored by the Hammersmith Branch, SL, at Kelmscott House, Hammersmith.

Source: *Ham. Min. Book.*

Text: see this volume, pp. 126–153.

1–8–88—An open-air speech for the Hammersmith Branch, SL, at Acton Green, Acton.

Source: *Ham. Min. Book.*

1–8–88 (evening)—"The Political Outlook," delivered at a meeting sponsored by the Clerkenwell (Central) Branch, SL, at the SL Hall, 13 Farringdon Road, London.

Source: *Commonweal,* Jan. 14, 1888, p. 16.

Text: as [The Present Outlook in Politics], see this volume, pp. 199–216.

1–15–88—"Useful Work *versus* Useless Toil," delivered before the Fulham Branch, SL, at the Branch rooms, Fulham, London.

Source: *Commonweal,* Jan. 21, 1888, p. 24.

Text: see Appendix II, item 41.

1–21–88°—Morris was scheduled to perform the role of the Archbishop of Canterbury in *The Tables Turned; or, Nupkins Awakened* at the SL Hall, 13 Farringdon Road, London.

Source: Handbill (B.M. Collection).

1–22–88—"The Social Problem" (also advertised as "The Social Revolution"), delivered at a meeting sponsored by the Chelsea Branch, SDF, at the Alham Rooms, Kilbolton Row, Fulham Road, London.

Source: *Justice,* Jan. 28, 1888, p. 6.

1–29–88—"The Revolt of Ghent," delivered at a meeting sponsored by the Hammersmith Branch, SL, at Kelmscott House, Hammersmith.

Sources: *Commonweal,* Jan. 28, 1888, p. 32; *Ham. Min. Book.*

Text: see Appendix II, item 122.

2–5–88—"What Socialists Want," delivered before the Fulham Branch, SL, at the Branch rooms, 8 Effie Road, Walham Green, London.

Source: *Commonweal,* Feb. 11, 1888, p. 48.

Text: see this volume, pp. 217–33.

2–7–88—A lecture, delivered at the Parish Hall, Chelsea.

Source: *Ham. Min. Book.*

2–19–88 (morning)—An open-air meeting for the Fulham Branch, SL, at Walham Green, Fulham.

Source: *Ham. Min. Book.*

2–19–88° (evening)—"Monopoly" was scheduled for delivery at a meeting sponsored by the Progressive Association, in the Penton Hall, Pentonville Hill, London.

Sources: *Commonweal*, Feb. 18, 1888, p. 56; letter to Jane Alice Morris, Feb. 19, [1888] (*Letters*, p. 280).

Text: see Appendix II, item 103.

2–22–88—"Monopoly," delivered at a meeting sponsored by the Thornton Heath Liberal Club, at the Seneca Hall, Thornton Heath, London.

Sources: Letter to Jane Alice Morris, Feb. 23, 1888 (B.M. Add. MS. 45340); *The Croydon Echo*, March 1, 1888, p. 3.

Text: see Appendix II, item 103.

2–26–88—An open-air speech, delivered for the Fulham Branch, SL, at Walham Green, Fulham, London.

Sources: *Commonweal*, March 3, 1888, p. 72; *Ham. Min. Book*.

3–7–88—A lecture, delivered at the Hammersmith Central Club.

Source: *Ham. Min. Book*.

3–11–88—"Monopoly," delivered at a meeting sponsored by the St. Pancras Branch, SDF, at the Athenaeum Hall, George St., London.

Source: *Justice*, March 18, 1888, p. 6.

Text: see Appendix II, item 103.

3–19–88—A speech, delivered at the annual Paris Commune Celebrations, sponsored by combined London socialist and anarchist groups, at Store Street Hall, London. H. M. Hyndman was chairman.

Sources: *Justice*, March 24, 1888, p. 5; *Commonweal*, March 24, 1888, p. 92; Handbill (*Nettlau Coll.*).

3–21–88—"Monopoly," delivered at a meeting sponsored by the Rev. Forrest, at Clerk's Lane Church, Kilmarnock, Scotland.

Sources: *Commonweal*, April 7, 1888, pp. 106–7; *The Kilmarnock Standard*, March 31, 1888, p. 4; letters to Rev. J. Glasse, Jan. 9, Feb. 20, and March 17, 1888 (*Man and Myth*, pp. 90, 92–3, 95).

Text: see Appendix II, item 103.

3–23–88—An open-air speech, delivered for the Edinburgh Branch, SLLL, at Leith, Scotland.

Source: see above.

3–24–88—A speech, delivered for the Edinburgh Branch, SLLL, at West Calder, Scotland.

Sources: see 3–21–88.

3–25–88—"Art and Industry in the Fourteenth Century," delivered at a meeting sponsored by the Glasgow Branch, SL, at Waterloo Hall, Galsgow.

Sources: *Commonweal*, March 31, 1888, p. 104; letter to May Morris, March 26, 1888 (B.M. Add. M.S. 45341); see also 3–21–88.

Text: as "Art and History in the 14th Century," see Appendix II, item 107.

3–26–88—"The Society of the Future," delivered at a meeting sponsored by the Edinburgh Branch, SLLL, at the Trades' Hall, 142 High St., Edinburgh.

Sources: *Commonweal*, March 24, 31, 1888, pp. 96, 104; *The Edinburgh Evening News*, March 27, 1888; see also letters to Rev. Glasse (entry for 3–21–88).

Text: see Appendix II, item 117.

3–27–88—A lecture, delivered at a meeting sponsored by the SLLL, at Buchan's Hall, Barrack St., Dundee, Scotland.

Sources: *Commonweal,* April 7, 1888, p. 106–7; *The Dundee Courier and Argus,* March 28, 1888; see also letters to Rev. Glasse (entry for 3–21–88).

3–28–88—"Monopoly," delivered before the Aberdeen Branch, SLLL, at the Lecture Hall, Café, Aberdeen, Scotland. The Rev. Alexander Webster was chairman.

Sources: *Commonweal,* April 7, 1888, pp. 106–7; *The [Aberdeen] Weekly News,* March 31, 1888, p. 5; *The [Aberdeen] Daily Free Press,* March 29, 1888, p. 6; *The Aberdeen Journal,* March 29, 1888, p. 6; J. Leatham, *William Morris, Master of Many Crafts* (Turiff, 1899), pp. ix–x.

Review: [Editorial], *The Aberdeen Journal,* March 30, 1888, p. 4.

Text: see Appendix II, item 103.

4–2–88*—"Socialism" was scheduled for delivery to the Fulham Branch, SL, at the Branch rooms, 8 Effie Road, Walham Green, London.

Source: *Commonweal,* April 21, 1888, p. 128.

Text: see Appendix II, item 66.

4–5–88—A speech, delivered at an open debate sponsored by the Ball's Pond Radical Club, at Ball's Pond, London.

Source: *Commonweal,* April 14, 1888, p. 119.

4–8–88 (morning)—An address, in lieu of an open-air speech, the weather being bad, at the Fulham Branch Rooms, Walham Green, Fulham.

Source: *Ham. Min. Book.*

4–8–88 (evening)—"What Socialists Want," delivered at a meeting sponsored by the Clerkenwell and Islington Branches, SDF, at Claremont Hall, Penton St., London.

Source: *Justice,* April 14, 1888, p. 6.

Text: see this volume, pp. 217–33.

4–15–88 (morning)—An open-air speech, delivered for the Fulham Branch, SL, opposite the Liberal Club, Fulham.

Source: *Commonweal,* April 21, 1888, p. 128.

4–15–88 (evening)—"Art and Industry in the Fourteenth Century," delivered at a meeting sponsored by the Hammersmith Branch, SL, at Kelmscott House, Hammersmith.

Sources: *Commonweal,* April 7, 1888, p. 112; *Ham. Min. Book.*

Text: see Appendix II, item 107.

4–17–88—"What Socialists Want," delivered at a meeting sponsored by the Mile-End and Bethnal Green Branches, SL, at the Mile-End Socialist Hall, 95 Boston St., Hackney Road, London.

Source: *Commonweal,* April 28, 1888, p. 134.

Text: see this volume, pp. 217–33.

4–29–88—An open-air speech for the Hammersmith Branch, SL, at Beadon Road, Hammersmith.

Source: *Ham. Min. Book.*

5–6–88—An open-air speech for the Hammersmith Branch, SL, at Beadon Road, Hammersmith.

Source: *Ham. Min. Book.*

5–8–88—An open-air speech for the Fulham Branch, SL, at Walham Green, Fulham. The SL choir attended and sang.

Source: *Ham. Min. Book.*

5–13–88—An open-air speech, delivered for the Fulham Branch, SL, at Walham

Green, opposite the Liberal Club, Fulham, London.

Sources: *Commonweal,* May 19, 1888, p. 160; *Ham. Min. Book.*

6–3–88 (morning)—An open-air speech for the Hammersmith Branch, SL, at Latimer Road Station, Notting Hill.

Source: *Ham. Min. Book.*

6–3–88 (evening)—"The Hopes of Civilization," delivered at a meeting sponsored by the Hammersmith Branch, SL, at Kelmscott House, Hammersmith.

Source: *Ham. Min. Book.*

Text: see Appendix II, item 67.

6–8–88—A speech, proposing the formation of the NAAA. The meeting, sponsored and presided over by the Duke of Westminster, was held at Grosvenor House, London.

Source: *The Architect,* June 15, 1888, pp. 338–9.

6–17–88 (morning)—An open-air speech, delivered for the Fulham Branch, SL, opposite the Liberal Club, Fulham, London.

Source: *Commonweal,* June 23, 1888, p. 200.

6–17–88* (afternoon)—An open-air speech was scheduled for delivery at Victoria Park, as part of the SL East-End agitation.

Source: *Commonweal,* June 16, 1888, p. 192.

6–20–88—"The Revolt of Ghent," delivered at a meeting sponsored by the Clerkenwell (Central) Branch, SL, at the SL Hall, 13 Farringdon Road, London.

Source and Review: *Commonweal,* June 30, 1888, p. 207.

Text: see Appendix II, item 122.

6–24–88—An open-air speech, delivered for the Fulham Branch, SL, opposite the Liberal Club, Fulham.

Source: *Commonweal,* June 30, 1888, p. 207.

6–31–88—An open-air speech, delivered for the Fulham Branch, SL, outside the Branch rooms, 8 Effie Road, Walham, London.

Source: *Commonweal,* July 7, 1888, p. 215.

7–1–88* (mid-day)—"Misery and the Way Out" was scheduled for delivery before the Fulham Branch, SL, at the Branch rooms, 8 Effie Road, Walham, London.

Source: *Commonweal,* June 30, 1888, p. 208.

Text: see Appendix II, item 50.

7–1–88 (evening)—An open-air speech for the Fulham Branch, SL, at Walham Green, Fulham.

Source: *Ham. Min. Book.*

7–8–88 (morning)—An open-air speech, delivered for the Fulham Branch, SL, in Fulham, London.

Sources: *Commonweal,* July 14, 1888, p. 223; *Ham. Min. Book.*

7–8–88 (early evening)—An open-air speech delivered for the Fulham Branch, SL, at Weltje Road, London.

Source: *Ham. Min. Book.*

7–8–88 (night)—"The Society of the Future," delivered at a meeting sponsored by the Battersea Branch, SDF, at the Sydney Hall, 36 York Road, Battersea, London.

Source: *Justice,* July 14, 1888, p. 6.

Text: see Appendix II, item 117.

7-22-88—An open-air speech, delivered as part of an anti-sweating demonstration sponsored by the SL, the SDF, and other London socialists, at Hyde Park, London.

Sources: *Commonweal,* July 28, 1888, p. 237; *Justice,* July 28, 1888, p. 5.

7-29-88 (morning)—An open-air speech for the Hammersmith Branch, SL, at Starch Green, London.

Source: *Ham. Min. Book.*

7-29-88—"From Chattel to Wage Slavery," delivered at a meeting sponsored by the Hammersmith Branch, SL, at Kelmscott House, Hammersmith.

Sources: *Commonweal,* July 28, 1888, p. 240; *Ham. Min. Book.*

8-5-88 (morning)—An open-air speech, delivered for the Hammersmith Branch, SL, at Latimer Road, London.

Sources: Letter to Jane Alice Morris, Aug. 9, 1888 (*Letters,* pp. 293–4); *Ham. Min. Book.*

8-5-88 (evening)—An open-air speech, delivered for the Hammersmith Branch, SL, at Weltje Road, London.

Sources: see above.

8-12-88 (noon)—An open-air speech, delivered as part of the SL and SDF Norwich demonstration, in the Market Place, Norwich.

Sources: *Commonweal,* Aug. 25, 1888, p. 268; letter to Jane Alice Morris, Aug. 18, 1888 (B.M. Add. MS. 45340).

Review: "Socialist Demonstrations at Norwich," *Eastern Evening News,* Aug. 13, 1888, p. 3.

8-12-88 (afternoon)—An open-air speech, part of the Norwich demonstration (see above), near the Wellington Statue, Market Place, Norwich.

Sources: *Commonweal,* Aug. 25, 1888, p. 268; letter to Jane Alice Morris, Aug. 18, 1888 (B.M. Add. MS. 45340); *Eastern Evening News,* Aug. 13, 1888, p. 2.

8-12-88 (evening)—"Monopoly," delivered as part of the Norwich demonstration, at the Gordon Hall, Norwich. Prof. C. J. Faulkner was chairman.

Sources: see above.

Review: [Editorial], *Eastern Evening News,* Aug. 14, 1888, p. 3.

Text: see Appendix II, item 103.

8-13-88 (noon)—An open-air speech, as part of the Norwich demonstration, in the Market Place, Norwich.

Sources: *Commonweal,* Aug. 25, 1888, p. 268; letter to Jane Alice Morris, Aug. 18, 1888 (B.M. Add. MS. 45340); *Eastern Evening News,* Aug. 14, 1888, p. 3.

8-13-88 (early evening)—An open-air speech, delivered as part of the Norwich demonstration, in the Market Place, Norwich.

Sources: see above; letter from C. J. Faulkner to Emery Walker, Aug. 14, 1888 (*Cockerell Papers*).

8-13-88 (late evening)—Chairman for a lecture by Mrs. Annie Besant, as part of the Norwich demonstration, at St. Augustine's Boys Board School, Norwich.

Sources: Letter to Jane Alice Morris, Aug. 18, 1888 (B.M. Add. MS. 45340); *Eastern Evening News,* Aug. 14, 1888, p. 3.

Review: [Editorial], *Eastern Evening News,* Aug. 14, 1888, p. 2.

8-19-88 (morning)—An open-air speech, delivered for the Hammersmith Branch, SL, at Weltje Road, London.

Sources: Letter to Jane Alice Morris, Aug. 21, 1888 (B.M. Add. MS. 45340); *Ham. Min. Book.*

8–19–88 (evening)—A lecture from notes, "A Chapter in the History of Rome," on the German historian Theodore Mommsen, delivered at a meeting sponsored by the Hammersmith Branch, SL, at Kelmscott House, Hammersmith. Sources: see above.

9–2–88 (morning)—An open-air speech for the Hammersmith Branch, SL, at Latimer Road, London.
Source: *Ham. Min. Book.*

9–2–88 (evening)—An open-air speech for the Hammersmith Branch, SL, at Weltje Road, London.
Source: *Ham. Min. Book.*

9–9–88*—An open-air speech for the Hammersmith Branch, SL, was scheduled for Weltje Road, London.
Source: *Ham. Min. Book.*

9–16–88—An open-air speech, delivered for the Hammersmith Branch, SL, at Weltje Road, London.
Source: *Commonweal*, Sept. 22, 1888, p. 303.

9–22–88*—Morris was scheduled for poetry readings at an entertainment sponsored by the SL at the International Club, 40 Berner Street, Commercial Road, London, for the benefit of the Yarmouth Free-Speech Fund.
Source: Handbill (*Nettlau Coll.*).

9–23–88—An open-air speech, delivered for Battersea Branch No. 2, SDF, at Battersea Park, London.
Source: *Justice*, Sept. 29, 1888, p. 6.

9–30–88 (morning)—An open-air speech, delivered for the Fulham Branch, SL, opposite the Liberal Club, Fulham, London.
Source: *Commonweal*, Oct. 6, 1888, p. 320.

9–30–88 (afternoon)—"Equality," delivered in the open-air for the Clapham Common Branch, SDF, near the millpond on Clapham Common, London.
Source: *Justice*, Oct. 6, 1888, p. 6.
Text: see Appendix II, item 128.

10–14–88 (morning)—An open-air speech, delivered for the Fulham Branch, SL, opposite the Liberal Club, Fulham, London.
Sources: *Commonweal*, Oct. 20, 1888, p. 335; *Ham. Min. Book.*

10–14–88 (afternoon)—An open-air speech, delivered for the local branch, SL, in Hyde Park.
Source: see above.

10–21–88—An open-air speech, delivered for the local branch, SL, at Regent's Park, London.
Source: *Commonweal*, Oct. 27, 1888, p. 343.

11–1–88—"Tapestry and Carpet Weaving," delivered as part of a series sponsored by the ACES, during the first exhibition, at New Gallery, Regent St., London.
Sources: Letter to Jane Alice Morris, Oct. 17, 1888 (B.M. Add. MS. 45340); *The Artist*, IX (Nov., 1888), 344; *The Times*, Nov. 2, 1888, p. 10; *Arts and Crafts Exhibition Society Catalogue, 1888*, p. 12.
Reviews: "Mr. Morris on Tapestry," *The Artist*, IX (Dec., 1888), 362; "Mr. Morris on Tapestry," *PMG*, Nov. 2, 1888, p. 6.

11–4–88 (morning)—An open-air speech, delivered for the Fulham Branch, SL, opposite the railroad station, Fulham, London.

Sources: *Commonweal,* Nov. 10, 1888, p. 359; *Ham. Min. Book.*

11–4–88*—An open-air speech for the Hammersmith Branch, SL, was scheduled for Weltje Road, London.
Source: *Ham. Min. Book.*

11–10–88—A speech, welcoming Mrs. Albert Parsons, widow of one of the executed Chicago anarchists. The meeting, sponsored by combined London socialist and anarchist groups, at St. Paul's Café, was presided over by R. B. Cunninghame-Graham, M.P.
Sources: *Commonweal,* Nov. 17, 1888, p. 364; *Justice,* Nov. 17, 1888, p. 5; letter to Jane Alice Morris, Nov. 17, 1888 (*Letters,* pp. 302–3).

11–11–88—An open-air speech, delivered at a Bloody Sunday memorial demonstration sponsored by London socialist and anarchist groups, in Hyde Park, London.
Sources: *Justice,* Nov. 17, 1888, p. 5; letter to Jane Alice Morris, Nov. 17, 1888 (*Letters,* pp. 302–3).

11–12–88—Chairman at a Bloody Sunday memorial meeting sponsored by combined London socialist and anarchist groups, at the Store Street Hall, London.
Sources: see above.

11–13–88—An open-air speech, delivered for the Clerkenwell (Central) Branch, SL, at Clerkenwell Green, London.
Source: Letter to Jane Alice Morris, Nov. 17, 1888 (*Letters,* pp. 302–3).

11–18–88 (morning)—"Monopoly," delivered at a meeting sponsored by the Nottingham Socialist Club, at the Secular Hall, Beck St., Nottingham. The Rev. Prof. Symes was chairman.
Sources: *The Nottingham Daily Guardian,* Nov. 19, 1888; letter to Jane Alice Morris, Nov. 17, 1888 (*Letters,* pp. 302–3).
Text: see Appendix II, item 132.

11–18–88 (evening)—"Equality," delivered at a meeting sponsored by the Nottingham Socialist Club at the Secular Hall, Beck St., Nottingham. Mr. W. H. Farmer was chairman.
Source: *The Nottingham Daily Guardian,* Nov. 19, 1888, p. 8.
Text: see Appendix II, item 128.

11–20–88*—An open-air speech was scheduled for delivery for the Hammersmith Branch, SL, in back of the Walham Green Church, London.
Source: *Commonweal,* Nov. 17, 1888, p. 368.

11–25–88*—"Equality" was scheduled for delivery at a meeting sponsored by the Fulham Branch, SL, at the Branch rooms, 8 Effie Road, Walham Green, London.
Source: *Commonweal,* Nov. 24, 1888, p. 376.
Text: see Appendix II, item 128.

11–29–88—A speech, delivered at a farewell meeting for Mrs. Albert Parsons. Combined London socialist and anarchist groups sponsored the meeting at South Place Institute, London.
Source: *Commonweal,* Dec. 8, 1888, p. 388.

12–2–88 (afternoon)—"The Society of the Future," delivered at a meeting sponsored by the Ancoats Recreation Committee at New Islington Hall, Ancoats, Manchester.
Sources: *Commonweal,* Dec. 15, 1888, p. 396; letter to Jane Alice Morris, Dec. 4, 1888 (*Letters,* pp. 303–4); *The Manchester Examiner and Times,* Dec. 4, 1888, p. 3.

Text: see Appendix II, item 117.

12–2–88 (evening)—"Monopoly," delivered at a meeting sponsored by the Manchester Democratic Club, SDF, at the Manchester Club Rooms, 20 Pilling St., Rochdale Road, Manchester.

Sources: *Justice,* Dec. 8, 1888 p. 6; letter to Jane Alice Morris, Dec. 4, 1888 (*Letters,* pp. 303–4).

Text: see Appendix II, item 103.

12–3–88—"Art and Socialism" delivered at a meeting sponsored by Bolton socialists, in Bolton.

Sources: *Commonweal,* Dec. 15, 1888, p. 396; letter to Jane Alice Morris, Dec. 4, 1888 (*Letters,* pp. 303–4).

Text: see Appendix II, item 42.

12–4–88—"What Socialists Want," delivered at a meeting sponsored by the Lancashire Council, SDF, at the Spinners' Hall, Saint Peter's St., Blackburn.

Sources: *Commonweal,* Dec. 15, 1888, p. 396; *Justice,* Dec. 1, 1888, p. 7; letter to Jane Alice Morris, Dec. 4, 1888 (*Letters,* pp. 303–4).

Text: see this volume, pp. 217–33.

12–5–88—"Art and Its Producers," delivered during the annual conference of the NAAA, at the Rotunda, Liverpool.

Sources: *Commonweal,* Dec. 15, 1888, p. 396; letter to Jane Alice Morris, Dec. 4, 1888 (*Letters,* pp. 303–4); "Applied Art at the Art Congress," *The Architect,* Dec. 14, 1888, pp. 333–5.

Review: *Liverpool Daily Post,* Dec. 6, 1888, p. 5.

Text: see Appendix II, item 134.

12–6–88—"Monopoly," delivered at a meeting sponsored by the Rochdale Social Democratic Club, SDF, at 46 Packer St., Rochdale.

Sources: *Commonweal,* Dec. 15, 1888, p. 6; *Justice,* Dec. 15, 1888, p. 6; letter to Jane Alice Morris, Dec. 4, 1888 (*Letters,* pp. 303–4).

Text: see Appendix II, item 103.

12–12–88*—"The Future of the Middle Classes" was scheduled for delivery at a meeting sponsored by the Hammersmith Branch, SL, at Kelmscott House, Hammersmith.

Source: *Commonweal,* Dec. 8, 1888, p. 392.

12–16–88—A lecture, delivered at a meeting sponsored by the Nottingham Socialist Club, at Swan's Buildings, Nottingham.

Source: *Justice,* Dec. 22, 1888, p. 3.

12–23–88 (morning)—An open-air speech, delivered for the Fulham Branch, SL, at Walham Green, London.

Source: Letter to Jane Alice Morris, Dec. 23, 1888 (*Letters,* p. 305).

12–23–88* (evening)—"Equality" was scheduled for delivery at a meeting sponsored by the Hammersmith Branch, SL, at Kelmscott House, Hammersmith.

Sources: *Commonweal,* Dec. 22, 1888, p. 408; letter to Jane Alice Morris, Dec. 23, 1888 (*Letters,* pp. 305–6).

Text: see Appendix II, item 128.

1889

1–6–89—"Socialism" delivered at a meeting sponsored by the Fulham Branch, SL, at the Branch rooms, 8 Effie Road, Walham Green, London.

Source: *Commonweal,* Jan. 12, 1889, p. 15.

Text: see Appendix II, item 136.

1–13–89—An open-air speech for the Hammersmith Branch, SL, at Weltje Road, London.

Source: *Commonweal,* Jan. 19, 1889, p. 23.

1–16–89*—Morris was scheduled to speak at the annual meeting to commemorate the Paris Commune at a meeting sponsored by the SL and the SDF at South Place. Hyndman was to be chairman.

Source: Handbill (*Nettlau Coll.*).

1–20–89—An open-air speech, delivered for the Hammersmith Branch, SL, at Weltje Road, London.

Source: *Commonweal,* Jan. 26, 1889, p. 31.

1–30–89—"Socialism," delivered at a meeting sponsored by the Hammersmith Branch, SL, at Kelmscott House, Hammersmith.

Source: *Commonweal,* Feb. 2, 1889, p. 39.

Text: see Appendix II, item 136.

2–3–89—An open-air speech, delivered for the Hammersmith Branch, SL, at Walham Green, London.

Source: *Ham. Min. Book.*

2–10–89—"The Society of the Future," delivered at a meeting sponsored by the Glasgow Branch, SL, at the Albion Hall, Glasgow.

Sources: *Commonweal,* Feb. 16, 1889, p. 55; letter to Jane Alice Morris, Feb. 8, 1889 (B.M. Add. MS. 45340).

Text: see Appendix II, item 117.

2–11–89—"Gothic Architecture," delivered at a meeting sponsored by the Haldane Trustees, at the Corporation Galleries, Glasgow. Prof. Veitch was chairman.

Sources: *The Journal of Decorative Art,* IX (April, 1889), 58; *Glasgow Evening News,* Feb. 12, 1889, p. 2; *The Architect,* Feb. 15, 1889, pp. 93–4; letters to Jane Alice Morris, Feb. 8, 16, 1889 (B.M. Add. MS. 45340).

Text: see Appendix II, item 137.

2–12–89—"Arts and Crafts," delivered before the Glasgow School of Art, at the Corporation Galleries, Sauchiehall St., Glasgow. Mr. F. H. Newberry, headmaster, was chairman.

Sources: *Commonweal,* Feb. 16, 1889, p. 55; letter to Jane Alice Morris, Feb. 16, 1889 (B.M. Add. MS. 45340); "The Arts and Crafts," *The Architect,* Feb. 15, 1889, pp. 7–8.

Text: see Appendix II, item 138.

2–13–89—"Equality," delivered at a meeting sponsored by the Edinburgh Branch, SLLL, at the Queen Street Hall, Edinburgh. Mr. L. Melliel was chairman.

Sources: *Commonweal,* Feb. 23, 1889, p. 63; letter to Jane Alice Morris, Feb. 16, 1889 (B.M. Add. MS. 45340); *Edinburgh Evening News,* Feb. 14, 1889.

Text: see Appendix II, item 128.

2–14–89—A speech "on art education," delivered at the annual distribution of prizes of the Macclesfield School of Art and Science. Mr. John May, J.P. and president of the school, was chairman.

Sources: Letter to Jane Alice Morris, Feb. 16, 1889 (B.M. Add. MS. 45340); *The Macclesfield Courier and Herald,* Feb. 23, 1889, p. 3; *The Macclesfield Chronicle,* Feb. 15, 1889, p. 5.

Text: see Appendix II, item 139.

2–17–89 (morning)—An open-air speech, delivered for the Hammersmith Branch, SL, at Weltje Road, Hammersmith.

Source: *Commonweal*, Feb. 23, 1889, p. 63.

2–17–89 (evening)—A lecture, delivered before the West Kensington Park Club, in Kensington.

Source: see above.

2–24–89—An open-air speech, delivered for the Hammersmith Branch, SL, at Latimer Road, London.

Source: *Commonweal*, March 2, 1889, p. 71.

3–1–89—"How Shall We Live Then?" delivered at a meeting sponsored by the Fabian Society, in Bloomsbury Hall, London. Mr. William Clarke was chairman.

Source: *To-Day*, XI (April, 1889), 120–21.

3–3–89—"How Shall We Live Then?" delivered at a meeting sponsored by the Hammersmith Branch, SL, at Kelmscott House, Hammersmith.

Source: *Commonweal*, March 9, 1889, p. 79.

3–31–89*—"Equality" was scheduled for delivery at a meeting sponsored by the Southwark and Lambeth Branches, SDF, at the Nelson Coffee Tavern, Westminster Bridge Road, London.

Source: *Justice*, March 30, 1889, p. 4.

Text: see Appendix II, item 128.

4–9–89—"Gothic Architecture," delivered at a meeting sponsored by the Guild and School of Handicraft and held in the Lecture Room of Toynbee Hall, for students of the University Settlements scheme. The lecture was illustrated with lantern slides.

Sources: Diary of Sydney Cockerell, entry for April 9, 1889 (*Cockerell Papers*); *The Toynbee Record*, I (May, 1889), 89.

Text: see Appendix II, item 137.

4–14–89*—"Equality" was scheduled for delivery to the Fulham Liberal Club, at Walham Green, London.

Source: *Commonweal*, April 13, 1889, p. 119.

Text: see Appendix II, item 128.

4–20–89—An open-air speech, delivered for the Hammersmith Branch, SL, at the Bridge-end, Hammersmith.

Source: *Ham. Min. Book.*

4–22–89—A lecture on architectural restoration, delivered before the Art Workers' Guild, at Barnard's Inn Hall, London.

Sources: Letter to Jane Alice Morris, April 21, 1889 (B.M. Add. MS. 45340); *Massé*, p. 105.

4–27–89—An open-air speech, delivered for the Hammersmith Branch, SL, at Weltje Road, London.

Source: *Commonweal*, May 4, 1889, p. 143.

5–5–89—An open-air speech delivered for the Hammersmith Branch, SL, at Beadon Road, London.

Source: *Commonweal*, May 11, 1889, p. 151.

5–12–89 (morning)—An open-air speech, delivered for the Hammersmith Branch, SL, at Beadon Road, London.

Source: *Commonweal*, May 18, 1889, p. 159.

5–12–89 (evening)—A lecture on Edward Bellamy's *Looking Backward* and

Grant Allen's article "Individualism and Socialism" (*Contemporary Review*, LV [May, 1889], 730–41), at a meeting sponsored by the Hammersmith Branch, SL, at Kelmscott House, Hammersmith.

Sources: *Commonweal*, May 18, 1889, p. 159; letter to J. Bruce Glasier, May 13, 1889 (*Walth*. MS., J-122).

Text: see Appendix II, item 142.

5–19–89 (morning)—An open-air speech, delivered for the Hammersmith Branch, SL, at Beadon Road, Hammersmith.

Source: *Ham. Min. Book*.

5–19–89 (evening)—An open-air speech, delivered for the Hammersmith Branch, SL, at Weltje Road, Hammersmith.

Source: see above.

6–2–89 (morning)—An open-air speech, delivered for the Hammersmith Branch, SL, at Beadon Road, Hammersmith.

Source: *Ham. Min. Book*.

6–2–89 (evening)—An open-air speech, delivered for the Hammersmith Branch, SL, at Weltje Road, London.

Sources: *Commonweal*, June 8, 1889, p. 183; *Ham. Min. Book*.

6–4–89*—"Monopoly" was scheduled for delivery before the Northern Radical Club and the Southwark and Lambeth Branches, SDF, at 108 Westminster Bridge Road, London.

Sources: *Commonweal*, June 1, 1889, p. 175; *Justice*, June 1, 1889, p. 4.

Text: see Appendix II, item 103.

6–10–89*—Morris was scheduled for poetry readings at an entertainment in the SL Hall for the benefit of the SL Propaganda Fund.

Source: Handbill (*Nettlau Coll.*).

6–16–89—An open-air speech, delivered for the Hammersmith Branch, SL, at Beadon Road, Hammersmith.

Source: *Ham. Min. Book*.

6–27–89*—"Monopoly" was scheduled for delivery before the New Labour Club, 5 Victoria Park Square, Bethnal Green, London.

Source: *Commonweal*, June 22, 1889, p. 199.

Text: see Appendix II, item 103.

6–30–89*—An open-air speech was scheduled to be delivered for the Hammersmith Branch, SL, at Weltje Road, London.

Source: *Ham. Min. Book*.

7–7–89—An open-air speech, delivered for the Hammersmith Branch, SL, at Weltje Road, London. George Bernard Shaw also spoke at this meeting.

Source: *Commonweal*, July 13, 1889, p. 223.

7–16–89—A speech, against the amalgamation of the Possibilist and the International Socialist Conferences, delivered at the International Socialist Working-Men's Congress, Salle Horel, 13, rue Au Maire, Paris.

Source: *Commonweal*, Aug. 3, 1889, p. 242.

Text: see Appendix II, item 144.

7–18–89—A report on the progress and condition of English socialism, delivered at the International Socialist Working-Men's Congress, Salle Horel, 13, rue Au Maire, Paris.

Sources: *Commonweal*, Aug. 3, 1889, p. 242; *The Daily News*, July 19, 1889.

Text: see Appendix II, item 145.

7-29-89—An open-air speech, delivered for the Hammersmith Branch, SL, at Weltje Road, Hammersmith.

Source: *Ham. Min. Book.*

8-11-89 (morning)—An open-air speech, delivered for the North Kensington Branch, SL, at Latimer Road, London.

Source: *Commonweal,* Aug. 17, 1889, p. 263.

8-11-89* (evening)—An open-air speech was scheduled for delivery for the Hammersmith Branch, SL, at Walham Green, Fulham.

Source: *Ham. Min. Book.*

8-28-89—"Monopoly," delivered at a meeting sponsored by the Yarmouth Branch, SL, at the Cora Hall, Yarmouth. Mr. C. Reynolds was chairman.

Sources: *Commonweal,* Sept. 7, 1889; *The Yarmouth Mercury,* Aug. 31, 1889; *The Yarmouth Gazette,* Aug. 31, 1889; *The Yarmouth Independent,* Aug. 31, 1889.

Text: see Appendix II, item 146.

10-13-89*—"The Class Struggle" was scheduled for delivery at a meeting of the Hammersmith Club, in Hammersmith.

Source: *Commonweal,* Oct. 12, 1889, p. 327.

Text: see Appendix II, item 147.

10-20-89*—A lecture was scheduled for delivery before the Yarmouth Branch, SL, at Yarmouth.

Source: see above.

10-27-89—"Why Working Men Ought to Be Socialists," delivered at a meeting sponsored by the North Kensington Branch, SL, at the Clarendon Coffee Tavern, London.

Source: *Commonweal,* Oct. 26, Nov. 2, 1889, pp. 343, 351.

10-29-89—"The Art of Dyeing," delivered at a meeting of working men sponsored by the NAAA as part of the annual art congress. Lord Provost Boyd presided over this meeting, which was held in the Museum of Science and Art, Edinburgh.

Sources: *The Edinburgh Evening News,* Oct. 30, 1889; letter to Rev. J. Glasse, Sept. 9, 1889 (*Man and Myth,* p. 97).

Review: "The Art Congress," *Commonweal,* Nov. 16, 1888, p. 364.

Text: see Appendix II, item 149.

10-30-89 (morning)—"The Arts and Crafts of Today," delivered as the presidential address to the Applied Art Section of the NAAA, at a meeting held in the Queen Street Hall, Edinburgh.

Sources: see above.

Review: see above.

Text: see Appendix II, item 150.

10-30-89 (afternoon)—Chairman of a meeting of the Applied Art Section of the NAAA, at the National Portrait Gallery, Edinburgh.

Source: *The Edinburgh Evening News,* Oct. 31, 1889.

10-31-89—Chairman of the general conference of NAAA sections, at the National Portrait Gallery, Edinburgh.

Sources: *The Edinburgh Evening News,* Oct. 31, 1889; *The Architect,* Nov. 8, 1889, pp. 264-8.

11-1-89—A lecture on socialism, delivered at a meeting sponsored by the Edinburgh Branch, SLLL, at the Oddfellows' Hall, Forrest Road, Edinburgh. Mr. Walter Crane was chairman.

Sources: *Commonweal*, Nov. 16, 1889, p. 364; *The Edinburgh Evening News*, Nov. 2, 1889.

Text: see Appendix II, item 151.

11–2–89—"Of the Origins of Ornamental Art," delivered at a meeting sponsored by the Glasgow Branch, SL, and the Edinburgh Branch, SLLL, at the Albert Hall, Edinburgh. The Rev. John Glasse was chairman.

Sources: *Commonweal*, Nov. 16, 1889, p. 364; *The Architect*, Nov. 8, 1889, pp. 7–8; *The Edinburgh Evening News*, Nov. 2, 1889; letter to Rev. J. Glasse, Sept. 9, 1889 (*Man and Myth*, p. 97).

Text: see this volume, pp. 136–57, and Appendix II, item 87.

11–3–89—Chairman for a lecture by Walter Crane, at a meeting sponsored by the Glasgow Branch, SL, at the Waterloo Hall, Glasgow.

Sources: *Commonweal*, Nov. 9, 1889, p. 359; letter to J. Bruce Glasier, Oct. 16, 1889 (*Letters*, p. 319); *Glasgow Evening News*, Nov. 4, 1889, p. 5.

11–7–89—"Gothic Architecture," delivered at a meeting sponsored by the ACES, at the second exhibition, in New Gallery, Regent St., London.

Sources: *Commonweal*, Oct. 19, 1889, p. 331; *Arts and Crafts Exhibition Society Catalogue, 1889*, p. 16.

Text: see Appendix II, item 152.

11–10–89 (afternoon)—"Monopoly," delivered at a meeting sponsored by the Liverpool Secular Society at the Lower Concert Hall, Lord Nelson Street, Liverpool.

Sources: *The Liverpool Daily Post*, Nov. 11, 1889, p. 11; letter to Kenworthy, Nov. 6, [1889], (*Tamiment*); letters to E. C. Chapman, Nov. 6, Nov. 8, 1889 (*Texas*).

Text: see Appendix II, item 103.

11–10–89 (evening)—"The Class Struggle," delivered at a meeting sponsored by the Liverpool Secular Society, at the Lower Concert Hall, Lord Nelson St., Liverpool.

Sources: see above.

11–11–89—A speech, delivered at a Bloody Sunday memorial meeting sponsored by the combined London socialist groups, at South Place Institute, Finsbury, London.

Sources: *Commonweal*, Nov. 16, 1889, p. 365; *Freedom*, Dec., 1889.

11–17–89—"Monopoly," delivered at a meeting of the Chesterfield Discussion Society in Chesterfield. Morris began the meeting with a reading of his poem "The Message of the March Wind."

Sources: Letter to John Glasse, Nov. 21, 1889 (*Man and Myth*, p. 101); *The Derbyshire Courier*, Nov. 23, 1889.

Text: see Appendix II, item 103.

11–18–89—"Socialism," delivered at a meeting sponsored by Sheffield socialists, at the Cambridge Hall, Sheffield.

Sources: *Commonweal*, Nov. 23, 1889, p. 375; letter to Rev. J. Glasse, Nov. 21, 1889 (*Man and Myth*, p. 101).

Text: see Appendix II, item 66.

11–20–89*—"Gothic Architecture" was scheduled for delivery at a meeting sponsored by the Hammersmith Branch, SL, at Kelmscott House, Hammersmith.

Source: *Commonweal*, Nov. 16, 1889, p. 367.

Text: see Appendix II, item 152.

11–24–89*—"Socialism" was scheduled for delivery before the Star Radical Club, 8 Mayall Road, Herne Hill, London.
Source: *Commonweal*, Nov. 23, 1889, p. 375.
Text: see Appendix II, item 66.

11–30–89—"The Class Struggle," delivered at a meeting sponsored by the Manchester Social Democratic Club, SDF, at the Secular Hall, Rusholme Road, Manchester.
Sources: *Commonweal*, Dec. 7, 1889, p. 391; *The Manchester Examiner and Times*, Dec. 2, 1889, p. 5.
Text: see Appendix II, item 147.

12–1–89 (afternoon)—"The Revolt of Ghent," delivered at a meeting sponsored by the Ancoats Recreation Committee, at New Islington Hall, Ancoats, Manchester. Mr. Charles Rowley was chairman.
Sources: *Commonweal*, Dec. 7, 1889, p. 391; *The Manchester Examiner and Times*, Dec. 2, 1889, p. 5; *The Manchester Guardian*, Dec. 2, 1889, p. 8.
Text: see Appendix II, item 122.

12–1–89 (evening)—A speech, delivered at a meeting sponsored by the Ancoats "At Home" Committee, at New Islington Hall, Ancoats, Manchester.
Source: *The Manchester Examiner and Times*, Dec. 2, 1889, p. 5.

12–10–89*—A lecture was scheduled for delivery to the New Fellowship, at the SDF Hall, 337 Strand, London.
Source: *Justice*, Dec. 7, 1889, p. 4.

1890

1–19–90—An open-air speech, delivered for the Hammersmith Branch, SL, at Weltje Road, Hammersmith.
Source: *Ham. Min. Book.*

1–22–90—"How Shall We Live Then?" delivered before the North London Branch, SL, at 6 Windmill St., Tottenham Court Road, London.
Source: *Commonweal*, Feb. 1, 1890, p. 39.

2–2–90 (afternoon)—"How Shall We Live Then?" delivered before the Leicester Radical Club, at the Club rooms, Vine St., Leicester.
Source: *Commonweal*, Feb. 8, 1890, p. 47.

2–2–90 (evening)—"What Socialists Want," delivered at a meeting sponsored by the Leicester Branch, SL, at the Co-operative Hall, Leicester.
Source: *Commonweal*, March 8, 1890, p. 79.
Text: see this volume, pp. 217–33.

2–9–90*—"Equality" was scheduled for delivery at a meeting sponsored by the Hammersmith Branch, SL, at Kelmscott House, Hammersmith.
Source: *Commonweal*, Feb. 8, 1890, p. 47.
Text: see Appendix II, item 128.

2–12–90*—Morris was scheduled to be chairman of the semi-annual meeting of the Socialist Co-operative Federation, at the SDF Hall, 337 Strand, London.
Source: see above.

3–2–90—"How Shall We Live Then?" delivered at a meeting sponsored by the North Kensington Branch, SL, at the Clarendon Coffee Tavern, London.
Source: *Commonweal*, March 8, 1890, p. 79.

3–11–90—"The Class Struggle," delivered at a meeting sponsored by the Leicester

Branch, SL, at the Co-operative Hall, High St., Leicester. Mr. T. Barclay was chairman.

Sources: *Commonweal,* April 12, 1890, p. 127; *The Midland Free Press,* March 15, 1890, p. 6; *The Leicester Daily Mercury,* March 12, 1890, p. 4.

Text: see Appendix II, item 147.

3–16–90—An open-air speech, delivered for the Hammersmith Branch, SL, at Walham Green, Fulham.

Source: *Ham. Min. Book.*

3–19–90—A speech, delivered at a Paris Commune memorial meeting sponsored by combined London socialist and anarchist groups, at South Place Institute, Finsbury, London.

Source: *Commonweal,* March 29, 1890, p. 101.

3–25–90—"The Class Struggle," delivered at a meeting sponsored by Leeds socialists, at the Grand Assembly Rooms, Leeds.

Sources: *Commonweal,* April 5, 1890, p. 111; *The Leeds Mercury,* March 26, 1890; placard in the Mattison Collection, Leeds University.

Text: see Appendix II, item 147.

3–31–90—An open-air speech, delivered for the Hammersmith Branch, SL, at the Bridge-end, Hammersmith.

Source: *Ham. Min. Book.*

4–12–90—"Gothic Architecture," delivered before the Artists' Club, at the Club rooms, Eberle St., Liverpool.

Sources: *The Liverpool Daily Post,* April 14, 1890, p. 6; letter to Kenworthy, Feb. 17, [1890] (*Tamiment*).

Text: see Appendix II, item 152.

4–13–90 (afternoon)—"The Development of Modern Society," delivered at a meeting sponsored by the Liverpool Socialist Society, at the Rodney Hall, Liverpool.

Sources: see above, also *Commonweal,* April 19, 1890, p. 127.

Text: see Appendix II, item 155.

4–13–90 (evening)—"The Social Outlook," delivered at a meeting sponsored by the Liverpool Socialist Society, at the Rodney Hall, Liverpool.

Source: see above.

4–27–90—An open-air speech, delivered for the Hammersmith Branch, SL, at the Bridge-end (near Kelmscott House), Hammersmith.

Source: *Commonweal,* May 3, 1890, p. 143.

5–1–90—A speech, delivered from a socialist platform in Hyde Park, London, as part of the May Day Celebrations organized by various trade union, radical, socialist, and anarchist groups.

Source: *Commonweal,* May 10, 1890, p. 150.

5–2–90—"Gothic Architecture," delivered at a meeting sponsored by the FS, at the St. James's Hall Restaurant. Mr. Ernest Radford had been scheduled to lecture on Morris, but his illness necessitated the substitution of Morris himself.

Source: *The Christian Socialist,* VIII (June, 1890), 88.

Text: see Appendix II, item 152.

5–11–90—An open-air speech, delivered for the Hammersmith Branch, SL, at the Bridge-end, Hammersmith.

Source: *Commonweal,* May 17, 1890, p. 159.

5–18–90—An open-air speech, delivered for the Hammersmith Branch, SL, at the Bridge End, Hammersmith.

Source: *Commonweal,* May 24, 1890, p. 167.

6–1–90 (morning)—An open-air speech, delivered for the Hammersmith Branch, SL, at the Bridge-end, Hammersmith.

Source: *Commonweal,* June 7, 1890, p. 183.

6–1–90 (evening)*—Morris was scheduled to open a discussion on "The Effect of the Socialist Movement on Imperial Politics" at the Hammersmith Branch, SL, Kelmscott House, Hammersmith.

Source: *Ham. Min. Book.*

6–8–90*—Morris was scheduled to be chairman of the anniversary celebration of the International Workingmen's Club, at 40 Berner St., London.

Source: *Justice,* June 7, 1890, p. 3.

6–15–90—An open-air speech, delivered for the Hammersmith Branch, SL, at the Bridge End, Hammersmith.

Source: *Ham. Min. Book.*

6–25–90—Speech seconding the adoption of the SPAB Annual Report, delivered in the Old Hall, Barnard's Inn, Holborn. Mr. Walter Crane was chairman.

Sources: *SPAB Reports, 1890* (London, 1890); *The Times,* June 26, 1890, p. 9.

Text: see Appendix II, item 158.

7–11–90—Morris opened a discussion on "The Present Strikes of Police, Postmen & Guards" for the Hammersmith Branch, SL, at Kelmscott House, Hammersmith.

Source: *Ham. Min. Book.*

7–13–90—An open-air speech, delivered for the Hammersmith Branch, SL, at Walham Green, Fulham.

Source: *Ham. Min. Book.*

9–7–90—An open-air speech, delivered for the Hammersmith Branch, SL, at the Bridge-end, Hammersmith.

Source: *Ham. Min. Book.*

9–21–90*—"The Hope of the Future" was scheduled for delivery at a meeting sponsored by the North Kensington Branch, SL, at the Clarendon Coffee House, Clarendon Road, London.

Source: *Commonweal,* Sept. 20, 1890, p. 303.

10–20–90—"Art for the People," delivered at a meeting sponsored by the "Commonweal" Branch, SL, at the Athenaeum Hall, Tottenham Court Road, London.

Source: *Commonweal,* Oct. 25, 1890, pp. 342–3.

Text: as "Of the Origins of Ornamental Art," see this volume, pp. 136–57.

11–1–90—An open-air speech, delivered at a meeting called by combined London socialist and anarchist groups to protest against "the persecution of Jews in Russia." The meeting was originally planned for the Great Assembly Hall, Mile-End; but official prohibition on the night of the meeting forced the speakers out to Mile-End Waste.

Source: *Commonweal,* Nov. 8, 1890, p. 359.

11–7–90—Morris opened a discussion on "Thrift from a Socialist Standpoint" for the Hammersmith Branch, SL, at Kelmscott House, Hammersmith.

Source: *Ham. Min. Book.*

11–11–90—A speech, delivered at a Bloody Sunday memorial meeting sponsored by combined London socialist and anarchist groups, at Milton Hall, London.
Source: *Commonweal*, Nov. 22, 1890, pp. 372–3.

12–11–90—Speech on the protection of ancient buildings at a meeting sponsored by the SPAB and the Master of Trinity College at Trinity College, Cambridge. Dr. Porter, the Master of Peterhouse, was chairman.
Sources: *The Trident* (Trinity College), I (March, 1891), 286–87; *SPAB Report, 1891.*

1891

2–13–91—Morris opened a discussion of the "legal maximum [price] and minimum [wage]" for the HSS at Kelmscott House, Hammersmith.
Source: *Ham. Min. Book.*

2–15–91*—"Idiots and Idiocy" was scheduled for two deliveries, the first, in the morning, at Bridge-end, and the second, in the evening, in the lecture hall of the HSS at Kelmscott House, Hammersmith.
Source: *Justice,* Feb. 14, 1891, p. 4.

6–10–91—Speech moving a vote of thanks to W. B. Richmond for a paper read before the Fourteenth Annual Meeting of the SPAB at the Old Hall, Barnard's Inn, London. Philip Webb was chairman.
Source: *SPAB Report, 1891,* p. 46.

7–21–91—Morris opened a discussion on "Gambling" for the HSS, at Kelmscott House, Hammersmith.
Source: *Ham. Min. Book.*

8–2–91—Morris read from and opened a discussion on *News from Nowhere* at a meeting sponsored by the HSS, at Kelmscott House, Hammersmith.
Source: *Ham. Min. Book.*

8–30–91—"Seven Years Ago and Now," delivered at a meeting sponsored by the HSS, at Kelmscott House, Hammersmith.
Sources: *Justice,* Sept. 5, 1891, p. 1; *Ham. Min. Book.*
Text: see Appendix II, item 165.

10–2–91—"Address on the Collection of Paintings of the English Pre-Raphaelite School," delivered at a private showing of the exhibition arranged by the Birmingham Museum and Art Gallery Committee, at the Corporation Gallery, Birmingham. Deputy Mayor Sir Thomas Martineau was chairman.
Sources: *Journal of Decorative Art,* XI (Nov., 1891), 171; *The Birmingham Daily Post,* Oct. 3, 1891, p. 5; *The Times,* Oct. 3, 1891, p. 11.
Text: see Appendix II, item 166.

10–4–91 (afternoon)—"Socialism up-to-date," delivered at a meeting sponsored by the Ancoats Recreation Committee, at New Islington Hall, Ancoats, Manchester.
Sources: *Journal of Decorative Art,* XI (Nov., 1891), 171; *The Manchester Guardian,* Oct. 5, 1891, p. 8.
Text: see Appendix II, item 167.

10–4–91 (evening)—A lecture on French and English cathedrals, delivered at a meeting sponsored by the Ancoats "At Home" Committee, at New Islington Hall, Ancoats, Manchester.
Sources: see above.

Text: see Appendix II, item 168.

11–18–91*—A lecture was scheduled for delivery at a meeting sponsored by the HSS, at Kelmscott House, Hammersmith.

Source: *Ham. Soc. Rec.,* Nov., 1891, p. 4.

11–20–91—"On the Influence of Building Materials on Architecture," delivered before the Art Workers' Guild, at Barnard's Inn, London.

Source: *The Master's Book of the Art Workers' Guild* (unpublished).

Text: see Appendix II, item 169.

12–9–91—"Real Socialism," delivered at a meeting sponsored by the HSS, at Kelmscott House, Hammersmith.

Sources: *Ham. Soc. Rec.,* Dec., 1891, p. 4; *Ham. Min. Book.*

1892

1–26–92—"The Woodcuts of Gothic Books," delivered before the Applied Art Section of the Society of Arts, at the Society's rooms, John St., Adelphi, London. Morris used lantern-slide illustrations.

Sources: *Journal of Decorative Art,* XI (June, 1892), 82; *The Artist,* XIII (March, 1892), 74; *The Times,* Jan. 25, 28, 1892.

Review: "The Society of Arts," *The Architect,* July 8, 1892, p. 18.

Text: see Appendix II, item 171.

2–21–92*—A lecture was scheduled for delivery at a meeting sponsored by the North Kensington Branch, SDF, at the Clarendon Coffee Palace, Clarendon Road, London.

Source: *Justice,* Feb. 20, 1892, p. 4.

5–29–92—"Town and Country," delivered at a meeting sponsored by the HSS at Kelmscott House, Hammersmith.

Sources: *Ham. Soc. Rec.,* May, 1892, p. 4; *Ham. Min. Book.*

Text: see Appendix II, item 172.

6–28–92—A speech, delivered at the annual conference of the SPAB, at Barnard's Inn, London. Judge Lushington was chairman.

Source: *SPAB Report, 1892,* p. 1.

6–28–92—Speech moving a vote of thanks to Judge Lushington, chairman, and making an appeal for funds, delivered at the Fifteenth Annual Meeting of the SPAB at the Old Hall, Barnard's Inn, London.

Sources: *The Architect,* July 1, 1892, pp. 13–14; *The Times,* June 29, 1892, p. 11.

8–14–92—A lecture, delivered at a meeting sponsored by the HSS, at Kelmscott House, Hammersmith.

Source: Letter to Jane Alice Morris, Aug. 15, 1892 (B.M. Add. MS. 45340).

8–21–92*—"Communism, i.e. Property" was scheduled for delivery at a meeting sponsored by the HSS, at Kelmscott House, Hammersmith.

Source: *Ham. Soc. Rec.,* Aug., 1892, p. 4.

Text: see Appendix II, item 175.

1893

1–?–93—"Town and Country," delivered at a meeting sponsored by the Ancoats Recreation Committee, at New Islington Hall, Ancoats, Manchester. Mr. Charles Rowley was chairman.

Source: *The Journal of Decorative Art,* XIII (April, 1893), 106.

Text: see Appendix II, item 172.

2–3–93—Morris opened a discussion on "the attitudes of Trades Unionism to Socialism," at a meeting sponsored by the HSS, at Kelmscott House, Hammersmith.

Sources: *Ham. Soc. Rec.,* Feb., 1893, p. 4; *Ham. Min. Book.*

2–19–93*—"Communism" was scheduled for delivery at a meeting sponsored by the HSS, at Kelmscott House, Hammersmith.

Sources: see above.

Text: see Appendix II, item 177.

2–23–93—Chairman of the first meeting of the Joint Committee of Socialist Bodies, to which the FS, the SDF, and the HSS sent representatives, at Kelmscott House, Hammersmith.

Sources: *The Fabian News,* III (March, 1893), 2; *Ham. Soc. Rec.,* March, 1893, p. 2.

3–10–93—"Communism," delivered at a meeting sponsored by the "Freedom" Publication Fund Committee, at the Grafton Hall, London.

Sources: *Journal for 1893; Freedom,* May, 1893, p. 24.

Review: *Freedom,* Aug., 1893, p. 52.

Text: see Appendix II, item 177.

4–30–93—An open-air speech, delivered at a meeting on behalf of the striking Hull dockers at Ravenscourt Park, London.

Source: *Ham. Min. Book.*

5–7–93—An open-air speech, delivered at the May Day celebrations sponsored by combined London socialist and anarchist groups in Hyde Park, London. Morris spoke from the SDF platform.

Sources: *Justice,* May 13, 1893, p. 5; *Ham. Min. Book.*

6–6–93—A speech against the restoration of St. Mary's Church, Oxford, at a convocation called by the University's Vice-Chancellor to discuss the issue. The meeting was in Oxford.

Sources: Letter to Philip Webb, June 6, [1893], (*Letters,* pp. 354–5); *The Architect,* June 9, 1893, pp. 373–4; *The Oxford Review,* June 7, 1893, p. 3.

6–19–93—"The Ideal Book," delivered before the Bibliographical Society, in London.

Source: *Trans. Biblio. Soc.,* I (1893), 179.

Text: see Appendix II, item 179.

7–18–93—Chairman, at the annual meeting of the SPAB, at Barnard's Inn, London.

Sources: *The Architect,* July 21, 1893, pp. 37–8; *SPAB Report, 1893,* pp. 53–4; *The Times,* July 19, 1893, p. 5.

10–21–93—"Printed Books, Ancient and Modern," delivered at a meeting sponsored by the Manchester Technical Instruction Committee, in the Lord Mayor's Parlour, Manchester.

Sources: *The Manchester Guardian,* Oct. 23, 1893, p. 5; *The Manchester Examiner and Times,* Oct. 23, 1893, p. 6.

10–22–93—"The Dangers of Restoration, with Special Reference to Westminster Abbey," delivered at a meeting sponsored by the Ancoats Recreation Committee, at New Islington Hall, Ancoats, Manchester.

Sources: *The Architect,* Oct. 27, 1893, pp. 259–60; *The Manchester Guardian,* Oct. 24, 1893.

11–2–93—"On the Printing of Books," delivered at a meeting sponsored by the ACES, during the exhibition at New Gallery, 121 Regent St., London.
Sources: *The Times*, Nov. 6, 1893, p. 4; *Arts and Crafts Exhibition Society Catalogue of the Fourth Exhibition, 1893*, p. 4.
Text: see Appendix II, item 182.

12–10–93 (afternoon)—"Waste," delivered at a meeting sponsored by the Burnley Branch, SDF, at the St. James Hall, Burnley. This lecture and the one immediately following were in support of H. M. Hyndman's contest for the Burnley Parliamentary seat.
Source: *The [Burnley] Socialist*, Dec. 15, 1893, p. 8.

12–10–93 (evening)—"What Shall We Do Now?" delivered at a meeting sponsored by the Burnley Branch, SDF, at the St. James Hall, Burnley (see above).
Source: *The [Burnley] Socialist*, Dec. 15, 1893, p. 5.

1894

1–14–94—"Early England," delivered at a meeting held at the South London Art Gallery, Peckham Road, London.
Source: *The [London] Daily Chronicle*, Jan. 15, 1894.
Text: see this volume, pp. 158–78.

2–20–94—A speech, delivered at a meeting sponsored by the Lansbury Campaign Committee, at the Jesmond St. School, Walworth, London. This speech was in support of George B. Lansbury's Walworth candidature.
Source: *Justice*, Feb. 24, 1894, p. 1.

2–21–94 (afternoon)—"The Woodcuts of Gothic Books," delivered at a meeting sponsored by the Birmingham Municipal School of Art, at the Birmingham and Midlands Institute, Birmingham.
Source: *The Birmingham Daily Post*, Feb. 22, 1894, p. 5.
Text: see Appendix II, item 171.

2–21–94 (evening)—"Address at the Distribution of Prizes," delivered at a meeting of the Municipal School of Art, at the Birmingham and Midlands Institute, Birmingham.
Sources: *The Architect*, March 2, 1894, pp. 148–50; *The Birmingham Daily Post*, Feb. 22, 1894, p. 5.
Text: see Appendix II, item 187.

3–11–94 (morning)—"What Shall We Do Now?" delivered in the open-air, at Trafford Bridge, Manchester, for the South Salford Branch, SDF.
Sources: *Justice*, March 10, 17, 1894; *The Manchester Guardian*, March 13, 1894.

3–11–94 (afternoon)—"Waste," delivered at a meeting sponsored by the South Salford Branch, SDF, at the Large Free Trade Hall, Manchester.
Sources: see above.

7–30–94—Morris testified as a character witness at the trial of Thomas Cantwell of the SL, in the Old Bailey, London.
Source: *The Times*, August 1, 1894, p. 3.

8–5–94*—An open-air speech was scheduled for delivery at a universal suffrage demonstration, sponsored by combined London socialist and radical groups, in Trafalgar Square.

Source: *Justice,* Aug. 4, 1894, p. 5.

11–18–94—"Makeshift," delivered at a meeting sponsored by the Ancoats Recreation Committee, at New Islington Hall, Ancoats, Manchester.

Sources: *The Ancoats Recreation Committee Winter Programme, 1894–5* (placard, B.M. Collection); *The Manchester Guardian,* Nov. 19, 1894.

Text: see Appendix II, item 189.

1895

1–5–95—A lecture, delivered at a meeting sponsored by the HSS, at Kelmscott House, Hammersmith.

Source: *Journal for 1895.*

3–31–95—"What We Have to Look for," delivered at a meeting sponsored by the HSS, at Kelmscott House, Hammersmith.

Sources: see above, also lecture list of the HSS (placard, B.M. Collection); a note on p. 13 of the MS.

Text: see Appendix II, item 190.

5–1–95—An open-air speech, delivered as part of the May Day celebrations sponsored by the SDF and other London socialists, in Hyde Park, London.

Sources: *Justice,* May 11, 1895, p. 4; *The Daily Chronicle,* May 2, 1895.

5–5–95—A lecture, probably delivered at a meeting sponsored by the HSS, at Kelmscott House, Hammersmith.

Source: *Journal for 1895.*

5–13–95—A speech, delivered at a meeting sponsored by the George B. Lansbury Campaign Committee, in the Browning-Hall, Walworth. Mr. Will Thorne was chairman.

Source: see above, also *The Times,* May 14, 1893, p. 10.

7–8–95*—A speech was scheduled for delivery in support of George B. Lansbury's Walworth candidature, at St. Stephen's Hall, Boyson Road, Walworth, London.

Source: *Justice,* July 6, 1895, p. 8.

8–18–95—A "talk on the Socialist Party," delivered at a meeting sponsored by the HSS, at Kelmscott House, Hammersmith.

Source: *Journal for 1895.*

9–15–95—A lecture, delivered at a meeting sponsored by the HSS, at Kelmscott House, Hammersmith.

Source: see above.

10–6–95—Chairman for a lecture by George Bernard Shaw, delivered at a meeting sponsored by the HSS, at Kelmscott House, Hammersmith.

Source: see 8–18–95 above.

10–30–95—"What We Have to Look for," delivered at a meeting sponsored by the Oxford and District Socialist Union, at the Central School (now the bus station), Gloucester Green, Oxford.

Sources: *Justice,* Nov. 9, 1895, p. 6; *Journal for 1895; The Oxford Review,* Oct. 31, 1895, p. 3; *Jackson's Oxford Journal,* Nov. 2, 1895, p. 5; *The Oxford Times,* Nov. 2, 1895, p. 3.

Text: see Appendix II, item 190.

12–1–95—A lecture, with lantern-slides, delivered at a meeting sponsored by the HSS, at Kelmscott House, Hammersmith.

Source: *Journal for 1895.*

12–14–95—"The Woodcuts of Gothic Books," delivered at a meeting sponsored by the Technical Education Department of the London County Council, at the Bolt Court Technical School, Fleet St., London.
Sources: see above, also *The Art Journal,* LIII (Jan., 1896), 31.
Text: see Appendix II, item 171.

12–28–95—A funeral oration for Sergius Stepniac, delivered in the open-air, at Waterloo Station, London.
Sources: *Justice,* Jan. 4, 1896, p. 6; *The Times,* Dec. 30, 1895.

1896

1–3–96—A speech at a New Year's meeting sponsored by the SDF, at the Holborn Town Hall, London. Harry Quelch was chairman.
Sources: *Justice,* Dec. 21, 1895, p. 4; Jan. 6, 1896; Chushichi Tsuzuki, *H. M. Hyndman and British Socialism* (London, 1961), p. 125.

1–5–96—"One Socialist Party," delivered at a meeting sponsored by the HSS, at Kelmscott House, Hammersmith.
Sources: *HSS Handbill* (B.M. Collection); *Journal for 1896.*

1–31–96—A speech, delivered at the annual meeting of the National Society for Checking the Abuses of Public Advertising, at the Society of Arts, John St., Adelphi, London. Alfred Waterhouse, R.A., was chairman.
Source: *The Architect,* Feb. 7, 1896, p. 89.
Review: *A Beautiful World,* III (Dec., 1896), 10.
Text: see Appendix II, item 197.

7–19–96—Morris's lecture "How We Live and How We Might Live," read by R. Catterson-Smith at a meeting sponsored by the HSS, at Kelmscott House, Hammersmith.
Source: *Ham. Min. Book.*
Text: see Appendix II, item 53.

APPENDIX II:

A Bibliographical Checklist of Morris's Speeches and Lectures

The two purposes of this list are to itemize all those of Morris's speeches and lectures for which there are known titles, subjects, or texts, and to provide detailed references to manuscript or printed texts where they exist. Entries are arranged chronologically in the order of scheduled first deliveries, to indicate the most likely order of composition; and after the heading "Deliveries," each entry includes dates in numeral form—month-day-year (e.g., 12–4–77 means December 4, 1877). These dates serve as cross references to Appendix I, the Calendar, where details of specific deliveries and sources of information concerning them can be found. As in the Calendar, an asterisk following the date indicates that a speech or lecture was scheduled but that there is no subsequent evidence of delivery. For the published lectures cited here each entry includes an exhaustive list of the various printed versions in the order of their publication. Unless otherwise indicated, each publication listed has the complete text, and versions described as "[Portions]" are included only when the edition referred to comprises a substantial part of the lecture or when the portion listed is the only surviving remnant of the text. Headings in quotation marks or brackets are titles. All other headings are based on the subjects discussed on specific occasions. Where titles of lectures are used as headings, they are taken, generally, from the manuscripts or from the most generally known authorized versions that appeared in Morris's lifetime, the object here being to use the titles most likely to represent Morris's latest intention. Where the manuscript has no title and where there are no printed versions, titles have been taken from newspaper accounts and given here (as elsewhere in this volume) in square brackets. Where Morris gave more than one lecture under the same title, or where he gave several untitled speeches on the same subject (e.g. the Annual Reports to the SPAB), the particular occasion and text—if there is one —is indicated by a Roman numeral following the heading. Variant titles of published versions are given, preceded by "As," in the reference to the individual publication; and where no title appears as part of the detailed reference to a published version, it should be understood that the title is as in the heading to that entry. Some translations are listed, but that part of the list should be taken as a handlist only. Abbreviations are expanded in the List of Abbreviations, pp. 8–10.

1: "The Lesser Arts"

Delivery: 12–4–77.
Publication:
> [Pamphlet], as *The Decorative Arts: Their Relation to Modern Life and Progress*. London, [1878]. Reprinted the same year with the date on the cover.
> As "The Decorative Arts," *The Architect*, Dec. 8, 1878, pp. 308–12.
> *Hopes and Fears*, pp. 1–37.
> *Dual Golden Type Edition*, pp. 1–18.
> *Collected Works*, XXII, 3–27.
> *Selected Writings*, pp. 494–516.
> *Victorian Prose*. Edited by F. W. Roe. New York, 1947, pp. 517–29.
> *On Art and Socialism*, pp. 17–37.
> *Penguin Edition*, pp. 84–105.

2: Speech on the Eastern Question

Delivery: 12–19–77.
Publication: no text remains.

3: "Address to English Liberals"

Delivery: 1–16–78.
Publication:
> *Artist, Writer, Socialist*, II, 370–82.

4: Speech on the Opening of the Dardanelles

Delivery: 1–7–78.
Publication: A MS in the Emery Walker house, Hammersmith, appears to match very closely the reported speech, but the published account is not sufficiently detailed for positive identification.

5: Address at the Cambridge School of Art

Delivery: 2–21–78.
Publication:
> As "Cambridge School of Art," *The Cambridge Chronicle and University Journal*, Feb. 23, 1878, p. 4.
> [Portions], as "Cambridge School of Art," *The Cambridge Express*, Feb. 23, 1878, p. 8.

6: Report at the First Annual Meeting, SPAB

Delivery: 6–21–78.
Publication:
> *The Architect*, July 6, 1878, pp. 7–8.

As "The Report," in The First Annual Meeting of the Society. *Report of the Committee thereat read.* London, 1878. Pp. 9–18.

7: *"The Art of the People"*

Delivery: 2–19–79.
Publication:
[Untitled], *The Birmingham Daily Post*, Feb. 20, 1879, p. 5.
[Pamphlet], as *An Address Delivered in the Town Hall, Birmingham.* . . . Birmingham, Osborne, 1879.
[Portions], as "Art: Its Ideal & Its Possibilities. An Address by William Morris, M.A., Numerically Arranged for Reporting Practice for Rates of Speed of 120 and 140 Words per Minute," in *Numeric Dictation Book for Time Practice in Reporting.* Edited by Bramley Barrington. 2nd Edition. Birmingham, 1888.
[Portions], *The Humanitarian Review*, I (July, 1900), 99–109.
Hopes and Fears, pp. [38]–70.
[Pamphlet], Chicago: Ralph Fletcher Seymour, 1902.
Dual Golden Type Edition, pp. 19–34.
[Booklet], Riverside (Conn.); Hillacre Press, 1914.
Collected Works, XXII, 28–50.
Selected Writings, pp. 517–37.
Victorian Prose, Edited by F. W. Roe. New York, [1947], pp. 529–40.
On Art and Socialism, pp. 38–56.

8: *"The History of Pattern Design"*

Deliveries: 4–8–79, 2–23–82.
Publication:
[Portions], as "Mr. William Morris on Egyptian, Greek, and Roman Art," *The Architect*, April 9, 1879, pp. 236–7.
Lectures on Art Delivered in Support of the Society for the Protection of Ancient Buildings. London, 1882, pp. [127]–73.
Architecture, Industry, and Wealth, pp. 1–36.
Collected Works, XXII, 206–34.

9: *Report at the Second Annual Meeting, SPAB*

Delivery: 6–28–79.
Publication:
As "The Report," in *Society for the Protection of Ancient Buildings. The Second Annual Meeting of the Society.* London, 1879. Pp. 8–17.

10: *Speech Seconding a Resolution Against Restoration*

Delivery: 6–28–79.
Publication:
[Untitled], in *Society for the Protection of Ancient Buildings. The Second Annual Meeting of the Society.* London, 1879. Pp. 30–36.

As "Address at the Second Annual Meeting, 28 June, 1879," in *Artist, Writer, Socialist,* I, 119–24.

11: Speech on the Restoration of St. Mark's, Venice—I

Delivery: 11–6–79.
Publication: no text remains.

12: Speech on the Restoration of St. Mark's, Venice—II

Delivery: 11–13–79.
Publication: no text remains.

13: Speech on the Restoration of St. Mark's, Venice—III

Delivery: 11–15–79.
Publication: no text remains.

14: [Our Country, Right or Wrong]

Delivery: It is not certain whether Morris ever delivered this lecture, but the MS bears an inscription in Morris's hand: "W. M. Jan. 30, 1880. 2.30 A.M. Kelmscott House, Upper Mall, Hammersmith." If this is, as it seems, a note to indicate completion of the text, it was probably delivered soon after to a liberal or radical group.
Publication:
The complete text is available in Morris's MS (B.M. Add. MS. 45334[4]).
[Portions], as "War and Peace," in *Artist, Writer, Socialist,* II, 53–62.

15: "The Beauty of Life"

Delivery: 2–19–80.
Publication:
B.M. Add. MS. 45332 (8) appears to be an early version of this lecture.
[Pamphlet], as *Labour and Pleasure versus Labour and Sorrow.* Birmingham, [1880].
Hopes and Fears, pp. [71]–113.
Dual Golden Type Edition, pp. 35–55.
Collected Works, XXII, 51–80.
Selected Writings, pp. 538–64.
Victorian Prose. Edited by F. W. Roe. New York, [1947], pp. 554–64.
On Art and Socialism, pp. 57–81.
The Victorian Age. Edited by John W. Bowyer and John L. Brooks. New York, 1954, pp. 648–60.

16: [Address to the Men and Women's College, Queen's Square]

Delivery: There is no clear indication when this lecture was delivered, but internal evidence suggests a date in 1880.

Publication:
   The complete text is available in Morris's MS (B.M. Add. MS. 45331[1])
   [Portions], *Artist, Writer, Socialist,* II, 63–72.

17: A Speech Proposing an International Committee for the Preservation of St. Mark's, Venice

Delivery: 5–31–80.
Publication: no text remains.

18: Speech Seconding a Resolution on Women's Rights

Delivery: 6–15–80.
Publication: *The Women's Union Journal; Organ of the Women's Protective and Provident League,* V (July, 1880), 69–70.

19: Annual Report of the SPAB—III

Delivery: 6–28–80.
Publication:
   As "Annual Report," in *Society for the Protection of Ancient Buildings. The Third Annual Meeting of the Society.* London, 1880. Pp. 10–18.

20: "Making the Best of It"

Deliveries: 11–13–80, 12–8–80.
Publication:
   [Resumé], *The Artist,* I (Dec., 1880), 356.
   [Resumé], *The Architect,* Nov. 20, 1880, p. 318.
   As "Hints on House Decoration," *The Architect,* Dec. 18, 25, 1880, pp. 384–7, 400–2.
   Hopes and Fears, pp. 114–68.
   Dual Golden Type Edition, pp. 56–82.
   Collected Works, XXII, 81–118.

21: Speech Supporting a Proposal to Form the Radical Union

Delivery: 1–15–81.
Publication: no text remains.

22: "Speech at a Meeting of the Kyrle Society"

Delivery: 1–27–81.
Publication:
   The Women's Union Journal, VI (Feb., 1881), 13–16. Reprinted as a broadsheet, 1881.
   Artist, Writer, Socialist, I, 192–97.

23: "The Prospects of Architecture in Civilization"

Delivery: 3–10–81.
Publication:
  Hopes and Fears, pp. 169–217.
  Dual Golden Type Edition, pp. 83–106.
  [Portions], as *Not for Leisure Alone.* . . . Riverside (Conn.), 1912.
  Collected Works, XXII, 119–52.
  On Art and Socialism, pp. 245–72.
  [Italian translation], in *Architettura e socialismo.* Bari, 1963, pp. 3–42.

24: Speech before the Nottingham Kyrle Society

Delivery: 3–16–81.
Publication:
  As "Nottingham Kyrle Society, 1881," in *Artist, Writer, Socialist,* I, 197–205.

25: Speech on the Restoration of the Campo Santo, Florence

Delivery: 3–31–81.
Publication: no text remains.

26: Annual Report of the SPAB—IV

Delivery: 6–24–81.
Publication:
  As "Annual Report," in *Society for the Protection of Ancient Buildings: Fourth Annual Report of the Committee.* London, 1881, pp. 7–18.

27: "Art and the Beauty of the Earth"

Delivery: 10–13–81.
Publication:
  As "The Condition and Prospects of Art," *The Architect,* Oct. 29, Nov. 5, 1881, pp. 282–4, 297–8.
  [Pamphlet], as *An Address Delivered in the Town Hall . . . Burslem.* (Wedgewood Institute Reports) Burslem, 1881.
  [Printed in the Golden Type at the Chiswick Press], London, 1899.
  Modern Eloquence. Phila., [1900], pp. 891–910.
  [German translation], Leipzig, 1901, pp. 1–31.
  Collected Works, XXII, 155–74.
  On Art and Socialism, pp. 156–72.
  [Pamphlet], ed. H. P. Smith (Adult Education and Society Series Documentary: 7), Oxford, 1962.

28: "Some Hints on Pattern Designing"

Delivery: 12–10–81.
Publication:
  The Architect, Dec. 17, 24, 1881, pp. 391–94, 408–10.
  [Printed in the Golden Type at the Chiswick Press], London, 1899.
  Collected Works, XXII, 175–205.

29: *"The Lesser Arts of Life"*

Delivery: 1–23–82.
Publication:
> *Lectures on Art Delivered in Support of the Society for the Protection of Ancient Buildings.* Edited by J. H. M. London, 1882, pp. [174]–232.
> *Architecture, Industry and Wealth,* pp. 37–79.
> [Dutch translation], in *Kunst et Maatschappij,* Rotterdam, [1903], pp. 31–76.
> *Collected Works,* XXII, 235–69.

30: *Testimony before the Royal Commission on Technical Education*

Delivery: 3–17–82.
Publication:
> As "Mr. Morris," in *Second Report of the Royal Commission on Technical Education,* Vol. III. London, 1884, pp. 150–61.
> [Portions], *The Architect,* Feb. 21, 1895, pp. 120–22.
> *Artist, Writer, Socialist,* I, 205–25.

31: *Annual Report of the SPAB—V*

Delivery: 6–9–82.
Publication:
> As "Annual Report," in *Society for the Protection of Ancient Buildings. The Fifth Annual Meeting of the Society.* London, 1882, pp. 7–20.

32: *Speech Seconding a Vote of Thanks to the Hon. James Bryce, M.P.*

Delivery: 6–9–82.
Publication:
> [Untitled], in *Society for the Protection of Ancient Buildings. The Fifth Annual Meeting of the Society.* London, 1882. Pp. 46–7.

33: *"The Progress of Decorative Art in England"*

Delivery: 10–20–82.
Publication:
> As "Mr. William Morris on Art Matters," in *The Manchester Guardian,* Oct. 21, 1882.
> As "Mr. William Morris on English Decorative Art," in *The Architect,* Oct. 28, 1882, pp. 262–3.
> As *Mr. William Morris on Art Matters* (Reprinted from the *Guardian*). London, 1961.

34: *[Art: a Serious Thing]*

Delivery: 12–12–82.
Publication: This title appears to be written on the MS in W. R. Lethaby's hand.

[Portions], *The Leek Times,* Dec. 16, 1882.
See also this volume, pp. 36–53.

35: *"Art, Wealth, and Riches"*

Delivery: 3–6–83.
Publication:
  The Manchester Quarterly, II (April, 1883), 153–75. Off-printed, 1883.
  Architecture, Industry and Wealth, pp. 80–104.
  [Dutch translation], in *Kunst en Maatschappij,* Rotterdam, [1903], pp. 77–103.
  Collected Works, XXIII, 143–63.
  On Art and Socialism, pp. 115–31.
  [Italian translation], in *Architettura e socialismo.* Bari, 1963, pp. 43–66.

36: *"Art and the People: A Socialist's Protest Against Capitalist Brutality; Addressed to the Working Classes (1883)"*

Delivery: There is no clear evidence when or where this lecture was delivered, but comparison of internal evidence with Morris's calendar of lectures in 1883 suggests it may have been read on April 1 or May 3 of that year.
Publication:
  Artist, Writer, Socialist, II, 382–406.
  [Portions], in *Victorians on Literature and Art.* Edited by Robert L. Peters. New York, 1961, pp. 279–90.

37: *Annual Report of the SPAB—VI*

Delivery: 6–6–83.
Publication:
  As "Report of the Committee," *SPAB Report, 1883.* London, 1883, pp. [7]–29.

38: *Speech in Support of the DF Program*

Delivery: 9–26–83.
Publication: no text remains.

39: *"Art under Plutocracy"*

Deliveries: 11–14–83, 11–16–83, 12–4–83, 1–22–84, 2–25–84.
Publication:
  [An Abstract by Morris], as "Mr. Morris on Art under Plutocracy," *The Cambridge Review,* Dec. 5, 1883, p. 122, and *The Cambridge Chronicle and University Journal,* Dec. 7, 1883.
  To-Day, I (Feb., March, 1884), 79–90, 159–76.
  Architecture, Industry and Wealth, pp. 164–97.
  As *Art, Labour, and Socialism.* (SPGB Library, No. 3) London, 1907.

(Reprinted from *To-Day,* without beginning and ending paragraphs). Reprinted, [1962], with "A Modern Assessment."
Collected Works, XXIII, 164–91.
On Art and Socialism, pp. 132–55.
[Italian translation], in *Architettura e socialismo.* Bari, 1963, pp. 67–99.

40: "The Origins of Decorative Art"

Deliveries: 11–24–83, 12–21–84*.
Publication: The lecture, as reported, seems to have been an earlier version of "Of the Origins of Ornamental Art," which was, however, greatly changed in the recasting, the first half being almost completely changed. References to St. George's Chapel and to Windsor in the later lecture suggest that toward its end some of the writing was taken from this earlier one. One fragmentary MS (B.M. Add. MS. 45334[9]) may be the concluding paragraphs of this lecture, but the reports are not definite enough for positive identification.

41: "Useful Work versus Useless Toil"

Deliveries: 1–16–84, 1–21–84, 2–17–84, 2–22–84*, 3–19–84, 3–23–84*, 4–27–84, 7–6–84, 9–5–84*, 11–2–84, 2–22–85*, 1–15–88.
Publication:
[Pamphlet], (Socialist League Platform, No. 2) London, 1885. Reprinted, 1886.
Signs of Change, pp. 141–73.
[Pamphlet], London, The Freedom Press [1890]. Reprinted, 1907.
Lee, pp. 208–33.
[Pamphlet], London, HSS, 1893.
[Pamphlet], Glasgow, The Labour Literature Society, 1893.
[Pamphlet], London, The "Torch Library," [1898].
Dual Golden Type Edition, pp. 70–85.
[Pamphlet], (No. 48 of "The Pocket Library of Socialism"). Chicago, [1909?].
Collected Works, XXIII, 98–120.
[Pamphlet], Sydney, The Judd Publishing Co., 1919.
Selected Writings, pp. 603–23.
Victorian Prose. Edited by F. W. Roe. New York, [1947], pp. 554–64.
On Art and Socialism, pp. 175–93.
Russian Edition, pp. 450–72.
Penguin Edition, pp. 117–36.

42: "Art and Socialism"

Deliveries: 1–23–84, 2–3–84*, 6–4–86.
Publication:
[Pamphlet], as *Art and Socialism: The Aims and Ideals of the English Socialists of To-day.* (Leek Bijou Reprints, No. 7) Leek, [1884].
Architecture, Industry and Wealth, pp. 105–32.
[Dutch translation], in *Kunst en Maatschappij.* Rotterdam, [1903], pp. 105–135.

Collected Works, XXIII, 192–214.
A Modern Book of Aesthetics, ed. Melvin M. Rader. New York, 1935, pp. 426–46 (omits the last three paragraphs).
On Art and Socialism, pp. 96–114.
Russian Edition, pp. 391–414.
[Italian translation], in *Architettura e socialismo*. Bari, 1963, pp. 100–127.

43: Debate on Socialism as the Remedy for "the Present Anarchy"

Delivery: 2–5–84.
Publication: no text remains.

44: "The Gothic Revival [I]"

Delivery: 3–3–84.
Publication:
  [Untitled Portions], *Artist, Writer, Socialist*, II, 629–30.
  See this volume, pp. 54–73.

45: "The Gothic Revival [II]"

Delivery: 3–10–84.
Publication:
  See this volume, pp. 74–93.

46: "Art and Labour"

Deliveries: 4–1–84, 5–18–84*, 8–17–84, 9–14–84, 9–21–84, 10–22–84, 11–16–84, 12–14–84, 3–3–85, 5–12–86.*
Publication:
  See this volume, pp. 94–118.

47: Speech at a Picture Show

Delivery: 4–8–84.
Publication:
  The entire text is available in Morris's MS (B.M. Add. MS. 45334[10]).
  [Portions], as "At a Picture Show," in *Artist, Writer, Socialist*, II, 164–69. Reprinted in *Victorians on Literature and Art*. Edited by Robert L. Peters. New York, 1961, pp. 290–96.

48: "Architecture and History"

Delivery: 7–1–84.
Publication:
  As "Paper Read by Mr. Morris," *SPAB Report, 1884*. London, 1884. Pp. 49–76.
  [Portions], as "Medieval and Modern Craftsmanship," *The Architect*, Sept.

13, 1884, pp. 171–73. The same portions were reprinted in *The Clarion,* Oct., 1884.

[Printed at the Chiswick Press in the Golden Type], as *Architecture and History and Westminster Abbey.* London, 1900, pp. 1–33.

[Dutch translation], in *Kunst en Maatschappij.* Rotterdam, [1903], pp. 1–30.

Collected Works, XXII, 296–317.

As "Paper Read at the Seventh Annual Meeting of the SPAB, 1 July, 1884," in *Artist, Writer, Socialist,* I, 124–45.

49: "Textile Fabrics"

Delivery: 7–11–84.
Publication:
> *The Architect,* July 19, 26, 1884, pp. 43–5, 50–53.
> [Pamphlet], London, International Health Exhibition, 1884.
> *Architecture, Industry and Wealth,* pp. 133–63.
> *Collected Works,* XXII, 270–95.

50: "Misery and the Way Out"

Deliveries: 9–8–84, 9–27–84*, 9–28–84*, 10–19–84*, 11–9–84, 11–17–84, 12–5–84, 12–7–84, 12–19–84*, 2–23–86*, 2–30–86*, 3–7–86*, 5–18–86*, 7–1–88*.
Publication:
> The entire text is available in Morris's MS (B.M. Add. MS. 45334[8]).
> [Portions], *Artist, Writer, Socialist,* II, 150–64.

51: "Iceland, Its Ancient Literature and Mythology"

Delivery: 9–14–84.
Publication:
> No full text remains, but the subject and date match well with MS notes now in the Morris Collection at Walthamstowe. The same subject was treated in a later lecture, "The Early Literature of the North—Iceland", (see this volume, pp. 179–98).

52: "At a Picture Show, 1884"

Delivery: 9–20–84.
Publication:
> *Artist, Writer, Socialist,* II, 406–19.

53: "How We Live and How We Might Live"

Deliveries: 11–30–84*, 12–13–84*, 12–26–84*, 1–11–85, 2–1–85*, 2–8–85*, 4–26–85, 6–28–85, 1–7–86*, 1–15–86, 3–6–87, 7–19–87.
Publication:
> *Commonweal,* June 4, 11, 18, 25, July 2, 1887.
> *Signs of Change,* pp. [11–36.

Lee, pp. [135]–62.
Dual Golden Type Edition, pp. 1–18.
[Pamphlet], Riverside (Conn.), Hillacre Press, 1914.
Collected Works, XXIII, 3–26.
Selected Writings, pp. 565–87.
[Spanish translation], Barcelona, [n.d.]. Pp. 1–33. Reprinted, 1936, by "Tierra y Libertad."
Russian Edition, pp. 425–49.
Penguin Edition, pp. 158–79.

54: *"Work, as It Is and as It Might Be"*

Deliveries: 1–4–85*, 3–8–85, 4–25–85, 4–27–85, 5–24–85.
Publication: no text remains.

55: *Speech to Open Edward Aveling's Lecture Series on Marx's* Das Kapital

Delivery: 2–7–85*.
Publication: no text remains.

56: *"Slaves and Slave Holders"*

Delivery: 2–15–85.
Publication: no text remains.

57: *Address to the Oxford Socialist Society*

Delivery: 2–25–85.
Publication:
This, according to Morris, was his "first long speech without book" (*Letters,* p. 231). Though, of course, no text remains, there are detailed summaries in *Jackson's Oxford Journal,* Feb. 28, 1885, and *The Oxford Times,* Feb. 25, 1885.

58: *Testimony on the Restoration of Westminster Hall*

Delivery: 3–11–85.
Publication:
[Untitled], *Report from the Select Committee on Westminster Hall Restoration.* London, 1885. Pp. 89–92.

59: *Speech on the Paris Commune—I*

Delivery: 3–22–85.
Publication: no text remains.

60: *"Commercial War"*

Deliveries: 3–27–85, 4–12–85*, 4–19–85*.
Publication:

The complete text is available in Morris's MS (B.M. Add. MS. 45333–4[16]). [Portions], *Artist, Writer, Socialist,* II, 311.

61: "Socialism"—I

Delivery: 3–29–85*.
Publication:
In the absence of detailed reports, the identification of this text is uncertain. Morris gave several lectures under this title (see *Man and Myth,* p. 59), and this one may or may not be the one published as "Socialism" (see item 66), though their nearness in time makes that likely.

62: Speech Moving a Socialist Rider to an Anti-War Resolution

Delivery: 4–2–85.
Publication: no text remains.

63: "How Can We Help?"

Deliveries: 5–8–85*, 5–10–85.
Publication: no text remains.

64: Speech to Protest "The Demolition of Churches at York"

Delivery: 5–30–85.
Publication: no text remains.

65: Speech to Open the Eighth Annual Meeting—SPAB

Delivery: 6–4–85.
Publication:
[Untitled], *SPAB Report, 1885.* London, 1885. Pp. 45–54.

66: "Socialism"—II

Deliveries: 6–9–85, 6–28–85, 10–10–85, 11–15–85*, 1–12–86, 1–24–86, 2–14–86*, 3–8–86, 4–13–86, 4–18–86, 6–28–86, 11–8–87.
Publication: The complete MS. is preserved in BM. Add. MS. 45333(1).
[*Norwich*] *Daylight Supplement,* March 13, 1886 (a broadsheet reprinted from a *Daylight* version published also in 1886).
[Portions], *Artist, Writer, Socialist,* II, 193–97.

67: "The Hopes of Civilization"

Deliveries: 6–14–85, 7–11–85, 9–1–85*, 6–3–88.
Publication:
Signs of Change, pp. 84–116.
Lee, pp. 163–88.

Dual Golden Type Edition, pp. 42–57.
Collected Works, XXIII, 59–80.
On Art and Socialism, pp. 279–97.

68: [*The Depression of Trade*]

Deliveries: 7–12–85, 8–16–85, 9–9–85, 10–18–85*.
Publication: see this volume, pp. 119–35.

69: *Speech Supporting Free Speech for the Manchester Socialist Union*

Delivery: 7–13–85.
Publication: no text remains.

70: *Speech on W. T. Stead's Exposé of London Prostitution*

Delivery: 8–5–85.
Publication:
No text remains, but the *Commonweal* (Sept., 1885) includes a résumé and an editorial by Morris on the subject.

71: *"Commercial Depression"*

Delivery: 8–16–85.
Publication:
No text remains under this title, but it is likely, considering the subject matter and date, that this is the same lecture as that given on other occasions as [The Depression of Trade]. See this volume, pp. 119–35.

72: *Speech at the "Hyde Park Demonstration for the Protection of Girls"*

Delivery: 8–22–85*.
Publication: no text remains.

73: *"What's to Become of the Middle Classes?"*

Delivery: 8–23–85.
Publication: no text remains.

74: *"The Guilds of the Middle Ages"*

Delivery: 9–20–85*.
Publication: no text remains.

75: *A Speech Seconding the Manchester Socialists' Free Speech Resolution*

Delivery: 9–26–85.
Publication: no text remains.

76: "The Larger Hope"

Delivery: 9–30–85*.
Publication: no text remains.

77: A Speech Welcoming John Williams

Delivery: 10–11–85.
Publication: no text remains.

78: "The Dawn of a New Epoch"

Deliveries: 11–10–85, 11–20–85*, 6–6–86*, 8–24–86, 10–18–86, 11–3–86, 11–27–86.
Publication:
Signs of Change, pp. 174–202.
Lee, pp. 234–56.
Dual Golden Type Edition, pp. 86–100.
Collected Works, XXIII, 121–40.

79: "Socialism, the True Road to Individual Development"

Delivery: 11–13–85*.
Publication: no text remains.

80: "The Political Outlook"

Deliveries: 1–10–86*, 1–13–86*, 1–27–86*, 2–2–86*, 2–10–86, 4–10–86, 4–17–86, 5–17–86.
Publication:
The complete text is available in Morris's MS (B.M. Add. MS. 45333[11]).
[Portions], *Artist, Writer, Socialist*, II, 277–87.

81: "Socialism, in Relation to the London Riots"

Delivery: 3–2–86.
Publication: no text remains.

82: "The Aims of Art"

Deliveries: 3–14–86, 3–31–86, 4–9–86, 5–16–86, 7–2–86.
Publication:
[Pamphlet], London, Office of "The Commonweal," 1887.
[Portions], *The Artist*, VIII (Sept., Oct., Nov., 1887), 283–85, 316–18, 346–48.
Signs of Change, pp. 117–40.
Lee, pp. 189–207.
Dual Golden Type Edition, pp. 58–69.

[Dutch translation], in *Kunst en Maatschappij.* Rotterdam, [1903]. Pp. 137–59.
Collected Works, XXIII, 81–97.
Selected Writings, pp. 588–602.

83: Speech Opening a Debate on "Socialism: What Is It?"

Delivery: 4–10–86.
Publication: no text remains.

84: "The Present and Future of the Working Classes"

Delivery: 4–19–86.
Publication:
> Morris's letter to J. L. Mahon (*Man and Myth,* pp. 59–60) makes it clear that his text for this lecture was a revised version of "The Dawn of a New Epoch" (see item 78).

85: "Our Policy"

Delivery: 4–25–86.
Publication:
> Although no text of this lecture remains, Morris wrote an article for *Commonweal* about this time that expresses his position. See "Our Policy," *Commonweal,* March, 1886, pp. 17–18.

86: "Competition"

Delivery: 4–28–86*.
Publication: no text remains.

87: "Of the Origins of Ornamental Art"

Deliveries: 5–19–86, 9–26–86, 1–1–87, 10–30–87, 12–11–87*(?), 1–1–88, 11–2–89, 10–20–90.
Publication:
> [Portions], *The Manchester Guardian,* Sept. 27, 1886, p. 6. See this volume, pp. 136–57.

88: Speech Seconding a Resolution to Establish a Fund for the Repair of Ancient Buildings

Delivery: 6–8–86.
Publication: no text remains.

89: "Whigs, Democrats, and Socialists"

Delivery: 6–11–86.
Publication:

Commonweal, June 26 and July 3, 1886, pp. 97–8, 106–7.
Signs of Change, pp. 37–54.
Dual Golden Type Edition, pp. 19–27.
Collected Works, XXIII, 27–38.

90: *"True and False Society"*

Deliveries: 6–23–86, 6–24–86, 6–25–86, 9–5–86, 1–23–87, 1–25–87*, 4–3–87, 4–17–87, 5–4–87*, 6–1–87, 6–9–87, 6–12–87*.
Publication:
   [Pamphlet], as *The Labour Question from the Socialist Standpoint.* (Claims of Labour Lectures.) Edinburgh, 1886. Offprint from the volume listed below.
   As "The Labour Question from the Socialist Standpoint," in *The Claims of Labour.* Edinburgh, 1886. Pp. 155–85.
   [Pamphlet], (The Socialist Platform, No. 6) London, 1886. Reprinted 1888.
   [Pamphlet], London, HSS, 1893.
   [Pamphlet], Glasgow: Labour Literature Society, 1893.
   [Dutch translation], Amsterdam, 1898, pp. [1]–32.
   As "The Labour Question from the Socialist Standpoint," in *Modern Socialism,* ed. R. C. K. Ensor. London, 1904, pp. 65–89.
   As "The Labour Question from the Socialist Standpoint," in *Representative Essays in Modern Thought,* ed. Harrison R. Steeves and Frank W. Ristine. New York, 1913, pp. 930–53.
   Collected Works, XXIII, 215–37.
   On Art and Socialism, pp. 293–316.

91: *"Education"*

Deliveries: 7–11–86, 7–18–86, 9–15–86.
Publication:
   No full text of this lecture remains, but an extensive résumé was printed in *The Architect,* Sept. 17, 1886, pp. 170–71.

92: *"Our Tactics"*

Delivery: 8–22–86.
Publication: no text remains.

93: *Speech "Against the Party of Compromise"*

Delivery: 9–17–86.
Publication:
   This speech was in defense of a rider against Fabian political tactics, a rider Morris tried, unsuccessfully, to attach to Mrs. Annie Besant's motion to establish a socialist political party. The text of the rider is quoted in *Our Corner,* VIII (Oct., 1886), 252–53.

94: *"Socialism: the End and the Means"*

Deliveries: 9–27–86, 9–28–86, 10–11–86, 10–15–86, 10–17–86, 11–2–86, 11–21–86, 12–1–86, 1–23–87*, 3–14–87, 4–8–87, 4–24–87*.
Publication:
    [*Norwich*] *Daylight,* Oct. 16, 1886, pp. 2–4.
    As "The End and the Means," *Artist, Writer, Socialist,* II, 420–34.

95: *Lecture on Pattern-Designing*

Delivery: 10–1–86.
Publication:
    In the absence of reports on this lecture, the text remains unidentified.

96: *"The Birth of Feudalism in Scandinavia"*

Delivery: 10–3–86*.
Publication: no text remains.

97: *"Early England"*

Deliveries: 12–12–86, 1–2–87*, 1–14–94.
Publication:
    See this volume, pp. 158–78. This lecture was the first of three on "England, As It Was, As It Is, and As It May Be." The last two in the series, "Feudal England" (item 101) and "Art and History in the Fourteenth Century" (item 107), have been published elsewhere.

98: *Speech Against the Eviction of Glenbeigh Crofters*

Delivery: 1–26–87.
Publication: no text remains.

99: *Speech at a Debate on the "Class War"*

Delivery: 2–4–87.
Publication: no text remains.

100: *Address to Protest Against "The Coming War" between Germany and France*

Delivery: 2–8–87.
Publication: no text remains.

101: *"Feudal England"*

Deliveries: (as "Mediaeval England," the MS title) 2–13–87, 2–16–87, 3–22–87.
Publication:
    This lecture was the second in the trilogy on "England, As It Was, As It Is, and As It May Be" (see also items 97 and 107).

Commonweal, Aug. 20, 27, and Sept. 3, 10, 1887, pp. 266–67, 274, 282, 290–91.
Signs of Change, pp. 55–83.
Dual Golden Type Edition, pp. 28–41.
Collected Works, XXIII, 39–58.

102: Speech on Monopoly

Delivery: 2–20–87.
Publication:
No reports of this lecture are sufficiently detailed to permit definite identification of the text, but the subject and the time suggest it may have been the same as the one later published as "Monopoly; or, How Labour Is Robbed" (see item 103).

103: "Monopoly; or, How Labour Is Robbed"

Deliveries: 2–20–87(?), 3–13–87, 3–20–87, 3–27–87, 4–5–87, 6–27–87, 8–21–87, 10–2–87, 10–16–87*, 10–30–87, 2–19–88*, 2–22–88, 3–11–88, 3–21–88, 3–28–88, 8–12–88, 12–2–88, 12–6–88, 6–4–89*, 6–27–89*, 8–28–89, 11–10–89.
Publication:
Reports suggest that Morris gave at least two different lectures under the general title "Monopoly." This one, the first and the more often used, was also changed in part from time to time by the addition of topical allusions.
[Serialized], as "Monopoly," *Commonweal,* Dec. 7, 14, 21, 1889, pp. 388–89, 394, 401–2.
[Pamphlet], (Socialist Platform No. 7) London, 1890. Reprinted 1891.
[Pamphlet], London, The Freedom Press [n.d.]. Reprinted 1907.
[Dutch translation], Amsterdam, Steringa [n.d.], pp. 1–16.
[Czech translation], Prague, Social Democratic Party [n.d.], pp. 1–24.
[Pamphlet], London, HSS, 1893.
[Pamphlet], Glasgow, The Labour Literature Society, 1893.
[Pamphlet], London, The "Torch Library" [1898].
Collected Works, XXIII, 238–54.
On Art and Socialism, pp. 194–207.

104: Speech for the Anniversay of the Paris Commune—II

Delivery: 3–17–87.
Publication: no text remains.

105: "Socialism and the Labour Struggle"

Delivery: 4–7–87.
Publication: no text remains.

106: Speech Against the "Latest Irish Coercion Bill"

Delivery: 4–13–87.
Publication: no text remains.

107: "Art and Industry in the 14th Century"

Deliveries: 5–15–87, 4–15–88.
Publication: This lecture was the last in the trilogy on "England, As It Was, As It Is, and As It May Be" (see also items 97 and 101). Published versions are all considerably altered from the MS of this lecture, which is preserved as B.M. Add. MS. 45331(9).
As "Art and History in the 14th Century," in *Time: a Monthly Magazine*, I, n.s. (Jan., 1890), 23–36.
Architecture, Industry and Wealth, pp. 138–49.
As "Art and Industry in the Fourteenth Century. An Article in 'Time,' November [*sic*], 1890," *Collected Works*, XXII, 375–90.
[Italian translation], in *Architettura e socialismo*. Bari, 1963. Pp. 151–69.

108: Speech Against Coercion of the Irish

Delivery: 5–21–87.
Publication: no text remains.

109: Speech in Support of a Motion to Establish a Fund for the Protection of Ancient Buildings

Delivery: 6–8–87.
Publication:
[Untitled], in *SPAB Report, 1887*. Pp. 56–57.

110: "The Policy of Abstention"

Deliveries: 7–31–87, 8–24–87.
Publication:
Artist, Writer, Socialist, II, 434–53.

111: Speech in Support of Free Speech in Ireland

Delivery: 9–25–87.
Publication: no text remains.

112: Speech Against the Execution of the Chicago Anarchists—I

Delivery: 10–6–87.
Publication: no text remains.

113: "The Early Literature of the North—Iceland"

Delivery: 10–9–87.
Publication:
See this volume, pp. 179–98.

114: Speech Against the Execution of the Chicago Anarchists—II

Delivery: 10–14–87.
Publication: no text remains.

115: "What Socialists Want"

Deliveries: 11–6–87*, 2–5–88, 4–8–88, 4–17–88, 12–4–88, 2–2–90.
Publication:
See this volume, pp. 217–33.

116: Speech for an Orderly Demonstration in Trafalgar Square

Delivery: 11–13–87.
Publication: no text remains.

117: "The Society of the Future"

Deliveries: 11–13–87*, 11–20–87, 12–1–87, 3–26–88, 7–8–88, 12–2–88, 2–10–89.
Publication:
Commonweal, March 30, April 6, 1889, pp. 98–9, 108–9, 114–15.
Artist, Writer, Socialist, II, 453–68.

118: Speech on "Socialism and the London Disturbances"

Delivery: 12–2–87.
Publication: no text remains.

119: Speech at the Funeral of Alfred Linnell

Delivery: 12–18–87.
Publication:
No full text remains, but the *Commonweal* account (Dec. 24, 1887, p. 413)
contains a detailed paraphrase.

120: [The Present Outlook in Politics]

Deliveries: 12–18–87, 1–8–88.
Publication:
See this volume, pp. 119–216.

121: "The Social Problem" (also advertised as "The Social Revolution")

Delivery: 1–22–88.
Publication: no text remains.

122: "The Revolt of Ghent"

Deliveries: 1–29–88, 6–20–88, 12–1–89.
Publication:
> *Commonweal*, July 7, 14, 21, 28, and Aug. 4, 11, 18, 1888.
> [Pamphlet, with the portion from no. 136 of *Commonweal* inadvertently omitted], Huddersfield, James Leatham, 1911.

123: Speech for the Anniversary of the Paris Commune—III

Delivery: 7–29–88.
Publication: no text remains.

124: Speech Moving the Formation of the NAAA

Delivery: 6–8–88.
Publication: no text remains.

125: Speech Against "Sweating" Practices in London Industries

Delivery: 7–22–88.
Publication: no text remains.

126: "From Chattel to Wage Slavery"

Delivery: 7–29–88.
Publication: no text remains.

127: "A Chapter in the History of Rome": A Lecture on Theodore Mommsen

Delivery: 8–19–88.
Publication:
> This lecture was delivered from notes, and no text remains.

128: "Equality"

Deliveries: 9–30–88, 11–18–88, 11–25–88*, 12–23–88*, 2–13–89, 3–31–89*, 4–14–89*, 2–9–90*.
Publication:
> The complete text of this lecture is preserved in the original MS (B.M. Add. MS. 45333[10]).
> [Portions], *Artist, Writer, Socialist*, II, 197–203.

129: "Tapestry and Carpet Weaving"

Delivery: 11–1–88.
Publication: no text remains.

130: Speech Welcoming Mrs. Albert Parsons

Delivery: 11–10–88.
Publication: no text remains.

131: Speech to Commemorate "Bloody Sunday"—I

Delivery: 11–11–88.
Publication: no text remains.

132: "Monopoly"—II

Delivery: 11–18–88.
Publication:
> This lecture differed considerably from the one published under the same title (see item 103). No text of this later version remains.

133: Speech of Farewell to Mrs. Albert Parsons

Delivery: 11–29–88.
Publication: no text remains.

134: "Art and Its Producers"

Delivery: 12–5–88.
Publication:
> In *Transactions of the National Association for the Advancement of Art and Its Application to Industry.* Liverpool, 1888. Pp. 228–36.
> In *Art and Its Producers and the Arts and Crafts Today: Two Addresses delivered before the National Association for the Advancement of Art.* London, 1901. Pp. 1–20. (Set in the "Golden Type" at the Chiswick Press.)
> *Collected Works,* XXII, 342–55.
> *On Art and Socialism,* pp. 208–19.

135: "The Future of the Middle Classes"

Delivery: 12–12–88*.
Publication: no text remains.

136: "Socialism"—III

Deliveries: 1–6–89, 1–30–89.
Publication:
> Morris's text for this lecture differed from both the earlier lectures given under the same title. It is possible that he gave a quite different lecture here

with this changed title (see *Man and Myth,* p. 59, where Morris indicates that he sometimes gave the same lecture under different titles). But reports of this particular occasion are not sufficiently detailed for positive identification.

137: "Gothic Architecture"—I

Deliveries: 2–11–89, 4–9–89.
Publication:
> Reports indicate that this lecture, while similar to that delivered later in the same year at the Arts and Crafts Exhibition (see item 152), was not identical with the later version. A MS of what may be an earlier version, much longer than the printed text, is preserved in B.M. Add. MS. 45332(9).

138: "Arts and Crafts"

Delivery: 2–12–89.
Publication:
> Though no full text remains under this title, it is likely that this is an early version of the lecture "The Arts and Crafts Today" (see item 150).

139: Speech "On Art Education"

Delivery: 2–14–89.
Publication:
> As "Mr. Morris on Art Education," *The Macclesfield Courier and Herald,* Feb. 23, 1889. No MS version of this lecture survives, but this printed text seems to be complete. Variations from Morris's usual practice in punctuation suggest that it comes from a shorthand report.

140: "How Shall We Live Then?"

Deliveries: 3–1–89, 3–3–89, 1–22–90, 2–2–90, 3–2–90.
Publication: no text remains.

141: Lecture on Restoration

Delivery: 4–22–89.
Publication: no text remains.

142: Lecture on Bellamy's Looking Backward *and* Grant Allen's Essay "Individualism and Socialism"

Delivery: 5–12–89.
Publication:
> Although no text of this lecture remains, Morris's views of Bellamy's work were published in a review, "Looking Backward," *Commonweal,* June 22, 1889.

143: *Address at the Twelfth Annual Meeting, SPAB*

Delivery: ?
Publication: May Morris's title and date are not corroborated by the *SPAB Report, 1889.*
As "Address at the Twelfth Annual Meeting, 3 July, 1889," *Artist, Writer, Socialist,* I, 146–57.

144: *Speech Against Amalgamation of Possibilist and International Socialist Conferences*

Delivery: 7–16–89.
Publication:
[Without title], in *Protokoll, Internationalen Arbeiter-Congresses zu Paris. Abgehalten vom 14. bis 20. Juli 1889. Deutsche Uebersetzung. Mit einem Vorwort von Wilhelm Liebknecht.* Nurnberg, 1890. Morris's speech is here reported in condensed form, p. 17.

145: *Speech on the Progress and Condition of English Socialism*

Delivery: 7–18–89.
Publication:
E. P. Thompson notes (*Romantic to Revolutionary*, p. 626) that "Morris's contribution is given in full in the Protocol of the Congress, published in Paris (1889)." This editor has not seen a copy of this, however.
[German translation as in the previous entry], pp. 39–43.

146: *"Monopoly"—III*

Delivery: 8–28–89.
Publication:
The reports of this occasion indicate that Morris's text, in most respects the same as the published "Monopoly" (see item 103), had been revised by the addition of fresh topical references.

147: *"The Class Struggle"*

Deliveries: 10–13–89*, 11–10–89, 11–30–89, 3–11–90, 3–25–90.
Publication:
[Portions], *The Leeds Mercury,* March 26, 1890.

148: *"Why Working Men Ought to Be Socialists"*

Delivery: 10–27–89.
Publication: no text remains.

149: *"The Art of Dyeing"*

Delivery: 10–29–89.
Publication:

Though reports of this occasion do not provide enough information to identify the text positively, Morris published an essay on the same subject and with a very similar title: "Of Dyeing as an Art," in *Arts and Crafts Essays by Members of the Arts and Crafts Exhibition Society.* London, 1893. Reprinted in 1899 and 1903 by Longmans, Green, and Co., pp. 196–211.

150: "The Arts and Crafts Today"

Delivery: 10–30–89.
Publication:
As "The Presidential Address," in *Transactions of the National Association for the Advancement of Art and Its Application to Industry.* London: The Society, 1890, pp. 189–212.
In *Art and Its Producers and the Arts and Crafts Today.* London, 1901, pp. 21–47. (Set in the "Golden Type" at the Chiswick Press.)
Collected Works, XXII, 356–74.
On Art and Socialism, pp. 229–44.
[Italian translation], in *Architettura e socialismo.* Bari, 1963, pp. 128–50.

151: Lecture on Socialism

Delivery: 11–1–89.
Publication: no text remains.
This lecture was probably impromptu. See Morris's letter to the Rev. John Glasse, Sept. 9, 1889 (*Man and Myth,* p. 97).

152: "Gothic Architecture"—II

Deliveries: 11–7–89, 11–20–89*, 4–12–90, 5–2–90.
Publication: See also item 137.
[Printed at the 1893 Exhibition of the ACES at New Gallery], London, The Kelmscott Press, 1893. Pp. 1–68.
Selected Writings, pp. 475–93.
Artist, Writer, Socialist, I, 266–86.

153: Speech to Commemorate "Bloody Sunday"—II

Delivery: 11–11–89.
Publication: no text remains.

154: Speech for the Anniversary of the Paris Commune—IV

Delivery: 3–19–90.
Publication: no text remains.

155: "The Development of Modern Society"

Delivery: 4–13–90.
Publication:

Commonweal, July 19, 26, Aug. 2, 9, 16, 1890, pp. 225–6, 237, 244, 253, 260–61.

156: "The Social Outlook"

Delivery: 4–13–90.
Publication: no text remains.

157: Speech for May Day—I

Delivery: 5–1–90.
Publication: no text remains.

158: Speech Seconding the Motion to Adopt the Annual SPAB Report

Delivery: 6–25–90.
Publication:
[Untitled], in *Society for the Protection of Ancient Buildings. The Thirteenth Annual Meeting of the Society. . . .* London, 1890, p. 70.

159: "The Hope of the Future"

Delivery: 9–21–90*.
Publication: no text remains.

160: Speech to Protest Against "The Persecution of Jews in Russia"

Delivery: 11–1–90.
Publication: no text remains.

161: Speech to Commemorate "Bloody Sunday"—III

Delivery: 11–11–90.
Publication: no text remains.

162: Speech on the Protection of Ancient Buildings

Delivery: 12–11–90.
Publication: no text remains.

163: "Idiots and Idiocy"

Delivery: 2–15–91*.
Publication: no text remains.

164: Speech Moving a Vote of Thanks to W. B. Richmond

Delivery: 6–10–91.
Publication: no text remains.

165: "Seven Years Ago and Now"

Delivery: 8–30–91.
Publication: no text remains.
> This lecture, being Morris's farewell to the SL, may also be the basis of a later essay, "Where Are We Now," in *Commonweal*, Nov. 15, 1890. Reprinted in *Artist, Writer, Socialist*, II, 512–18. The report is too sketchy, however, to allow positive identification.

166: "Address on the Collection of Paintings of the English Pre-Raphaelite School"

Delivery: 10–2–91.
Publication:
> [Pamphlet], Birmingham, E. C. Osborne and Son [1891].
> *Artist, Writer, Socialist*, I, 296–310. Error in title, "Oct. 24, 1891."
> In *Victorian Poetry and Poetics*, ed. Walter E. Houghton and G. Robert Stange. Boston, 1959, pp. 600–605. Repeats title error.

167: "Socialism Up-to-Date"

Delivery: 10–4–91.
Publication:
> The opening passages of this lecture were written out in full, but the remainder took the form of topic headings. The entire MS is preserved (B.M. Add. MS. 45333[1]).
> [Portions], *Artist, Writer, Socialist*, II, 341–43.

168: Lecture on French and English Cathedrals

Delivery: 10–4–91.
Publication: no text remains.
> The reports indicate that this was an extempore lecture with lantern-slide illustrations.

169: "On the Influence of Building Materials on Architecture"

Delivery: 11–20–91.
Publication:
> *Century Guild Hobby Horse*, VII (Jan., 1892), 1–14.
> *Architecture, Industry and Wealth*, pp. 247–64.
> *Collected Works*, XXII, 391–405.

170: "Real Socialism"

Delivery: 12–9–91.
Publication: no text remains.

171: "The Woodcuts of Gothic Books"

Deliveries: 1–26–92, 2–21–94, 12–14–95.
Publication:
> As originally delivered, this lecture was accompanied with 38 lantern-slide illustrations. Unless otherwise indicated the following published versions include a selection of these.
> In *The Journal of the Society of Arts*, Feb. 12, 1892, pp. 247–60.
> [No illustrations], *The Architect*, Feb. 26, March 4, 1892, pp. 145–47, 154–59.
> *The Journal of Decorative Art*, XII (June and July, 1892), 82–7, 102–3.
> [Portions], as *Some German Woodcuts of the Fifteenth Century*. Edited by Sydney C. Cockerell. London, 1897.
> [Pamphlet], New Rochelle (N.Y.), The Elston Press, 1902.
> [No illustrations], *Artist, Writer, Socialist*, I, 318–38.

172: "Town and Country"

Deliveries: 5–29–92, 1–?–93,—not 1894, as J. W. Mackail asserts (*Mackail*, II, 301–2).
Publication:
> [Portions], *The Journal of Decorative Art*, XIII (April, 1893), 106.
> [Portions], *Mackail*, II, 301–6.

173: Speech at the Fifteenth Annual Meeting, SPAB

Delivery: 6–28–92.
Publication: no text remains.

174: Speech Moving a Vote of Thanks to Judge Lushington

Delivery: 6–28–92.
Publication: no text remains.

175: "Communism,—i.e. Property"

Delivery: 8–21–92*.
Publication:
> The complete text, which concludes with topic headings, is preserved in Morris's MS (B.M. Add. MS. 45333[12]).
> [Portions], *Artist, Writer, Socialist*, II, 345–52.

176: Speech Opening a Discussion on "The Attitudes of Trades Unionism to Socialism"

Delivery: 2–3–93.
Publication: no text remains.

177: "Communism"

Deliveries: 2–19–93*, 3–10–93.
Publication:
> [Pamphlet], George Bernard Shaw, Editor. Fabian Tract, No. 113. London, 1903. Reprinted, 1907.
> *Collected Works,* XXIII, 264–76.
> *On Art and Socialism,* pp. 325–35.
> *Russian Edition,* pp. 478–90.

178: Speech Against the Restoration of St. Mary's, Oxford

Delivery: 6–6–93.
Publication: no text remains.

179: "The Ideal Book"

Delivery: 6–19–93.
Publication:
> *Trans. Biblio. Soc.,* I (1893), London, Dove Press, 1900, 179–93.
> London, 1900.
> In *Zeitschrift für Bucherfreunde,* V (1900).
> In *The Art and Craft of Printing.* New Rochelle (N.Y.), The Elston Press, 1902. Pp. [47]–[55].
> [Pamphlet], London, 1907. Dated 1908 in Colophon. Reprinted 1957.
> New York, Calumet Press for George H. Broughton, 1909.
> New York, Limited Edition Club, 1931.
> *Artist, Writer, Socialist,* I, 310–18.
> [Portions], as *The Ideal Book . . . Being Part of an Address Delivered before the Bibliographical Society. . . .* Floral Park (N.Y.), The Experimental Press, 1937.

180: "Printed Books, Ancient and Modern"

Delivery: 10–21–93.
Publication: no text remains.

181: "The Dangers of Restoration, with special Reference to Westminster Abbey"

Delivery: 10–22–93.
Publication: no text remains.

182: "On the Printing of Books"

Delivery: 11–2–93.
Publication: no text remains.
> The major ideas of this lecture are probably contained in an essay on printing by Morris and Emery Walker published by the ACES. See "Printing," in *Arts*

and Crafts Essays by Members of the Arts and Crafts Exhibition Society (London, 1899), pp. 111–33. Reprinted in *Artist, Writer, Socialist*, I, 251–60.

183: "Waste"

Deliveries: 12–10–93, 3–11–94.
Publication: no text remains.

184: "What Shall We Do Now?"

Deliveries: 12–10–93, 3–11–94.
Publication: no text remains.

185: "What Is: What Should Be: What Will Be: What May Be"

Delivery: sometime in 1893.
Publication: Morris's MS is preserved (B.M. Add. MS. 45333[8]), but it consists largely of topic headings.
[Portions], *Artist, Writer, Socialist*, II, 356–57.

186: Speech in Support of George B. Lansbury for Parliament—I

Delivery: 2–20–94.
Publication: no text remains.

187: "Address at the Distribution of Prizes to Students of the Birmingham Municipal School of Art on Feb. 21, 1894."

Delivery: 2–21–94.
Publication:
As *An Address delivered by William Morris at the Distribution of Prizes to Students of the Birmingham Municipal School of Art, on the 21st of February,* [1894]. Birmingham, The Municipal School of Art [1894], pp. 1–21. [Printed in Kelmscott Press Golden Type at the Chiswick Press], London, 1898.
[German translation], Leipzig, 1901, pp. iv–28.
Collected Works, XXII, 421–37.
In *Fourteen Addresses Delivered to Students at the Birmingham Municipal School of Art*. Birmingham, The School of Art, 1924, pp. 56–72.

188: Speech on Universal Suffrage

Delivery: 8–5–94*.
Publication: no text remains.

189: "Makeshift"

Delivery: 11–18–94.
Publication:
Artist, Writer, Socialist, II, 469–83.

190: "What We Have to Look For"

Deliveries: 3–31–95, 10–30–95.
Publication:
> The complete text is preserved in Morris's MS (B.M. Add. MS. 45333[3]).
> [Portions], *Artist, Writer, Socialist,* II, 357–61.

191: Speech for May Day—II

Delivery: 5–1–95.
Publication: no text remains.

192: Speech in Support of George B. Lansbury for Parliament—II

Delivery: 5–13–95.
Publication: no text remains.

193: Speech in Support of George B. Lansbury for Parliament—III

Delivery: 7–8–95*.
Publication: no text remains.

194: Talk "On the Socialist Party"

Delivery: 8–18–95.
Publication: no text remains.

195: Funeral Oration for Sergius Stepniak

Delivery: 12–28–95.
Publication: no text remains.

196: "One Socialist Party"

Delivery: 1–5–96.
Publication: no text remains.

197: Speech Against the Abuses of Public Advertising

Delivery: 1–31–96.
Publication:
> ["A very imperfect text," according to the editor], in *A Beautiful World,* III
> (Dec., 1896), 16–18.

INDEX

Eugene D. LeMire is professor of English,
University of Windsor. He received his Ph.B. and M.A. from
the University of Detroit (1951, 1954), and his Ph.D. from
Wayne State (1962).

The manuscript was edited by Robert H. Tennenhouse.
The book was designed by Joanne Colman. The type face for
the text is Linotype Caledonia, designed by W. A. Dwiggins,
cut in 1937; display faces include Bookman introduced by
American Type Founders in 1903 and Lombardic initials.
The book was printed on S. D. Warren's Old Style Antique
paper and bound in Columbia Mills' Fictionette Natural Finish
cloth over binders board. Manufactured in the United States
of America.